BL 3446693

D1425520

LL·PAM

History & Crime

WEEK LOAN

$\ell\beta$

BIRMINGHAM CITY
UNIVERSITY
DISCARDED

Key Approaches to Criminology

The *Key Approaches to Criminology* series was established in order to bring together different but related disciplines. It is impossible to study criminology or criminal justice without dipping into other subject areas, yet it is often the case that criminological discussion is impoverished through a lack of proper understanding of these fields. Each book in the series help readers to make intellectual connections between subjects and disciplines, and to understand the importance of studying crime and criminal justice within a broader context. The books are authored by scholars who are ideally – perhaps even uniquely – placed to write them.

History & Crime is no exception. Although criminology undeniably has been enriched by historical analysis, and historical perspectives are the subject of renewed interest within contemporary criminological studies, there has not yet been a text that synthesizes historical and contemporary criminological issues and comprehensively underlines the importance of understanding the past to make sense of the present. Barry Godfrey, Paul Lawrence and Chris Williams put this right, exploring many of the most pertinent issues of our times, among them: immigration, surveillance, governance, prostitution, media and public perceptions of crime, and the state of our prisons. Using fascinating case studies and numerous illustrations from the past, the authors show us the importance of historical contexts and continuities to ongoing debates about crime, justice and punishment. Like the other books in the series *History & Crime* will be required reading on a wide and diverse range of undergraduate and postgraduate degree courses and is a valuable addition to the *Key Approaches to Criminology* series.

Yvonne Jewkes
Series Editor

Other books in the series:

Media and Crime (2004) Yvonne Jewkes (University of Leicester)

Globalization and Crime (2007) Katja Franko Aas (University of Oslo)

Gender and Crime (2008) Marisa Silvestri (London South Bank University) and Chris Crowther-Dowey (Sheffield Hallam University)

History & Crime

Barry S. Godfrey
Chris A. Williams
Paul Lawrence

SAGE Publications
Los Angeles • London • New Delhi • Singapore

BIRMINGHAM CITY LIBRARY UNIVERSITY

© Barry S. Godfrey, Chris A. Williams, Paul Lawrence

First published 2008

Apart from any fair dealing for the purposes of research or
private study, or criticism or review, as permitted under
the Copyright, Designs and Patents Act, 1988, this publication
may be reproduced, stored or transmitted in any form,
or by any means, only with the prior permission in writing
of the publishers, or in the case of reprographic reproduction,
in accordance with the terms of licences issued by
the Copyright Licensing Agency. Enquiries concerning
reproduction outside those terms should be sent to the
publishers.

SAGE Publications Ltd
1 Oliver's Yard
55 City Road
London EC1Y 1SP

SAGE Publications Inc.
2455 Teller Road
Thousand Oaks, California 91320

SAGE Publications India Pvt Ltd
B 1/I 1 Mohan Cooperative Industrial Area
Mathura Road
New Delhi 110 044

SAGE Publications Asia-Pacific Pte Ltd
33 Pekin Street #02-01
Far East Square
Singapore 048763

BIRMINGHAM CITY UNIVERSITY

Book no.   34466924

Subject no   364.9 God

LIBRARY

British Library Cataloguing in Publication data

A catalogue record for this book is available
from the British Library

ISBN 978-1-4129-2079-7
ISBN 978-1-4129-2080-3

Library of Congress Control Number:

Typeset by C&M Digitals (P) Ltd., Chennai, India
Printed in Great Britain by The Cromwell Press, Trowbridge, Wiltshire
Printed on paper from sustainable resources

Contents

1

Introduction

Why write this book? We like the popular metaphor of 'the elephant in the room' – a large issue which nobody mentions even though it is difficult to ignore. In criminology and crime history we appear to have two elephants in a very small room which both ignore each other. This volume intends to explore the relationship (mainly in Chapter 2) and to explore some areas where historical study can offer much to criminological understanding, and vice versa.

This book could have chosen any number of topics to explore. Each of the topics we finally selected will illustrate the utility of combining criminological and historical knowledge, but there are many others that would be equally valid that we have left unexplored for reasons of space. We have in fact limited ourselves to six subjects which meet most if not all of the following criteria:

- The topics are (hopefully) interesting and entertaining as self-contained enquiries.
- They are perennial criminological concerns which have not benefited from a dialogue between historians and criminologists, e.g. the construction and validity of criminal statistics (Chapter 3) or the history of surveillance (Chapter 7).
- The topics have been prematurely consigned to the dustbin of history, e.g. the local control and governance of the police (Chapter 4); the problem of mass incarceration and the possibilities of decarceration (Chapter 8).
- They are 'live topics' in that they are currently perceived as important criminological topics – street crime, public disorder, immigration (Chapters 5 and 6).

The book is meant to be accessible to a wide range of people: undergraduates and postgraduates; academic experts working at the intersection of crime history/criminology; or those with a general interest. To that end we have devised a clear structure, with further reading for those who want to deepen their interest, and suggestions for study questions.

Following this introduction, in Chapter 1 we attempt to describe the separate developments of crime history and criminology, and how they have overlapped and converged in recent years. The chapter presents a chronology which can be found in the standard textbooks, but raises some contentious questions about who and what have been included under the auspices of history and what has been ruled in and ruled out of the discipline of criminology. Subsequent chapters then explore the contribution that historical perspectives can make to modern criminological studies, and pressing issues of crime, policing, surveillance and punishment in the twenty-first century.

Chapter 3 interrogates the reasons why criminal statistics were originally compiled and the uses to which they were put. Positivistic, interactionist and pessimistic approaches to crime statistics are discussed. Each of those perspectives has a view on the accuracy, validity and possible manipulations of crime numbers and crime rates. The chapter concludes by insisting that taking a longer perspective on the collection of crime data can inform us not so much about trends and amounts as the underlying rationales for collecting, collating and studying crime statistics.

The validity of crime statistics is a long-standing one in both historical and criminological circles. Police governance, however, has drifted in and out of fashion as a topic of study. Chapter 4 explains how local control over police forces has been eroded in recent years – and is far from the structure envisaged by nineteenth-century models of governance. Yet, the topic is set to re-emerge in the near future, with the reorganization of police forces into larger adminis-trative units that cross County jurisdictions, and with the possibility of a national force controlled by the Ministry of Justice.

Chapter 5 explores a subject that has been debated by psychologists, psychia-trists, social investigators, criminologists, historians and cultural theorists for over 100 years. These debates over the persistent or habitual offenders have been given a new twist latterly with New Labour's determination to stamp down on 'the hard core of offenders who blight our inner cities' within a general rhetoric of inclusivity and social welfare. This chapter, and Chapter 6, both chart the processes of exclusion for the poor, marginalized and immigrant members of British society. They show how conceptions about the nature of criminals, and about ethnic minorities, have directed the criminal justice system towards iniq-uitous and unjust dispositions.

Chapter 6 attacks the idea that the settled peaceable kingdom has been peri-odically unsettled by waves of unruly, uncivilized violent immigrants (Irish and East European Jewish settlers in the nineteenth century, the West Indian and Commonwealth immigration of the 1960s and 1970s, and more recently, again, fears about Eastern Europeans). The chapter unpicks attitudes towards social change, and how the criminal justice system has often been the instrument used to control 'problem' communities.

Chapter 7 also takes a long view, this time of the growth of surveillance in society. It outlines some prevailing models of surveillance and control that evolved in the nineteenth-century factory system. It then traces the faltering steps of CCTV to the point where there are now 4 million cameras in the UK – more than there are in the whole of the United States. Lastly, it re-evokes and re-examines Bentham's Panopticon, the 'ideal prison' of the eighteenth-century imagination, and one that has proved influential over social theorists in recent decades.

Chapter 8 concludes the book with a examination of mass imprisonment – how did we get to the position of having the highest ever number of people imprisoned in this country in 2007, and one of the highest per capita rates of imprisonment in the Western world? It traces the development of forms of pun-ishment, together with the aims of deterrence, rehabilitation and incapacitation that drove them. It ends by questioning whether, at the seemingly height of the power and use of the prison, we are actually about to enter a period when decarceration and community penalties can actually dominate the punitive landscape?

2

History, Criminology and 'Historical Criminology'

Chapter Contents

OVERVIEW

Chapter 2:

- Provides an introduction to the history of criminology and the development of historical studies of crime.
- Questions whether historians and criminologists are now beginning to use similar methodological and theoretical models to study crime and policing.
- Asks whether the relationship can be characterized as an overlap, collision or convergence of interest; and what the implications are of the growing relationship between history and criminology. This chapter attempts to answer this question with reference to extracts of criminological and historical writing.

KEY TERMS

criminology   crime history   historical criminology   discipline

Despite the fact that interest in the topic of crime and policing has developed significantly within the **discipline** of history during the last 20 years, and that many criminologists have also come to appreciate the value of a historical approach to their own discipline, there has actually been very little published which considers the mutual advantage of association between these two 'disciplines' or 'sub-disciplines'. The underlying rationale for this chapter is to answer or at least begin to answer a set of questions – have crime history and criminology grown closer together as they have evolved, and do they now share many of the same methods, theories, concepts and aspirations? If they have (to some extent) converged or overlapped, where do they meet? And do they meet? What would be the advantages of 'historically contextualized criminology', and what are the advantages for 'histories of crime' that are informed by criminological theory?

First, however, it is valid to ask whether criminology and crime history have anything in common at all. After all, both criminology and crime history have employed very different empirical and theoretical frameworks, and used them at different levels, in different ways, and for different purposes. Neither use the same terminology for apparently similar research methods – the 'oral history interview' seems remarkably similar to the 'survey interview', for example. Both groups of scholars seem to have been imprisoned in their own silos, or parishes, as Burke puts it:

Historians and social theorists have the opportunity to free each other from different kinds of parochialism. Historians run the risk of parochialism in an almost literal sense of the term. Specializing as they usually do in a particular region, they may come to regard their 'parish' as completely unique, rather than as a unique combination of elements each one of which has parallels elsewhere. Social theorists display parochialism in a more metaphysical sense, a parochialism of time rather than place, whenever they generalize about 'society' on the basis of contemporary experience alone, or discuss social change without taking long-term processes into account. (Burke, 1992: 2)

However, as Burke states, both groups can substantially benefit from appreciation of the other. Both disciplines seek similar insights into the functioning and regulation of past and present societies, and just as most historians have become familiar with theory, most criminologists would now say that an understanding of historical contexts is essential. As C. Wright Mills stated in *The Sociological Imagination* in 1959, 'Every social science – or better, every well considered social study – requires an historical scope of conception and a full use of historical material' (1959: 145). The caveat is essential. There are some criminologists who, although very good on their own ground, are a bit shaky when they think historically. Loose phrasing by criminologists – 'our forebears', 'in times gone by', or 'in the [unidentified] past', for example – are likely to make historians wince (King, 1999). In many criminological studies and criminology textbooks, the history of crime merely provides an introduction to the 'main' chapters that follow. There has been a prevailing sense that historical studies can be bracketed off, left behind – their authority and explanatory power contained within 'the past' and its historically specific conditions – before modern studies then explain crime and its control. As Burke lamented, historians have been perceived as antipathetic to theory, with only a few exceptions:

Relatively few historians utilize theory in the strict sense of the term, but larger numbers employ models, while concepts are virtually indispensable... The distinction between practice and theory is not identical with the distinction between history and sociology... some students of these disciplines produce case studies in which theory plays only a small role. On the other side some historians, notably the Marxists, discuss theoretical issues with vigour. (Burke, 1992: 1)

Historical studies are accepted as providing context, but the ideas they contain are somehow presented as less relevant; as dead issues. At least that has been the case until recently: because crime history and criminology seldom spoke the same language, and did not constructively interact until the late twentieth century, the relationship was characterized as a 'dialogue of the deaf' (Braudel, 1958; see also Skocpol, 1984) which neither 'side' wanted to change. For example, Hay stated that: 'Recent histories of crime and criminal law make little use of criminology, partly because it is noticeably indifferent to what interests historians most: cultural, political and economic change. More importantly, much criminology still seems to be infected with the belief that the civilised legal order must represent the healthy, or the collective conscience, or some more recent formulation of the norm' (Hay, 1980: 45). However, that comment was written over a quarter of a century ago, and perhaps we can now suggest that historians and social scientists, particularly criminologists, are at last learning to listen to each other. 'Despite not being the "best of neighbours" historians and sociologists are both concerned with the study of human behaviour' (Burke, 1992: 2). In fact, we can be more specific: the vast majority of historians and social scientists are both concerned with the way society is constructed, operated, functions, fails to function, changes, alters, interacts and otherwise affects human beings. We can also be more positive: they may be more like neighbours chatting over the garden fence, to borrow Burke's analogy, than lovers entwined in each other's arms, but historians and criminologists do now seem to be beginning to share a common framework, use similar methods and, in many cases, to reference the same social theorists (Elias and Foucault notably). Where empirical approaches are concerned, while striving for quasi-scientific rigour, both disciplines have been required to address the problems of objectivity and interpretation of evidence. Historians now think of the ethical considerations of their work much more than they once did, and both sets of scholars are sometimes required to submit their research proposals to ethics committees of one kind or other. Moreover the ecumenical instincts of many modern crime historians and criminologists have meant that their intellectual enquiries have begun to significantly interact in the last few decades. Crime history often has its own stream at criminology conferences (The British Criminology Conference, and the Australian and New Zealand Society of Criminology Conference), and crime history is now taught on the vast number of criminology and criminal justice studies courses – each year Keele University teaches crime history to 250 undergraduate criminologists, for example.[1] The pace of convergence seems to be gathering. However, because conversations between crime historians and criminologists are such recent features, it is appropriate that this chapter first provides a lengthy overview of the separate development of modern crime history and of criminology; only then will it consider how the two disciplines are coming together, and what elements of each discipline are necessary for a rigorous 'historical criminology' to flourish (if that is indeed possible and desirable).

> Criminology is the body of knowledge regarding crime as a social phenomenon. It includes within its scope the processes of making laws, of breaking laws, and of reacting towards the breaking of laws. (Sutherland and Cressey, 1955: 3)

This statement by Sutherland and Cressey established the modern conception of criminology, detaching it from a scientific format and ushering it into the social sciences – into the realm of norms, transgressions, processes, institutions and policy. Yet even this expansive if fairly prosaic description of criminology seems constraining for the subject of criminology today.

Before the development of undergraduate criminology courses, dedicated academic journals and criminological textbooks, the teachers and theorists of criminology were drawn from geography, history, biology, psychology, political sciences, law and economics. Indeed they still are. Criminology as a discipline, a subject, a practice, a set of intentions, once again interacts with a broad range of social sciences and humanities. What it has lost in disciplinary cohesiveness it may have made up for in a healthy diversity and interaction of empirical, methodological and theoretical discussions. Possibly. That is perhaps a topic for a different debate. This chapter will contribute to discussions by describing the progress of criminology as a distinct subject from the nineteenth century onwards; and by describing how crime history has made its own distinct contribution to criminology, especially in recent years. It describes the rise of classical criminology and its adherents (Beccaria, Bentham) through to the 'scientific criminology' (Lombroso) of the late twentieth century, but ends before the penal-welfarist more pragmatic/administrative criminology changed the field in the early to mid twentieth century.[2] This is a somewhat traditional history of the criminological enterprise, but the chapter will also include (albeit to a limited extent due to space[3]) the tradition of inchoate English amateur social inquiry into crime which has been rather ignored by orthodox histories (Plint, 1851; Pike, 1876; Mayhew, 1851–61).

A sub-discipline itself, crime history, like criminology, is also diverse and tends to interact with broader histories of the social, with political and economic history, geography, literary and cultural studies. Like criminologists, crime historians come in many shapes and forms – those who favour quantitative analyses; qualitative, literary and oral historians; empiricists and theorists; modernists and post-modernists; those concerned with the institutions of criminal justice, the penal-welfare complex, the agencies of control; those focusing on social order, regulation and surveillance; those who study legislation or particular types of crime; and those that study the offender, or the victims of crime. In describing how crime history developed, this chapter will chart the optimistic Whig histories that described the inevitable progress of the criminal justice system and its power to deliver peaceful society (Radzinowicz, 1948; Critchley, 1967, 1970; Reith 1943). It then describes the challenge that arose to those views in the 1970s and 1980s by radical or Marxist historians (Hay, 1975; Thompson, 1975; Linebaugh, 1991), before showing how the field 'exploded' in the last few decades, with crime history for the first time both producing a critical mass of researchers and research students and also reaching out to criminology in a way which should propel the field forward into new and exciting areas.

A word or warning: this chapter reflects our personal and possibly idiosyncratic history of the intellectual area that the authors inhabit and explore. Some – on both sides: criminologists and historians – will take issue with our characterization of our joint disciplinary history, and some will be surprised to find Henry Mayhew (the Victorian social investigator and journalist) and Thomas Holmes (the late nineteenth-century police court missionary) contained within the history of criminology; whilst Michel Foucault (the influential French social theorist) is enlisted as a historian. Crime history, unlike criminology in this respect, has not quite yet coalesced into a distinct sub-discipline with those who guard its intellectual borders. That process has begun, with review essays and crime history textbooks beginning to rule some topics in, and some topics out. Even broad churches have walls, but whilst crime historians are still inclined to continue expanding intellectual horizons, we will press on with our characterization of the development of crime history, and be prepared to continue discussions on this and other points.

The history of the criminology

As Garland has noted (2002), the division of criminology into periods such as classicism and positivism is a common feature of textbooks, but the application of such labels is misleading. The periods that historians might prefer to call, say, 'the Enlightenment' and *'fin de siecle'* (there are a number of terms that could be applied with equal validity) are labels that can only be applied retrospectively when layers of intellectual endeavour and historical conditions have been identified and 'named'. Since the criminological project can only be really clearly identified as beginning in the late nineteenth century (Lombrosian positivism especially), the corralling of writers like Beccaria and Bentham into a neat history of the discipline is particularly problematic. This chapter does not seek to comprehensively document the history or pre-history of criminological theory – there are a hundred textbooks that can do that. In general we can say that early modern writers were concerned with vagabonds, unruly apprentices, lawless mobs and highway robbers. In the eighteenth century, those concerns largely continued but they were joined by social commentators who were advocating change to the arbitrary use of power, and the greater calibration of punishment to the offence caused. It is these commentators that have received the greatest attention from modern criminologists and for that reason they have been dragooned into some histories of criminology. We do it ourselves in this book, in fact, when discussing **Jeremy Bentham's Panopticon** (see Chapters 6 and 7).

We do try to remember, however, that although the theories of Beccaria and Bentham are given prominence by modern criminologists, the vast number of eighteenth- and nineteenth-century contemporaries perceived crime as a moral issue and therefore saw greater or harsher punishments as the answer to criminality (Bailey, 1993; Godfrey and Lawrence, 2005). Criminologists have ignored these views largely because they are not 'progressive' in any sense, and are a dead-end in criminological theory. Historians, however, have been keener to take into account those commonly held opinions, and those that researched them – social investigators such as Henry Mayhew.

Henry Mayhew (1812–87) was a journalist and sometime editor of *Punch* magazine, who published three volumes intending to document the lives of London's working classes in the 1850s. He carried out interviews with a wide range of street workers and street dwellers which showed the labouring poor in the main to be hard working, uneducated but well-meaning. Although the chapters were formed using the words of the interviewees, Mayhew's editorializing shines through, and he has cut, clipped and trimmed interviews to form a narrative that (largely) supports social reform of the kind he advocated – relief and support for the deserving poor and the respectable labouring classes. The last volume in his series, however, focused on those who were even further at the margins of polite society than the domestic servants, costermongers, street traders and street entertainers he had previously encountered:

> To show the class of characters usually frequenting these lodging houses, I will now give the statement of a boy – a young pickpocket – without shoes or stockings. He wore a ragged, dirty, and very thin great coat... designedly made – in the outer garment were slits through which the hand readily reached the pockets of the inner pockets of the inner garment, and could there deposit any booty. (Mayhew, 1861)

The 15-year-old boy described his apprenticeship in a pottery, and his life living on the streets after being dismissed from work for clumsily breaking pots. He therefore fitted Mayhew's theory that misfortune led to crime, and that orphans especially were prone to becoming thieves. After being recruited and trained in the 'art' of pick-pocketing, he was imprisoned 13 times.

> Every time I come out harder than I went in. I've had four floggings; it was bad enough – a flogging was – while it lasted; but when I got out I soon forgot it. At a week's end I never thought again about it. If I had been better treated I should have been a better lad. I could leave off thieving now as if I had never thieved, if I could leave without. (Mayhew, 1861)

Mayhew comments in the text that he doubts the veracity of that last sentence. Mayhew, like his contemporaries, saw crime as a moral failing, a weakness in the character of those who fell into gambling, drunkenness, prostitution and theft because they lacked the will to lead an honest working life (Mayhew's volume on criminals, *London's Underworld*, published in 1862, was originally entitled 'Those who will not work'.) The boy expected to be transported to a penal settlement, a device supposed to sweep criminals away from Britain's shores rather than have any rehabilitative effect. Mayhew interviewed one ex-convict who made the long trip back, with old age, rather than the penal experience, bringing the end of his criminal career.

> I was two years and a half at this same trade. One week was very like another – successes and escapes, and free-and-easies, and games of all sorts, made up the life. At the end of the two years and a half I got into the way of forged Bank-of-England notes... I saw Cashman hanged for [robbing] that gunsmith's shop on Snow-hill, and I saw Fauntleroy hanged [the last man to be hanged for forgery, in 1824], and a good many others, but it gave me no uneasiness and no fear. The gallows had no terror for people in my way of life. (Mayhew, 1861)

Despite casting doubt on the effectiveness of contemporary systems of transportation, corporal and capital punishment, Mayhew was influential in helping to cement the idea of a criminal 'class' who lurked in urban areas, and who were essentially unreformable, but he was only reflecting a new *zeitgeist*.[4] For example, a decade before Mayhew's volume was published, the Leeds social reformer, Thomas Plint, described the criminal class in *Crime in England* (1851) in similar terms and Charles Dickens, who was an important social reformer as well as successful author, disseminated ideas about the criminal class to a large middle-class audience. The ideas of Mayhew, Plint and a mass of newspaper writers who took up their ideas, helped to create a conceptual divide between those who deserved help from government and philanthropists, and those who had placed themselves beyond society – a group who only necessitated punishment and constant surveillance (see Chapter 6).

The 'criminal class', and changing perceptions of criminality, are described more fully in Chapter 4. However, with hindsight, one could identify the 1850s and 1860s as the start of the 'othering' process which created a cultural milieu where criminals were defined as separate from respectable society – and when the criminology of the other, rather than the criminology of the self truly began. It could be said, therefore, that Mayhew, and others like him, have been unduly written out of the history of criminology.

Socio-historical processes of identification and categorization that Mayhew employed were reinforced and accelerated by the new 'science' of criminology and the scientific/historical conjunctions that supported it between the 1870s and the First World War. As the 'science' developed and recruited more adherents across first Europe then the world, it coalesced into a form of enquiry substantial enough to warrant its own historians, and to regularly feature in standard histories of criminology. Let us briefly chart the history of scientific criminology – which as we shall see relied on the measurement of physical characteristics, and taxonomic categorization. Those people who were being 'left behind' or 'left out' of a dynamic Victorian economy were attracting attention from medical psychologists, biologists and social policy-makers as much as they were from criminologists. The 'residuum' of nineteenth-century society caused such concern both to those who wished to give them a helping hand up the social scale, and those who wanted to keep them down.[5] Those poor devils – the insane, the vagrant, the homeless, the criminal, the disillusioned, the downtrodden, the poor – that were chewed up and spat out by mature capitalism in the Victorian period, the lowest and most unproductive members of society, that Karl Marx considered the non-productive working class. That is where the criminological gaze started to fall.

In 1876, Cesare Lombroso of Turin University produced his best-known work, *L'uomo delinquente*, and one frequently cited as the origin of scientific criminology. The conclusions he drew from his series of autopsies on criminals drew heavily on the theories of Charles Darwin. His book *On the Origin of Species* (1859) suggested a biologically determined path of human development rather than one of 'divine creation'. The erosion of religious authority that Darwin's work implied was first taken on board by scientists. Lombroso's views were that criminality was not a rational choice or a moral failing but could be the result of a hereditary trait passed through the generations, reinforcing the inability of some to adapt to civilized society – their physical appearance and the criminality and vice being the proof of that theory. Lombroso's theories struck a chord with many influential thinkers across Europe (and particularly with continental European police forces). Darwin had asserted the importance of hereditary and environmental factors in the sphere of biology, and had implied that such factors were potentially more important than 'the will of the individual' in the development of humanity. Lombrosian theory therefore seemed to fit well with modern understandings of biological determinism, and consequently his theories on criminality achieved credibility. His belief that certain physical stigmata were apparent within national groupings, and in prostitutes and criminals (e.g. a deviation in head size and shape from the types common to ethnic groups, eye defects and peculiarities, pouches in the cheeks like those of some animals, the abundance, variety and precocity of wrinkles) promoted an anthropocentric criminology which lent itself to scientific investigation, measurement, categorization, cause and effect. Scientific criminology seemed to offer the opportunity to identify criminals before the crime had been committed; it therefore appeared (however fallaciously we now view those theories) to be a hugely valuable weapon in the Victorian and Edwardian war against crime. Although they never wrote about the darker possibilities of their theories, Lombroso's and

Darwin's theories were as unsettling as they were reassuring because they also fitted frighteningly well into emerging theories of degeneracy in the 1890s.

If, as Darwin had proved, the course of human history was not divinely ordained, then 'progress' was not assured. If mankind could evolve, could it not also 'degenerate'? As Godfrey and Lawrence note:

> The Second Law of Thermodynamics in 1851, and the concomitant discovery of 'entropy' (the idea that the universe had a finite life, and that energy could eventually be dissipated), while obviously having no immediate implications for Victorian society, did perhaps augment the notion both that 'progress' was not assured in human affairs, and that the 'will of the individual' was insignificant when set against the environmental constraints acting upon him/her. Certainly, the impact of the development of notions of 'degeneration' is vital to an understanding of changing perceptions of criminals in the nineteenth century. Degeneration theory was a diffuse current of social thought. It was, broadly speaking, concerned with the underbelly of progress, with the notion that modern, urban, industrial life was inherently unhealthy (both mentally and physically) and would eventually produce a 'degenerate' race of humans, weak, debilitated, morally corrupt and incapable of decisive social interaction. (Godfrey and Lawrence, 2006)

Psychiatry, as well as criminology and a host of other social sciences, was developing in this period, and much of what has been written about degeneration has come from practitioners seeking to use degeneration as an explanation for the 'feeble mindedness' of inmates in mental institutions. For example, the work of Henry Maudsley, who emerged in the 1870s as the leading psychologist of the era, was very influential. He noted that:

> in consequences of evil ancestral influences, individuals are born with such a flaw or warp of nature that all the care in the world will not prevent them from being vicious or criminal, or becoming insane... No one can escape the tyranny of his organisation; no one can elude the destiny that is innate in him, and which unconsciously and irresistibly shapes his ends, even when he believes that he is determining them with consummate foresight and skill. (Maudsley, 1873: 76)

The theories promoted by Maudsley, as a psychiatrist, were almost indistinguishable for proto-criminologists like L. Gordon Rylands for example (Rylands, 1889: 35; Wiener, 1990; Leps, 1992; and see also Chapter 4).

The theory of degenerative genetic criminality was not monolithic, nor was it static. For example, in 1906, Dr. T.S. Clouston, President of the Royal College of Physicians, explained that inherited conditions did not lead directly to criminality, but that over time, problematic inherited characteristics could allow temptation to overwhelm the weak of will.

A bad nervous heredity means mental unresistiveness to the causes of mental weakness and ill-health. The margin of security is less. While a man who has good heredity may with impunity take many liberties in the way he uses his brain, this is not safe if he has a bad heredity. There are modes of upbringing, of education, and of conduct in life that should be avoided where a man is handicapped by bad heredity... While heredity implies a potentiality towards good and evil it commonly needs a special exciting cause or combination of causes to bring out visible effect. Take the excessive use of alcohol as an example – the father and mother of a boy have indulged in it before and during his life *in utero*, he has been poisoned *in embryo*, they have both acquired an uncontrollable craving for it, the boy has thereby acquired a weak constitution, probably neurotic in its character, and his development of body and mind has not been perfect. Few students of heredity would say that he had necessarily acquired the special craving for alcohol from his parents. All that is affirmed is that his power of mental inhibition would probably be weak and his defences generally below par. He would not be able to withstand social temptations, and alcohol would have a quicker and worse effect on him than on his parents. But on the other hand, if his health in childhood and youth were specially attended to, and his body and brain thereby strengthened, if his education were made a specially suitable one, if he selected an open-air occupation, if he took no alcohol, if during adolescence especially he were guarded from severe temptation, all these influences would be likely so as to strengthen his mental inhibition and antagonise his heredity that he would not fall into the alcoholic condition, and *might* even procreate mentally healthy children. (Clouston, 1906: 61–62, emphasis added)

So there we have it, in brief. Until scientific criminology came along with all of its faults, particular views on criminality privileging moral failings as the cause of vice were given credence by religious figures, and a range of dispersed voices occasionally ventured ways that the authorities could prevent the spread of immorality. New scientific criminological discourses in the 1890s then placed authority in the hands of a small group of experts: psychiatrists, geneticists and, yes, 'criminologists'. We could continue the history of scientific criminology up to the present day with discussions of the criminal gene, and how it may or may not cause or enable criminality in particular individuals. Indeed it is the central platform of this book that debates that have taken place in the past continue to have a resonance today. However, let us now leave the *progression* of criminological theory, to instead pose some different and perhaps provocative questions.

In reviewing the orthodox history of criminology, it is clear that criminology as a discipline could not claim a common methodological approach – Lombroso employed scientific rationalism, Beccaria and Bentham were philosophers who developed their ideas on punishment without empirical research (as will be seen in Chapter 6). This is unsurprising, and criminologists today employ a wide range of methodologies – ethnography, participant observation survey, and interviews.

This last method was also employed, of course, by Mayhew; and so we return again to ask why Mayhew has not yet found a regular spot within criminology textbooks. Second, the development of criminology as a discipline does not seem dissimilar to that of the disciplines of medicine, psychiatry, psychology and sociology, and yet the histories of those professional groups (and the development of ideas associated with those expert groups in their formative stages) are all contained comfortably within the province of traditional history syllabuses. Why should the history of criminology remain so resolutely outside the realm of social history and its researchers? If historians of crime are not writing about the history of criminology, then what on earth are they writing about?

Histories of crime

Historians of crime – particularly low level and non-political crime – have been slow off the mark. Crime seldom rates an entry in the contents (or even in the indexes) of general histories of British society before the 1980s, even the 1990s. Crime history has attempted to understand the processes and interactions between how people perceived crime and its impact at particular moments in history; how it was represented in sources of information (such as newspapers, pamphlets, and popular songs); how the authorities reacted; and what changed over time. But the interest in these issues has been slow to grow, and has developed in particular directions, as the following paragraphs will illustrate, starting with the Whig view of crime.

In 1948 Sir Leon Radzinowicz published an authoritative history of the criminal law and its operation. In his preface to *A History of English Criminal Law*, he implicitly identified three key concerns of 'early' crime historians – progressive reform (from the eighteenth century onwards); presentism (that the lessons of the past can assist the modern criminal justice system); and the close relationship between criminal history and wider contexts of social history. The chapters that followed his Preface kept to these guidelines, and his description of the development of policing and the law is bathed in the golden light of the eighteenth-century Enlightenment:

> Child of the Common Law, nourished and moulded by Statute, the criminal law of England has always been sensitive to the needs and aspirations of the English people, and it has continuously changed under the impact of the predominant opinion of the day. Yet while it has never been static, its rate of growth has been uneven, and the main features which it presents today were built up from the movement for reform which began in the middle of the eighteenth century. To that development the forces of morality, of philosophical thought and of social consciousness all made their contribution. (Radzinowicz, 1948: ix)

There is no doubt that this work stood alone as an important work which would substantially influence and inform post-war historians. It formed part of what has come to be known as the Whig view of history. This form of history is usually portrayed as championing the inevitable progress of the United Kingdom towards refinement, order, social contentment and peaceable living. The police were pictured in this theory as key instruments of the State which could bring this desirable and contented situation about. Whig history is now often parodied, but its adherents were not simply viewing the world through rose-tinted glasses, nor were they bad or inadequate historians. However, they, like all scholars, were products of their time, personal educational and occupational backgrounds, and social conditions. Reith was writing when German bombs were falling, and notions of English civilization and progressive reason were everywhere juxtaposed against brutal totalitarianism. Critchley wrote his works when the post-war consensus was virtually intact. He saw the 1950s and 1960s as the era of 'Dixon of Dock Green', when police efficiency was such that constables could arrest the odd bad lot who didn't fit into the generally law-abiding citizens of the 1950s and 1960s. No wonder Reith (1943), Critchley (1967) and others looked back at eighteenth- and nineteenth-century policing agencies as earlier, inferior, but essentially recognisable versions of the twentieth-century police force. They looked to the future with optimism, looking forward to building on the strong foundation provided by past successes.

The Whig view was not so much revised as swatted away by the radical historians of the 1970s and 1980s. Marxist scholars used studies of the eighteenth-century Bloody Code and eradication of customary rights in the countryside and in the workplace to illustrate the class bias they believed permeated the criminal law (and society as a whole). Brilliant scholars (Doug Hay and Raphael Samuel especially) ripped apart the consensual positivistic views of crime history. Peter Linebaugh (1991) and Doug Hay showed how the discretionary nature of capital punishment empowered local elites, and how the criminal code generally supported 'the ruling classes'. Edward Thompson demonstrated with clarity and powerful arguments that industrial capitalism had reconfigured the customary world, and that the criminal justice system was the motor for increased discipline in society. We could not mention discipline without considering the contribution of Michel Foucault who provided a different but equally challenging view of the relationship between crime, knowledge and power.

Foucault's *Discipline and Punish* (1975) examined power in relationship to both knowledge and the physical body, focusing on what he saw as the coercive technologies of control over it. He argued that institutions such as the army, the factory and the school disciplined bodies thorough surveillance techniques (either real or merely assumed to exist). He mapped the emergence of a disciplinary society and its new articulation of power by analyzing Jeremy Bentham's infamous prison design, the Panopticon (see Chapter 7 and Chapter 8).

Somehow these histories – 'Albion's Fatal Tree' (1975), 'Whigs and Hunters' (1975), 'Discipline and Punish' (1977) – suited the times. However, the ideological direction that crime history had been thrust in had tended to limit the horizon. For example, the decline of the customary world was blamed on the industrial organization of labour and the increasing power of nineteenth- and twentieth-century disciplinary institutions, but few were interested in empirical studies of factory discipline (aside from Thompson's 1967 article). Foucault's work was criticized for lacking not only a gender perspective, but also much of the empirical evidence that could support the theoretical model. Whilst some types of crime (poaching, workplace theft) and some punishment types (capital punishment, prison designs) had received considerable attention, the everyday offences – property offences, interpersonal violence, low-level nuisances – had been ignored. The daily traffic of magistrates courts (which dealt with virtually all offenders then as now) seemed to have been ignored. However, at the end of the twentieth century, the idea of crime history caught the wind.

It would be reasonable to speak of an explosion of crime history in the 1990s and the 2000s. A cohort of Ph.D students in the 1990s produced detailed empirical studies of crime and policing in various towns and cities across Britain. To these were added important studies of juvenile offending (Shore, 1999), policing in Victorian towns (Taylor, 2002), gender and victimisation (D'Cruze, 1998), gangs (Davies, 1998), interpersonal violence (Wood, 2004) and the criminal justice system (King, 2000). We have limited ourselves to a small indicative list, and the fact that we have left out references to a huge number of important works merely supports our point that the field has expanded so dramatically. Modern crime problems also seemed to inspire historical research. The recent concern over predatory paedophiles must surely have provoked some to investigate the past (Brown and Barratt, 2002; Jackson, 2000). If the evidence of piles of books and hundreds of crime history articles are anything to go by, there is therefore no reason to think that interest in crime history will subside over the next few decades.

Crime historians have now begun to define themselves and the boundaries of their subject. Reviews of the field have been published – three editions of Clive Emsley's *Crime and Society in England 1750–1900* have appeared between 1986 and 2004 – and they have been joined by Taylor (1998), Rawlings (1999) and Godfrey and Lawrence (2005). How the processes of defining the subject and the topics within it affect the growing relationship between crime history and criminology remains to be seen, and is indeed the focus of the next section of this chapter.

Overlap, collision or convergence?

In the previous two sections we have produced a chronological categorization of crime history and criminology. We suggest in this section that the development of crime history and of criminology have intertwined significantly in recent years. We hope to show now that crime history is part of a living and vital criminological tradition which presents historical data along with, not to prove or support or challenge, modern research. We therefore place historical enquiry on an equal footing with social scientific research.

It seems to us that crime history and criminology have now come to terms with each other, and are now creating their own history of interaction. For example, it does not make much sense to classify John Lea's work as criminological or historical, as they are so closely interwoven in his study of crime and modernity (2002). The same could, quite obviously, be said for Garland's *Punishment and Welfare* (1985) and other books (Sim, 1990; and Loader and Mulcahy, 2003, for example). Pearson's (1983) study of cyclical fears of youth crime and 'hooliganism' weaves together historical evidence to debunk the myth of the British Golden Age in a book which is read equally by historians and criminologists:

> This book aims to cast some old light on new problems. It is about street crime and violence. But it is also about myth and tradition: the myth of the 'British way of life' according to which, after centuries of domestic peace, the streets of Britain have been suddenly plunged into an unnatural state of disorder that betrays the stable traditions of the past. What I hope to show, by contrast, is that real traditions are quite different: that for generations Britain has been plagued by the same fears and problems as today; and that this is something which should require us to reassess the shape of our present difficulties and the prospects for the future... But the English have been blaming their violence on someone else for a century or more, and in the past street crime and disorderly conduct have been foisted on to any number of alien influences – 'street Arabs', 'hot-blooded' ruffians, the 'offscouring of the Continent', discharged Foreign Legionnaires, 'Americanised television violence', and so on – with a particularly fixed tradition of groaning English fears about Americanisation which stretches back to the mid-nineteenth century as part of this effort to uphold the illusion of a peaceful inheritance in which violence is entirely foreign to the English national character. Indeed, it is wonderfully apt that in a key moment of this tradition, when late Victorian London christened its own unruly offspring... an 'Irish' name was chosen, providing the key term in the discourse: *hooligan*. (Pearson 1983: ix–xi)

Without historical perspective Jock Young could not achieve his aim to trace 'the rapid unravelling of the social fabric of the industrialized world in the last third of the twentieth century, charting the rise of individualism and of demands for social equality which emerged on the back of the market forces that have permeated and transformed every nook and cranny of social life. It notes the slow but steady erosion of deference whether it is in politics, in public life, in the classroom or in the family' (Young, 1999: vi). Nor would John Pratt's study of social and penal policy make much sense without historical data: 'dangerousness, as it were, is a concept of risk and its strategies of management found their way into the social fabric of the late nineteenth century. From that time onwards, dangerousness has been given a continuous momentum by the fears and anxieties attendant upon the conditions of modern life' (Pratt, 1997: 6). A last example is Godfrey et al.'s (2007) exploration of the impact of structural factors experienced at individual level, particularly employment opportunities and relationship-formation, to desistence from offending. They use historical data sets running over long periods of time and criminological theory to try to piece together the lives of offenders with results they hope are relevant to social policy-makers today:

> Naturally, we were constrained to considering only those factors that we had access to data about, and these, of course, were 'social' (rather than psychological or psychosocial) in nature. Marriage and having children, as modern commentators have found, appear to act as mechanisms for reforming men who wish to please or win approval from their spouses or who generally accept the responsibility that parenthood brings. We suggested that in times when gender inequalities are less pronounced than they were in the late nineteenth and early twentieth centuries, females are able to exert (willingly or otherwise) a greater degree of control over their boyfriends and husbands (and for that matter, maybe over their fathers and brothers too). However, our data led us to conclude that because the nature of marriage in the late nineteenth and early twentieth centuries was different to its modern meaning, the impact it had on male behaviour was not so strong, not so persuasive...

> ...we seek to draw lessons from our studies of the late nineteenth and early twentieth centuries which may be of use to those studying these issues in the contemporary. But why, first of all, ought criminologists studying desistance using contemporary data be concerned with what was happening around 100 years earlier? We think that there are a number of reasons why they might wish to take an interest in studies such as our own.

> ...Crewe in 2004, just as we commenced our fieldwork, was in some respects little different from Crewe in 1904. The railway is still an important part of 'what' Crewe was (even if it had been severely cut back in the 1990s). The Works are, along with Rolls-Royce/Bentley, a major employer (although with a much reduced number of employees), and Crewe is still a major hub for train travel in the North West and along the west coast main line from London to Glasgow. There is still a sizeable locomotive depot to

the south of Crewe station and a large set of sidings further south still. Much of the housing stock is still Victorian terraces, although this too is changing as new houses are built to meet local housing needs. Many people in Crewe live and work there or in the immediately surrounding area and there are still parts of Crewe where crime appears more likely to occur, and still places where it is less likely to occur – and these regularities appear to have changed little over 100 years or so. Many of the buildings built by or at the time of the Works' ascendancy are still standing (the market, Lyceum theatre, and Town Hall, for example). On the other hand, it is a very different place. There are fewer jobs related to the locomotive building industry, fewer public houses, less rented accommodation, more police officers, a university campus and a host of other social changes.

...These changes help us to make sense of crime and offending as part of a social process as well as simply the outcome of a series of individual choices. Societies change, and 'change' at that level is often about change in structural factors foremost and individual-level change which follows it. As societies change they reveal continuities and discontinuities which can help us to make sense of the processes at play when individuals desist from criminality. This is not to suggest that we ought to exclude from our consideration all individual-level processes, but rather that when we are able to explore processes of desistance over 100 years ago, it is inevitably the structural factors which will draw our focus. (Godfrey et al., 2007)

Therefore, society is, one could state, always part way through one kind of structural change or other, or more usually a plethora of simultaneous structural changes. Consequently, perspective helps to clarify and monitor the direction as well as the dimensions of 'change'. Godfrey et al.'s use of criminological theory and historical data will hopefully become part of a larger collection of studies and publications that take a similar line. Time will tell.

Summary

We have, in this chapter, outlined the development of crime history and criminology. Although they have experienced different intellectual forces, somewhat but not wholly different methodologies, and been preoccupied with different forms of criminality and formations of social order at times, it is clear that the disciplines have grown closer together. Whether the subjects approached in this book (see Chapters 3 to 8) should properly be situated within a 'history' or 'criminology' book is an interesting but ultimately fruitless enquiry. Indeed we have asserted that some recent studies of crime cannot be solely categorized as criminology or history, the extent of convergence is that great. That situation, we believe, will become more and more common, as seems to be the wish of both historians and criminologists. Perhaps the last word should go to Gary Lafree in his 2006 Presidential Address to the American Society of Criminology:

> I argue that our field would be strengthened by expanding the domain of criminology in five directions: 1) by providing more emphasis on historical data and analysis, 2) by broadening the scope of emotions we test for among offenders, 3) by doing more cross-national comparative analysis, 4) by bringing situational variables into our research, and 5) by making criminology more interdisciplinary. (Lafree, 2007)

We could not agree more.

STUDY QUESTIONS

1 What have been the main developments in criminological theory from the eighteenth to twentieth centuries?
2 How has crime history developed from the Second World War to the twenty-first century?
3 How and in what ways have the two disciplines grown closer together?
4 What are the future possibilities for historically informed criminology and criminologically informed history?

FURTHER READING

Emsley, C. (2005) *Crime and Society in England, 1750-1900*, 3rd edition, Longman: Harlow.
Garland, D. (1985) 'The Criminal and His Science. A Critical Account of the Formation of Criminology at the End of the Nineteenth Century', *British Journal of Criminology*, 25(2): 109-37.
Godfrey B. and Lawrence, P. (2005) *Crime and Justice 1750-1950*, Cullompton: Willan Publishing.
Rock, P. (1988) *A History of British Criminology*, Clarendon Press: Oxford.
Rock, P. (2003) 'Sociological theories of crime', in M. Maguire, R. Morgan and R. Reiner, *The Oxford Handbook of Criminology*, 3rd edition, Oxford University Press: Oxford, pp. 51-83.

Notes

1 Where once one would struggle to find a course containing a history of crime element, it is now extremely common for criminal justice and criminology courses to include modules on crime history or the history of deviance, as well as on the foundations of criminology itself. History

degree courses too, even when not specifically addressing the issue of crime, usually include modules on large-scale disorders (industrial disputes and labour relations; food riots and the economy; political movements which were heavily policed, and so on).

2 It is not our intention to describe a complete history of criminology from early developments through scientific criminology, to post-modern criminology. A visit to any academic bookshop will reveal many textbooks which give adequate attention to the history of criminology.

3 For a more fulsome description of the contributions made to the discipline by proto-criminologists, see Mannheim, 1960; Fattah, 1997; and Garland, 2002.

4 The existence of such widely held ideas about a criminal class should not be taken to mean that such a 'class' ever actually existed. In fact, most historians would now argue, as Bailey (1993: 246) does, that 'whatever Victorians thought, very few Victorian criminals were full-time "professionals"'. Emsley (2005: 177) agrees that, 'the more historians probe the reality of such a class, the more it is revealed to be spurious'. Rather than the bulk of crime being committed by small, professional gangs, it is far more probable that most crimes were committed by ordinary working people who needed to supplement their paltry wages. It is also unlikely that most offenders were culturally or socially very different from other members of the working class. See Chapter 4 for a greater understanding of ideas on the 'criminal class'.

5 Although mainly associated with the 1880s and 1890s, the idea of an unproductive 'social problem group' which included the mentally ill, the criminally divergent and the physically disabled actually continued in one form or another up until the Second World War. For example, the Wood Committee on Mental Deficiency concluded in 1929 that, while 'low grade defectives' (defined as idiots and imbeciles) were evenly distributed throughout society, what it termed the 'higher-grade feeble minded' were concentrated at the bottom of society, in a 'social problem group' clearly distinct from the bulk of the working class (Macnicol, 1987: 302).

3

The History of Criminal Statistics

Chapter Contents

OVERVIEW

Chapter 3:

- Provides the history of statistical collection of crime data. It asks, which crimes were statistically recorded and why? The chapter explores how statistics also increasingly came to be manipulated by a variety of agencies.
- Analyses the nature of British historical criminal statistics. What credence can we place in the statistics? How much spin was involved in presenting statistics? What part did labelling play in distorting the crime statistics?
- Reveals problems in interpreting crime data. How can criminologists and historians explain what the statistics 'mean'? We consider positivist, interactionist and pessimistic approaches towards criminal statistics.
- Concludes by examining how and why past debates about criminal statistics continue to hold their relevance today.

KEY TERMS

criminal statistics	positivism	pessimism
crime trends	interactionism	

Many of the most important questions in historical criminology are quantitative. Is crime, as an indicator of wider social problems, on the rise? Did crime, particularly violent crime, decline during the nineteenth century, and is it rising now? Have the aggregated characteristics of criminality remained the same throughout history? Just about all the discussion of the state of criminal justice in the present makes an explicit reference to the past. Almost always this is to point to a relatively crime- or violence-free past and contrast this to the present (Pearson, 1983; Hitchens, 2003). Another thing that many social commentators have done is to talk about 'rates' of crime. Whether they mention actual numbers or not, they are making claims about the total amount of crime: a measure that we can only arrive at through adding up lots of discrete incidents to produce a total. 'Statistics', defined as 'the science of collecting and analysing numerical data' (*The Concise Oxford Dictionary*), are what we end up with when we aggregate together large numbers of events. Naturally then, there is a constructed aspect to all statistics. However, for the last 200 years, statistics of all kinds have been a central element in the way that advanced societies are governed, and the way that political adjustments to that governance have been advocated and justified. Statistics tend to be taken to be scientific, independent and therefore accurate.

This chapter will look at the ways that criminal statistics have been defined and used; both by contemporaries who published them and discussed them, and later by historians who have tried to see what conclusions can be drawn from them. It will begin with an overview of the genesis and development of data about crime and criminality, consider in detail some of the many debates which crime statistics have engendered, and raise some sceptical questions about the validity and authenticity of crime statistics.

It is tempting to perceive the history of criminal statistics as one of progress and growing sophistication, but is this actually the case? From their inception (which happened in 1805 in the UK), crime statistics have been used to support specific policy aims, and this chapter will consider the many ways in which the concerns of those gathering data about crime may have shaped the nature and reliability of the information collected.

Rather more than many of the other chapters in this book, this one will talk explicitly about the debates among historians over statistics of crime. These debates arise from the difficulty in agreeing what the official figures mean, and what genuine lessons we can learn from them. The main lesson to come out of these debates between historians is 'beware': the official returns certainly do not give us an obvious and accurate picture of the levels of crime in the past. A few historians have argued that certain sets of official figures (but not all of them) can tell us some things about crime rates at some times. Most, though, take the position that official statistics are most useful for telling us about the activity of the criminal justice system, rather than the 'state of crime'. But whatever we choose to use them for, the more we know about why and how they were collected, the better our conclusions will be. The use of criminal returns to calculate 'objective' crime rates has been, and remains, fraught with difficulty and only with the relatively recent arrival of large-scale victim report surveys, such as the British Crime Survey, can a reasonable (though still imperfect) estimate of real crime rates and trends be made.

Different sorts of crime

In order to understand how crime has been counted in the past, we need to appreciate that in Britain there were two different ways that suspects could be dealt with. The first was the simple way, generally reserved for the less serious crimes, of dealing with them via *summary* means, through the action of a justice or justices in a local magistrates' court which sat daily or weekly. This was quick and cheap, but the penalties that could be handed down were limited. More serious crime was dealt with 'on *indictment'*. The suspect would be held until the next county Quarter Sessions (where s/he would face a bench of justices), or for very serious crimes the next county Assize Court. Some crimes, notably assault, could be tried in either way.

Before the middle of the nineteenth century, there was no system of public prosecution in England: it was the responsibility of the victim to initiate the law's pursuit of the offender, and once they had been caught, to finance a prosecution. If successful, they would be paid reasonable expenses from public funds, but the expense of mounting a prosecution naturally deterred many victims from doing so. Historian Peter King has exhaustively studied the way that the criminal justice system worked in the eighteenth century, and has come to some startling conclusions about the proportion of crime that was ever followed up with a prosecution. Working from diaries and personal papers, he estimated the number of times that victims of theft (a serious crime with harsh penalties, but one which was difficult and expensive to prosecute) ever reported the crime to the authorities, and pursued their suspects through the courts. He concluded that fewer than 1 in 20 (5%) of thefts resulted in a prosecution (King, 2000). This is just one example of what has become notorious as the 'dark figure' of unknown crime, a problem which has stalked crime statistics since their inception.

The birth of criminal statistics

The word 'statistics' first appeared in the late eighteenth century, referring to knowledge used to improve the running of the state (Hoppit, 1996: 517). Its modern meaning, of specifically numerical knowledge, developed in the early nineteenth century when the first statisticians to apply mathematical techniques to the analysis of data concentrated initially on crime and criminality. Thus it is unsurprising that policing, a vitally important exercise of state power, has always been bound up with statistics. The criteria and forms of collection have changed many times over the years. Nevertheless, despite the changes, studies of criminal justice statistics maintain common themes: the ways that counting crimes has served as a spur to reform of policing and punishment; the ways that statistics have then been deployed by police forces and prison authorities to justify their existence; and the way that numerical information has been used *within* the criminal justice system as a means of control and supervision of employees as well as of inmates.

In England and Wales, the first nationally collated set of figures related to crime was instituted in 1810, when the House of Commons ordered the collection of details of all those committed to trial for indictable offences: the first run of numbers went back to 1804. Comprehensive statistics of the criminal justice system in France were published by the Department of Justice from 1827, and these became the model for Belgium, Sweden, Austria and several German and US states. These appear to have helped prompt the UK's Home Office to collect more information. In 1834 they grouped the offences for which they were recording committals into six broad categories, which were used until the 1980s: crimes of violence against the person; non-violent property crime; property crime involving violence; forgery and offences against the currency; malicious offences against property (e.g. criminal damage); and miscellaneous crimes. Also prompted by the French returns in the 1830s, the Belgian statistician Adophe Quetelet began to combine the collection of information with the advanced mathematical techniques that could be used to analyse it. Quetelet publicized the idea of the normal distribution of measurements of natural phenomena around a mean, as derived from the annual reports of crimes and the courts' responses to them. He summed this up in a much-quoted phrase:

> We can count in advance how many individuals will soil their hands with the blood of their fellows, how many will be swindlers, how many poisoners, almost as we can number in advance the births and deaths that will take place... Here is a budget which we meet with a frightful regularity – it is that of prisons, convict stations, and the scaffold. (Quetelet, 1831: 80–81 cited in Radzinowicz, 1965: 1047).

Quetelet's prominence in the international statistical movement, and the central place of crime in his analysis, meant that for much of the nineteenth century it was this movement that shaped the demand for changes in the ways that crimes were recorded, and the ancillary information that was also gathered. There was often a greater concern to obtain information that would enable the emerging science of criminology to identify the environmental predispositions towards crime, or the 'criminal type', than there was attention to the activities from which these numbers were derived. Nevertheless, it was the demands of the International Congress of Statisticians which led to the centralization and publication of police (as distinct from court) statistics in the UK from 1857.

Through the second half of the nineteenth century, successive international conferences of statisticians and penologists advocated that criminal statistics be collected on a firmer basis in each state, and on a comparable basis internationally. This was one reason why in Britain the 1857 format for returns went beyond the recording of the activity of the criminal justice system. The desire to define and fix the 'criminal type', deriving from the work of the Italian criminologist Lombroso, found expression in the returns which each police force had to make, giving the number of thieves, prostitutes and other 'bad characters' at large in their jurisdiction, and the numbers of their haunts. Reflecting the nineteenth century's re-discovery of juvenile delinquency, these numbers were divided into those under and over 16. Although the numbers of miscreants at large were the basis for many contemporary pronouncements about the extent of crime, these 'labelling' returns of dangerous people and places were the product of subjective judgements by police officers that varied markedly from place to place.

Because it appears to be closest to the figure of real crime, and thus the most accurate guide to the state of the problem, many commentators throughout the last two centuries have focused on the number of serious (indictable) crimes reported to the police. This figure is bound to include some crimes for which nobody was charged, and thus gives a bigger number, and one closer to 'real crime' than can be derived from the numbers of people actually charged. For the nineteenth century and much of the twentieth, the crimes that were counted in the 'reported crime' figures were mainly property offences – overwhelmingly non-violent theft. In the UK, this figure was first compiled nationally in 1857, and thus it forms what appears to be a very full run of crime rates. However, this data is notoriously uneven. Analysis of comparable data in large British cities in the late nineteenth century has shown that changes in the rate of indictable crime correlate best with changes in the person occupying the office of Chief Constable (Tobias, 1967: 296–308).

All methods to record statistics about crime and criminals need to confront a number of fundamental problems. The most basic is that the process of defining an action in a certain way is not automatic but depends heavily on the discretion of the relevant witness – be they a police officer or a member of the public. The police role is unique in the extent to which it gives discretion to the officer at the bottom of the organization's hierarchy. One of the ways in which this discretion is exercised is in the process by which the complexities of social reality are fitted into one of the many ostensibly watertight legal definitions of 'crime' or 'offence'. This process of labelling is necessarily open to manipulation in the interests of the individual officer or of the organization to which they belong. Events can additionally be manipulated; for example, in the 1960s, British police were loath to arrest perpetrators of domestic violence for assault charges which were unlikely to be substantiated (Jackson, 2006). On the other hand, if a drunken participant in a domestic quarrel could be lured outside, they could then be arrested for being drunk in a public place: an offence for which no other witnesses were required. This produced an arrest, but no statistical measure of action taken against violence (Young, 1991).

For national or international comparisons to have any validity, they must be based on the application of a consistent standard, which is difficult when only one police force is involved, but even more so when multiple agencies, often with different immediate operational concerns, is involved. Once the definition of the action has been arrived at, other questions remain, notably those of multiple offences. If a number of different offences are committed as part of the same incident, are all counted, or just the most serious? To take one example, which shows why comparative international studies can be misleading, the US federal crime recording standards recorded an event that involved a number of different perpetrators as several different crimes – but if just one of those suspects was ever brought to justice, the entire event would be labelled as 'solved'. So should crimes involving more than one person be enumerated according to the number of different perpetrators or the number of victims? Counting systems designed to monitor the internal work of the criminal justice system tend to favour the former, while the more recent move towards the greater involvement of victims implies that the latter measurement ought to be the basic building block.

A Home Office Departmental Committee met in 1892 and concluded that the counting rules regarding reported crime were highly inconsistent between different police jurisdictions, which cast doubt upon the value of this measure as a means of comparison. Throughout the twentieth century, each central government intervention in Britain was designed to impose comparability by tightening up the counting rules. Inevitably, all the moves in this direction – each one accompanied by expressions of confidence in the resulting figures – had the effect of raising the 'official' crime rate. Another factor which may have led to an increased propensity to report crime is the rise of the domestic insurance business from the 1930s onwards. Insurance companies will only pay out if a crime has been logged with the police. In addition to the increase in the rate of indictable (serious) offences, as proportionally more resources were allocated to the criminal justice system, police had time to record more minor crimes. This was encouraged in part by the emerging disciplines of probation and social work, which created minor punishments for some offences and thus had the effect of drawing into the criminal justice system events which would previously have been regarded as too trivial.

'Cuffing': police efforts to conceal crime rates

In the nineteenth and twentieth centuries, in most advanced countries, rates of reported crime were very low by modern standards. Perhaps low reported rates were produced by low crime rates, but another explanation is an official unwillingness (largely on the part of police forces) to record crimes. In these countries, the rise in official crime rates that began in the second quarter of the twentieth century was in part a consequence of more 'honest' recording procedures. In some jurisdictions, notably the USSR, official crime rates were kept at a low level by dint of more overt official fiat. Despite their presumed position as the measurement closest to the figure of 'real crime', the figures for serious crimes reported to the police are so problematic as to be unusable as a guide to the number of crimes committed.

Let us consider one aspect of this process – the historic reluctance of British police to record crimes, in order to produce a reassuringly high clear-up rate. In the 1960s and 1970s, Malcolm Young worked in the Criminal Investigation Department (CID) of Newcastle-upon-Tyne City Police. While a policeman he studied anthropology, and, after retiring from the police as a senior detective, used his anthropological training to analyse his career. One aspect of CID work which he saw as very important was the fact that detectives are judged on their 'clear-up' rates – the proportion of officially reported crimes on their patch which are solved in one way or another. A detective's working life was thus a constant battle to get results on paper which will satisfy the force's statistical office.

There were a number of processes that could be used to construct a high clear-up rate. These involved bureaucratic manoeuvres such as recording an incident as one offence if nobody was arrested for it, but as several different offences if they had 'a body' – a suspect in custody. For example, take the theft of milk bottles from the door-steps of 50 houses on a street: a minor crime common in the 1960s. This could be logged as a single crime, or as 50. If there was a suspect in custody, the detectives would be inclined to count it as 50 separate solved crimes. If there was no suspect, the detectives would resist attempts to record it at all, or if necessary write it up as one unsolved crime. At the extremes, 'cuffing' offences involved such practices as burning old report sheets, or persuading criminals to admit to offences which they may not have committed. But the key to the process was an extreme reluctance to record reports of crimes as crimes unless it was clear that they would be cleared up. As Young puts it in this account of the mid-1950s:

> My first instruction on my first day as a cadet on the CID front desk was given to me by a seasoned detective, who often left me to 'hold the fort' for long periods while he adjourned to a nearby pub: 'remember kid, nothing is stolen unless I say ... everything is "lost", so send them all downstairs to lost and found property' – unless of course there was a possible 'body'. By such straightforward omissions in recording, the incidence of 'crime' was kept artificially low and although the victim still reported the 'crime' and saw the particulars written down on a message pad, the lost property register or some other document, it never became a crime statistic. How the report was 'recorded' was considered immaterial to the injured person, but it was crucial to the institutional presentation of social reality. It was simply not something the public needed to know about. Whether the report was eventually counted as a crime in the annual lists, or was omitted to present an acceptable level of local villainy was of no public concern. (Young, 1991: 319)

Later, Young concluded that very little had changed between the start of his police career and its end in the 1990s. The detection rate – now much lower because counting was more honest – remained the number one test of detectives' effectiveness, and a key indicator of how the force was perceived in public:

> These [Home Office] counting rules have created a growth industry concerned with counting, measuring and classifying relatively petty and minor criminal acts, and then presenting them in such a way as to create the best statistical impression of efficiency... [T]he newly-emergent management oriented hierarchies in the forces... have found themselves hamstrung by the cultural strength of the numbers game and the significance of the detection rates. For this system of counting what policemen do has such a hold on the culture that it seems impossible to dislodge from its central place as *the* primary means of determining practical effectiveness. (Young, 1991: 267)

Was this practice unique to the 1960s? Hardly: in 1855 the Sheffield Watch Committee (the police authority of the time) conducted an investigation into the working of the town's police force. Among other recommendations, they ordered that all reports of crime be written up into a book, rather than on loose sheets (Sheffield Watch Committee Minutes, 1855: 6). It is obvious from this instruction that they were concerned that reports of some crimes were getting 'lost'. The effects of cuffing were not confined to English cities either: many 'low crime' rural areas in the UK appear to have attained this status as much through the deliberate suppression of official awareness of crime as through the repression of crime itself. In the late nineteenth century, an Assize judge (a senior judge based in London, who periodically travelled round the country to hear the most serious criminal cases) arrived in a Welsh court to find that he had no criminals to try. Such an event was called a 'maiden Assize' and the judge was expected to celebrate it by wearing white gloves. But this judge was not impressed, and addressed the local grand jury (local landowners who had to vet all prosecutions for legal accuracy) thus: 'Gentlemen, I would willingly congratulate you on the non-existence of crime in your several counties IF it did not exist, but as I believe it does exist, though, by some means it is not brought before me, my congratulations must assume a modified form' (Jones, 1992: 3).

If the tendency of the criminal justice system to suppress the reports of crime was consistent across time and space, we could allow for it and be confident that the figures that we had were a constant percentage of 'real crime', and thus still use them as good guides to which areas had high or low crime rates. Unfortunately, we know that this is not true either. Since records began in the 1850s, Nottinghamshire has historically recorded a high crime rate, and in the 1980s its recorded crime was twice that of its neighbouring counties. In 1985, criminologists launched a research project to try to find out if this was because crime was twice as prevalent or not (Bottomley and Pease, 1986: 39–41). First they conducted a survey of a random sample of the local population, to see what proportion of them had been victims of crime. This was a local version of the British Crime Survey, which was already in existence on a national basis. The survey suggested that most categories of crime were higher in Nottinghamshire than in the rest of the country, but only by 25–30%: not nearly enough to explain the discrepancy in reported crime. The researchers also analysed the way that crimes initially came to light in the various counties in the area and discovered that in Nottinghamshire a quarter of the known crimes were the result of admissions of guilt by suspects directly to the police. In the neighbouring county of Leicestershire, less than 5% were identified in this way. Nottinghamshire police, therefore, were putting much more effort into recording crime which had not been reported by the public. They also looked at the value of items reported stolen in Nottinghamshine compared to neighbouring counties, and found that in that county, 25% of stolen property was valued at less than £1, whilst in Leicestershire, the proportion was just 5%: the obvious conclusion was that in Nottinghamshire, minor thefts were recorded more often, whereas in neighbouring counties, police would not record thefts of items which had – to them – a trivial worth. The researchers concluded that differing police willingness to record crime could account for the majority of Nottinghamshire's apparent propensity for crime.

Nottinghamshire police clearly set a lower limit on the value of stolen property which was worth enough to be worth reporting. But the fact that most items have a monetary value means that this kind of analysis is at least possible in the case of theft: theft is a crime which is easy to define, the definition of which has not changed at all in the last few centuries. In this, it is a rarity – most other crimes have been subject to shifting legal definitions and many are additionally at the mercy of shifts in social mores and values. This is particularly the case for crimes of violence.

There is strong evidence that levels of violence which were felt by most Britons to be acceptable in the early nineteenth century were subject to a successively harsh clampdown by the forces of law and order over the next century and a half. This action involved the progressive criminalization of the 'fair fight', the suppression of duelling among the wealthy, and the increasing unwillingness of the state to overlook (some) domestic violence. Perhaps most importantly, the right of the head of the household to use 'reasonable force' to discipline women, servants and children came under attack from the law. In the early nineteenth century any responsible adult was often seen as competent to use force – within limits – to discipline children misbehaving in public. For example, in 1839 some respectable inhabitants of Sheffield brought before the magistrates two boys whom they had caught fighting in the street. The magistrate was not glad of this business, and said 'it would have been much better than bringing them before the Bench [magistrates' court] had some person taken a stick and given the boys a sound flogging' (Williams, 1998: 281).

The other end of the shift in attitudes to violence against juveniles was summed up in 1956. Two police officers in Scotland assaulted a 16-year-old boy who had been arguing with them. Their reaction would probably have passed without comment a few decades earlier, but in this case it ended with questions being asked in Parliament, national publicity about the 'Thurso Boy', and a public inquiry which found the case against the policemen 'not proven'. By the end of the 1950s low-level violence by authority figures, which had not even been seen as criminal at the start of the century, was now identified as a crime, and increasingly became the subject of critical media and parliamentary debate.

The result of the shift in definitions of violent crimes was summed up by the Home Office's chief statistician, the Criminal Registrar, in his 1909 report:

> There is no... clear rule, and (it may be said) no uniform practice as to the degree of violence which makes it proper to prosecute an assault as an indictable offence... Many of the common assaults and still more of the assaults on police constables, now disposed of summarily, amount in reality to malicious wounding, causing grievous bodily harm, or even felonious wounding, and if they were sent for trial, would go to swell the number of indictable offences against the person. (Home Office, 1909: 12–13).

So although the offence of 'assault' has been recorded and counted for over 200 years in Britain, there is great doubt that this consistent label is referring to a consistently defined group of events (see Godfrey, 2003: 345).

Ways of looking at statistics: positivist, interactionist and pessimist

So are all the 'reported crime' figures entirely worthless? Are the figures driven by changing definitions of which activities constitute a breach of the peace, or cause harm to someone, and which harms are then turned into crimes – a process known as 'criming' by the police? One response is to argue that even if we assume that under-reporting makes it difficult to draw distinct conclusions about different areas, we can still get some idea of general national trends from them. One group of historians has taken such a *positivist* approach to the figures for reported crime, holding that, if used with care, some of them can tell us about the state of crime. The most convincing example of this approach was that taken by Gatrell and Hadden in their work on the decline of theft and violence in Britain in the later nineteenth century (Gatrell and Hadden, 1972; Gatrell, 1980). This is one of the very few periods when people writing about crime have proclaimed that, in general, things are getting better rather than worse (Pike, 1875). They set out to see if the fall in reported crimes was real or merely a product of the system. First, they examined all the other factors which might be expected to affect the crime rate. Over this period, a number of developments occurred which made it likely that crime rates would rise. The number of police increased, making it easier for members of the public to report crimes. Police increasingly took on the task of prosecutors, making the process of private prosecution less of a disincentive, and prosecution costs were reimbursed if the prosecution was successful. Thus, given all these factors making reporting and prosecution easier, it would be reasonable to expect reported crimes to rise. Instead they fell, and thus Gatrell and Hadden concluded that the only explanation left is that is was a result of a real fall in crime during this period.

As well as drawing conclusions about the overall movement of crime, Gatrell and Hadden also used criminal statistics in a positivist way to see if any of the Home Office's measurements of crime could be correlated with movements in the business cycle. To do this, they explored whether trends in particular sorts of crime matched up with economic trends, to test the hypothesis that in times of hardship, people are more likely to turn to property crime. Conversely, in times of relative wealth, with more money available to spend on alcohol, we could expect more crimes of violence and disorder. Sure enough, Gatrell and Hadden found such a correlation. In this case, whatever the long-term variations in the proportion of crimes that are recorded, or the variations in reporting caused by changes over time in police policy, and the difference in practice between jurisdictions, the underlying influence of the economy on the numbers of reported crimes was such that it still left a pattern on the figures.

Another group of historians (maybe even the majority of historians of crime) takes an *interactionist* approach to criminal justice statistics. The 'interactionist' view is that quantitative data can tell us about crime but only through the medium of changes in the criminal justice system: thus it is better for giving a picture of the interaction between state institutions and social forces. David Philips concluded that: 'Offences cannot be treated as simple entities on their own, but must be considered in the context of their reciprocal relationship with the law and law enforcement' (Philips, 1977: 41–3). So, for example, when reported instances of property crime rose massively in the mid-twentieth century, an interactionist perspective would be to state that this *might* be due to more criminals stealing goods, but we know that changes in public willingness to report crime, and police willingness to register it, were so large that we cannot draw any firm statements about increases in criminality. What we can do is point to the way that the criminal justice system evolved to cope with many more offenders, which is an interesting topic in itself.

If we take a close look at one place for which we have data covering arrests as well as indictments and convictions, we can see the broad picture that emerges of the activity of the criminal justice system. We have data for all these measures from Sheffield between 1844 and 1855.

The Sheffield figures show that although, in theory, all property crime ought to have been dealt with on indictment, in practice, a lot of it was dealt with summarily, without an expensive wait for a higher court to convene. One eighth of all arrests for property crime culminated in charges for offences like 'Robbery in Gardens, &c'; 'Obtaining Money or Goods by false pretences'; 'Pawning or disposing of property illegally'; 'Embezzlement'; and 'Frauds'. The characteristic pattern for this 'summary robbery' is of conviction rates which, at 60%, were very high for summary offences. The majority of property crime (4,928 arrests in 1844–55) was prosecuted on indictment as 'larceny' (the legal term for non-violent theft). But although many people were arrested for this crime, many of them were released by the lower courts without facing trial. It is likely in these cases that the police or the victim regarded the incident as not serious enough to justify the considerable expense of a trial. The characteristic pattern here was of a high discharge rate at petty sessions, and a low rate of committal to later trial. A very small proportion (205 arrests) were arrested for property crime that was violent, or potentially so. This was prosecuted under the categories of: 'Robbery from the person by force or threat', 'Burglary', and 'Assaults, with intent to commit robbery'. Of those arrested, only 37% were discharged by the magistrates in petty sessions, and the rest were committed for trial on indictment – so those arrested for violent theft were far less likely to walk free from the initial hearing. Of those committed for trial in the higher courts however, only 70% were convicted, so violent theft had a lower conviction rate than those for non-violent indictable property crime (81%) and summary property crime (87%).

Where does this leave criminal statistics? The problem is that if 'committals for indictable offences' is used to measure crime, it is likely that this is not measuring changes in the number of crimes committed, but changes in willingness to prosecute for crime. The practice of convicting people summarily in local petty sessions courts rather than on indictment in higher courts was made general in 1855, when an Act of Parliament allowed summary conviction for theft of items under a certain value. Naturally, this led to the number of prosecuted thefts shooting up as prosecution became easier – a fact which some subsequent historians mistook for a crime wave. Before the 1855 Act, about two thirds of the people arrested for theft were released without charge, and the rest went on to face trial. Once the Act was passed, the pattern changed, and less than 40% were released. Instead, a quarter faced trial on indictment for serious theft, and the rest were convicted by the magistrates in the lower courts (Williams, 2000). As well as a wider net for crimes of property, we have also seen that more and more people are drawn into the criminal justice system over the course of the twentieth century owing to a diminution of the tolerance of the use of violence as a summary punishment of juveniles by figures in authority.

A third position is a totally *pessimistic* view towards the statistics, seeing them only as one ingredient in a debate on crime, and an ingredient which need not have any relationship to reality. This line is taken by Rob Sindall, who has studied the issue of street robbery in mid-Victorian Britain. He argues that the statistics are so flawed that the only credible approach to take is:

> to view the statistics not as a reflection of a phenomenon but as a phenomenon in themselves. It was on the criminal statistics, not the actual state of crime, that both individuals and institutions based their beliefs about the actual state of crime. Thus to look at the criminal statistics is to look at the statistics that the Victorians themselves used to gauge the state of crime in their society. There is no dispute that viewed from this perspective the criminal statistics are real enough. As the cause of certain reactions, such as self-protection, increased policing and new legislation, they are immensely useful in explaining the reactions themselves. The statistics are therefore a measure, not necessarily of what was happening, but of what people believed was happening. It was through the knowledge of such statistics, rather than the observation of criminal acts themselves, that Victorians could conclude in the 1840s that 'the progress of wickedness is so much more rapid than the increase of the numbers of people' and in the 1890s that, 'we have witnessed... a decline in the spirit of lawlessness. (Sindall, 1990: 20)

John Tobias, who also holds this pessimist position, studied the returns of crimes committed in detail. After analysing the returns of reported crime from several police force areas, he came to the conclusion that fluctuations in this measurement were largely random and could not be relied upon to give a picture of crime. Thus, in order to find out about the general picture of crime in the nineteenth century, he would ignore all statistics, and instead pay attention to the written statements of various contemporary commentators, who could be assumed to know what they were talking about. Tobias was criticized by David Philips, who pointed out that, in relying on what contemporary observers said about the nineteenth century, Tobias was not in fact freeing himself from dependence on the statistics. Philips showed that the Victorian commentators whom Tobias was relying on for information – politicians, prison governors, social scientists, civil servants and police officers – were themselves reading and commenting on criminal statistics, and using these numbers to inform their views about whether and when crime was rising and falling, and why this might be the case. Philips argued that rather than take the commentators' word for it, modern historians may as well go back to the only data that they had access to.

In looking at the three positions (positivist, interactionist and pessimist), we have so far deliberately confined ourselves to the figures for 'reported' crime. On the face of it, these look like the most reliable measure of crime, since they are the ones that are closest to 'real crime'. But it is important not to mistake this particular measure for 'the criminal statistics' as a whole: in fact, there are many other measures of activity which we can also use. Many of these are about the activity of the criminal justice system, such as records of arrests, trials, verdicts and sentences. These are generally reliable, in that they record events which it is reasonable to suppose took place (although one historian, Howard Taylor, whose claims will be discussed below, has claimed that they do not even do this).

Other runs of numbers, though, are less immediately reliable. Most of these concern information about criminals, which is of a different order to information regarding what the criminal justice system did to them. Two of the most significant are those dealing with the characteristics of arrested offenders, and the numbers of offenders or other 'bad characters' at large.

Statistics that measure 'labelling'

In the 1830s, an influential group of public commentators and what we may term 'early criminologists' (see Chapter 2) began to investigate the criminal justice system. The new prisons and the new police were advancing, but so was criminal activity, which was increasing at an alarming rate. For some, the solution would be found in the progress of universal primary education: for others what mattered more was religion. It was as a result of this debate that in 1836 the annual returns of people committed (sent) to prison was begun. For the first time, this did not merely calculate the numbers of men and women sentenced for each crime, but included evidence as to their character: their age, sex, 'degree of instruction' (education) and the number of times that they had been committed previously. This information formed the basis for a number of competing views about the efficacy – or not – of the Victorian prison. But as several commentators pointed out, it was far less reliable than the basic counts had been. Sex was (usually) easy to determine, but age could be under- or over-stated by offenders who appreciated that the young and the very old were generally treated more leniently by the courts. 'Degree of instruction', which was largely concerned with whether the inmate could read and/or write, also depended on the co-operation of the prisoner. As for the information about previous committals, it was in the prisoner's interest to conceal these, since repeat offenders generally received longer sentences. Registers of 'habitual criminals' from the late nineteenth century show that most of them went under one or more aliases, and before the introduction of fingerprinting at the turn of the century, it was very difficult to accurately determine the identity of a prisoner, and thus their age and whether or not they had previous convictions.

There was a similar link between the shape of the crime statistics and contemporary debates when a national network of police forces was introduced for the first time by the 1857 Police Act. This will be covered in depth in the next chapter, but for now we need to understand that one of the factors which precipitated this legislation was a growing public fear that the numbers of vagrant criminals

in the country was rising, and that the *status quo* in policing – whereby some jurisdictions had reformed their police, and others had not – was leading to criminals
'migrating' to under-policed areas. Before 1857, police forces had been financed
entirely from local rates: the central government hence had no hold over them,
and although there was a theoretical requirement that they file quarterly returns
of their activity, few did; and no returns have survived. After this date, though,
they were eligible for a grant for a quarter of their costs from general taxation (in
1873 this went up to a half) and thus central government wanted a statistical
record of the activity that it was funding. A similar mechanism was at work in the
United States, although in this case almost all law enforcement (except the FBI)
was locally financed and controlled until the later twentieth century, which meant
that nationwide police statistics date from comparatively recently. In Britain, what
Parliament, which had voted the money, wanted to hear was how well the various local police forces were doing. As well as records of arrests and summary convictions, they also asked for the police to collect annual returns of 'criminals at
large'. This was divided by gender and into those over and under 16, and into five
categories: known thieves and depredators; receivers of stolen goods; prostitutes;
suspected persons; vagrants and tramps. Also shown were: houses of bad character; resorts of thieves and prostitutes – public houses, beer shops, and coffee shops;
brothels and houses of ill fame; and tramps' lodging houses.

Such 'labelling' is too susceptible to changing definitions on the part of the
police force to be considered as any reliable reflection of reality. It would have
had to utilize the subjective opinions of many different men and be liable to
change with changes of policy and personnel. This is illustrated by odd jumps
in the statistics from year to year. To take the example of Sheffield, the number
of 'known thieves and depredators' under the age of 16 dropped from 25 boys
and 10 girls in 1867 to 4 boys and no girls in 1868, before climbing again to 18
and 9 respectively in 1869. In 1858, 95 'receivers of stolen goods' were living in
17 'houses of receivers of stolen goods'. By 1867, 44 were living in 51 houses.
Something had certainly changed, but it is most likely to have been the criteria
used, rather than any 'actual' alteration in the number of fences and their residences. 'Female receivers of stolen goods' stood at 6 in 1859, 20 in 1860 and 7
in 1861. Tobias and Sindall are certainly right in this particular case: changes in
definition – subjective and unrecorded – can have so much impact as to render
any study of other putative changes impossible.

Statistics and spin

'Pessimist' analysis of historical criminal statistics can still offer a useful perspective on the criminal justice system – asking questions such as: which statistics

Table 3.1   *Returns from Birmingham Police for 23–30 June 1840*

	Discharged, prosecutor refusing to prosecute	Remanded	Reprimanded and discharged	Summarily convicted	Committed for trial	Total
Felony	16	2	26		9	53
Misdemeanour	5		29	35		69
Drunkenness	1		24	24		49
Vagrancy			4	1		5
Total	22	2	83	60	9	176

Source: *Birmingham Journal*, 4 July 1840.

were collected? How were they aggregated? Why and in what ways were categories such as 'Strangers' and 'Irish' separated from the totals? How were the numbers 'spun'? The answers to all these questions are important because, as Superintendent Malcolm Young noted in the 1980s, in the modern era, numbers are an important measurement of success. New police forces, including the Metropolitan police, were keen to use numerical measures to bolster their claims to legitimacy (Reynolds, 1998: 161). For example, from its inception in 1839 the first reformed police force in Birmingham was unpopular and contentious. It had been foisted by central government on an unwilling town chiefly to keep an eye on the radical Chartist National Convention which was meeting in the city. The force took positive steps to bolster its public image in Birmingham. The police Superintendent responsible for prosecutions made sure that each week the record of local arrests and their outcomes was published in the *Birmingham Journal*, one example of which is given in Table 3.1.

The Commissioner of the Birmingham Police acknowledged in his reports to his immediate superior, the Home Secretary, that his primary mission – maintaining public order in the face of the activity of Chartists in the city – was made easier by his force's usefulness in controlling petty and serious crime (Weaver, 1994: 307). The message sent out by the continual presentation of results in the Birmingham press was a defensive one, designed to show that the police were active: even if only a few men were committed to trial for serious offences, the police were doing their part of the job, by bringing large numbers of criminals up before the magistrates. High numbers were the measure of success, and hence legitimacy.

In the late 1990s, historian Howard Taylor argued an even more radical (and to the criminologist, depressing) view of criminal statistics. He claimed that they were worthless, even as a measure of the effort of the criminal justice system. So whereas Young had claimed that crime rates and clear-up rates were numbers produced by police shoe-horning real events into different categories, and using every bureaucratic means possible to refuse to count some altogether,

Taylor claimed that many of them were fictions, plucked out of thin air by police who were using them to justify their existence. Taylor challenged the idea that the count of murders is the most reliable of all official indicators of crime. In his view, the Treasury set a cash limit on the number of (expensive) murder trials that could be funded annually, and this led to the police forces in Britain 'rationing' the number of murder trials to average around 150 per year.

Taylor's views have received a robust response from historian Robert Morris. Morris's riposte mainly concerns the earlier period. While conceding that it is highly likely that coroner's courts almost certainly missed a substantial number of homicides, he shows that Taylor's accusation that the Treasury capped the costs of murder trials (and hence their number) is based on a misunderstanding of the way that British government worked, and in fact no such cap existed. Even if it had, it is hard to imagine how the 150 or so forces in Britain at the time – each with a very strong tradition of local independence from the centre – could have been organized to implement a quota of murders without complaining or leaving any mark in the historical record. Overall, it seems that until Taylor can come up with a 'smoking gun' – evidence of large-scale and long-term *fabrication* of the police returns on crime – his charges must be regarded as 'not proven'.

Victim surveys: a new departure

With the growth of sociological interest in the issue of crime from the 1960s onwards, the flawed nature of criminal statistics became increasingly obvious. The response in Britain was to follow the lead of the US, where a victim survey, the National Crime Victimization Survey (NCVS) was adopted in 1972, during a period when the liberal consensus about crime control was being challenged, and the US Department of Justice was becoming far more active in its relation-ship with police forces at the state, city and local level. It involved interviewing of over 80,000 people twice a year about their experience of crime or that of their household. In 1982, the British Crime Survey was begun, initially every two years. To nobody's great surprise, the pattern that the BCS has revealed is that even serious offences such as major assaults, robbery and burglary are sig-nificantly under-reported: far more of these take place every year than ever fea-ture in 'crimes reported to the police'. Minor offences are still less likely to make it to the official statistics. But the BCS still does not record every offence that the official statistics do. At the time of writing, for example, it only records the victimization of people aged 16 or over, so crimes committed on youths below this age will not show up on it, although a proportion of them will be reported and form part of the police-derived figures. This is significant given that in the early years of the twenty-first century, theft of mobile phones and other items of personal electronic equipment from juveniles became a widespread problem:

the BCS cannot track it at all. In addition, the BCS, as a household survey, cannot record crimes where the victim is a company or other institution rather than an individual. Thus it does not track shoplifting and other thefts from business premises, which between them form a substantial proportion of reported theft. And it cannot track homicide! Nevertheless, the existence of the BCS after 1982 gives us an important corrective to the official statistics of crime. Historians of the future are going to find it invaluable.

Before we conclude, let us explore in depth some documentary evidence showing how contemporaries compiled and viewed criminal statistics. Allowing historical sources to speak on their own terms can often be the most illuminating form of historical research. Below is the start of an article by prison reformer Mary Carpenter. More well-known as a pioneer of the use of reformatories for juvenile delinquents, here she is challenging the pattern of available criminal statistics.

On the Importance of Statistics to the Reformatory Movement, with Returns from Female Reformatories, and Remarks on them. By Mary Carpenter.

Journal of the Statistical Society of London, (Mar., 1857) 20(1): 33–40. [Based upon a Paper read before Section F.–Economic Science and Statistics of the British Association for the Advancement of Science at Cheltenham, August, 1856; with additions.]

The position which Reformatory Schools at present hold with regard to the State, renders it of the first importance that as much light as possible should be thrown by statistics on the real numbers of the juvenile criminal population of the country, and that official returns should be henceforth so arranged that accurate information may be obtained as to the actual success or failure of the plans adopted.

The want of such information has led to very serious and alarming apprehensions relative to the inadequacy of any possible supply of reformatories to cope with the enormous multitude of young thieves which is supposed to exist. Reference has been made to criminal returns of convictions, throughout the country, of young persons under the age of 16, and it has been imagined that we must make provision for such an annual supply. Two points have, however, been left out of view: first, that the number of either *commitments* or *convictions* by no means shows the number of criminal individuals, since many have been committed several times during the year; and secondly, that according to the old system of imprisonment for juveniles, the same individual not only would be recommitted two or three times in the same year, but might remain from year to year until transported, not only himself swelling the annual list of convicts, but drawing others into his vortex, and thereby multiplying crime in a fearful ratio; whereas, when the reformatory system is fully carried out, no young person will be allowed to be more than a second time convicted, and frequently all who are likely to be exposed to a second will be removed at the first, and thus each year the list must be greatly lessened numerically. Not only so, but it has been found that a deterring influence has already been exerted in those towns where the Juvenile Offenders' Act has been carried into active operation. At the late meeting in Bristol of the National Reformatory Union, an important communication was made by the chief constable of Berwick, that there had been considerable diminution in juvenile crime since the Juvenile Offenders' Act came into operation; and it was stated by the chaplain of the Liverpool Gaol, 'that since the Liverpool magistrates began to act with their present determination of availing themselves of the Youthful Offenders' Act in all its provisions, both for the protection of the child and for enforcing the parental responsibility in every suitable case, a manifest anxiety amongst the criminal population had been created, and that the number of juveniles in the gaol, of which he had been for some years chaplain, is less than during any period within his recollection.'

Carpenter here is using this section of the article to do two things: first, she claims that new and better statistics need to be collected in order to properly assess the impact of reformatories. Second, she also draws attention to one of the perennial problems of any attempt to aggregate events and draw conclusions about people: what is the number of repeat offenders? If all that is counted is committals, then 100 could be the result of 100 different juveniles each going to prison once, 20 going five times, or many more combinations. The Home Office's presentation of criminal statistics, by comparison, offers a very different perspective on the accuracy and meaning of the figures of crime.

The extract below comes from the preamble to the official Home Office Criminal Statistics for 1893. This section of the publication was the opportunity for the Registrar of Criminal Statistics, the senior civil servant in the Home Office with responsibility for the production of the numbers, to write about what he considered were the significant features of the mass of figures that would follow in the returns proper. It also gave him an opportunity to explain how the compilation of the returns had been changed since the previous year, especially in ways that brought them closer to international norms.

Introduction to the Criminal Statistics for the year 1893. HMSO: London, 1895.

1. The INCREASE or DECREASE of CRIME.

The question whether crime is increasing or decreasing has been much discussed in recent years, and very contradictory inferences have been drawn from the Criminal and Prison Statistics.

The first step in attempting to arrive at a sound conclusion is to determine what class of figures can be accepted as a trustworthy index to the amount of crime. No set of figures should be used for this purpose without carefully examining all the conditions and circumstances or without making due allowance for influences, other than actual increase or decrease of crime, which affect the figures; but in some cases the disturbing influences are so great as to deprive statistics, which at first sight might seem to show the growth or diminution of criminality, of all value from this point of view.

Thus the total number of convictions on indictment, or of persons tried on indictment, has often been treated as if it afforded an index to the amount of crime; but the value of this test has been destroyed by those changes in procedure introduced by the Summary Jurisdiction Act, 1879, by which a large but uncertain number of cases that would formerly have been tried on indictment, are now brought within the jurisdiction of justices in Petty Sessions.

Others again have taken the totals of all convictions, whether on indictment or on summary procedure, as their guide: forgetting that there are large classes of cases dealt with summarily which are not really criminal, and that the number of these is so great as to determine the increase or decrease of the totals. For instance, the number of convictions under the Education Acts has risen from 13,662 in 1874 to 50,235 in 1893.

The prison population, another criterion which has often been adopted, gives even more misleading results. Its rise and fall is affected not only by the creation of new offences not really of a criminal character, such as offences under the Education Acts and Vaccination Acts and under county and borough byelaws, but also, and to a very much greater extent, by the tendency to impose long or short sentences.

On the whole the best criterion of the amount of criminality is the total, not of crimes tried on indictment, but of *indictable* crimes. All serious crimes are included in the list of indictable offences and none are included that are not really criminal, except perhaps a few under the head of nuisances which are too small in number to affect the totals in any appreciable degree. The great changes in procedure within the last 20 years, which have so largely affected the number of cases actually tried on indictment, have not in any way affected the definitions of indictable crimes; and in the few cases where new indictable offences have been created the necessary allowances can easily be made.

If we take the total number of indictable offences as the best-general criterion of the amount of crime, it is immaterial whether the figures we use be those of offences committed (i.e. reported to the police), of persons tried; or of convictions: The conclusions to be drawn from them as to the increase or decrease of crime are substantially the same. The figures quoted in this Introduction represent the number of *persons tried for indictable offences*.

...

[The next section contained a number of tables, each giving the number tried for various indictable offences between the years 1874 and 1893, and the proportion that this made of each 100,000 inhabitants.]

…

Summing up these results we arrive at the following conclusions: that during the 20 years from 1874 to 1893, the number of crimes of violence against the person has diminished in a very marked degree; and though 'crimes against morality' have apparently increased, the increase is, in part at any rate, due to the creation of new offences by legislation; that all classes of crimes against property show a diminution in the actual figures, and a marked diminution as compared with the population; and, though in the case of larceny and kindred offences this diminution is complicated by changes of legal procedure, in the cases of crimes of violence and also in the case of offences against the currency where there has been no change of procedure, the diminution is very marked indeed; and that the miscellaneous offences included in Class VI, with the exception of attempts to commit suicide, have shown a considerable diminution. On the whole, therefore, there is good ground to think the decrease in crime, though not so great as it has often been represented, though by no means comparable for instance to the decrease in prison population, is nevertheless real and substantial.

Similar results may be obtained in the case of the minor offences, which are within the ordinary jurisdiction of Courts of Summary Jurisdiction. I do not propose to extend to them the detailed examination that has been undertaken with regard to indictable offences, but the following figures from Table D show the tendency to diminution, particularly under the heads of assaults, malicious damage and drunkenness.

Proportion of Persons tried per 100,000 inhabitants

	1874–78	1879–83	1884–88	1889–93
Assaults	402	320	289	268
Stealing animals, fruit, &c.	19	22	20	13
Malicious damage	97	80	76	65
Vagrancy Acts	121	157	153	14.1
Game Laws offences	52	41	40	30
Drunkenness	–	–	812	698
Education Acts offences	103	272	218	285

…

4. Crime in RELATION TO AGE AND SEX.

…

The proportion of persons convicted on indictment who are women is 13 per cent, of persons convicted summarily for indictable offences, 19 percent. There appears, therefore, to be a distinct tendency to send for trial a smaller proportion of women than of men, and the true results as regards crime can only be obtained by taking in one view all cases whether settled summarily or sent for trial.

Taking all indictable crimes, it will be found that 82 percent of the persons convicted are men, against 18 percent of women, but the proportion of women varies very much in different classes of crime:

Crimes	Proportion of women (%)
Violence against the person	11
Crimes against morals	4
Procuring abortion and concealment of birth	91
Child stealing and cruelty to children	70
Burglary	3
Robbery and extortion	10
Crimes against property without violence	19
Malicious injuries to property	15
Forgery	9
Coining, &c.	18
Miscellaneous offences	16

Generally speaking, in crimes involving the use of force, the proportion of women is smaller. In crimes of violence against the person the proportion falls, as stated above to 11 percent. Under the head of robbery it is 10 percent; while in the case of burglary, housebreaking, &c., the proportion of women is less than 3 percent. On the other hand, in the case of offences against property without violence, the proportion committed by women rises to 19 percent. It is much higher under one or two heads, notably larceny from the person, 27 percent, and receiving stolen goods, 31 percent. The number of women convicted of forgery is small, only 9 percent; while under the head of coining and passing counterfeit coin the proportion rises to 18 percent. Under the head of attempting suicide the proportion of women is exceptionally large – 27 percent.

...

How far these figures represent the tendency to crime – to acts of dishonesty and violence – in the two sexes is a question which goes somewhat beyond the scope of this Introduction. On the one hand the tendency to treat women more leniently than men – not to prosecute a woman for an offence for which a man would be prosecuted; not to convict a woman on evidence on which a man would be sent to prison – may be responsible for some lowering of the percentage of female criminals. On the other hand, it has to be borne in mind that women – weaker physically, and having fewer means of employment – are more likely than men to be driven to those offences which are due less to criminal instincts than to stress of circumstances.

As you might expect, positivist ideas dominate this piece: the Registrar is confident that the numbers collated here are representations of actual crime. But there is also evidence of an interactionist view – he is aware of changes in counting rules, and the potential problems with leniency towards women which meant that the figures for women's convictions would not stand direct comparison with those for men's as a measure of their inherent criminality: thus the figures are not a picture of crime, but a picture of the interaction between criminals and the criminal justice system. We would not expect the Registrar to be a pessimist about the returns, but if we subject them to a 'pessimist' analysis, ignoring the numbers and just looking at them as an ingredient into (and a reflection of) the debate on criminal justice, then historians and criminologists can gain much from studying them.

Summary

There are reams of historical criminal statistics: exact numbers, related to identifiable geographical areas, compiled painstakingly, and analysed minutely. If only we could simply use them in an uncomplicated and straightforward manner to answer some of the big questions of criminology. Are we getting more or less criminal? Why are women far less likely to be criminals? What is the relationship between crime and social class? Is a high level of crime an inescapable result of modernity? What we have learned from this chapter, though, is that there are great limits to the questions that can be answered from criminal statistics. We can certainly learn a great deal about the nature of the criminal justice system by adopting an 'interactionist' approach to them. If we look at them in a 'pessimistic' way, we can find out about which topics were the live issues of the day, and learn about the political reasons behind the ways that statistics were presented. For certain periods and certain very general questions, a 'positivist' approach is justified: but overall the most important thing to remember about the crime statistics is what they cannot tell us.

STUDY QUESTIONS

1   Why were criminal and judicial statistics originally compiled, and have those aims changed now?
2   What can crime statistics tell us about levels of crime, and trends in crime rates?
3   What are the major problems of crime statistics, and how have these problems manifested themselves or changed over time?
4   How have the three main analytical frameworks (positivistic, interactionist, pessimist) attempted to make something from crime statistics?

FURTHER READING

Gatrell, V.A.C. (1980) 'The decline of theft and violence in Victorian and Edwardian England', in V.A.C. Gatrell, B. Lenman and G. Parker (eds) *Crime and the Law: the social history of crime in early modern Europe*, Europa: London.

Gatrell, V.A.C. and Hadden, T. (1972) 'Criminal statistics and their interpretation', in E.A. Wrigley (ed.) *Nineteenth Century Social History: essays in the use of quantitative methods for the study of social data*, Cambridge University Press: Cambridge.

Morris, R.M. (2001) '"Lies, Damned Lies, and Criminal Statistics": Reinterpreting the criminal statistics in England and Wales' in *Crime, Histoire & Sociétiés/Crime, History & Societies*, 5(1): 111–27.

Sindall, R. (1986) 'The criminal statistics of nineteenth-century cities: a new approach', in *Urban History Yearbook 1986*, pp. 28–36.

Williams, C.A. (2000) 'Counting Crimes or Counting People: some implications of mid-nineteenth-century British police returns' in *Crime, Histoire & Sociétiés/Crime, History & Societies*, 4(2): 77–93.

4

Police Governance – Enforcement, Discretion, Professionalism and Accountability

Chapter Contents

OVERVIEW

Chapter 4:

- Provides an examination of how local control was exerted over the police between 1800 and 1914, and how different systems developed in London, the counties, and the towns and cities of England.
- Reveals the pressures for centralization after the First World War. It describes the development of a national officer class and the increasing power of the Home Office which led to the eclipse of local democracy in 1964.
- Explains how terms such as 'modernizing' the police have hidden tensions between democracy and professionalism in policing for the last two centuries. This chapter outlines some of the key debates.
- Examines the re-emergence of (some) local control. What lessons does the past hold for the new systems of local control?

KEY TERMS

governance	enforcement	professionalism	local accountability

In a phrase written in the 1970s, which has been much quoted since (albeit largely by sociologists), American researcher Egon Bittner defined the police as 'a mechanism for the distribution of situationally justified force in society' (Bittner, 1975: 39). However, more recently Johnston and Shearing (2003: 9) have argued that changes in policing practice have moved it in an increasingly decentralized and complex direction. Their view is that Bittner's definition is obsolete, and rather than think of 'the police' as an *institution* we should pay more attention the *process* of 'policing', which they define as all 'programmes for promoting peace in the face of threats that arise from collective life'. This new theoretical definition is indeed useful as a way of tracking recent changes in policing, but, for us, Bittner's definition still has much mileage in it. For most of the last 200 years, policing has been what the police did, and 'the police' were that uniformed body of men (and from 1914 in the UK, women) whose specific job it was to enforce the law, protect public order, and defend the state within its borders, using force if necessary. Even now (2007), despite the growth in policing activities by various central and local 'non-police' state agencies, and an increase in the number of private security personnel, the vast majority of those who carry out this function in the UK's public places are members of the 50 or so police forces which trace their institution ancestry back 150 or more years.

The contemporary study of policing involves far more than merely attempting to arrive at the most effective definition for the subject area. There are a large number of theoretical and practical issues regarding policing which are topics of concern to researchers and policy-makers. These involve, for example, looking at gender; which is not just about how police deal with women, but also concerns how much they are influenced by an ethos of masculinity (Westmarland, 2001). This has particular relevance following the ongoing discovery of the problem of domestic violence. There is also a focus on policing and race, which is especially salient given that the most contentious issues in British policing in the last 30 years have derived from problematic relationships between police and members of ethnic minority communities (Whitfield, 2004; also see Chapter 6). Since the defeat of the organized British working class in the 1980s, the question of the policing of industrial disputes has become less relevant. However, the recent rise in 'anti-terrorist' operations, and their accompanying vast increase in police powers and surveillance technologies (see Chapter 7), has given new force to the question of how these can be balanced with political liberties such as freedom of movement and protest (Waddington, 1994). While these issues are important, the basic questions of police practice and efficiency also occupy the attention of many researchers. Effectiveness at fighting crime and disorder, and at allaying public fear of crime, often expressed through initiatives like neighbourhood watch and the clamour for more bobbies on the beat, remains central to the debate over policing (Innes, 2003; Loader and Muclcahy, 2003).

Much of this work of analysis and interpretation of the police's activity, though, comes back to the central question of how the police institution fits into the wider society. How does it respond to public demand, and how does it judge which public demands are legitimate and which are not? For example, up until the last decade or so, most British police had a tacit policy of not getting involved in domestic violence, unless it had reached a highly injurious level (Edwards, 1989). This was not necessarily because they subscribed to a patriarchal ideal and thought that wife-beating was reasonable. It had as much, if not more, to do with the extreme difficulty of getting convictions following arrests for domestic violence, given that the victim hardly ever agreed to give evidence in court. Convictions are one of the most important measures of police activity, and an arrest that is unlikely to produce one thus involves a large outlay of time and effort for a limited result (see Chapter 3). One major recent change in policing policy is the move towards a culture of arresting the perpetrators of domestic violence, and of pressing charges even if the victim is opposed to the process. This is an instance of government (in this case central government) forcing a change in policing policy which has the effect of limiting the choices that the individual police officer on the spot can make, using their discretion.

Discretion is one of the most significant aspects of policing, because it is so important. A police officer responding to an incident has a very wide degree of latitude. The law has a broad scope, and this is not merely the product of present-day emergency and quasi-civil powers, but has always been present, given the existence of powerful statute laws like the Vagrancy Acts, and common law arrestable offences such as breach of the peace. The officer has to decide whether to attempt to defuse a situation and move on, to arrest for a trivial offence such as a public order offence, or (sometimes) to declare a major incident and look for evidence that a serious crime has been committed. So, for almost all the interactions between police and public, policing is inherently difficult to supervise, and this has always been the case. It is very hard to formulate a set of rules which will apply to the infinite variety of situations that most police officers need to deal with. Thus, rather than a complete concentration on the policy that comes down to police officers from the top, there are a number of factors that exercise massive influence on how policing is carried out: the background of police officers and their attitudes, the history of police practice contained in the organization's culture, the training programme, and the formal instructions and rules (Reiner, 1991: 349).

'Discretion' works at the level of the individual officer, but it is also important in the disposition of the force as a whole. This chapter will look at the historical record to examine the ways that police discretion, operations and powers have been controlled in Britain. It ought to provide the necessary background information to any informed discussion about the theory and practice of contemporary policing.

Local control or central authority – modern debates

In liberal democracies, there is a built-in tension in policing between 'democratic control' and 'bias'. Few people would disagree with the statement that police need to be close to the communities they serve in order to carry out their job, but equally, most would argue that it would be a bad thing for the police to be merely a tool of some sections (even of a majority) in those communities if it meant that the law was not fairly enforced. If the police are too closely controlled by the people, this leaves them open to the charge of 'politicization' or bias, but if not the people, then who should control them?

The British doctrine for much of the twentieth century, zealously repeated by police and politicians alike, is that police are professionals responsible only to the law: they are not under the control of one politician or another. Local and national politicians may be responsible for providing adequate resources for policing, to be able to set out guidelines for the police, and have the right to demand reports about police activity (thus making the police 'accountable'), but in order to avoid 'politicization' they cannot give them day-to-day orders. Perhaps the most eloquent, and certainly the most extreme, exponent of this doctrine was the journalist Charles Reith, who wrote a series of very influential histories of the British police in the 1930s and 1940s. He claimed that:

> One of the most striking features of the behaviour of the British police is their success in preventing their dependence on public approval from interfering with the efficiency of their service to Law, and thus overcoming what might appear, in theory, to be a fundamental weakness of their organization. They never forget their dependence on public approval, and they secure it, not by pandering to the local or temporary demands of a section of the public at any temporary moment, but by a strict impartiality in their behaviour, and by providing a consistent service of unbiased support of laws, and resistance to their breach, regardless of the nature or justness of the laws. The consistent aloofness of the police from political bias, and their sustained indifference to any other aspect of a law than its need of being observed are frequently the cause of temporary embarrassment and unpopularity, but they are the real foundation of the immense confidence with which the public regards the police, and on which their value and their strength depend. (Reith, 1943: 7)

Reith's eulogies to the acceptability of policing were based on an unstated consensus view of what it was reasonable and desirable to expect police to do. Thus, Reith's ideas had much greater purchase in the 1950s, when the overall level of social consensus was itself higher. This view of policing as unproblematic adherence to the law is far less powerful when society (or at least those parts of it with access to the media) is divided over what police ought to be doing. To take just one example, the policing of industrial disputes in the 1980s led to controversy over the way that police forces should be controlled, precisely because there was no general agreement that this was a proper allocation of police resources. Writing in the early 1990s, Robert Reiner pointed out:

> The bottom line of any controversy about policing is who governs Who has the power to determine the policies which will actually be implemented? As policing has become more controversial in the last quarter-century, so police accountability has become an ever more hotly debated topic. By the 1980s two clearly polarised camps had developed. (Reiner, 1991: 249)

Before we go into the historical detail of how the way that Britain's policing structure evolved, it is worth considering the issues that we will be examining. There are different forms of power over police. These include the power to:

- set wages and terms and conditions of employment;
- write instructions about the procedures that police must follow;
- determine training programmes;

- hire and fire police – which might extend to selecting merely the chief, the senior officers, or every recruit;
- distribute police resources geographically, such as by setting patrol patterns; and
- order police to carry out a particular task.

If we look at the history of policing in Britain, we can see that, at various times, there are many different ways that these powers have been divided up between police chiefs, central government and local government. Despite all the rhetoric, there is not really any single 'British way' of controlling police. The rest of this chapter will examine the history of policing in England and Wales[1] to show how the actual way that police were controlled, and the balance of power between police chiefs, local government and national government, has shifted in the last 150 years. As will be seen, there are periods of stability and periods of rapid change, each the product of a different combination of circumstances. Although the overall direction has been to concentrate power in the hands of police officers and central government at the expense of local government, the last decade has seen this process go into reverse in some respects. The historical development is certainly *not* a story of gradual movement in one direction and for one reason.

In the early years of the twenty-first century, the notion that the police were overly centralized regained respectability in British political debate. In the 1980s, the Conservative government reflexively supported police chiefs against their (often Labour-controlled) **police authorities**, but this position has now changed. A comprehensive report commissioned by a Conservative-linked think tank called Policy Exchange was issued in 2003 (Loveday, 2003). This argued that the American model of policing – where democratically elected local governments control the make-up and the policies of the police in their **jurisdiction** – was one that the UK ought to adopt. The Conservatives even fought the 2005 General Election on a platform of electing local police chiefs: a return to a version of the local democratic structures that had been replaced over 40 years previously.

The history of policing and local government

The earliest police were the **parish constables** and (in towns only) the local **night watch** forces. These were in theory composed of **householders** who took it in turns to carry out these duties unpaid. By about 1750, almost all of the night watch, and many parish constables were no longer householders but paid substitutes; the watchmen working for a low wage, the parish constables for fees. Watchmen patrolled a short urban beat, or stood in a kiosk, at night time only, usually carrying a lantern and a staff, and calling out the time as they patrolled. The work was steady, but not especially well paid, and in consequence, while in the main they gave a satisfactory service, the quality of the personnel was sometimes low. Unlike watchmen, parish constables were almost always literate – in an age when about half of the male population was not. They rarely patrolled the streets, but instead followed up complaints of crime. They were ultimately answerable to local justices of the peace, though they were not closely supervised by them – or, indeed, by anyone. Instead, they could be sued or fined if they failed to perform their duty adequately; an expensive and time-consuming process which was rarely invoked. They did not receive wages, but could claim their expenses, and rewards (sometimes very large) for prosecuting criminals. The constable could serve warrants, search premises and arrest suspects, but the initiative in prosecuting serious crime was almost always taken by the victim.

Constables were close to their communities, which was a source of pride for most theorists of British government at the time, who also favoured them since they could not act as agents of any potential oppressive government (Rawlings, 1999: 74). However, this closeness was a problem to many early police reformers, who argued that because they were embedded in their communities, and lacked a supervisory structure, constables were unable or unwilling to enforce unpopular laws, such as those concerning smuggling, poaching and many causes of disorder such as licensing laws. Not only that, but their essentially amateur nature meant that many of them were not competent to act against criminals, and those constables who were full-time were suspected of corruption, since their dependence on rewards gave them an incentive to ignore minor crimes and, in some cases, to connive in setting up major ones.

In practice, these criticisms were over-blown, and most of the 'old police' system worked well most of the time. Nevertheless, as is well-known, in the period between 1800 and 1860, new salaried and uniformed police forces were founded all over Britain. They made a virtue of their ability to prevent crime and to secure the streets from disorder. It was claimed that they were professional, in that they applied a constant standard to all members of the public, without regard to their ability to pay for their services. These **new police** organizations had various structures of accountability, but they tended to follow a standard pattern of organization and activity, which marked a great break from the system of parish constables. They were assigned to a 'beat' which it was their duty to patrol, generally along a set route. Their performance of this task was supervised by a series of higher ranking officers, each reporting verbally or (more often) in writing to the one above. They were subject to military-style discipline, and their training involved drill and marching: abilities which were useful for intervening in riots and political demonstrations. No more would British policing largely be in the hands of a mainly amateur group of responsive individuals who merely reacted to reports of crime: the ethos of the new police was to prevent crime and disorder by a continual presence on the streets.

The practice of policing

For the second half of the nineteenth century and, for most police, the majority of the twentieth, the way that they did their job was through walking a beat. This was as likely, or sometimes more likely, to be at night time as in the day, since it was at night that much property crime – such as theft, robbery and burglary – took place. The evenings were also the time that there was a risk of disorder related to drinking and other pastimes. But the main threats to order happened in daylight, and police were routinely deployed in larger numbers to control crowds and enforce the law at major public events such as races and fairs. Although the policeman on the street was legally very powerful, police authority was limited in private space. This of course meant that those people (such as the middle classes) who conducted most of their lives in private space were unlikely to be interfered with by police, whereas those who were more likely to be found in public, largely from the working classes, felt the policeman's presence far more strongly. In the early days of the new police this conflict over the use of the streets led to extreme opposition by working-class people. Perhaps the best known is the case of the Lancashire mill town of Colne, where:

> By April 24, 1840, a flash-point was reached. During the afternoon small knots of men began to collect in different parts of the town; by sundown a large crowd numbering several hundreds had congregated. The events of that evening showed evidence less of a 'spontaneous' riot than of real tactical planning. Every lamp in Colne was put out. At about 9 pm, the police formed up to clear the streets. One segment of the crowd pretended to flee ahead of them to the east. At length on a given signal this group turned 'and in a disciplined manner' began to stone those policemen who had been lured away from the main body. The police, split into two bodies, were driven from the streets. (Storch, 1975: 80)

Legally powerful in some respects, the policeman was physically and morally at a disadvantage: especially in rural areas, he was often miles from aid, and also from supervision. For this reason, many rural forces prohibited their constables from entering pubs alone: they were forced to observe them through the window. For although the 'new' policeman was in theory a man apart from the temptations of community life, the dilemma was that he also needed to be part of that community if he was to have any chance of enforcing the law on his own.

Perhaps because of their vulnerable position, police tended to apply different standards to the 'respectable'. As Carolyn Steedman has found, following her research into the policing of the Victorian countryside:

In 1862, just after the Night Poaching Act came into force, the chief constable of Buckinghamshire ordered his men to exercise 'extreme caution and discretion' in apprehending people, only to approach respectable persons if they felt 'assured in their own minds' that an action could be carried through. 'I expressly pointed out,' said the chief constable of Cumberland and Westmoreland 'that the police should be very careful never to interfere with anybody whom they knew to be a respectable man... (Steedman, 1984: 149)

In theory, police powers – to prevent obstruction, maintain order, search on suspicion, and to arrest if evidence was present – were structured in such a way that it was the poorest Britons who felt their presence the strongest, while (before the arrival of the motor car) the rich and respectable were more likely to see them as servants than masters.

Towns and cities

The power of towns to police themselves was re-defined by the 1835 Municipal Corporations Act which for the first time gave them a legal obligation to set up a police force under the control of a Watch Committee: but it set no standards as to the size of the force. Many **boroughs** took a long time to set up their forces, but they all did eventually, and some of them (such as Liverpool and Birmingham) were among the most strongly policed areas in the country. By the second half of the nineteenth century, the 150-odd boroughs of England and Wales set great store by controlling their own police force. Watch Committees were elected annually from the newly elected local council, but once in place it was the Committee, not the council, who were the police authority. They had the power to promote, hire and fire any member of the force, right up to the top, and the local chief (often called a 'head constable' or 'superintendent') could not fine his men more than one day's pay without the watch committee's involvement. They wrote the rules and regulations for their force (Williams, 2003).

This system also made the police responsive to the issue of what we would now call 'anti-social behaviour' – low-level disorder. Watch Committee members could hear of the complaints of their friends or constituents, and pass these on to the head constable at one of their weekly meetings: he had an obligation to obey their instructions. Nearly all borough head constables were policemen who had risen from the ranks and were seen as servants (albeit skilled and necessary) by the committees. Practically, this meant that local councils had direct control over how the law over many important local issues was enforced. These included licensing laws, the regulation of traffic, and the imposition of sexual morality through the ability to tolerate (or not) brothels.

In 1890 the issue of who was in ultimate charge – policeman or committee – was tested in Liverpool when a pro-**temperance** group, the Vigilance Association, gained a majority on Liverpool city council and hence its Watch Committee. They ordered the city's chief constable, William Nott-Bower (a rare example of an 'officer-class' city chief), to close down the city's brothels, which though technically illegal had long been tolerated in certain areas. Nott-Bower protested that this would merely spread the problem of prostitution throughout the city and lead to more police work; he made this claim based upon the fact that he was a professional police officer with a better grasp of the priorities of his job than the Committee. But when the police chief appealed to the Home Office, they backed the Watch Committee and confirmed that it had the power to give him detailed orders (Nott-Bower, 1926: 140–146): political control over-rode professional claims. The policeman was eventually vindicated when the inhabitants of the areas into which the trade had moved put enough pressure on the Watch Committee that they tacitly reversed their zero-tolerance policy.

Of course, there were limits to how democratic this system was. The vote in local elections was limited to rate-paying householders, which meant that the electorate was overwhelmingly male, and included very few of the working classes. The councillors themselves had to meet a property qualification, and this was zealously imposed to keep the radical poor from the council, while those radicals who did get elected found themselves excluded from Watch Committees (Williams, 2004). It was perhaps for this reason that, until 1914, the system of extreme local control was backed up by Whitehall. When questions over police matters outside London were raised by MPs in Parliament, Home Secretaries regularly disclaimed all responsibility for them, and merely advised them to take their complaints to the relevant local police authority; the correspondence of the Home Office shows that this attitude was replicated in private.

Counties

In the counties, the first police forces were set up in 1839 when, alarmed by the threat of Chartism (the radical working-class movement for democratic reform) the government passed legislation which enabled counties to set up 'new' police forces in their counties, if they so chose. Providing a police force became an obligation for the counties in 1857.

In the counties, the police were overseen by a committee of the county quarter sessions bench of Justices of the Peace. These men were responsible for the police not because they sat in courts, but because they were the local government. Since the sixteenth century, each county of England and Wales was administered by the local Justices of the Peace, who met four or six times a year to consider local government issues as well as dispense justice in **quarter sessions.** As well as policing and judicial matters, Justices were also responsible for highways, prisons, bridges, asylums and markets. They were overwhelmingly members of the landowning elite of the county – or at least that subset of it which felt an obligation of high social rank was to aid in the governance of the locality. Often, members of parliament would also be active Justices, and some government ministers tended to act as well: thus the men at the centre of the police system also had experience of the localities within it (Storch and Philips, 1998: 67). Sometimes, especially in semi-urban areas where there was much call for their services, there were numbers of Church of England clergymen on the bench, but these men too were mainly younger sons of landowners, and shared most if not all of the attitudes of their fellows.

The Justices' Police Committees were not as active as Watch Committees, and did not enjoy the same level of legal control. They tended to meet quarterly, and concerned themselves with providing the necessary money, equipment and property for their chief constable to run the force efficiently. Their most important function was to appoint the chief constable, and in some counties even this was very rarely exercised, since county chiefs were often appointed very young, and retired or died in office many decades later. The reason that they were appointed at such as young age was that the vast majority of them were not professional policemen who had risen through the ranks, but younger sons of the gentry, who shared their background and pre-occupations with the county bench of justices, even when they did not serve in their native county. Often they had already had experience as army officers; very few had specific police experience, and of those that did, the majority had gained it in the Empire or in Ireland. Within their forces, county chief constables tended to gain a reputation as autocrats, and it was they, rather than the police committee, who were responsible for hiring and firing the subordinate members of their force.

The majority of county policing was done by police dispersed to villages in their ones and twos, many with only daily or less frequent contact with sergeants or fellow officers, patrolling lonely rural beats which took in several villages. But this was not the whole picture: nearly all counties contained some substantial urban centres which the 'rural' force policed, and many (such as Staffordshire, Lancashire and the West Riding of Yorkshire) had large semi-urban industrial districts to patrol. So it was in its style and structure of accountability that county policing displayed the most contrasts with borough policing. This was notable in the balance of power between the police authority and the chief constable, but the factor which linked both types of system was that policing was the responsibility of local government.

The London Metropolitan force

For nearly all of its life, the London Metropolitan police (the 'Met') has been an exception to the general rule about the way that British police were controlled. In 1785 the Prime Minister, William Pitt, proposed a single centrally controlled police force for London. This proposal never went anywhere, chiefly because it infringed upon the jealously guarded independence of the self-governing **City of London**. In the square mile of the City, policing was already relatively effective, but it was the threat to the City's political autonomy which mobilized it against Pitt's police bill rather than any considerations of policing effectiveness. This pattern was repeated many times in the course of the transition from 'old' to 'new' police, outside London as well as within it (Williams, 2000; Paley, 1998: 104). Policing is too important to be considered merely in terms of crime, or even of broader issues of law and order. In any political system, even one as stable as that of Great Britain, control over the police is a highly significant exercise of state power. Local considerations and local politics were always very important in the eclipsing of the old police.

In 1829, London's local authorities acquiesced in the creation of a new police force for the entire capital except for the square mile of the City. The Met controlled a network of stations across London, from which police constables were based, the vast majority of them patrolling beats. The ethos of the force was to prevent crime by virtue of their presence on the streets – although this did not stop them making numerous arrests. The detective force was non-existent until 1842, and very small after that until the 1870s. Despite this orientation towards passive uniformed policing, the force was controversial for a number of reasons. In many parts of London, the parish vestries which had previously run the watch had created efficient and effective bodies of men: some places were better patrolled before 1829 than after it. Londoners paid for the Met, but they had no control at all over the way that the force operated. In establishing its credentials as a riot-control force, it acquired a reputation for heavy-handedness and brutality. This view of policing can be seen in the aftermath of the Cold Bath Fields riot of 1833, when an **inquest jury** decided that owing to the unprovoked attack of the police on a demonstration, the death of a Constable who was stabbed in the ensuing fight was 'justifiable homicide'. The initial years were clearly rocky, but afterwards, the Met began to gain general acceptance in London.

The Met was then under the control of two (from 1859, one) Commissioners of police, responsible to the Home Secretary. In London, the Home Secretary was himself (the first female Home Secretary was appointed in 2007) the police authority. This state of affairs persisted until 2000, when the Metropolitan Police Authority was created. This had the same amount of control over the Commissioner as other provincial police authorities, and marked the end of the Met's exceptional situation. Some of the MPA's members were elected from the Greater London Authority; others were appointed. Despite this reform, the Home Secretary still has greater control over the Metropolitan Police than other forces, reflecting the fact that the Met plays national roles such as combating political crimes and protecting foreign diplomats.

Professionalism and centralization

The nineteenth century's structures of policing were the product of a particular political system, and as that system evolved, so did they. As local government became more and more democratic, Britain's ruling elites grew worried that this might leave radicals or the working classes in control of policing, and took steps to prevent this. Other pressures for change were less overtly political, and came from a desire to control crime and disorder better by the compulsory amalgamation of small forces, and the imposition of a basic regime of central inspection on them.

The very small size of some of the borough forces was seen by many police reformers as an obstacle to the creation of an integrated national system of police. Partly this concern was driven by the 'migration theory': that criminals would leave areas where the police force was strong, and instead take refuge in those areas where it was weak. Hence, weak police forces in one area were the responsibility of all. A Parliamentary Committee considered this issue in 1853: an extract from the 1853 Report is reprinted at the end of this chapter. In 1854 and 1856 the Home Office's attempts to pass police bills that limited the rights of boroughs to control their own police forces were defeated by an alliance of Watch Committees, who sent down representatives to join their borough MPs in a mass delegation to the Home Secretary. All but the smallest boroughs won; the 1857 Act paid a quarter of the costs of 'efficient' forces provided that they policed a population of more than 5,000. This Act also created the Inspectorate of Constabulary: two (later three, later more) senior police officers working for the Home Office to check that forces were indeed 'efficient'. This, though, was narrowly defined as meeting a certain ratio of police to population, and reaching an acceptable standard of parade-ground drill. Some boroughs even decided to ignore the grant altogether, although this attitude tended to change from 1874, when the government grant was raised to half of the costs.

In the counties, a precedent was set in 1888 that would have far-reaching consequences. The Local Government Act that year took political power away from the Justices of the Peace (though they remained magistrates in legal cases), and gave it to elected county councils. But the one power which was not transferred was that over the police force. The dominant Conservative wing of the Unionist government overruled the desires of the Liberal Unionists to replicate the democracy of the cities in the counties. The Prime Minister Lord Salisbury wrote: 'The civilization of many English counties is sufficiently backward to make it hazardous for the Crown to part with power over the police; even if that power should be looked on as a proper municipal attribute, which I am inclined to doubt' (Dunbabin, 1963: 250). County police authorities – 'standing joint committees' – were created, with their membership divided between magistrates and elected members. Given that some of the elected members of almost every county were upper-class magistrates, this gave the landowners a built-in majority on the police committees. The crucial point was that for the first time outside London, policing was no longer defined as just another power of the ordinary institutions of local government, but instead as something with which democratic local government could not be trusted.

The impact of the First World War

The First World War brought new responsibilities for police forces and, above all, for the Home Office. Home Office civil servants, needing to work through the police, became increasingly concerned that the large number of forces, of varying sizes and quality, were an imperfect instrument for carrying out their instructions. Consequently, more centralization and the compulsory amalgamation of more forces became a top Home Office priority. 'War is the health of the state', and faced with the imperative demands of a war, all states tend to pay more attention to effectiveness, at the expense of conserving traditions or adhering to political norms such as an attachment to democratic control. Policing was just one of many policy areas where the expanded state responsibilities of the two world wars would set a benchmark for what could be done, and provided a point for policy-makers and administrators to aim for.

During the war, police wages were frozen at a time of rising inflation, and although police had many more duties to perform, forces were denuded of men by the armed services. These developments galvanized the underground police union into action. This body had arisen in the preceding decade, having emerged out of a growing self-consciousness among rank and file police officers, which first arose in the agitation in the 1880s for an entitlement to a pension, and had been strengthened by the opposition to often oppressive and arbitrary discipline. The Union's first strike in 1918 was short, effective and victorious. The Home Office promised a pay rise, a review of pay and conditions, and the right to join a staff association which would negotiate with employers. They did not, though, recognize the Union as legal, and in 1919 there was another strike, largely confined to Liverpool and London, over the issue of Union recognition. This time, the government took a hard line, and sacked all the strikers, never to reinstate them.

The review produced the Desborough Report, whose conclusions were the basis of the 1919 Police Act. This unified pay and conditions for police nationally. Thus it took away from the local police authorities the right to set the levels of pay for their forces, and also established a national body (the Police Council). The rank-and-file side of the negotiations was taken by the new staff association, the Police Federation. The official side of the negotiating body was co-ordinated by the Home Office, which of course meant that central government had a lot more power over policing; it also involved the creation for the first time of an official group of chief constables, who took their own place round the table for consultations. During the interwar period, the government increasingly began to pay for 'common police services', such as training facilities, the first forensic science laboratories, and technical collaboration over issues like radio.

By the end of the nineteenth century, county chief constables kept a club in London for their use, and the borough chiefs also organized annual dinners (on a less opulent scale) but these relationships between senior officers tended to be social rather than professional. Over the length of the twentieth century, however, police chiefs consistently increased their degree of professional autonomy (Deflem, 2002: 457), which meant that they were increasingly able to set the policing agenda, usually in alliance with the Home Office, and at the expense of the power and position of the local police authorities. In the tense atmosphere of the 1920s, the spectre of Bolshevism and the appearance in local government of its apparent (to some) shadow, the Labour Party, led to an increase in political battles between police authorities and their chiefs. Disputes involving Labour-controlled authorities Monmouthshire and St Helens were both settled when the Home Office came down against the authority: in the county by withholding funds, and in the borough by setting up an inquiry that exonerated the chief constable. The expansion in the 'security state' during the 'red' scares of the early 1920s saw an unprecedented level of peacetime planning for counter-insurgency and maintenance of supplies. The Home Office took increasing responsibility for producing a class of leaders for police forces, and thus intervened increasingly in matters of training, promotion and appointment. The Home Office began to intervene more in the appointment of chief constables; the Hendon Police College, which had a national impact, was set up in 1933. By the 1950s **Whitehall** introduced a policy of refusing to appoint any chief constable who had only one experience in force; this was clearly designed to create a more homogenous and professionalized group of senior police officers.

The main new issue which prompted Whitehall to take this line was the rise of the left, in the shape of the trade unions and their political wing, the Labour Party. The unions were increasingly militant in the post-war period, and in response the Home Office became the centre of increasingly sophisticated plans for emergency powers and counter-insurgency. Not unnaturally, this process was very difficult to plan without a high degree of centralization. Whitehall needed to know who to deal with in the provinces, and to know that they were competent; police forces needed to be able to work together. For the first time since the 1840s, the organized working class posed a potential threat to the political control of the state as a whole, rather than merely a threat to public order in one area or another. One answer to this problem was the development of the system of mutual aid between forces, so the public order response could be co-ordinated; a process that culminated in the use of the central National Reporting Centre (operated by the Association of Chief Police Officers) during the 1984/85 miners' strike.

As well as the heightened demands on the police system stemming from industrial unrest, the Home Office was also worried by the influence of the Labour Party, which was beginning to take a significant degree of power in many towns and cities and in a few counties such as Durham. The system of local control which had been politically unproblematic when Watch Committees could be controlled by Liberal or Conservative majorities became a threat when it appeared that they could fall into the hands of Labour politicians who might be less willing to use them to preserve order against strikers.

The decline of local autonomy

After its failed attempt to bring the borough police forces under its control in the 1850s, the Home Office left them alone until well into the twentieth century. But in the new post-war climate, the department's policy (which was adopted or followed passively by every successive Home Secretary) was to increase the control it exercised over the provincial forces. Its initial gambit was to propose that all small borough forces should be amalgamated with county forces as part of the overall post-war cuts in public expenditure, but this policy did not pass. During the 1920s, successive Home Secretaries, anxious to avoid conflict in the

House of Commons, decided against introducing new legislation to end the independence of the boroughs. Instead, the Home Office changed tack, and proclaimed the independence of chief constables through the courts rather than statute law. The decision by Whitehall to support the authority of the independent chief constable (both borough and county) was justified by referring to the doctrine that since the ordinary constable was ultimately responsible to the law rather than to his superiors, thus the chief constable was also. Local executive control of the police was therefore portrayed as 'political' and hence suspect. In a speech in November 1928, the Home Office's Permanent Secretary, Sir John Anderson, spelt out that: 'the policeman is nobody's servant... it is the Law... which is the policeman's master'.

Although Anderson claimed that this doctrine was long-standing, it was in fact innovative. In the period before 1914, the Home Office had made it clear that in the boroughs at least, the policeman – even the police chief – was the servant of the Watch Committee. The legal framework which set the situation up – the 1835 Act with minor later amendments – had not changed. The issue of who controlled the constable was addressed, though not to everyone's satisfaction, in 1930, with the legal verdict in the case of 'Fisher vs Oldham'. A man named Fisher was wrongly arrested following incorrect information provided by the Oldham borough police. He sued Oldham Corporation for damages, on the basis that the police force was their responsibility (Emsley, 1996: 164). In a judgement which raised eyebrows even at the time, Lord Justice McCardie ruled that since an individual police constable took an oath to uphold the law, the police force as a whole were not the servants of the borough, but of the Crown, and hence the borough could not be held responsible for their actions. This ruling cemented Anderson's view of constabulary independence into law for the first time. So when Charles Reith wrote the glowing view of the British police's subordination to the law alone which was quoted earlier in this chapter, he was describing a state of affairs that was less than 20 years old.

By establishing this 'constitutional principle', and massively enhancing its role at the centre, the Home Office transformed its powers. T.A. Critchley, a Home Office civil servant at the time, thought that during this period the police became more of a national than a local service and:

> the prolific 'advice' and 'guidance' contained in Home Office circulars on all manner of subjects became a euphemism for 'direction'; and chief constables, resentful of any attempt at interference from the outside, would look to an informal exchange with the Home Office to settle almost any problem. Thus, for good or ill, the department had worked itself into a position of exercising great power without formal responsibility. (Critchley, 1967: 219)

The introduction of radio and police cars meant that for the first time central-ization could lead to significant improvements in efficiency. Issues such as mak-ing sure that radio frequencies were compatible also provided another reason for it. During the 1920s, the British police service as a whole became increas-ingly pre-occupied with the challenge to its traditional modes of operation presented by the increasing use of the motor car. More police needed to be detached on to traffic patrol and enforcement duties, leading to strained rela-tions with many middle-class motorists who were not happy in their new roles as the objects of police attention (Emsley 1993). As well as this, criminals threat-ened to move faster than police, not least because they could easily cross bound-aries between local forces. In the words of one chief constable, before slum clearance 'one knew with some certainty where to look for suspected persons in relatively circumscribed areas' (Popkess, 1936: 186).

Although the image of the 1950s is one of social peace and a consensus soci-ety, policing became increasingly contentious in this period. Unease over polic-ing derived from two main sources: accusations of police incivility and sometimes excessive violence towards members of the public, and corruption scandals involving local chiefs and police authorities. The result was a Royal Commission on the Police, which sat from 1960 to 1962. It had a mandate to investigate 'the constitution and function of local police authorities; the status and accountability of members of police forces, including chief officers of police; and the relationship of the police and the public and the means of ensur-ing that complaints by the public against the police are effectively dealt with'. In practice though, under heavy influence from the Home Office, the Commission skated over the question of the relationship with the public and concentrated on administrative structures. The Home Office agenda from the outset was clear – the Secretary of State should be made more responsible for policing outside London. Watch Committees ought to be more like the county police authorities, and thus exercise far fewer powers. The result was the 1964 Police Act, which subsumed city forces into counties, and so replicated the weak sys-tem of local accountability found in the county police forces.

Beginning in the mid-1960s, and reaching what many saw as an unpleasant crescendo in the 1980s, chief constables began to develop a political profile in their own right, usually but not always associated with the Right of the political spectrum. Following the urban riots of 1981, several clashed with their police authorities over how they should be equipped: the chief constables, backed by the Home Office, favoured the adoption of a more paramilitary style of riot policing, and although a number of police authorities protested that this was not their desire, the chief constables' policies prevailed. Tension increased following the miners' strike of 1984/85, which saw a complex pattern of mutual aid between forces, co-ordinated through ACPO's National Reporting Centre. The police were subject to accusations that they had allowed themselves to be dragged into supporting the government side of the dispute, rather than merely enforcing the law. They denied these accusations, but many senior officers felt that being identified too closely with one political party was not healthy in the long run for the police.

Many adopted a more nuanced and professional style, moving away from 'law and order' rhetoric towards the idea of 'community policing', which was initially made prominent by John Alderson, the chief constable of Devon and Cornwall police. This idea meant different things to different people, but it was largely justified in terms of adopting police tactics and forms of organization which brought the police 'back' into close touch with those that they policed. It tended to be an issue of tactics rather than democratic control. Nevertheless, a new focus towards basic order maintenance policing and closer contact with the 'community' characterized the 1990s, and informed most recent develop-ments in policing. In organizational terms, the most striking feature of the 1990s and the early twenty-first century has been the rise of the Basic Command Unit: this is a police district containing between 100,000 and 300,000 people, and is led by a chief superintendent. The Home Office now col-lects statistical data at the level of the BCU rather than the force. In addition, the Inspectorate of Constabulary can (and does) conduct its inspections at BCU rather than force level. Thus the old county forces are seeing their pre-eminence challenged from above with the increasing power of the Home Office, and from below by the increasing autonomy of their territorial units. Alongside this process, the 1998 Crime and Disorder Act also brought local gov-ernment back into the policing process: at the BCU level, each police force must now agree to consult representatives of the local authority on the nature of an annual plan to reduce crime and disorder, and the 'Crime and Disorder Reduction Partnership' provides another line of accountability for the police. However, unlike that enjoyed by Watch Committees, this accountability does not concern everything that police forces do, but merely those activities relat-ing to the fulfilment of the plan.

Continuity in the discussion of police organization

The format of this book is to introduce and compare historical documents, and below there are excerpts from two documents which illustrate continuity in the ways that policing has been discussed from the 1850s to the early twenty-first century. The first is a number of extracts from the proceedings of a Parliamentary Select Committee which considered the issue of how to reform police in the

1850s. The second is an extract from a 2005 report by HM Inspectorate of Constabulary on the best form of police organization for the twenty-first century.

The 1853 Select Committee

Second report from the Select Committee on Police Together with the proceedings of the committee, minutes of evidence and appendix. Ordered by the House of Commons to be printed, 5 July 1853.

1 (a) Evidence of Willis

Edward Willis was Head Constable (at the time this was the preferred designation of their police chiefs by many boroughs) of Manchester between 1842 and 1857, and acted under the close supervision of the Watch Committee.

> Evidence of Capt Edward Willis, Head Constable of Manchester, 10 June 1853, p. 22, Vol 2.
>
> 2902. Supposing they had a separate police and separate districts, taking Manchester as a separate county, do you think Lancashire and Manchester could be under the direction of one chief constable? – There is certainly at present a want of co-operation and a want of union; the police forces know very little of what each other is doing, and there is very little intercommunication except when very serious robberies are committed. I think it would be a benefit to the counties; as most of the thieves reside in large towns, from whence they go out to commit their depredations.
>
> ...
>
> 2904. [Chairman.] Is the district round the Manchester police district half rural and half manufacturing? – Yes.
>
> 2905. In the vicinity of large towns, like Manchester, do you think those districts would be attached to the Manchester district? – I think so.
>
> 2906. Do you think it would tend to the prevention of crime? – I think it would.

1 (b) Evidence of McHardy

John McHardy was an officer in the Customs Service when he was recruited by the county of Essex to set up their force in 1839. Since his force was among the largest of those founded in this period, and close to London, he became an influential voice advocating professionalism and hence centralization.

> Evidence of J.B.B. McHardy, 27 May 1853, p. 49, Vol 1.
>
> I would propose...that England be divided into four districts...

728. [Chairman.] In speaking of four divisions, do you include Wales and Scotland? – No; I would have one for Wales, and two for Scotland.

729. And only two for England? – Four for England; north, south, east and west; Wales one, and Scotland two.

730. In proposing the appointment of these inspectors, am I to understand that you are not in favour of centralization in London? – Decidedly I am not in favour of entire centralization. I think, for numerous reasons, it would be anything but advisable; you would lose the great advantage of local supervision; for every police constable has several superintendents, particularly with the smaller ratepayers, who are ready to point out any irregularity.

...

733. You have mentioned the number of policemen in your force; are you enabled to train recruits thoroughly before entrusting them with the responsibility of their duties? – No, from the constant demand for constables.

734. By whom is that demand made? – By the public; it is an increasing demand.

Resolution

This resolution formed a part of the recommendations of the Committee.

Resolved, 6. That the efficiency of all existing Police Forces is materially impaired by the want of co-operation between the Rural Constabulary and the Police under the control of the authorities of boroughs, or other local jurisdictions. That, in order to secure that co-operation which uniformity can alone afford, Your Committee are of opinion, that the smaller boroughs should be consolidated with districts or counties for Police purposes, and that the Police in the larger boroughs should be under a similar system of management and control to that of the adjoining district or county, and (where practicable) under the same superintendence, by which arrangement a considerable saving would be effected in the general expenditure.

In 2005, HM Inspector of Constabulary Dennis O'Connor (who had in the course of his career served in the Metropolitan, Kent and Surrey forces), supported by the staff of HM Inspectorate, reported on the suitability of the organization of the 43 police forces in England and Wales for the specific functions of investigating major crimes and terrorism. Like the Select Committee of 1853, he linked improvements in efficiency and professionalism to centralization. Home Secretary Charles Clarke initially proposed that many of these forces should amalgamate swiftly, but these plans proved highly unpopular in most localities, and when he resigned in 2006 (over a separate issue) his successor quickly shelved the plans.

The 2005 Inspectorate report

Excerpt from the 'Executive summary' (i.e. the recommendations).

Design considerations for restructuring

> 1.40 The existing 43 force structure is over 30 years old. It matches local government structures and has emphasised the need to drive down volume crime and provide local policing, with considerable success, but current scope and scale now act as constraints to improve protective services and the economics associated with them. Models of democratic policing vary between the disaggregated, and layered such as in the United States or France, to all purpose, integrated bodies, as presently exist in the United Kingdom and the Netherlands.

> 1.41 The practical advantages of integrated units in facilitating intelligence, operational control and clarity of responsibility are compelling in an environment of unprecedented uncertainty. This was evidenced in the ACPO response on police reform discussions in 2004, which showed that a laminate model, that envisages an integrated approach to policing, was superior to disaggregated models.

> 1.42 Community affinity for policing services above the BCU level is also of value in demonstrating commitment to the needs of wider recognisable localities; and putting a human, accessible, accountable face on the imposing institution of policing.

> 1.43 In creating a structure that is fit for purpose the overall goal should be the creation of organizations that are large enough to provide a full suite of sustainable services, yet still small enough to be able to relate to local communities.

> 1.44 It would be possible to disaggregate certain functions – giving one force the role of investigating major crimes for two or three neighbours for example – but with the possible exception of counter-terrorism, this risks blurring important lines of accountability at a time when the service instead needs to take a clear, balanced view of the police mission...

> 1.45 BCUs are the critical building blocks of both the current structure and a possible new arrangement. They deliver the vast bulk of everyday policing services and many are now sufficiently large and have secured coterminosity such that they can be left largely intact during a move towards a more streamlined structure.

> 1.46 Particular design considerations around combinations of forces in whatever form they take include:

- *Size* – the review indicates minimum size of over 4,000 police officers, but must be cognisant of the need to design-in resilience and spare capacity.
- *Mix of capability* – any structural change must take account of the graded capability of potential 'partners' (i.e. forces that could be amalgamated or work more collaboratively) as indicated through both performance on volume crime and the Protective Services Review.
- *Criminal markets* – it is fundamental to understand the underlying criminal markets and context in which any new entity is to operate.
- *Geography* – the scale and demography may require a measure of pragmatism in proposals for change.
- *Risk* – it is essential that opportunities to reduce risk are maximised by considering current capability and consolidating to generate new strengths.
- *Co-terminosity* – it is essential to consider established political and partners' boundaries.
- *Identity* – whilst accepting the local focus of public perception, historical and natural boundaries should be maximised where possible.

...

'1.60 ...when viewed from the context of the range of challenges and future threats now facing the service and the communities it polices, the 43 force structure is no longer fit for purpose. In the interests of the efficiency and effectiveness of policing, it should change. Whilst some smaller forces do very well, and some larger forces less so, our conclusion is that below a certain size there simply is not a sufficient critical mass to provide the necessary sustainable level of protective services that the 21st century increasingly demands.

61 The position is likely to worsen rather than improve as time progresses. The costs and professional sophistication needed to provide adequate standards of protective services will become ever harder to deliver for smaller forces and we now firmly believe that some reorganisation of forces and re-configuration of protective services is inescapable.[2]

The 2005 report was obviously justified by the perceived need to combat terrorism: what is less obvious is that the 1853 Committee was also influenced by international issues. Parliamentarians were reflecting wider fears about the potential threat to social peace posed by soldiers who would be demobilized after the Crimean War. Anxiety about post-war disorder has been common in Britain and beyond for centuries. The Select Committee ended up producing a blueprint for radical centralization of policing, in the shape of the 1855 Police Bill. An outcry, largely orchestrated by the boroughs that stood to lose their autonomy, led to its defeat, and to the 1857 Act (described above). There are significant points of similarity between the two documents. These include the following:

- The impact or threat of war – policing is hardly ever considered in isolation on its merits. Almost every other policy area development or crisis can have an impact on, policing; indeed in may cases, an issue is judged to be significant or not insofar as it has an impact on policing.
- Big is beautiful – the desire to make things efficient by cutting central costs, to make them effective by improving communication within the organization, and to make them powerful by having a large force: the 10% strategic reserve in a force of 10,000 men is enough to control the largest crowd; in a force of 2,000 men, it is not.
- Effectiveness is seen as the most important factor. Others, such as the constitutional position of the police (which loomed so large in the eighteenth century), are not referred to, or are referred to as subsidiary factors which ought not stand in the way of police effectiveness in the fight against crime.

But as well as the similarities, there are significant differences in the context of each extract:

- The nature of police forces – in the nineteenth century there were very few specialist roles within the police, aside from a very few detectives. Then, nearly all police were grouped in similar units, exercising similar skills, which were essentially those of beat patrol. Now we have a far bigger CID, Special Branch, traffic, traditional foot patrol, and cars that respond to incidents. Each produces a very different kind of job and potentially different styles of policing.
- The complexity of organization – in the period covered by the first extract, each area was policed by only one territorial police force. In the modern day, there is effectively a two-tier structure, which is acknowledged in the report, consisting of the forces, and the BCUs beneath them. As we have seen, these are a relatively new introduction.

Summary

To take us right back to the beginning of this chapter, discretion remains at the heart of police practice, both for the officer on the beat, and the officer or committee who is charged with assigning police to beats, and setting procedures and standards. The problems inherent in squaring the exercise of this discretion with control in a liberal democracy are perennial in the history of British police, although over the years they have been addressed (they are inherently hard to *solve*) in a variety of different ways. One message from a consideration of the historical evidence, therefore, is that we cannot consider policing as an abstract ideal which can be divorced from the social and, above all, political conditions of the society around it. In order to explain it, then or now, we must understand the main external forces that act together to shape the nature of the police institution.

STUDY QUESTIONS

1   How did different systems of local control emerge in London, the counties, and the towns and cities of England between 1800 and 1914?

2   What part did the Home Office play in eclipsing local democracy in 1964?

3   What have been the major barriers to local governance of policing in the nineteenth and twentieth centuries?

4   Does the emergence of community safety offer the possibility of increased local control in the future?

FURTHER READING

Brogden, M. (1982) *The Police: Autonomy and Consent*, Academic Press: London.

Emsley, C. (1996) *The English Police: a political and social history*, 2nd edition, Longman: Harlow.

Loveday, B. and Reid, A. (2003) *Going Local – Who Should Run Britain's Police?* Policy Exchange: London.

Lustgarten, L. (1986) *The Governance of the Police*, Sweet & Maxwell: London.

Reiner, R. (1991) *Chief Constables: Bobbies, Bosses, or Bureaucrats?*, OUP: Oxford.

Wall, D. (1998) *The Chief Constables of England and Wales: the socio-legal history of a criminal justice elite*, Ashgate: Aldershot.

Notes

1   The constitutional position was slightly different in Scotland, notably owing to the lower level of independence of borough forces, and to the existence in Scotland of a separate public prosecutor's office (the Procurator Fiscal) which pre-dates the England and Wales Crown Prosecution Service (established in 1985) by several hundred years. Otherwise, though, the main developments are similar, although the dates of the relevant Acts are slightly different.

2   O'Connor D. (2005) *Closing The Gap: A Review Of The 'Fitness For Purpose' Of The Current Structure Of Policing In England & Wales*, HM Inspectorate of Constabulary: London.

5

Changing Perceptions of Criminality

Chapter Contents

OVERVIEW

Chapter 5:

- Considers contemporary debates about a criminal 'underclass' – a hard core of offenders responsible for a large proportion of all crimes committed.

- Describes the origins of these debates, starting with perceptions of crime in the late eighteenth century.

- Questions how the concept of a dangerous revolutionary poor became transformed into the concept of a rising tide of professional criminals in the heart of English society.

- Discusses how, as the nineteenth century progressed, fears about degeneracy caused some to turn to biological explanations for crime. How did this scientific approach to criminality inform understandings of the causes of crime – and what is its legacy?

- Asks: What are the differences between contemporary discussions about 'problem families' and the 'ASBO generation' and historical discussions about criminals and how they were 'made'? The case studies, extracts of historical documents and the conclusion to this chapter reveal the close connections between the two sets of debates.

KEY TERMS

criminal class	residuum	degeneration	the 'underclass'

A perennial debate in the criminal justice field revolves around the question of 'who commits crime?'. More specifically, the media and the public (as well as criminologists and politicians) often debate whether there is a particular 'type' of person who is predisposed to criminality, and whether these putative individuals form an identifiable 'class' of criminals. One word which is often bandied loosely about in this connection is the term 'underclass', first popularized in the USA by the journalist Ken Auletta (1982). This rather vague, umbrella term refers to the notion that an identifiable class of individuals, usually poor, poorly educated, under-employed, often involved in substance abuse and from 'broken homes', are responsible for a disproportionate amount of criminality and other forms of anti-social behaviour. Also implicit in the term is the idea that this 'underclass' is somehow essentially 'different' and 'separate' from mainstream society in both its values and behaviour.

In a speech on 30 May 2001 Tony Blair pledged that New Labour would 'take further action to focus on the 100,000 most persistent offenders' who were 'responsible for half of all crime' and 'the core of the crime problem in this country'. Of these individuals, he claimed that 'nearly two thirds are hard drug users, three quarters are out of work [...] more than a third were in care as children [and] half have no qualifications' (Young, 2002: 463). While he did not explicitly use the term 'underclass', Blair's focus (using largely hypothetical figures) on crime as primarily the pursuit of an identifiable class of lazy, dissolute, anti-social individuals was clearly based on a long-standing social preconception.

Jock Young has identified three different variants of the underclass debate. In one version, the presence of a disaffected underclass is viewed as the end result of 'a sort of hydraulic failure of the system to provide jobs' (Young, 2002: 457). In the work of theorists such as Wilson (1987), a lack of jobs leads to social and spatial isolation for many. The alienation that this engenders has the end result that drug use and petty crime (and other 'anti-social' behaviours) became the norm in deprived areas. In this version of the underclass debate, it is 'the system' (primarily late-modern capitalism) which is to blame. In another strand of debate, typified by works such as Christian Parenti's *Lockdown America* (1999), it is the stigmatization of the employed and the stereotyping of certain socio-economic and racial groups as criminogenic which has produced an underclass. In this radical version of the debate, members of the underclass are again primarily victims of social injustice.

In the third version of the underclass debate, however, disadvantaged individuals are blamed for their own lack of motivation and 'self-exclusion' from mainstream society. One of the foremost exponents of this type of thinking has been Charles Murray, a policy analyst for a conservative American think tank (the American Enterprise Institute). Murray caused controversy in the early 1980s when he claimed to have identified a particularly problematic section of the American working class defined by its anti-social behaviour (1984). He believed he had distinguished three linked indicators – rising illegitimacy, rising crime and rising drop-out from the labour force – which defined a 'separate' and 'different' element at the lower end of the social spectrum. In 1989, and again in 1993, Murray was invited by the *Sunday Times* to assess the extent to which the United Kingdom was developing a USA-style 'underclass'. Here, again, Murray claimed to have identified an ostensibly 'new' and growing element of society marked by a divergent value-set (1989, 1994). It was here that he located high levels of crime and criminality, claiming that 'the habitual criminal is the classic member of an underclass. He lives off mainstream society without participating in it' (1989: 11). In other words, for Murray and others on the right, members of the 'underclass' define themselves as such by their wilfully anti-social behaviour.

Although he does have his supporters, customarily on the political right, Murray has been severely criticized on both sides of the Atlantic on grounds of his methodology and general use of inflammatory language. However, his work still stands as perhaps the most extreme example of a more general trend – the turning away during the 1980s (in some spheres) from collective explanations of crime based on economic and environmental factors. Even among criminologists not involved in the 'underclass' debate, there was a marked drift towards analyses of criminal activity which considered individual ethics. Gottfredson and Hirschi's 'control theory', for example, noted that 'criminal acts provide *easy or simple* gratification of desires. They provide money without work, sex without courtship, revenge without court delays'. Thus, for them, it also followed that 'people lacking in self-control will also tend to pursue immediate pleasures that are not criminal; they will tend to smoke, drink, use drugs, gamble, have children out of wedlock and engage in illicit sex' (1990: 89–90).

However, this chapter is not concerned with the question of whether or not an identifiable underclass actually exists. Still less is it an attempt to discern objective causes of crime. What is important here is that an underclass is perceived by many to exist, and that policy is often formed on the basis of these perceptions. But just how contemporary is this debate? Is the idea of an 'underclass' really the new, startling phenomenon that commentators such as Murray claim? How do current perceptions and debates over the causes of crime compare to those of the past? When, in fact, did public concern with the idea that a specific class of individuals commit most crime arise? In the following extracts, for example, Murray's work shows clear parallels with that of Patrick Colquhoun, a London magistrate writing two centuries earlier.

> [I]nevitably, life in lower class communities will continue to degenerate – more crime, more widespread drug and alcohol addiction, fewer marriages, more dropout from work, more homelessness, fewer young people pulling themselves out of the slums, more young people tumbling in. (Murray, 1999: 114)

> [T]he moral principle is totally destroyed among a vast body of the lower ranks of the People; for wherever prodigality [extravagance], dissipation [indulgence in vice], or gaming, whether in the Lottery or otherwise, occasions a want of money, every opportunity is sought to purloin public or private property. (Colquhoun, 1800: 11)

Despite being separated by a gulf of two centuries, the congruence between the perceptions of poverty and crime expressed by Patrick Colquhoun and Charles Murray is striking. Each reveals a focus on the poorer elements of society as the source and location of much crime and criminality, and as somehow essentially 'different' and 'separate' from mainstream society. Moreover, for both authors, the criminality of the poor is not merely a by-product of the environmental hardships associated with their poverty. Each complicates the issue by linking both poverty and criminality to a range of other 'lifestyle' factors such as personal morality, 'dissolution' and idleness. There are some clear similarities here, despite the nearly 200 years separating the two authors. However, as with all historical study, care must be taken not to draw glib conclusions and, in particular, not to assume that simply because a view pertains at two particular points in time, it was the same for the whole of the intervening period. What is required is a consideration of the changing ways in which criminality has been explained between Colquhoun and Murray.

Perceptions of crime in the late eighteenth century

As V.A.C. Gatrell has noted, 'for centuries in Britain, stealing from and hurting other people have been pursuits as common and traditional as drinking and fornicating' (1990: 243). This continuity does not, however, mean that *perceptions* of crime and criminals have always been the same. In fact, if one looks far enough back into the past, it is possible to encounter some very different perceptions of criminality. Prior to 1750, before the **Industrial Revolution,** England was largely rural and overwhelmingly agricultural. The vast bulk of the population could be considered 'poor'; rural communities tended to be places where outsiders could be easily identified; there was no mass media in the sense in which we use the term today; and the institutions of law and order were very different to our own (see Godfrey and Lawrence, 2005). While this certainly did not mean that theft, violence and murder were rare or unusual occurrences, it did perhaps mean that the social meaning of crime (the way it was perceived and discussed) was different.

Gatrell has argued that, prior to the late eighteenth century, while elites and the middle classes may well have worried in passing about lawlessness and 'the thieving instincts of the poor', they were relatively indifferent to crime as a generic 'social problem'. Essentially, he argues, prior to about 1780, 'crime' as a subject for public concern and discussion did not really exist. Where the term was used at all, it was usually in the context of personal depravity. In other words, there was no public debate about a 'crime problem' which was seen to be worsening or deteriorating and, more importantly for this discussion, 'the criminal' was not yet discerned as 'a social archetype, symbolic of the nation's collective ill-health' (Gatrell, 1990: 248). Crime was something which might affect one individually, but was not an issue which the government or the press might discuss in the abstract. Property-owning elites were generally more exercised of the threat of revolution and public disorder (particularly in the wake of the **French Revolution** of 1789) than by fears of crime.

However, from about 1780 onwards, the threat of crime did gradually become more of a focus of public concern, and debates about criminality began to be rehearsed. Crime quickly became a problem associated primarily with the poor. However, while the poor were readily associated with crime, this was not *because of* their poverty (for example, not because they *had* to steal to make ends meet). Poverty itself was widespread and, even at the end of the eighteenth century, was still accepted as inevitable by most social analysts. Edmund Burke, writing in 1795, claimed that 'the labouring classes are only poor, because they are numerous. Numbers in their nature imply poverty. In a fair distribution among a vast multitude, none can have much' (Poynter, 1969: xiv). Rather, the poor were associated with crime because of their supposed lax personal morality. For example, Henry Fielding, the novelist and Bow Street **magistrate**, believed that the typical robber was 'too lazy to get his Bread by labour, or too voluptuous [given to sensory gratification] to content himself with the produce of that Labour' (Fielding, 1751: 169). Fielding believed that rich and poor alike could suffer from poor standards of morality, but that this was only translated into crime among the poor whose income could not support their vices. Similarly, Patrick Colquhoun, in his influential treatise, identified 'the depraved habits and loose conduct of a great proportion of the lower classes of the people' as one of the primary causes of crime (Colquhoun, 1800: 3). As he noted:

> While in the higher and middle ranks of life a vast portion of Virtue and Philanthropy is manifested [...] it is much to be lamented that, among the lower classes, a species of profligacy and improvidence prevails, [...] To this source may be traced the great extent and increasing multiplication of crimes, insensibly generating evils calculated, ultimately, to sap the foundation of the state. (1800: 618)

Thus, by the start of the nineteenth century, crime was becoming a topic of public discussion and concern, and an issue which was overwhelmingly associated with the behaviour of the poor. In understanding this change, it is essential to consider the wider historical context. Initially, of course, it is important to recall the immense social and economic developments of the period. From the late eighteenth century the twin forces of industrialization and urbanization had generated tremendous wealth for some. However, this transformation had also entailed vast disruption in the living conditions of much of the population. In many new urban areas the spread of wage labour and cyclical unemployment, overcrowding and a lack of social infrastructure meant that the problems of poverty were glaringly apparent. Economic growth and its attendant benefits remained extremely unevenly distributed.

Perhaps more importantly, however, these changes in the structure of the economy were contributing to a decline in traditional, patriarchal views of the poorer classes. For example, a shift from farm workers as 'servants in husbandry', with the traditional obligations this entailed for employers, to mere wage labourers within a rural proletariat meant an increasing shift towards a market driven economy where traditional rights, duties and deference counted for little. Allied with this, the upheavals caused by rapid urbanization blurred the boundaries of society and contributed to increasingly fluid employment patterns in towns and cities. Thus, not only did this economic and social turmoil contribute to harsh living conditions for the bulk of the population (at least until around 1860), and hence trail crime and popular unrest in its wake, but the rapid and forced development of new types of social relations clearly led to fears of a breakdown in morality and the erosion of tradition forms of authority.

Another significant factor in the growth of concerns over crime was the advent (during the early part of the nineteenth century) of criminal and judicial statistics. As already discussed in Chapter 2, the growth of statistic collection generally (and of judicial statistics in particular) appeared to promise, for the first time ever, the possibility of quantifying crime and identifying 'types' of criminals. Of course, as the discussion in Chapter 2 makes clear, despite Adolphe de Quetelet's assertion of the 'constancy with which the same crimes are annually reproduced in the same order', these initial statistics did not necessarily reflect actual levels of crime but merely the practices and operation of the judicial system (Porter, 1981: 110). However, again, what is important is not the reality but the perception. The new statistics were *believed* to be identifying a group of repeat offenders, and hence public opinion and government policy were shaped accordingly.

Thus, the poor became the focus of many types of anxiety in a rapidly changing society. On the continent, fears over the 'dangerous classes' (the unruly poor) and their possible involvement in revolutionary activities continued. However, as Victor Bailey has argued, fear of social unrest was not something the propertied classes, even in London, worried that much about by the early nineteenth century. Rather, 'these years were characterised by the emergence of the notion (though not yet the phrase) of a "criminal class"' (Bailey, 1993: 232). While there were still residual concerns over the gangs of 'sturdy beggars' believed to tramp the countryside extorting money by intimidating villagers, it was the urban poor in particular who came under increasing scrutiny, and it was primarily in towns and cities that the 'criminal class' was judged to reside.

The 'criminal classes'

Although most prevalent during the 1860s, the notion of a 'criminal class' was a common theme among many mid-nineteenth-century writers. While hard to define with any precision, the term generally referred to a rather nebulous group of individuals (not just the poor or the working classes *en masse*, but rather a subgroup of these) who made their living from crime. The criminal classes were those who had largely foresworn the world of labour and immersed themselves in crime and vice of all kinds. Very often seen to be steeped in criminality from childhood, it was often claimed that the criminal classes had their own *argot* (or slang language), their own meeting places and their own customs and rituals. They were thus, in every sense of the word, 'separate' from respectable society – 'the enemies of the human race' as *The Times* put it. The Leeds reformer, Thomas Plint, in his 1851 book *Crime in England*, described them succinctly thus:

> The criminal class live amongst [...] the operative [working] classes, whereby they constitute so many points of vicious contact with those classes – so many ducts by which the virus of a moral poison circulates through and around them. They constitute a pestiferous canker [an infectious sore] in the heart of every locality where they congregate, offending the sight, revolting the sensibilities, and lowering, more or less, the moral status of all who come into contact with them. (Cited in Himmelfarb, 1984: 387)

The criminal classes, as portrayed in the middle-class press, had certain key characteristics. Firstly, they were overwhelmingly an urban phenomenon. As we have seen, cities were developing very fast during the first half of the nineteenth century. Often, therefore, their speed of growth outstripped the ability of municipal governments to provide an adequate infrastructure. Hence sewerage, lighting, road surfaces and housing stock were all hugely deficient. This made the new urban environments both threatening and anonymous. As Gareth Stedman Jones has argued, the poorer districts of cities thus became 'an immense *terra incognita* periodically mapped out by intrepid missionaries and explorers who catered to an insatiable middle-class demand for travellers' tales' (1976: 14).

These vast new agglomerations also appeared to pave the way for the erosion of 'personal' or 'individual' social relationships between the classes. Sir Charles Shaw, a former police chief of Manchester, described the residents of industrial cities as 'the debris, which the vast whirlpool of human affairs has deposited here in one of its eddies, associated, but not united; contiguous, but not connected' (Lees, 1985: 32). Clearly, the notion of *anomie,* the breakdown of rules and norms of expected behaviour during periods of social change (first proposed by the sociologist Durkheim and later developed by the sociologists Robert Parks and Robert Merton), was well-known, if as yet unnamed, during the period.

Secondly, the 'criminal classes' were closely associated with the lowest end of the social spectrum. Again, what must be stressed is the notion that it was not poverty itself which was associated with crime, but rather the poor, who were held accountable for their own situation. Many believed that it was idleness and a love of vice which led to poverty. Hence, if the poor then resorted to crime this was their own fault for ending up poor in the first place. As a Royal Commission of 1839 concluded:

> [W]e have investigated the origin of the great mass of crimes committed for the sake of property, and we find the whole ascribable to one common cause, namely the temptations of the profit of a career of depredation, as

compared with the profits of honest and even well paid industry [...] The notion that any considerable proportion of the crimes against property are caused by blameless poverty or destitution we find disproved at every step.

Gottfredson and Hirschi's proposal that criminality is more prevalent among those with low levels of self-control would thus have found widespread approval had it been promulgated a century earlier.

A final common theme of middle-class debates on the 'criminal classes' was that of the transmission of deficient values across the generations. John Wade, the radical journalist, in his well-known *Treatise on the Police and Crimes of the Metropolis* claimed that 'thieves are born such, and it is in their inheritance: they form a caste of themselves, having their peculiar slang, mode of thinking, habits, and arts of living' (1829: 158). Similarly, William Augustus Miles, in the Select Committee Report on Gaols (1835) noted that 'there is a youthful Population in the Metropolis devoted to crime, trained to it from Infancy, adhering to it from Education and Circumstances [...] a Race *sui generis* different from the rest of Society, not only in Thoughts, Habits, and Manners, but even in Appearance; possessing, moreover, a Language exclusively their own' (cited in Philips, 2003: 91).

Thus, in contemporary terminology, the mid-nineteenth-century criminal class might be defined as a marginalized segment of the working class, confined to certain slum areas of major cities, frequently unemployed, given over to drugs and drink, and often bringing up their children to the same type of life. At a cursory glance, at least, this description is not a million miles away from that of the 'underclass' supposedly 'discovered' in Britain and the USA during the 1980s. Again, it is important to stress that the reality of all this is rather unlikely. As Bailey has argued 'whatever the Victorians thought, very few Victorian criminals were full-time "professionals"' (1993: 246). Rather, the majority of crimes were committed by ordinary working people forced to supplement their meagre income with thefts of food, fuel or clothing. Most offenders were not markedly different in social or cultural background to the bulk of the 'honest poor'. That said, the notion that a marginalized group of the working class was turning away from the values of mainstream society and devoting itself to crime, idleness and vice came to have great purchase on the public psyche during the mid-nineteenth century. Why was this? A number of reasons might be posited.

Some authors have focussed on the idea of 'moral panic' as a way of explaining the mid-century preoccupation with a 'criminal class'. The idea of moral panic was first defined by Stanley Cohen as a phenomenon where:

a condition, episode or groups of persons emerges to become defined as a threat to societal values and interests: its nature is presented in stylised and stereotypical fashion by the mass media; the moral barricades are manned by editors, bishops and other right-thinking people; socially accredited experts pronounce their diagnoses and solutions. (Cohen, 2002: 9)

Usually implicit in the term is the idea that new legislation is rushed through as a result of the 'panic', which then quickly subsides. A number of historians (for example, Davis, 1980; Bartrip, 1981, and Sindall, 1987) have investigated the way in which fears over garotting (a form of violent street robbery) led, in 1862, to intense media scrutiny and a subsequent change in the law regarding **'ticket-of-leave men'**. The panic over garotting, initially precipitated by an attack on the M.P. Hugh Pilkington, who was assaulted on his way from the House of Commons to the Reform Club, certainly seems to have been 'one of those episodes in which public anxieties, especially as expressed and orchestrated by the press and by government actions, serve to "amplify deviance" and to promote new measures for its control' (Davis, 1980: 191).

However, the notion of a 'moral panic' is perhaps a little too simplistic to serve as a satisfactory explanation for a phenomenon as complex as the rise of fears of a 'criminal class'. A further development of the theory of moral panic has been provided by David Philips (1993, 2001, 2003), who has elaborated the notion of 'moral entrepreneurship'. For Philips, what is really significant about moral panics is the way in which they provide opportunities for 'moral entrepreneurs' to push for their own political and social agendas. Philips cites William Augustus Miles as an example. Miles, a 'self-proclaimed expert', worked for various House of Lords Select Committees. While trying to secure permanent paid government employment for himself he conducted many interviews with juvenile offenders, police and prison officers. Philips argues that Miles had 'a horrified fascination with the details of criminals, criminal areas and criminal life' and hence sought to fix in his readers' minds the image of a deceitful and predatory class who were 'constantly cheating and robbing the honest public' (2003: 92). More than this, however, Philips also contends that Miles 'deliberately' accentuated the size and threat of the criminal class in order to win support for his campaign for reform of the policing agencies. Miles had a clear vested interest in doing this, as he hoped to gain government employment in the agencies set up as a result of his recommendations.

Certainly, the rise of fears of a criminal class cannot be explained without reference to key individuals such as Miles (and also Colquhoun, mentioned above). However, it is also important to consider deeper, underlying reasons for these fears. Randall McGowen (1990), for instance, has sought to consider the social functions which narratives of a criminal class served in nineteenth-century England. He believes that the idea of a criminal class served to displace a general unease about the chaotic state of the nineteenth-century city, and to transform it into a specific anxiety. As he notes:

> By contrast with the disturbing sight of the urban masses or the dark reaches of the city, the habitual criminal had a known form [...] Amidst all the uncertainty produced by the idea of crime, its mysterious roots and its

lurking presence in the heart of the city, nonetheless here at least was some comfort, for one could recognize the criminal. For all the other fears associated with crime, it was reassuring to think that one had grasped it, measured it, figured it out, and could act upon it. (1990: 50)

Thus perhaps the true significance of the notion of a criminal class (and this holds true for the modern notion of an underclass too) is that it enables criminality to be defined as the actions of a class of people who commit crimes, not because of economic hardship or deprivation, but essentially because of weakness of character. This has the further implication that the remedies for criminality, therefore, are not to be found in any major economic or social reform, but in strengthening the agencies of policing, prosecution and punishment. Hence, avoiding any indictment of society as a whole or of the existing *status quo*, the notion of a criminal class meant that the problem of crime 'was essentially reduced to one of identifying and isolating that class' and dealing with it through the institutions of the police, the courts and the prison (Philips, 2003: 105). However, while the 'criminal class' was a useful notion for moral entrepreneurs, and may have helped the mid-nineteenth-century middle-classes to feel better about the rapid pace of change within English towns and cities, the concept was not a static one. Towards the end of the nineteenth century, with the advent of new fields of knowledge (particularly criminology, but also psychology and the pseudo-science of **eugenics**), new and very different perceptions of the form and nature of criminality arose.

Degeneration and the 'born criminal'

During the last third of the nineteenth century, prevalent attitudes towards criminality began to undergo considerable modification. Individualistic explanations of poverty and crime (which placed an emphasis on rational choice and the deficient morality of the working classes) were increasingly being superseded by more *collective* theories of degeneration and urban decay. Although most commonly associated with the work of the Italian criminologist Cesare Lombroso, Daniel Pick (1989) has demonstrated that the diffuse and ill-defined discourse of degeneration was a European-wide phenomenon. Originating in the work of the French doctor Morel on cretinism, degeneration theory focused on the detrimental effects of modern, urban life (both the effete luxury of the aristocracy, and the squalid, filthy existence of the poor) on the physical and mental health of individuals. Adverse environmental conditions not only led individuals towards physical and mental infirmities, but also predisposed them to criminality and vice. Moreover, many late nineteenth-century scientists and criminologists came to believe that such defects could then become hereditary, leading to an inexorable decline in the overall health of the nation. As Pick expressed it, 'degeneration was increasingly seen by medical and other writers not as the social condition of the poor, but as a self-reproducing force; not the effect but the cause of crime, destitution and disease' (1989: 21).

Thus public attention gradually shifted away from the notion of a wily, professional criminal class to consider the hereditary influences or environmental factors which shaped the destiny of all those at the very bottom of society. Typical of this view were the remarks of the social commentator Francis Peek in the 1880s:

> In many dismal alleys and fetid courts of our large towns, the impure and stagnant air depresses and enervates those who return home, already exhausted by work [...] Many families [...] have only one single room, in which parents and children of all ages and both sexes work, live and sleep. It is impossible to conceive that children brought up thus can fail to become unhealthy in body and depraved in mind and morals. (1883: 32)

While the degenerating effects of slum living were seen to affect many of the poor, particular concern was focused on what came to be called the '**residuum**' – a term which passed into common usage during the 1880s. The residuum was made up of all the most unproductive elements at the bottom of society. The residuum thus included criminals, but also lunatics, alcoholics, habitual vagrants and long-term paupers. The boundaries between these categories were both bridged and blurred by the concept of degeneration. All these types of individuals were believed to be 'inherently unable to help themselves, because of biological and physical "degeneracy"' (Harris, 1995: 67).

It is likely this significant shift in public discourse on the causes of crime was largely due to the influence of new forms of 'knowledge' and 'expertise'. In the field of science, to take but one example, the publication of Charles Darwin's *On the Origin of Species* (1859) suggested a biological path of human development rather than one of 'divine creation'. Darwin's exploration of the significance of hereditary and environmental factors in the sphere of biology implied that such factors were potentially more important than 'the will of the individual' in the development of society, too. Thus notions of free will and rational choice, which early 'moral' views of crime were based upon, came to be undermined. Moreover, Darwin's theory raised the unsettling idea that if the course of human history was not divinely ordained, then 'progress' was not assured. If mankind could evolve, could it not also 'degenerate'?

Medical writings, too, and in particular the new discipline of psychiatry, often seized upon the influence of hereditary factors in causing mental deficiency, and routinely linked this to criminality. The pioneering psychologist Henry Maudsley, for example, believed that some individuals were 'born with such a flaw or warp of nature that all the care in the world will not prevent them from being vicious or criminal, or becoming insane' (Maudsley, 1873: 76). Similarly, early criminologists also sought to forge links between modern living, vice and crime. The ability of the individual to shape his or her destiny was downplayed and the force of 'hereditary impulses' stressed. As Gordon Rylands, one of the new criminological writers, noted:

> Many unfortunate persons have bequeathed to them by their parents morbid affections of the brain which compel some to homicide, some to suicide, some to drunkenness and its consequent vicious and degraded mode of life, reducing others to idiocy or raving madness. In this sad class of cases it is obvious enough to any one that the criminal should be no less an object of our deep commiseration than the man who has been seized by a loathsome and painful disease. (Wiener, 1990: 237)

It can be seen, therefore, that when considering changing representations of crime and criminals, we must be aware that these were not constructed in a vacuum. Cultural trends, scientific developments and economic and social changes all have an impact on the construction of criminality. However, one important point to note here is that while the causes ascribed to criminality changed considerably towards the end of the nineteenth century, there had been much less change in the public's perception of criminals. New discourses of crime meant that the topic was discussed using new terminology. Criminality was thus no longer seen as residing among the ignorant and unrestrained 'dangerous classes', nor among the wily and mysterious 'criminal class'. By the end of the nineteenth century, the unhealthy and degenerate 'residuum' was the locus of fears about criminality. However, while the 'residuum' was perceived to be rather smaller than the 'dangerous classes' of the start of the century (largely due to growing faith in the responsibility of the honest working class), and while the causes attributed to criminality had changed, the persona of the criminal remained remarkably constant. The 'crime problem' was still located among the urban poor or, more specifically, in a deviant subset of the urban poor.

Crime was closely identified with a deprived class of individuals, living in unhealthy slum areas, partial to drink and drugs and unable to raise their children properly. Of course, not all commentators took such a view and even among those who did this did not preclude sentiments of sympathy. The Cambridge academic and economist Alfred Marshall argued that:

> Those who have been called the Residuum of our large towns have little opportunity for friendship; they know nothing of the decencies and the quiet, and very little even of the unity of family life [...] No doubt their physical, mental and moral ill-health is partly due to other causes than poverty: but this is the chief cause. (Welshman, 2006: 16)

Nevertheless, in the latter part of the nineteenth century, the residuum was seen by many as the social location of the bulk of criminogenic individuals. The first half of the twentieth century, however, was one of immense social change for those at the lower end of the social spectrum. Not only did the upheavals of the First World War produce dramatic socio-economic transformations, the period also witnessed the advent of the welfare state, the start of slum clearances and town planning, and the depressions of the 1930s. Given all this, did a more sophisticated debate about poverty and crime arise in the first half of the twentieth century? Or, to put it another way, what (if anything) links the concept of the residuum to the late twentieth-century 'underclass'?

The twentieth-century 'social problem group'

By the beginning of the twentieth century, the term 'residuum' was already falling out of common usage. It is tempting, perhaps, to infer from this that a more objective and analytical view of poverty and crime was beginning to develop. However, John Welshman has argued that, in fact, 'by the 1890s, the term "unemployable" had become a synonym for the residuum' – with many of the same adverse connotations (Welshman, 2006a: 586). For example, well-known social activists like Sidney and Beatrice Webb used the term 'unemployable' to refer to the sick and crippled, 'idiots and lunatics', the epileptic, the blind, deaf and dumb, criminals and the 'incorrigibly idle', and all those who were deemed 'morally deficient'. The Webbs advocated labour colonies to remove the burden of the unemployable from society as a whole. Likewise, even William Beveridge (a key figure in the founding of the British welfare state) believed that:

> There are social parasites most prominently represented by the habitual criminal and the habitual vagrant. Each of these is in truth as definitely diseased as are the inmates of hospitals, asylums and infirmaries, and should be classed with them. (Cited in Welshman, 2006b: 27)

Thus the now familiar linking of poverty, crime, and mental, physical and moral deficiency was alive and well in the pre-First World War period. While social surveys such as that undertaken by Joseph Rowntree (published in 1901) did show a growing awareness of the true nature of urban poverty, Welshman argues that they still contained an implicit 'behavioural interpretation of poverty and unemployment'. In other words, the belief that the poor could be held at least responsible for their own situation lingered into the twentieth century.

While the full employment of the First World War temporarily stilled debate over those at the bottom of society, the high unemployment of the post-war recession meant that the topic was quickly on the public agenda again. While economists and demographers were perhaps moving towards a more objective and neutral analysis of the labour market, the term 'unemployable' became incorporated into a new concept, the 'social problem group' of the 1920s. During a period of recession, at a time when the new professions of psychiatry and social work were securing their place within British society, the discovery of the 'social problem group' provided both a convenient scapegoat for poor economic performance and a legitimate object of enquiry for these newly professionalized groups.

The 'social problem group' was a term which was closely linked to the eugenics movement and which found its way into a number of governmental reports during the 1920s and 1930s. The term 'eugenics' was first coined by Francis Galton (Charles Darwin's half-cousin) in 1883. Prompted by discoveries in genetics and biology, scientists, social reformers and other 'eugenicists' asserted that the human race could (and should) be improved through the breeding out of deficiencies such as mental retardation and inheritable diseases. In the early part of the twentieth century, some British eugenicists advocated that pauperism, criminality, alcoholism and prostitution could also be tackled via eugenic methods, including forcible sterilization of deficient individuals. For example, C.T. Ewart, assistant medical officer at Claybury Asylum, claimed in 1910 that:

> Nothing is more wasteful than this army of degenerates who, when they are not living at the cost of the taxpayer in workhouses or prisons, are wandering at large, idling, pilfering, injuring property, and polluting the stream of national health by throwing into it human rubbish in the shape of lunatics, idiots, and criminals. (Cited in Stone, 2001: 405)

The eugenics movement never did get the legislation on sterilization and social cleansing they desired. Although a Departmental Committee on Voluntary Sterilization was set up by the Department of Health in 1932, the campaign was damaged by revelations of compulsory sterilization and euthanasia in Nazi Germany. However, the eugenicist discourse on hereditary deficiencies among the poor did find expression, albeit in diluted form, in a number of governmental enquiries and reports.

The Wood Committee, which was convened in 1924 to consider 'Mental Deficiency' (and which reported in 1929), concluded that 'higher grade feeble minded' were concentrated in the bottom 10% of society, and hence identified a coherent 'social problem group'. This 'subnormal' or 'social problem' group was seen to contain a much larger proportion of 'epileptics, paupers, criminals (especially recidivists), unemployables, habitual slum dwellers, prostitutes and other social inefficients' than other levels of society (Macnicol, 1987: 302). Thus, more than a quarter of the way though the twentieth century, the linking of poverty, crime, vice, and mental and physical defects remained intact.

In the aftermath of the Second World War, as Welshman argues, the concept of the 'social problem group' was largely replaced in public discourse by that of the 'problem family'. This notion still encompassed many of the attributes ascribed to the nineteenth-century residuum. The survey *Our Towns,* published by the Women's Group on Public Welfare (1943), for example, identified a putative 'submerged tenth' – a strata of 'problem families' at the bottom end of the social spectrum – 'always at the edge of pauperism and crime, riddled with mental and physical defects, in and out of the courts for child neglect' (Welshman, 2006b: 69). However, after 1945, the eugenic element of this debate diminished rapidly, and the focus of interest in poverty 'came to be cultural rather than biological' (Morris, 1994: 31). Partly, no doubt, the post-war period signified for many 'a new era of social awareness and optimism', during which it was thought that innovative welfare systems would alleviate both poverty and crime. Partly, also, it became increasingly common to find collective explanations for social ills which emphasized the role of environment and 'the system' over the culpability of individuals.

It was not really until the 1970s that what Macnicol terms another 'cycle of rediscovery' took place, and there was a resurgence of debate surrounding the problem of poverty and its relationship to social deviancy. This was initiated in England by Sir Keith Joseph, then Secretary of State for Health and Social Services, in the early 1970s. In a speech in 1972 he posited the existence of a 'cycle of deprivation' whereby deficient values were being transmitted among the poor across the generations. In another, better-known, speech in Birmingham in October 1974, he claimed that lower-class mothers were consistently 'producing problem children, the future unmarried mothers, delinquents, denizens of our borstals, subnormal educational establishments, prisons, hostels for drifters' and, echoing Colquhoun, predicted calamity, noting 'the balance of our population, our human stock, is threatened' (*The Times,* 21 October 1974: 3).

From the mid-1970s onwards, it is possible to note the genesis of the specific 'underclass' debates which formed the starting point for this chapter. Economic marginality, alternative values and deviant behaviour feature in most discussions of the underclass. However, it is the renewed focus on *individual* values and responsibility (rather than structural and state responsibility) which are of most interest here. The term 'underclass' was first popularized in the USA by the journalist Ken Auletta in an article in the *New Yorker* in the early 1980s. Auletta noted that 'at the heart of this age-old debate is the issue of social versus individual responsibility' but further claimed that 'whatever the cause [...] most believe that the underclass suffers from *behavioural* as well as income deficiencies' (Auletta, 1981: 91). Auletta's status as a journalist is perhaps noteworthy. It is certainly significant that the underclass debate has had a far greater public impact than previously discussed 'social problem groups' or 'cycles of deprivation', which were conducted largely among interested experts.

The underclass debate in Britain was initially more subdued than in the United States, and the term 'underclass' itself was rarely used until the mid-1980s. Ralf Dahrendorf was one of a prominent few arguing for the emergence of an underclass in Britain and his definition was much like Marx's 'lowest sediment within the reserve army of labour', with an emphasis on its relationship to Britain's 'moral hygiene' (Mann, 1994: 86). A very different approach came from the left, where the concept has been used in attempts to promote the interests of the poor and highlight social divisions. The Labour MP and former minister Frank Field, for example, claimed that it was a decline in concern about the welfare of the poor which produced an 'underclass', and that economic individualism promoted greed and indifference (Field, 1989). In general, in both England and the USA, the liberal left has emphasized the decline of staple industries in creating 'social isolation' for marginalized groups, while the right has focused more on the 'pathology' and 'culture' of the putative 'underclass'. In both countries the term has been eagerly appropriated by the media, which has often been keen to claim that 'the underclass has not only arrived: it dominates' (Jones, 1993). There is not space here for a detailed consideration of the underclass debate itself. A number of useful studies have already been mentioned (Macnicol, 1987; Mann, 1994; Morris, 1994; Young, 2002; Welshman, 2006). Enough evidence has perhaps been given here, however, to indicate that the idea of a problematic 'underclass', eating away at society's values from within, is nothing new. In one form or another, this is a debate that has been rehearsed in Britain for centuries.

Plus ça change, plus c'est la même chose?

On the surface, at least, it appears that there are many similarities in the debates over poverty and crime of the last two centuries. However, it is important to consider this point in detail. While it is easy to make glib comparisons based on a few seemingly similar quotations, just how much congruence is there across these debates? Is it possible to sustain a more detailed comparison? Two of the quotations in the introduction to this chapter appeared to show that the writings of Patrick Colquhoun and Charles Murray have a lot in common, despite the fact they were produced 200 years apart. As individuals, both men were politically conservative, socially influential and widely read. But what happens if their writings are subjected to a more in-depth analysis? For example, to what *type* of individual does each author attribute criminal tendencies? To what social factors does each author link crime? Do poverty and 'social exclusion' *produce* criminality?

Patrick Colquhoun (1800) *A Treatise on the Police of the Metropolis,* **pp. 311–364.**

Chapter XI: Of Criminal Offences

Offences of every description have their origin in the vicious and immoral habits of the people, and in the facilities which the state of manners and society, particularly in vulgar life, afford in generating vicious and bad habits [...]

Before a child is perhaps able to lisp a sentence, it is carried by its ill-fated mother to the tap-room of an ale-house; in which are assembled multitudes of low company, many of whom have been perhaps reared in the same manner. The vilest and most profane and polluted language, accompanied by oaths and imprecations, is uttered in these haunts of idleness and dissipation [...]

Reduced, from their unfortunate habits, to the necessity of occupying a miserable half furnished lodging from week to week, there is no comfort at home. [...]

Another cause of the increase of crimes, arises from the number of individuals in various occupations among the lower and middling ranks of life [...] who, from their own mismanagement and want of industry, or attention to their business, are suddenly broke down, and in some degree excluded from the regular intercourse with Society. Unable to find employment, from want of character, or want of friends, with constant demands upon them for the means of subsistence to themselves and families, they resort to Public-houses, under the influence of despondency, or to kill time which hangs heavy upon them [...]

Chapter XIII: The State of the Poor

Indigence, in the present state of Society, may be considered as a principal cause of the increase of Crimes [...]

But it is to be lamented, that in contemplating the mass of indigence, which, in its various ramifications, produces distresses more extensive and more poignant than perhaps in any other spot in the world, (Paris excepted) [...] though sometimes the result of unavoidable misfortune, it is perhaps more frequently generated by idleness, inattention to business, and indiscretion [...]

While the wretchedness, misery and crimes, which have been developed, and detailed in this work, cannot be sufficiently deplored, it is a matter of no little exultation, that in no country or nation in the world, and certainly in no other Metropolis, does there exist among the higher and middle ranks of Society, an equal portion of Philanthropy and Benevolence [...]

[But] it is not pecuniary aid which will heal this *gangrene*: this *Corruption of Morals.* [...] In spite of all the ingenious arguments which have been used in favour of a System admitted to be wisely conceived in its origin, the effects it has produced incontestably prove that, with respect to the mass of the Poor, there is something radically wrong in the execution [...]

A new era in the world seems to have commenced [...] The evil propensities incident to human nature appear no longer restrained by the force of religion, or the influence of the moral principle. On these barriers powerful attacks have been made, which have hitherto operated as curbs to the unruly passions peculiar to vulgar life: they must therefore be strengthened by supports more immediately applicable to the object of preserving peace and good order [...]

The first step is, to attend to the Morals and the Habits of the rising Generation; to adapt the Laws more particularly to the manners of the People, by minutely examining the state of Society, so as to lead the inferior orders, as it were, insensibly into better Habits, by gentle restraints upon those propensities which terminate in Idleness and Debauchery.

Charles Murray (1989) 'The Emerging British Underclass', *Sunday Times Magazine*, November.

'Underclass' is an ugly word, with its whiff of Marx and the lumpenproletariat. Perhaps because it is ugly, 'underclass' as used in Britain tends to be sanitised, a sort of synonym for people who are not just poor, but especially poor. So let us get it straight from the outset: the term 'underclass' does not refer to a degree of poverty but to a type of poverty.

It is not a new concept. I grew up knowing what the underclass was; we just didn't call it that in those days. In the small Iowa town where I lived, I was taught by my middle-class parents that there were two kinds of poor people. One class of poor people was never even called 'poor'. I came to understand that they simply lived with low incomes, as my own parents had done when they were young. Then there was another set of poor people, just a handful of them. These poor people didn't lack just money. They were defined by their behaviour. Their homes were littered and unkempt. The men in the family were unable to hold a job for more than a few weeks at a time. Drunkenness was common. The children grew up ill-schooled and ill-behaved and contributed a disproportionate share of the local juvenile delinquents [...]

Britain does have an underclass, still largely out of sight and still smaller than the one in the United States. But it is growing rapidly [...] I am not talking here about an unemployment problem that can be solved by more jobs, nor about a poverty problem that can be solved by higher benefits. Britain has a growing population of working-aged, healthy people who live in a different world from other Britons, who are raising their children to live in it [...] and whose values are now contaminating the life of entire neighbourhoods [...]

Charles Murray (1993) 'Underclass: The Crisis Deepens', *Sunday Times Magazine.*

When trying to estimate what's happening to the underclass I focus on three symptoms: crime, illegitimacy, and economic inactivity among working-aged men.

[...] Illegitimacy in the lower-classes will continue to rise and, inevitably, life in lower class communities will continue to degenerate – more crime, more widespread drug and alcohol addition, fewer marriages, more dropout from work, more homelessness, more child neglect, fewer young people pulling themselves out of the slums, more young people tumbling in [...] How are males to be socialised if not by an ethic centred on marriage and family? And if they are not socialised, how may we expect the next generation of young English males to behave? [...] In lower class communities, where the norm of marriage has already effectively been lost and a generation of boys is growing up socialised by a 'something else' ethic not centred on marriage and family [...] it is not just the economic head wind that will have to be bucked, but a cultural milieu that bears no resemblance to anything that English society has ever known. [...] I favour eliminating benefits for unmarried women altogether (for potential new entrants, while keeping the Faustian bargain we have made with women already on the system). A strong case can be made that [...] these radical changes would produce large reductions in the number of children born to single women [...] Many will find [...] this level of restraint on the welfare state unacceptable. But as you cast about for solutions, I suggest that one must inevitably come up against this rock. The welfare of society requires that women actively avoid getting pregnant if they have no husband, and that women once again demand marriage from a man who would have them bear a child. The only way the active avoidance and the demands are going to occur is if childbearing entails economic penalties for a single woman. It is all horribly sexist, I know. It also happens to be true. Other things happen to be true as well. Babies need fathers. Society needs fathers. The stake for England, as for the United States, is not to be measured in savings in the Social Security budget nor in abstract improvements in the moral climate. The stake is the survival of free institutions and a civil society.

Obviously, these short extracts can only convey a loose sense of the ideas of both Colquhoun and Murray. Both make forceful arguments. Colquhoun's *Treatise* extended to almost 700 pages, while Murray's was more concise but no less strident.

In relation to the questions posed above it would appear that both do focus on elements of 'the poor' as the perpetrators of a disproportionate amount of crime. However, it is clearly not simply poverty as an unfortunate economic state that exercises these commentators. Both Colquhoun and Murray focus on the standards of behaviour and morality of members of the poorer classes as significant in the causes of crime. Colquhoun refers to 'vicious and immoral habits' while Murray refers to healthy but idle individuals 'whose values are now contaminating the life of entire neighbourhoods'.

The social factors linked to crime are also similar, although there are differences. Both mention deficient socialization within the family, drinking and drugs, and unemployment, but with different emphases. For Colquhoun, it is clearly drink which is the chief culprit in leading the poor towards criminality. For Murray, it is illegitimacy and a consequent lack of male role models which leads young men towards deviant behaviour. Interestingly, both argue that welfare exacerbates the problem of an underclass rather than alleviating it. Colquhoun argued that 'it is not pecuniary aid which will heal this *gangrene*' while Murray advocated the elimination of benefits for unmarried mothers.

In answer to the key question as to whether 'social exclusion' produces criminality, the answer which can be inferred from the work of both commentators is, confusingly, both yes and no. Yes, both believe that it is among the socially excluded that crime is most prevalent. However, both deny that social exclusion (characterized by low wages, reliance on benefits, geographical segregation in run-down areas and so forth) necessarily leads to criminality. Rather, both at least imply that it is the deficient personal values of a subset of the poor (smaller for Murray than Colquhoun) which leads to social exclusion in the first place, and hence on to criminality. Both critiques are laden with value-judgements despite, particularly in Murray's case, assertions to the contrary. Colquhoun refers to 'unfortunate habits', 'want of industry' and 'the unruly passions peculiar to vulgar life'. While Murray makes the case that the State needs to provide a framework to enable young men and women to make the 'right' choices in their lives, implicit within his text is still a focus on morality and the traditional 'virtues' of marriage and hard work. There are, of course, differences of language and presentation. However, the two authors do have much in common, despite the separation of years. The perpetuation of the underclass discourse seems likely (for all the reasons discussed in the conclusion) to continue in one form or another for the foreseeable future. Few members of the general public are yet willing, as Young (2002: 484) suggests, to 'emphasize that crime occurs throughout the structure of society and that its origins lie not in a separate aetiology but in the structure of society and its values'.

Summary

Obviously, when considering both public debate and expert discourse, it is important to remember that there is never simply one unanimous 'point of view'. The historical perceptions and stereotypes discussed in this chapter were often contested, and it is always difficult to assess the impact that they had on policy formation and the actual operation of the criminal justice system. That said, it would appear that the image of the lower end of the social spectrum as 'separate' in values and behaviour from the rest of society, and as the location of a disproportionate amount of crime, deviancy and dependency, has (in one form or another) remained fairly constant over the last two centuries. However, what has perhaps changed over time are the *causes* to which criminality among this group has been attributed. More specifically, at the start of the nineteenth century, lax personal morality was generally seen as a cause of both poverty and crime. In the latter half of the nineteenth century, explanations of crime arose which placed more emphasis on hereditary characteristics and the environment in which the poor lived. During the mid-twentieth century, the focus shifted towards 'problem families' and the way in which a 'culture of poverty' sustained certain modes of behaviour. Towards the end of the twentieth century, however, the pendulum swung back (at least on the political right) to debates about the lack of moral responsibility among a relatively small group of socially deprived individuals.

There are a number of potential explanations for the somewhat circular nature of these debates, and for the recent resurgence of explanations of criminality among the poor which emphasize morality and rational choice. Most obviously, the problems of poverty and crime still persist. While noting the methodological difficulties associated with all kind of criminal statistics, it is undeniable that despite real advances in the provision of welfare, in general standards of living and in the sophistication of patterns of policing, few types of criminality have sensibly diminished since the Second World War and others have markedly increased in recent decades. Robert Reiner has claimed that 'from 1975 onwards, the rising crime-rate is justifiably referred to as being in a stage of "hyper-crisis"' (Reiner, 1990: 50). In the course of the last 40 years, high crime rates have become a normal social fact in most contemporary Western societies. Hence, the recent underclass debate must, at least in part, be an attempt to conceptualize a real problem. There has been an increasingly obvious failure of the 'penal-welfare' model, the state-centred policy suite which promised 'not just to punish legal violations, and quell internal unrest, but actually to govern in ways which would curb or cure the social problem of crime' (Garland, 1996: 449). This has, perhaps inevitably, led to a resurgence of speculation as to the nature and extent of the problem of criminality among the poor, and to a disproportionate desire to apportion blame.

However, Baguley and Mann (1992: 124) claim that this perpetuation of 'blame' is due to the fact that 'the dominant ideas of the day have been consistently used by the middle classes to facilitate a redefinition of the poor' and point to a need within the middle classes to justify their privileged place in society by identifying the 'failings' of the poor. They conclude that 'the underclass is the ideology of the dominant upper and middle classes', in the sense that conceptions of an underclass assist other groups within society to sustain relations of domination. Also on a theoretical level, Dario Melossi has attempted to account for the way in which, 'in a somewhat cyclical fashion, at least since the inception of modernity and criminological thought in the nineteenth century, representations of crime and criminals have been oscillating between different social attitudes' (Melossi, 2000: 296). In periods of relative prosperity, he contends, there has been a tendency towards liberalism, optimism and low imprisonment rates, with criminals even seen as 'innovators fighting an unjust and suffocating social order'. By contrast, since the early 1970s, rising unemployment and a profound restructuring of the economy have led to a concomitant 'deep *disciplining* of the working class', via what he terms 'revanche criminology', characterized by 'the ideological disconnection of the issue of crime from social circumstances' (2000: 308–10). When removed from its 'embeddedness in the complexity of social relationships', the whole question of crime thus inevitably becomes one of 'moral edification'.

It is also likely that this debate is linked to wider, long-term tensions between 'liberal' and 'collectivist' paradigms. Richard Cockett notes that it is possible to view the last two centuries in terms of an ideological struggle between liberalism and collectivism (1994: 6). He is primarily concerned with *economic* liberalism, but his thesis can arguably be applied more generally. He notes that, following the initial triumph of liberalism over feudalism from 1770 to the 1880s, economic liberalism (with its concomitant focus on individual freedom of action) became the mainstream 'orthodoxy'. Then, from the 1880s to the 1940s, there was a gradual sea-change in favour of collective explanations of phenomena, initiated largely by the Fabians. Subsequently, it is only recently, from the 1970s onwards, and co-incident with Thatcherism, that more individualistic explanations have again assumed a popular vogue, albeit always now within a referential framework of impersonal social forces. Cockett notes that 'one can [...] interpret this process in Hegelian terms as these cycles bear a close resemblance to the dialectic of thesis/antithesis/synthesis', and the parallels of this process with the debates outlined above are readily apparent.

STUDY QUESTIONS

1 What were the main explanations of the causes of criminality from 1750 to 1850?

2 How did the concept of a professional criminal class arise in the mid-nineteenth century?

3 What was the contribution of scientific criminology to understanding crime?

4 What are the similarities and differences between current and historical debates about the 'underclass'?

FURTHER READING

Bailey, V. (1993) 'The Fabrication of Deviance: "Dangerous Classes" and "Criminal Classes" in Victorian England', in J. Rule and R. Malcomson (eds) *Protest and Survival: The Historical Experience. Essays for E.P. Thompson*, Merlin Press: London, pp. 221–56.

McGowan, R. (1990) 'Getting to Know the Criminal Class in Nineteenth-Century England', *Nineteenth-Century Contexts*, 14(1): 33–54.

Pick, D. (1989) *Faces of Degeneration. A European Disorder, c.1848–1918*, Cambridge University Press: Cambridge.

Welshman, J. (2006) *Underclass. A History of the Excluded, 1880–2000*, Hambledon: London.

6

Immigration, Ethnicity, Race and Crime

Chapter Contents

OVERVIEW

Chapter 6:

- Provides evidence suggesting that race and ethnicity are significant in the operation of the contemporary criminal justice system. A presumed link between ethnicity and crime is a staple part of media reporting. This chapter describes current research in this area.
- Describes how, despite the contemporary focus on immigration from the Caribbean since 1945, there is a long history of migration to the British Isles.
- Describes historical studies of race and crime and presents primary historical evidence from a number of sources to identify common perceptions surrounding ethnic minorities and crime.

KEY TERMS

race   ethnicity   immigration   media stereotypes

The intertwined issues of immigration, race, ethnicity and crime are the subject of much contemporary debate. Fears that foreign arrivals to the United Kingdom might engage in criminal activities have become a staple part of media reporting on crime. Following a trio of teenage fatalities in London, for example, a leader article in *The Express* (16 February 2007) carried the headline 'How we surrendered our streets to the evil rule of foreign killers', and referred to the prevalence of 'Third World thuggery' in inner London. Similarly, in late 2006 the Home Office was publicly pilloried when it emerged that over 1,000 foreign criminals had been simply released from prison without being considered for deportation, with some going on to commit serious crimes.

This type of controversy is not, of course, confined to foreign nationals, nor found only in the media or the political arena. As regards British ethnic minorities, police forces often come under criticism for their stop-and-search procedures, which appear disproportionately to target young black men. Evidence also suggests that strip searches are more likely to be conducted where the suspects in custody are of African-Caribbean origin (Newburn et al., 2004). Moreover, research indicates that, all the way through the criminal justice system, young, black men are disproportionately represented. Perhaps the most startling evidence of this pertains to the end point of the criminal justice system – prison. In the year 2000, black British nationals formed 10% of the male prison population in England and Wales (and around 12% of all female detainees) despite comprising only 2% of the overall population (Phillips and Bowling, 2002: 579).

The upshot of this is that, if your skin colour is black, you are around five times more likely to be involved in the criminal justice system than if it were white. Citizens of African-Caribbean origin are also proportionately more likely to be the victim of a crime than their white counterparts (Clancy et al., 2001: 12). This over-representation of African-Caribbeans in particular is interesting, as it would appear that other ethnic minority groups (such as those of Asian origin) are subject to equal levels of societal prejudice, yet do not end up in the criminal justice system in disproportionate numbers (Smith, 1997: 725). It is thus incorrect to assert a simplistic correlation between race and involvement in the criminal justice system.

A number of reasons might be posited as to why men and women of African-Caribbean origin are more likely to end up in prison than any other ethnic group. As noted, it would be convenient to assume simple societal prejudice, but this does not explain the under-representation of Asians within the prison population. One might posit bias in arrest or sentencing. However, there is evidence to indicate that, although black men are more likely to be arrested and charged than their white counterparts, this discrepancy is ironed out somewhat as they pass through the criminal justice system, being proportionately more likely to have their case terminated by the CPS (Phillips and Bowling, 2002: 599–601).

One thing which is more widely agreed is that young men of African-Caribbean origin are proportionately more likely to be members of the lower socio-economic categories. There is a well-documented, strong correlation between these strata of society and involvement in the criminal justice system. Structural theories of crime, however, cannot provide a convincing explanation as to why some individuals turn to crime and others do not.

Clearly, immigration, race and crime are subjects of continuing debate. Contemporary criminological writings, however, often assume that these issues are of fairly recent advent, and tend to concentrate on the migration to Britain from colonial territories which occurred in the aftermath of the Second World War. The problematic involvement of African-Caribbean men with the police (and in the criminal justice system) is usually considered from the 1958 Notting Hill riots onwards. In fact, ethnicity, immigration and crime have been of public and official concern at many points during the last 200 years.

The first section of this chapter will give a brief overview of immigration and race in Britain since c.1800, as a necessary prerequisite to any consideration of the involvement of immigrants and ethnic minorities in the criminal justice system. While it is true to say that mass immigration to Britain from its colonies in Africa and the Caribbean was primarily a post-1945 occurrence, it is certainly not the case that black migrants were not present in England or involved in the criminal justice system before that time. Also, other waves of European immigrants should not be forgotten. The mass Irish immigration of the mid nineteenth century saw well over half a million resident in England by 1861.

They formed over 2% of the population (Holmes, 1988: 21), a figure comparable to current figures for all those of African-Caribbean descent. The arrival of Eastern European Jews towards the end of the century was also statistically, as well as culturally, significant. The post-Second World War colonial influx will also be outlined.

The second part of the chapter will then consider both media and public perceptions generated by these waves of immigrants. Obviously it will be impossible for a relatively brief treatment to consider all the perceptions and stereotypes attached to such a diverse set of communities, and hence the discussion will concentrate principally on attitudes pertaining to the criminal justice field. As today, the views of the media and of the public in framing the actions of the police and the judiciary are impossible to ignore.

The final section will evaluate what data is available about actual patterns of offending among ethnic minorities over the past two centuries. One of the problems besetting criminologists wishing to study contemporary issues of race and crime is the relative paucity of firm data. The 1991 census was the first to gather adequate data on ethnicity, and prison statistics which record ethnicity are only available from 1985. Problems with sources are obviously compounded the further back in time one peers. Hence, straightforward comparisons of offending or committal rates over time are impossible. However, historians are a resourceful bunch, and there have been a number of quantitative studies attempted, mainly using data compiled from sources not originally intended for that purpose. These will be considered here, along with qualitative data pertaining to issues such as the disproportionate use of police discretion where minority groups were concerned ('over-policing'), and the extent to which black, Irish or Jewish citizens were more likely to belong to the socio-economic groups customarily associated with criminality.

Immigration and race in British history

Towards the end of the eighteenth century a number of British cities (particularly London, but also other ports such as Liverpool) were becoming truly cosmopolitan, and attracting migrants from many countries. Most immigrants were at this stage from Europe but, by the 1780s, there were at least 5,000 black people living in London (Myers, 1996: 35). Some contemporary estimates placed this figure much higher, at 15,000 or even 20,000 (around 2% of London's population at the time). Many of these individuals had ended up in England as a result of the slave trade, which was at its peak during the eighteenth century. As traders and plantation owners made their fortunes overseas, it became common to transport slaves back from the colonies of the West Indies and North America.

For London's powerful elites, an 'exotic' servant was a symbol of status and a familiar sight on the streets of London.

Slaves in England were obviously in a unique legal position, almost entirely unprotected by the law. This changed somewhat with the 'Somerset Ruling' of 1772, a landmark test case where Charles Stewart, the owner of a runaway slave (James Somerset), attempted forcibly to remove Somerset from England and ship him back to Jamaica. The presiding judge (Lord Mansfield) ruled that, while slavery was legal in the colonies, it had no force in mainland England. Many took this to mean that slavery itself was declared illegal at this point. This was not true (it simply meant that slaves could not be removed from England against their will), but the case certainly did much to place the issue of emancipation on the political agenda and gave many slaves the confidence to strike out on their own (Gerzina, 1995: 132). Following a long abolition campaign, the Abolition of the Slave Trade Bill was passed by Parliament in 1807. Contrary to the impression given by the celebratory media events of the centenary anniversary of this event in 2007, the Act did not make slavery illegal, only the trade in slaves. Slavery still continued in British colonies. It was not until 1833 that the Slavery Abolition Act was passed, freeing all slaves in the British Empire.

Of course, not all of those of African-Caribbean origin who were resident in England at this time were slaves. Large numbers of black Londoners also arrived as sailors in the merchant navy and as soldiers in Britain's armed forces. After the end of the **American War** in 1783, many black men who had fought on the Loyalist (British) side were discharged at British ports, forming the first coherent black communities in the United Kingdom. Quite a number of black migrants also worked as domestic servants or labourers. Those black migrants who were not slaves also found themselves in a disadvantaged position legally. The **Poor Law** (or system of relief for the destitute) was regulated by place of birth. The parish where you were born was responsible for your upkeep should you fall on hard times. Obviously, those born overseas did not have access to these resources. Many were thus forced into highly visible begging, leading to poverty among the black community being a much discussed social issue by the start of the nineteenth century. We should recall, however, that (while unusual) it was perfectly possible for a black immigrant to rise to a position of considerable prestige within British society at this time. Freed slave Ignatius Sancho, for example, published poetry and a number of works on musical theory. Ottobah Cugoano and Olaudah Equiano (also freed slaves) were both prominent in the movement to end the slave trade. Tom Molineux was a successful black boxer in early nineteenth-century England, and Ira Aldridge became a celebrated actor.

While the black population in Britain during the early nineteenth century has been described as 'large' and 'significant' (Walvin, 1973: 84), the Irish were by far the largest immigrant minority in Britain during the first half of the nineteenth century. The legal status of the Irish in Britain was of course different to those arrivals from Africa and the Caribbean. Following the passing of the Act of Union of 1800, largely in response to a bloodily suppressed rebellion in 1798, Ireland was subsumed into the United Kingdom of Britain and Ireland, and Irish home rule abolished. Until 1922 the whole of Ireland was thus part of Great Britain, and ruled from Westminster. To an extent, therefore, it is more precise to speak of Irish 'migrants' rather than 'immigrants'. However, contemporaries perceived the Irish as ethnically different from the English, and certainly the Irish also viewed themselves that way. Hence, in the discussion that follows, arrivals to the mainland from Ireland in the nineteenth century will be analysed in much the same way as other immigrant groups.

The 1841 census recorded 189,404 Irish immigrants living in England and Wales (around 1.8% of the total population). By 1871 this figure had risen to 566,540, or 2.5% of the total population (Holmes, 1988: 2). This tally does not, of course, include second-generation migrants born in England, who might very well still have considered themselves Irish but were not counted as such. Although the Irish population in England and Wales diminished somewhat towards the end of the nineteenth century (with the 1911 census showing around 375,000 – 1% of the total population) the numbers involved and the relative rapidity of their arrival ensured they were the focus of both debate and scrutiny.

What were the reasons behind this massive influx? Again, one of the most basic reasons was exploitation – this time the exploitation of Ireland by the British. It used to be argued that the expropriation of goods and money from the Irish economy was so rampant that it was left unable to sustain its own population. Such a view is, however, too simplistic. For example, emigration was lowest from the poorest areas of Ireland, as individuals simply could not afford to leave. Famine in Ireland between 1845 and 1849 also forced many to emigrate – and Ireland saw its population drop from around 8 million to just 4.4 million by 1911. The famine was partly the result of catastrophic failures in the potato harvest. However, at a time of prosperity in England, and at a time when Ireland was under English control, the English must surely take some share of the responsibility here also.

While better than in Ireland itself, the conditions which met Irish arrivals to England and Wales left plenty to be desired. It is important to avoid stereotypes. Large numbers of Irish served in the British armed forces and in the police, too, towards the end of the century. There were also Irish lawyers and doctors. However, there is no doubt that such life experiences were not the norm. In the north of England, the Irish became closely associated with the agricultural sector of the British economy, where it was common for them to take on short-term work (at harvest time, for example). Further south, many also took up residence in towns and cities. Here, Irish immigrants clustered in semi-skilled and unskilled trades such as dock work and labouring. Irish women often worked in textile factories or in domestic service. This concentration at the lower end of the social spectrum can be traced to a range of causes – prejudice on the part of the English being at least as important as reasons such as illiteracy on the part of many of the immigrants (Swift and Gilley, 1989). Residential segregation was also a part of Irish urban social life. In areas such as Scotland Road in Liverpool and St Giles, London, Irish immigrants very often settled near their kin or acquaintances, thus creating densely populated 'Irish quarters'.

Towards the end of the century this influx from Ireland abated somewhat. However, soon the public gaze turned to a new set of arrivals, this time from Eastern Europe. In the 1880s, large numbers of immigrants began to arrive from Russian Poland (Poland having been partitioned in 1815 and a large part of it incorporated into and ruled by Russia). Most of these new arrivals were Jewish. There are no absolutely reliable statistics, but it has been estimated that around 40–50,000 Russian Poles (the vast majority, Jews) arrived in Britain between 1875 and 1901, eventually numbering 82,844, or 0.3 per cent of the total population. While numerically less significant than the Irish, these new arrivals again tended to congregate in specific areas of settlement (in particular the East End of London) and this made them more visible and hence increased the impact of their arrival.

Why did these individuals travel so far to reside in Britain? Again, exploitation and persecution provide part of the answer, although this time not on the part of the British. Most of these immigrants were drawn from the western boundary of Russia, the so-called 'Pale of Settlement'. They were denied employment by Russia outside of this area, and increasing population pressure meant worsening social conditions. In addition, however, and more significantly, Eastern European Jews were subject to unremitting persecution at the end of the nineteenth century, where 'governments seemed to be competing with one another over who could most mistreat the Jews' (Winder, 2005: 229).

On arrival in Britain, many Jewish immigrants clustered in particular professions, particularly the clothing trade, cabinet making and boot making. While numbers nationally were not perhaps that great, their geographical and occupational density (particularly in London and a few other major cities) meant that 'within [...] a short period of time the immigrants and refugees introduced a new, distinctive, immigrant cultural life into their areas of settlement' with the result that 'the East End and Stepney in particular became an island of immigrant Jewish culture' (Holmes, 1988: 46).

Such was the consternation generated by this very visible influx that Britain passed its first ever peace-time legislation restricting those who could come to the country – the Aliens Act of 1905. There had been legislation controlling entry to the United Kingdom before, but only during times of war. In 1793, for example, an Aliens Act (passed in response to war with France and fear of spies) had restricted access to those with appropriate documentation. After the war, however, the legislation was soon relaxed and was abolished by the 1830s. Towards the end of century, Britain was seen by many as perhaps the most tolerant country with regard to immigration, as even the USA had introduced some restrictions in 1882. The passing of the Aliens Act of 1905, however, sprung from deep antipathy towards Jewish immigration in particular, combined with fears that British-born workers would lose their jobs (Kershen, 2005: 14).

Following the passing of the act, the numbers of immigrants entering Britain fluctuated annually between 1906 and 1911 but, overall, there was a noticeable decline. Still more stringent restrictions were introduced after the First World War (in 1919). From this point on, work permits were required for the first time for those already resident in Great Britain. Indeed, during the 1930s, in stark contrast to the end of the nineteenth century, many of those hoping to flee to Britain from Nazi Germany and other parts of mainland Europe found their route impeded by restrictions introduced in 1919 and 1920.

After the Second World War, however, this restrictive climate was relaxed again somewhat. The reconstruction of the British economy after six years of war required manpower that the domestic market was unable to supply. More than a year after the end of the war, for example, Britain was still employing more than 350,000 prisoners of war, and in 1946 the Foreign Labour Committee (FLC) was created to explore ways of recruiting foreign labour (Whitfield, 2004: 12). In addition, the decades after the Second World War saw the 'retreat from Empire'; the gradual withdrawal and transfer of power in Indian and Africa. Thus between 1945 and 1971 (the date of final British withdrawal from the Middle East), a steady succession of immigrants and refugees arrived in Britain, and their cumulative impact led to important changes in the constitution of British society.

One of the most significant paths for immigration in the immediate post-war period was from the Caribbean to Britain. Life in the West Indies was at the time blighted by overcrowding and unemployment, and the 1948 British Nationality Act guaranteed West Indians free entry into the United Kingdom. These push-and-pull factors were decisive for many. The SS *Empire Windrush*, carrying the first group of immigrants from the region, arrived on 18 February 1949. When the USA restricted immigration from the Caribbean in 1952, this flow increased still further. The black population of Britain increased from around 10,000 in 1939 to approximately a million in 1964 (Whitfield, 2004: 22). Hundreds of thousands of immigrants also arrived from India and Pakistan during the same period.

London attracted large numbers of these new arrivals. However, Bristol, the Midlands (Birmingham, Derby, Leicester and Nottingham) and Yorkshire (Leeds) also saw significant immigrant communities spring up. Compared to the African and African-Caribbean immigrants of previous centuries, these new arrivals entered a wider range of occupations. However, most were still concentrated on trades where labour was scarce and, inevitably, this meant doing jobs that British workers were not that keen to fill. In London this meant public transport and general labouring. In the Midlands, this often entailed working in foundries and textile mills, particularly covering the night shifts.

Immigration from the Caribbean slowed somewhat after the passing of the Commonwealth Immigrants Act of 1962, which restricted immigration from former British colonies. Indeed, from this point on, a gradual hardening of social attitudes can be discerned in Britain. In the general election of 1964, a conservative candidate won the seat of Smethwick (West Midlands) with the racist slogan 'if you want a Nigger for a neighbour, vote labour' (Gilroy, 1987: 81). The National Front was formed in 1967 and a year later the conservative M.P. Enoch Powell made his notorious 'Rivers of Blood' speech, in which he predicted the fragmentation of British society and a rise in racial violence unless immigration was sharply curtailed. Against this background, entry controls were progressively strengthened with a new Commonwealth Immigrants Act in 1968 and the passing of the Immigration Act of 1971. While increasing restriction was the trend, it should also be remembered, however, that at the same time there was increasing social concern about racial prejudice and disadvantage in Britain. Significant legislation was passed in this area too, including the Race Relations Acts of 1965 and 1968 which made it illegal to discriminate on the basis of race.

During the latter part of the twentieth century, legal restrictions on immigration continued. In the 40 years following 1962, no less than ten acts relating to asylum and immigration control were passed by both Conservative and Labour governments. However, while immigration from former colonies significantly diminished during this period, the gradual drawing together of the European Union had a significant impact in facilitating the arrival of workers from mainland Europe. The Office of National Statistics (ONS) estimated the net annual inflow (of immigrants vs emigrants) was 47,000 in 1997. By 2004, however, this had increased to around 220,000. These figures have risen yet again following the accession of ten new countries to the EU in May 2004, with many new immigrants from (for example) Poland, again taking jobs that the UK labour market finds hard to fill.

As can be seen from this brief overview, immigration to Britain has always been a very diverse process, with the immigrants themselves also multifarious. However, while some new arrivals have been educated and prosperous, this was not the norm. Over the last two centuries, the majority of immigrants have been concentrated (at least after their arrival) in the lower socio-economic groups. Their social status has very often been inferior to the indigenous population and, even when legally equal (which was not always the case) this equality was often merely a thin veneer. While Britain had negligible controls on immigration for much of the period under discussion, even this brief overview highlights the various ways in which those coming to Britain from overseas have always had a struggle to establish a new life here. However, what were the indigenous perceptions of these successive groups of immigrants? How were they viewed by the public, the media, and officials such as the police and the judiciary? What common discursive tropes can be identified and how did they relate to the criminal justice sphere?

Public opinion and media stereotypes

As might be expected, a very broad range of opinions and stereotypes have been associated with immigrants to Britain during the past 200 years. These perceptions have routinely been extended to subsequent generations of immigrants' families. While usually legally British, they have often still been viewed and treated as ethnically different 'others'. There is not space here to cover the entire range of stereotypes applied to those perceived as different to the majority white population. However, this section will discuss the many associations made between immigrants, ethnic minorities and crime.

At the start of the nineteenth century, as we have seen, the absolute number of black immigrants in Britain was quite low. Many were slaves or former slaves, and as such were perceived very adversely by the indigenous population. Indeed, Norma Myers (1996) argues that they were often viewed as sub-human, a stereotype which served to legitimate their 'chattel' status under the system of slavery. While opinions had changed quite significantly by the start of the nineteenth century, perceptions of inferiority endured. For example, William Wilberforce, one of the driving forces behind the Abolition of the Slave Trade Act of 1807, invited black residents of London to a celebratory dinner following the passing of the act, but still required them to eat in a separate room.

However, Myers contends that public attitudes towards black immigrants at the start of the nineteenth century were best characterized by 'mixed antipathy and sympathy', and prejudice was not the only attitude on view (Myers, 1996: 51). Many new arrivals from the West Indies, Africa and America were poor, being relatively unprotected by the law and finding it hard to secure employment. Poverty and very visible begging among the black community of London generated considerable public sympathy. As early as 1786, for example, a 'Committee for the Relief of the Black Poor' was founded (which disbursed significant funding to black immigrants and 'Lascars' – immigrants from South East Asia).

As regards crime and criminal justice, the available evidence suggests that, while societal attitudes towards black immigrants were by no means wholly warm, there was no particular association made between Africans and African-Caribbean immigrants and criminality. Peter King has made a preliminary study of ethnicity and crime during the period 1780–1830 (as part of a broader work-in-progress), and finds that very little mention is made of specific ethnic groups in contemporary pamphlets and books about crime. Similarly, Myers finds that while black men and women were not handled entirely equally in court (often being treated in the same manner as minors who were too young to understand the nature of the oath) there was certainly no consistently hostile stereotype applied to black immigrants by the courts. Actual involvement in the criminal justice process will be covered in the next section. Suffice it to say here that what little evidence there is indicates that ethnicity was not yet central to discussions of crime, policing and justice. Partly, this may have been a function of the low numbers involved. Partly also it may have been because, as discussed in the previous chapter, there was little or no public discourse in the early nineteenth century concerning crime as a generic 'social problem' requiring state action.

However, by the time Irish immigration was reaching a peak in the mid nineteenth century, this had changed considerably. 'Crime' in the abstract (rather than any particular incident) had become well-established as a problem to be discussed by the media and the public. Irish immigrants attracted a lot of unwelcome and unflattering attention, and the notion that Irish men and women were somehow innately predisposed to crime and disorder was widespread. The historian, critic and writer Thomas Carlyle, for example, noted in 1839 that 'in his squalor and unreason, in his falsity and drunken violence', the Irishman was 'the ready-made nucleus of degradation and disorder' (cited in Swift and Gilley, 1989: 163). A Welsh radical journalist, writing about the social effects of illiteracy in 1846, still felt it acceptable to use the phrase 'thieving like an Irishman' (cited in O'Leary, 2002: 162). Similarly, the journalist and social investigator Henry Mayhew (writing later in the century) believed that, of the habitual criminals of London, 90% were 'Irish Cockneys' – individuals born in London to Irish parents (Mayhew and Binney, 1862: 402).

There was a specific association often made between the Irish, 'drink' and petty criminality. Excessive consumption of alcohol, particularly spirits, was seen to be an intrinsic Irish weakness, and such beliefs were not only confined to the press but also permeated the criminal justice system. The Select Committee on the Police of the Metropolis (1817), for example, was informed that 'the effects of liquor upon the Irish in every scene of depredation and murder, needs only to be adverted to'. Likewise, in 1834, a Manchester magistrate noted:

> If there be a company of English drinking in a beer-shop, they are very good friends if they get drunk together, and they can go home with each other and behave with the utmost kindness; but if it be a party of Irish drinking whiskey or spirits, they will quarrel or fight before they reach home. (Cited in Swift and Gilley, 1989: 167)

The idea that Irish immigrants were prone to violent quarrels (both within their own communities and without) was another prevalent belief. There was also a perception that they were likely to resist arrest, or even that other members of the community would intervene if the police arrived. A Superintendent of the Night Watch in Manchester, giving evidence to the Constabulary Commission of 1839 claimed that:

> It repeatedly happens that, in order to apprehend one Irishman in the Irish parts of town, we are forced to take from ten or twenty, or even more, watchmen. The whole neighbourhood will turn out with weapons, even women, half-naked, carrying brickbats and stones for the men to throw.

Clearly then, adverse perceptions of Irish immigrants were widespread throughout British society during the nineteenth century, with many sharing Friedrich Engels' view that all Ireland had supplied England and America with were 'pimps, thieves, swindlers, beggars and other rabble' (cited in Henderson, 1967: 95). The hostile reception the Irish received in Britain probably owed much to the timing of their arrival. Impoverished immigrants fleeing famine in Ireland in the 1840s came to a country where vagrancy, travelling labourers and poverty were already the focus of much public attention, with the 'Condition of England' question the subject of much media debate. In addition, the period after 1839 saw the reorganization of many provincial police forces in England, with many seeking particularly to crack down on travelling vagrants and 'suspicious characters'. Towards the end of the century, there may have been some amelioration of such prejudicial attitudes. However, anti-Irish sentiment could still flare up with dramatic consequences (such as the large-scale attacks on Irish property in Tredegar, Wales, in 1882). The suspicion that Irish immigrants were involved with the campaign for Irish independence, which was to result in formation of the IRA following the Easter Rising of 1916, also did little to improve the image of the Irish in England during the early part of the twentieth century.

Another group of immigrants often associated with underground political dissidence were those arriving from Eastern Europe in the latter part of the nineteenth century (particularly Jews from Russian Poland). As noted above, the public outcry over this influx was largely responsible for the passing of the Aliens Act of 1905, which restricted peace-time entry into United Kingdom for the first time ever. Between 1880 and 1905 there was a general sense of discontent that England was virtually the only nation to be accepting such refugees without restrictions, while many of the English working class were themselves emigrating. Even the socialist press (in 1894) felt that:

> the Old Word [is] depleting itself of its best and most adventurous blood [...] while we accept with open arms all the broken-spirited physical wrecks which Northern Europe cares to dump down. (Cited in Garrard, 1970: 19)

However, most of the prejudices directed against Eastern European Jews were not really concerned with crime or criminality. There were worries about over-crowding and the unsanitary conditions of many of the areas where these new arrivals lived (such as the East End of London). There were also economic concerns, as Jewish immigrants from Poland were believed to be causing unemployment among British workers. Certainly, the *East London Advertiser* claimed in the late 1880s that:

> Competition is at the bottom of this evil [unemployment]; foreign competition for the most part. The swarms of foreign Jews who have invaded the East End labour market are chiefly responsible. (Cited in Kershen, 2005: 3–4).

However, immigrants from Eastern Europe were *not* a population particularly linked to crime in the way that the Irish had been. The only significant association made between Jews from Eastern Europe and criminality was where **anarchism** and political dissidence were concerned. For a time the largest anarchist publication in the United Kingdom, the *Arbeiter Freind* (Worker's Friend) was published in Yiddish, and the support anarchist groups gave to strikes and other 'revolutionary' activities was of concern to the British government.

This lack of overt linkage between immigrants from Eastern Europe and criminality is interesting. Like the Irish, they were often poor and were usually socially segregated. They were perceived as being culturally and ethnically different from the indigenous 'white' population, and were subject to a high degree of prejudice. As we will see, a very similar pattern of prejudice can be traced in public fears and media stereotypes regarding African-Caribbean immigrants in the period after the Second World War. In this latter case, however, a strong link *was* gradually developed in the media and in the public psyche between these immigrants and various types of criminality and disorder. How can we account for this?

As previously described, the period between the docking of the SS *Empire Windrush* in 1948 and the passing of the Commonwealth Immigrants Act in 1962 saw the arrival of hundreds of thousands of African-Caribbeans (along with many thousands from India, Africa and other former colonial regions). As with all previous large-scale immigrations, these new arrivals were subject to various derogatory prejudices and stereotypes. However, initially at least, these concerns did not focus primarily on criminality per se. Rather, as with the Eastern European immigrants of half a century earlier, the lifestyles and cultures of the African-Caribbean arrivals were the primary focus of attention. As regards housing, there were concerns that immigrants from the Commonwealth were lowering the value of property and crowding white residents out of their homes (a key theme of Enoch Powell's 'rivers of blood' speech). Black culture was stereotyped as involving loud, prolonged parties and the use of drugs such as cannabis. There was also apprehension over the intermarriage of African-Caribbeans and white women, with black sexuality stereotyped as predatory.

Racial prejudices such as these were the trigger for the Notting Hill riots of 1958. Although police initially insisted that the events were not 'racial', the disorder is now known to have been triggered by crowds of youths, 300–400 strong, chanting 'Keep Britain White', and attacking West Indian residences (and indeed residents) in Notting Hill. Violent rioting raged over the bank holiday weekend before order was restored. In the immediate aftermath, an ITN news reporter visited the area to interview residents. He concluded that the majority view of white residents was that most West Indians were 'honest people doing an honest job'. Grievances were aired but, again, these revolved around housing, employment and loud clubs. While there was an association made between West Indians and 'girls on the game' – the assumption being that immigrants were often running brothels – our contemporary concerns such as street crime and theft were not mentioned at all. Thus, although a survey prior to the passing of the Race Relations Act of 1968 showed that racial discrimination in Britain 'ranged from the massive to the substantial' (Smith, 1992: 1050), associations were not routinely made between African-Caribbeans and crime during the 1950s and 1960s.

This changed fairly rapidly, however, during the 1970s. When the House of Commons Home Affairs Committee considered race relations and immigration in 1972, it consulted widely and the majority of witnesses 'tended towards the view that Afro-Caribbeans were less criminal than whites' (Smith, 1992: 1053). However, by the time Lord Scarman's report on the 1981 Brixton Riots was published, this opinion had been largely reversed. While Scarman famously concluded that the Metropolitan Police were not 'institutionally racist', he argued that many young black men felt alienated and excluded from British society, and linked crime, inner-city decay and the breakdown of consent between the police and local communities. Taking up this theme, the Home Secretary William Whitelaw spoke, in the aftermath of the 1981 riots, of the 'need to remove the scourge of criminal violence from our streets' – clearly connecting this with ethnic minority communities (Benyon and Solomos, 1990: 28). Thus, by the early 1980s, 'race' and 'law and order' were now issues to be discussed at the same time. But why was there this sudden change in public perceptions and media stereotyping? There is not space to fully investigate this here, but this shift from generalized prejudice towards a specific focus on the involvement of black youths in certain types of criminality has been much debated by criminologists and historians.

Certain key points should be noted. During the 1970s there were a series of high profile and widely reported confrontations between the police and members of African-Caribbean communities – most notably, perhaps, the Notting

Hill Carnival Riots of 1976, 1977 and 1978. Relations between the police and African-Caribbean communities were strained, to say the least, during this period. Also during the 1970s, the growing media focus on disorderly behaviour on the streets of African-Caribbean areas bled into the assertion that black youths were largely responsible for the newly termed crime of 'mugging'. In 1978, for example, Enoch Powell again made the headlines by highlighting the fact that recently released crime statistics appeared to indicate that mugging was a 'racial' crime, committed largely by black men, and this notion rapidly became a staple media trope.

The significance of these factors is, however, hard to unpick. There is no doubt that there were violent confrontations between the police and African-Caribbeans, and there is no doubt that the statistics released by the Metropolitan Police during the 1970s appear to show a sharp rise in mugging by black men. However, these 'facts' have been interpreted in various ways. Gilroy (1987), for example, has argued that the Metropolitan Police actively presented data on street crime in a manner calculated to show African-Caribbeans as a problem group, and thus enhance their own support base during a difficult period for the police. Similarly, Hall et al. (1978) claimed that the sudden appearance of mugging as a 'crime problem' allowed the police to scapegoat young blacks, and prepare the public for the introduction of more authoritarian policing during a period in which the state was undergoing a 'crisis of legitimacy'.

Others have taken a more moderate line. Waddington (1986) for example, argued that there was evidence to suggest that the official reaction to the 'discovery' of mugging in the 1970s was not disproportionate. Whitfield (2004) notes that policing during this period was characterized by a 'them and us' approach, which may well have contributed to a worsening of ethnic minority/police relations. What is not in doubt, however, is that from the early 1980s onwards, African-Caribbean communities, especially those in large cities, became the object of particular media attention and police scrutiny, and that young black men began entering the criminal justice system in disproportionate numbers.

To conclude, this overview of perceptions of immigration and crime has shown how successive waves of immigrants, usually residing in socially disadvantaged communities, have customarily been perceived as 'different' from the majority white population. This difference has been presented in terms of ethnicity, but also via a focus on the divergent cultures and behaviours attributed to immigrant groups (divergent, that is, from a perceived indigenous norm or ideal). Ethnicity was not really an issue linked to 'crime' in the early part of the nineteenth century. However, the rapid Irish immigration of the mid-nineteenth century, in tandem with the development of the daily press in the same period, meant that it quickly became one.

Interestingly, while all immigrant groups were subject to societal prejudice and stereotyping, not all became associated with criminality to the same extent.

Certainly the Irish were believed by many to be innately criminal. However, Eastern European immigration at the end of the nineteenth century, which was significant enough to generate Britain's first ever peace-time immigration controls, was not particularly associated with criminality. Likewise, the African-Caribbean immigrants of the post-war period were not initially associated with criminality. This perceived link only developed later. Part of the explanation for this may lie in a consideration of the notion of 'disorder'. The Irish quarters of the mid-nineteenth century, and the African-Caribbean communities of the later twentieth century, were widely perceived to be a threat to order on the streets of British cities. The Eastern European communities of early twentieth century, and the influx from the Caribbean in the 1950s, were not so perceived. It might be argued, therefore, that it is only once an ethnic minority population is believed to threaten the stability of the host society that it becomes linked to criminality in the public psyche. This issue will be discussed further in the conclusion. Now, however, it is time to turn from the suppositions of the media, the public and politicians, to investigate what has been written about the actual involvement of immigrants and ethnic minorities in the criminal justice system.

Immigration, ethnicity, crime and criminal justice

As discussed above, immigrants and ethnic minorities were subject to a wide range of prejudices in Britain in the past. As is arguably the case now, different stereotypes were applied to different ethnic/migrant groups. However, many of these groups were perceived to have been disproportionately criminal in comparison with the domestic 'white' population. Certainly, at various times, there were media and public fears about the involvement of Irish, African-Caribbean and Eastern European immigrants in crime, disorder and political activism. However, what does historical research indicate about the actual involvement of immigrants and ethnic minorities in the criminal justice system? To what extent can popular perceptions be said to have been 'justified'? What other factors might account for the over-representation of certain groups in the criminal statistics and the prison population?

It has already been argued that black immigrants were not particularly associated with criminality during the early part of the nineteenth century. The empirical studies available confirm this, and appear to indicate that, at this time, black immigrants were no more likely to be involved in the criminal justice system than white individuals of comparable social status. Of course, it is important to remember that the evidence here is quite scarce. Peter King, as part of a larger work in progress, has noted that the Old Bailey only recorded place of birth systematically for a brief period between 1791 and 1793. Taking this data, however, combined with other trial reports, fragmentary court, reformatory and prison records, he calculates that the black population of London 'may well have been under-represented' in the courts. Much depends on the population figures used. If the minimum figure of 5,000 black inhabitants of London in the 1790s is used, then black people were no more likely to be accused of a crime than whites. However, if the higher estimate of 15,000 is used, then they were very much *less* likely to be in court than whites. In terms of verdict and sentencing, King also finds that the black population was not unduly disadvantaged. His findings back up previous work by Myers (1996) – the only other study of the topic – who found that there was no evidence that the black population of London was particularly criminal. Patterns of black offending, rather, suggested 'poor people's crime, and poor people's punishment' (Myers, 1996: 98).

Quite a different picture emerges, however, when the offending patterns of Irish immigrants is considered later in the century. As argued above, the Irish were clearly linked in both the public and official mind with certain types of criminality. Certainly, most studies concur that they were over-represented for their population size in the criminal statistics. Roger Swift and Sheridan Gilley have noted that 'the Irish-born were almost three times as likely to face prosecution as their English neighbours' (Swift and Gilley, 1989: 165). A number of local studies of York, Bradford and Wolverhampton have demonstrated how the Irish comprised 20–30% of total prosecutions in the early 1860s, an index of over-representation relative to their population size of between 2.5 and 3.3 (Finnegan, 1982; Richardson, 1976; Swift, 1984). In Wales, too, O'Leary (2002: 170) confirms that the proportion of Irish-born criminals in Welsh prisons in the late 1860s meant that they were around three times more likely to face prosecution than their white neighbours.

Within this broad over-representation, moreover, it is possible to associate the Irish with particular types of offences. The authors cited above generally link Irish offenders with petty criminality and disorder. Irish appearances in court typically involved the lower magistrates courts (rather than the **Quarter Sessions**). Characteristic offences for which they were convicted were drunk and disorderly, assault and, to a lesser extent, petty theft, vagrancy and resisting arrest. Moreover, there is evidence to suggest that a lot of Irish appearances in court were for intra-ethnic assaults. Irish migrants were much less likely simply to assault strangers. Sectarianism (strife between Catholic and Protestant factions) was a problem in some areas at certain times. While it might be argued that the offending patterns of the Irish as revealed by criminal statistics do fit the stereotype of 'drunken, fighting Irish', this assertion has to be set in a wider social context. Assaults on the police, street fighting, and excessive drinking were all common white working-class traits during the period (Storch, 1976). It thus becomes hard to disentangle the over-representation of Irish in certain crime returns from their social status and the prejudice directed against them.

One point worth noting briefly is that the Irish were often associated with travelling people and 'gypsy' bands. The 1839 Royal Commission on a Constabulary Force for England and Wales noted that:

> three parts of those who are travelling now throughout the kingdom have Irish blood in them, either from father, mother, or grandmother [...] culti-vated minds are not to be looked for amongst such thieves as we are now describing, who for the most part are of no education, of Irish parents, totally unacquainted with, and therefore unable to perceive, their own degraded state.

Travellers of all kinds were increasingly 'suspect' during the mid-nineteenth century, when the working class was becoming increasingly static. Hence, foreign gypsies and travellers were assumed, almost without question, to be criminal (Lawrence, 2000). This applies equally to the gypsies who arrived from Eastern Europe in 1904–07, who provoked widespread antipathy from the working class and police alike (Holmes, 1988: 64).

The majority of new arrivals from Eastern Europe were not migratory once in Britain, however, and settled in the East End of London and other areas of major cities. As already discussed, the prejudicial stereotypes attached to these (mainly Jewish) immigrants did not initially revolve around crime. Official studies of criminality among this group at the end of the nineteenth century confirmed that they were 'on the whole a peaceful and law-abiding community' (HMSO, 1894: 61). A Board of Trade report from 1894 investigated the numbers of Russian and Polish immigrants in prison in London (for it was here that most of these were concentrated), and plotted this against the population size as a percentage of the London population. It found that in 1893 there were only 21 Russians or Russian Poles in prison, about 1 per 1,081 of the population. The average for the indigenous population was slightly lower – meaning the immigrants from the new group were slightly less likely to be in prison. Obviously, these numbers were so small and the population figures so approximate that they are largely meaningless. However, the figures clearly do not highlight crime as a particular issue affecting Eastern European immigrants.

This picture did change somewhat in the twentieth century. Giving evidence to the 1903 Royal Commission on Alien Immigration, Sir Alfred Newton, ex-Lord Mayor of London and a magistrate at Guildhall Police-Courts, stated that between 15–20% of all cases brought before him were Germans or Eastern Europeans. This would indicate a massive over-representation compared to population size (although it must be remembered that the immigrant population was very dense in some areas). Other legal witnesses, however, felt that there had been no recent increase in crime among immigrants and disputed these figures. What can be said with more certainty is that, despite involvement of Eastern European (Jewish) immigrants in some high-profile criminal cases (such as the

1911 **Siege of Sydney Street**), they were never as disproportionately involved in the criminal justice system as the Irish were before them, or as the African-Caribbean population were to become later in the century.

There is no doubt that the African-Caribbean immigrants who arrived in Britain after 1948 were subjected to widespread public prejudice. In the fields of housing and employment in particular, discrimination was rife, at least until the passing of the Race Relations Act of 1968 which gradually began to iron out the worst biases. During the early period of immigration, however, crime per se, was not an issue particularly associated with black communities. However, from the 1970s onwards, crime statistics began to indicate a link between young black men and particular types of crime – especially street crime. The use of the term 'mugging' dates from this period. Data on ethnicity and nationality in relation to the United Kingdom prison population has only been collected since 1985. From this point, however, there has been a steady rise here too. This is not the place for a lengthy debate on recent trends – this is well covered in criminological literature (see, for example, Phillips and Bowling, 2002; Holdaway, 1996; Mhlanga, 1997). Suffice it to say that African-Caribbeans have been, for some decades, over-represented in both arrest figures and in prison populations. This is particularly striking given that other ethnic minorities (such as South Asians) are likely to be subject to the same levels of societal prejudice (Daniel, 1968) but do not end up in criminal justice system in disproportionate numbers. It is also important to note that all available data shows that ethnic minorities and immigrants are more likely also to be the victims of a crime than white citizens. This is not necessarily due to racism but rather due to their poor life chances and socio-economic circumstances. This was as true in the early nineteenth century as it is now (Clancy et al., 2001).

How then are we to make sense of this rapid trawl through the offending patterns of immigrant communities in the last 200 years? A number of points stand out clearly. Firstly, immigrants have very often been part of the lowest socio-economic categories. This was true of the black population of early nineteenth-century England (Myers, 1996: 56–81) and is equally true of the African-Caribbean population of Britain today (Modood et al., 1997). Other distinctive immigrant groups, such as the nineteenth-century Irish and Eastern European Jews, have also been socially disadvantaged within British society. Given that there has traditionally been a clear association between the lower socio-economic groups and involvement in the criminal justice system among the indigenous population (see Chapter 4), it is perhaps not surprising to find that the same often also applies to immigrants and ethnic minorities.

This is not, however, an infallible rule. The example of the London's East End Jewish community shows that a socially disadvantaged ethnic minority is not inevitably drawn into the criminal justice system in disproportionate numbers. Similarly, current research indicates a striking difference in rates of imprisonment between South Asian and black people, despite the similarities in their socio-economic positions. Low social status can only form part of any analysis of ethnicity and crime. A consideration of the media stereotypes and public prejudices directed at different groups leads us towards a second reason why immigrants and ethnic minority groups were (and are) more likely to feature in criminal statistics: They were (and are) more likely to be watched by the police.

Social groups such as the Irish immigrants of the nineteenth century, and to a lesser extent the African-Caribbean population of the 1970s, lived in socially disadvantaged, geographically concentrated communities. As such, they were very 'visible' within contemporary society. This statement of course applies to most ethnic minority communities. However, as has been argued, the nineteenth century Irish and the African-Caribbean communities of 1970s were also widely believed to be culturally predisposed towards certain types of criminality. Hence, it is likely that these communities were 'over-policed' relative to their numbers. Certainly there is evidence that police officers of all levels during the nineteenth century shared working-class antipathy towards the Irish, and were ready to suspect them of crime. Equally, Whitfield (2004) notes that although the Metropolitan Police began racial-awareness training for recruits in 1964, this was for many years largely 'tokenistic'. There is also much evidence to suggest that, at least until the 1990s, young black men were far more likely to be stopped and searched without good cause than their white counterparts (Phillips and Bowling, 2002: 595–7). Both the issue of the long-term social disadvantage often suffered by immigrant minorities and the increased likelihood of intrusive policing demonstrate how deep the historical roots of the link between crime and ethnicity are.

The perpetuation of adverse ethnic stereotypes

It has been argued above that a major factor in the over-representation of ethnic minorities in the criminal justice system was (and is) their position in British society. Often languishing in the lower socio-economic groups, they are also often concentrated in segregated communities which become highly 'visible' and targeted (in the past at least) by intrusive patterns of policing. A broader variable behind this, it has been further argued, are the adverse associations made by the media and public opinion between ethnic minority communities and crime. By linking crime to 'foreign' elements, British society avoids the need to critically examine itself. Consider the following two extracts relating to ethnicity and crime. Although separated in time by almost 150 years, there are some noteworthy similarities – for example, the way ethnicity is linked to crime. Yet how reliable are these two different types of historical sources? Moreover, what effect might each of these publications have had on the operation of the criminal justice system?

Report of the Royal Commission on a Constabulary Force, 1839
Extract from pages 95–97, evidence for the Manchester region

97. Much of the new population of these districts consists of strangers who have immigrated [*sic*] from other parts of the United Kingdom [...] In Manchester alone there are nearly 30,000 Irish [...]

Mr S. Thomas, deputy constable of the township of Manchester:- 'The principal charge against the Irish is brutal and disorderly conduct, the result of their drunken rows. The beer shops are the source of a great deal of crime, and many of them are kept by the Irish. Illicit spirits are often clandestinely hawked about by the Irish women. We have sometimes fights and serious affrays, in which we are forced to show (though we never use) cutlasses with the Irish [...] It is extremely dangerous to execute a warrant in a **factory** where many Irish are employed; they will throw bricks and stones on the officers' heads as they are coming up stairs, and frequently succeed in driving them off [....]

The following is an extract from the evidence of Mr Aaron Lees, cotton manufacturer of Manchester, to the Factory Commissioners:

'What character do the Irish bear in Manchester?- They are the worst part of the population; usually the first to turn out, the first to commence riots, and, in fact, there is no recklessness of conduct which they do not at times display. I brought a mill a short time ago at Crompsall, and the first thing I did was to get every Irishman out of the cottages, giving them money as an inducement to depart quietly. In twelve of these cottages, built back to back, there were 131 people living in the greatest dirt and destitution. Their manners are so different to those of the English that, though they receive the same wages, they always live in misery and dirt, and addicted to spirituous liquors'.

The Times, 16 April 1981: p. 15, col F
Letters to the Editor – 'Brixton riots: the ethnic factors'

Sir, Some clear conclusions emerge from the recent riot. First [...] given the attitude of many young West Indians to the police, their apparently low threshold before violence, and the high level of crime in some areas of Brixton, the immediate cause is not the important cause. [...]

But it is not good enough to blame unemployment and poor housing. Areas of Glasgow, Liverpool and other big cities have endured such conditions without erupting into riot. Must we not recognize a specifically ethnic factor which predisposes West Indian youth – either through things uniquely done to them or through their own upbringing – to reject police and other authority, to turn more readily to crime, and to look to outside causes for their own misfortunes? [...] While analysis remains at its present superficial level, problems are unlikely to be improved by throwing even more money at them. [...]

Police ability to control riots is clearly inadequate. They suffered heavy casualties, much property was destroyed and crime proceeded without check for several hours. Their equipment and tactics need thorough investigating [...]

On the other hand, rioters themselves receive little deterrent. Their activities are rewarded by painless excitement, large amounts of loot and the prize of 200 injured policemen. Only a small proportion of those involved are arrested, and so far have received derisory sentences. [...]

Rioters will be assured of spiritual comfort from social workers, clerics and politicians who will declare the guilt of society and of the police for what happens. In view of the readiness with which such statements spring to the lips of the rioters themselves, it would be interesting to know what responsibility our social reformers bear for eroding inhibitions against such an outbreak of violence. Yours faithfully.

In considering the historical worth of both of these sources, caution should be exercised. The first extract is from a parliamentary Royal Commission report. As such, it forms part of the printed parliamentary record. One might think that this would guarantee a certain level of objectivity. Far from it, in this case. In 1836 the Home Secretary had agreed to Sir Edwin Chadwick's requests for a Commission to investigate rural policing. Chadwick was keen to extend the influence of central government and set up new police forces, and ran the Commission accordingly. He asked leading questions of witnesses and distorted the evidence presented to the Commission's other members (Storch and Phillips, 1999: 111–35). Hence, while still an interesting and potentially useful document, the 1839 Royal Commission Report should definitely be handled with care. The second extract is from the letters page of *The Times*. Clearly, *The Times* is an extremely prestigious newspaper. It has a small circulation, however, and very much represents the view of an elite 'establishment'. Moreover, the extract is drawn from the letters page. Hence, the value of this evidence is hard to assess. It might be argued that it is just the opinion of one reader. However, while the mechanism for which letters are selected for publication is opaque, the letter presumably expresses sentiments which are not entirely at odds with the paper's editorial line.

Both extracts show a clear focus on the criminality of particular ethnic groups – Irish and West Indians. However, neither displays a simple association between ethnicity and all types of crime. In the case of the evidence presented to the Royal Commission there is a view that drink is a major cause of crime (a perception which was also very common in relation to the English working class at the time). In addition, there is a strong focus on disorderly behaviour, fighting and even rioting. The Irish are perceived to be very resistant to the authority of the police and these issues are seen as part of a distinctive, and repellent, Irish culture. As one witness noted, 'their manners are so different to those of the English'. Very similar themes can be seen in the extract from *The Times*. The author of the letter clearly associates West Indians with crime, but again discounts economic factors (as in the extract on the Irish, where it was noted they 'receive the same wages as the English'). Rather, the author highlights an 'ethnic factor' – something uniquely West Indian – which predisposes this group to criminality. Components of this include a rejection of police and other authority, a low threshold before violence, and a love of 'painless excitement'. It might therefore be argued that there are a lot of similarities in the attitudes these two extracts reveal.

However, as regards the impact that perceptions such as these might have had on the operation of the criminal justice system, this is a much harder question to answer. Obviously, single pieces of evidence such as these would have had no individual impact at all. What is important is to assess how common such stereotypes were. If they were extremely common, then it is likely that the pressure of public opinion they represent would have had an impact on the actions of the police and central government. Here, perhaps, we may perceive a difference between the extracts. It is probably fair to say that the prejudices evident in the 1839 extract were shared by a significant section (if not a majority) of the English population. In 1981, the views expressed were probably rather less mainstream. In both cases, however, what we can say is that the background prejudices of the public in relation to crime and ethnicity were significant in informing the priorities of the police and of central government in relation to minority communities.

Summary

Immigration has a long history in Great Britain, and prejudice against racial and ethnic minorities is equally longstanding. What, however, can we pick out from this overview of the last two centuries which can help to interpret current debates on race and crime?

Firstly, it is noteworthy that during the early nineteenth century, there was no 'race and crime' issue. This was not due to a lack of minority groups, a lack of prejudice or indeed a lack of crime. Rather, it was because a) there were relatively few immigrants living in Britain; b) the daily press had yet to assume its current form (Hampton, 2004); and c) there was little discussion of crime as a generic, abstract social problem. All of these factors underwent rapid change by the mid-nineteenth century and from that point on ethnic minorities have usually been associated with criminality of one kind or another.

Secondly, large ethnic minorities have always attracted opprobrium of various kinds in Britain (although antipathy has never been the sole attitude on display). However, a study of the Irish of the mid-nineteenth century, and the African-Caribbean population of the 1970s and 1980s, reveals many similarities in perceptions and treatment. Both populations were seen as potentially criminal and both were the target of invasive patterns of policing. One other point of comparison stands out. Both were associated with disorderly behaviour, a trait which has traditionally drawn more swift official response than many other sorts of criminality.

This link provides one possible key as to why immigrants and ethnic minorities (and, in particular, *these* immigrants and ethnic minorities) have so often been linked to criminality. Orderliness is often considered as a quintessentially English virtue (primarily by the English, it has to be said). As Conley has argued, it was believed during the nineteenth century that 'civilized behaviour was what distinguished Englishmen from others' (Conley, 2005: 777). Certainly, a common discursive trope in discussions of criminality during the period was to view criminality as somehow 'foreign', in contrast to 'British' values of order, stability, politeness. For example, in 1872, a report in *The Times* of an Assize Court in the North of England described 'a succession of murder and minor outrages' as presenting 'a picture of drunken brutality such as might be more fitly expected in some savage island in the far Pacifics' (Conley, 2005: 777). Given this habit of describing crime, particularly violent, disorderly crime, as something essentially foreign to the British way of life, it is a relatively short step from this to actually associating criminality with immigrants and ethnic minorities within Great Britain. By defining criminality as something intrinsically alien to the British national character, it becomes thus something external to 'British society'. This enables internal social problems with violence, poverty and alienation to be externalized and effectively ignored.

Looking back, it becomes apparent that many of the issues discussed in contemporary criminological literature on race, ethnicity and crime have a long history. This deep past needs to be unearthed if contemporary patterns of offending and prejudice are to be combated. As Gilroy has argued, 'racism is not akin to a coat of paint on the external structures of social relations which can be scraped off if the right ideological tools and political elbow grease are conscientiously applied to the task' (Gilroy, 1987: 11). Racial prejudice, the linking of ethnicity and crime in the media and public opinion, and the patterns of policing and justice this has engendered, are intrinsic to social relations in Great Britain today. It is only via an appropriate awareness of the way in which these social relations have built up over successive decades that change in the future will be possible.

STUDY QUESTIONS

1   Over the last two centuries, what part has the media played in linking together immigration and crime?

2   What are the similarities and differences between the treatment of Irish immigrants in the nineteenth century, and West Indian settlers to the UK in the twentieth century?

3   How important have notions of British identity been to the construction of 'foreign' traits of criminality? And why does popular and press opinion tend to ignore structural factors such as poverty of recent immigrants?

4   Has racism shown itself to be endemic to the criminal justice system since the eighteenth century, or is it a more recent phenomenon?

FURTHER READING

Gilroy, P. (1987) *There Ain't no Black in the Union Jack*, Routledge: London.

Holmes, C. (1988) *John Bull's Island. Immigration and British Society, 1871-1971*, Macmillan: London.

Myers, N. (1996) *Reconstructing the Black Past. Blacks in Britain, c.1780-1830*, Frank Cass: London.

Swift, R. and Gilley, S. (eds) (1989) *The Irish in Britain 1815-1931*, Barnes and Noble: London.

7

Surveillance: From the Workplace to the Streets?

Chapter Contents

OVERVIEW

Chapter 7:

- Provides an overview of the current state of surveillance in the UK today. Over 4 million cameras watch over the citizens of the UK. To what end? How did surveillance over daily life grow to these proportions, and has increased surveillance delivered the benefits it promised?
- Follows the history of surveillance from the private to the public arena. The factory has provided a strong model for surveillance since the mid-nineteenth century, but how did the principles and practices of factory surveillance transfer to the streets?
- Explores the possibilities and achievements of surveillance from the growth of a national police system from 1829 to the introduction of CCTV cameras. Have surveillance techniques controlled crime and violence – or prevented terrorism?
- Concludes with Bentham's prison ideas and asks whether, in the twenty-first century, the UK has become 'the Panopticon society'.

KEY TERMS

| Surveillance | Big Brother | CCTV | Panopticon |

At the apex of the pyramid comes Big Brother. Big Brother is infallible and all-powerful... Nobody has ever seen Big Brother. He is a face on the hoardings, a voice on the telescreen. We may be reasonably sure that he will never die, and there is already considerable uncertainty as to when he was born... in the past no government had the power to keep its citizens under constant surveillance. [Now] every citizen, or at least every citizen important enough to be worth watching, could be kept for twenty-four hours a day under the eyes of the police and in the sound of official propaganda, with all other channels of communication closed. The possibility of enforcing not only complete obedience to the will of the State, but complete uniformity of opinion on all subjects, now existed for the first time. (Orwell, 1948).

Of course, we do not have TV screens in our houses reporting back every movement to a shadowy authority, but nevertheless, some allege that the routine recording of normal activities such as taking cash from an ATM, filling in forms that require a huge amount of biographical detail, using biometric passports, and the prospect of compulsory identity cards, all point to a growing control by the

State over the lives of ordinary people. Most notably there are the seemingly omnipresent CCTV cameras that watch over us and scrutinize our actions. In the past decade, the use of CCTV has grown to unprecedented levels. In Britain over £250 million per year is now spent on a surveillance industry resulting in an estimated 4.2 million cameras surveying public areas – far more cameras than there are in the whole of the United States. In fact, the UK has one camera for every 14 people. Even quiet backwaters and country villages with low crime rates are installing CCTV surveillance of public areas, housing estates, car parks and public facilities, and every year this market grows by 15–20% (Davies, 1996: 183).

It is not surprising that the growth of surveillance has been noticed by sociologists and criminologists, who have used Foucault's (1977) work on Bentham's ideal prison design of the 1780s to inform their own studies. As Rock (2003) noted: 'Michel Foucault's dramatic simile of Jeremy Bentham's model prison, the **Panopticon**, was put to massive use in criminology... Foucault and those who followed him wished to argue, modern society is coming to exemplify the perfection of the automatic exercise of power through generalized surveillance' (Rock, 2003: 64). Are we, as seems to be an accepted view, living in a Big Brother society, and if we are, how did we get to this position?

The eyes of God, or at least His earthly agents, had watched over medieval and early modern society, acting as a strong agent of social control bolstered by the military power of rulers. When embryonic nation states evolved throughout the globe in the modern period, and scientific rationalism started to make inroads against the dominance of religious conformity, armies of the State faced external enemies, and a host of agencies enforced laws at home against those who disturbed the peace or the prosperity of the powerful. After the introduction of the New Police in 1829 and the creation of County forces in 1856, there was not an un-policed space in the land, at least not in theory. This extension in surveillance over those considered to be problematic to good public order, and the extension in centralized governmental control that it seemed to facilitate, have been considered in Chapters 4 and 5 (along with the other implications of the introduction of formal uniformed policing). This chapter explores the history of policing (in its broadest terms) and surveillance as capitalistic society developed, and begins with an examination of the origins of surveillance in the workplace.

The factory ranks alongside the prison and the barracks as a totemic symbol of panopticism for social theorists. For Foucault (1977), Melossi and Pavarini (1981), and others, the differences between working conditions and prison conditions were minimal:

> 'For the worker the factory is like a prison' (loss of liberty and subordination); 'for the inmate the prison is like a factory' (work and discipline)... The ideological meaning of this complex reality can be summarised by the

attempt to rationalise and conceptualise a duel analogy: *prisoners must be workers, workers must be prisoners.* (Melossi and Pavarini, 1981: 188, emphasis added)

They believe that the factory did not consciously imitate the prison, nor the prison the factory, but both evolved from ideas concerning the control of time and space. Giddens (1995) stated that: 'The commodification of time, and its differentiation from further processes of the commodification of space, hold the key to the deepest transformations of day-to-day social life that are brought about by the emergence of capitalism'. Clearly, the factory environment with its overbearing surveillance was thought by some to benefit capitalistic society by encouraging workers to be disciplined, compliant and 'civilized' to middle-class standards of morality. However, the following section argues that social theorists have overstated their case somewhat, and that a review of empirical evidence may help to re-balance the theoretical position.

Workplace crime and workplace surveillance, 1750–2005[1]

In the industries of eighteenth-century England, many workers labouring as family units considered it a customary right to keep for themselves some part of the materials used in their stage of production (which was routinely carried out in their own cottages).[2] The taking of waste materials was rife, particularly in the textile industry of south west and northern England where it involved taking pieces of workplace material or some of the waste goods produced in manufacturing, i.e. the thrums (cloth or woollen waste). Indeed, most industries saw some form of appropriation of finished goods or raw materials. Perhaps the most discussed example of eighteenth-century **workplace appropriation** is the taking of 'chips' (pieces of wood) from the Royal Dockyards. However, Emsley (2004: 143–73), Styles (1983) and Rule (1981, 1986) have catalogued a series of out-worker appropriations – including 'bugging' by hatters and shoemakers (whereby cheap material was substituted for the more valuable material they were supposed to use). These practices were viewed as a kind of traditional entitlement or perquisite (perk) which had been passed down through the ages and, as such, they became part of the customary world that granted rights that were deeply entrenched in (particularly rural) communities.

However, in the late eighteenth and early nineteenth century, many of the traditional rights of countryside dwellers were gradually criminalized. These included gleaning (collecting corn left after harvesting), firebote (gathering small amounts of wood from forests for the fireplace), the rights of grazing (on common land), and the poaching of small game, which all became subject to the criminal code in the late eighteenth century.

Like the countryside, the workplace became a conceptual battleground between the rights of custom and tradition, and the rights of property (Godfrey, 1997). The 'rights' of workers to work at their own pace, take home waste material, and have some autonomy over the conditions of their employment, had been gradually eroded from the eighteenth century onwards. Linebaugh (1991) and Hobsbawm (1968) have asserted that both the eighteenth and nineteenth centuries saw the employers attempt to criminalize customary rights within the workplace (see also Davis, 1987 and 1989), just as other historians have argued that a parallel process was occurring in the countryside. Indeed, historians such as Linebaugh place the large body of eighteenth-century legislation against workplace frauds within the context of what they believe was a defining character of eighteenth-century criminal law – the transformation of a large number of infractions that had previously been violations of trust or corporate obligation into criminal offences against property. This view is typified in the work of Hay (1983: 27) who said:

> the custom of... payment in perquisites, either part of the product or raw materials, became the subject of extensive penal legislation. Employers did not always want to eliminate perks: allowing such appropriation by employees could be a way of escaping employers' wage-fixing agreements in times of labour shortage, and also a way of avoiding monetary wage payment during downturns in the trade cycle. At such times both capital and labour tacitly agreed on the custom, within limits, of taking perks. But those limits were always contested, and in the long term, with expanding inventories, larger workforces, and a sharpening interest in accurate book-keeping, employers requested, and received, criminal legislation that designated such appropriation as theft.

In 1777 the textile manufacturers of Yorkshire persuaded Parliament to enact legislation which outlawed customary perquisites, and established the Worsted Inspectorate to patrol the region, search suspects' houses, and apprehend those suspected of theft from work. Between 1840 and 1880 this agency (which was controlled by the Worsted Committee made up of leading manufacturers) prosecuted approximately 3,000 workers.[3]

However, the introduction of the factory system has been seen as the *key* weapon in the employers' fight to control the employee in the workplace. When workers were collected together in the centralized production areas of the factory it offered the employers the possibility of far greater control over their workers' time and behaviour. The factory facilitated higher levels of surveillance over employees, and allowed employers to use *both* informal punishments and the law to 'police' the behaviour of their workers. It established a complex and hierarchical system of managers, supervisors, foremen and overseers who could watch over the behaviour of the workers. The factory also had physical boundaries (gatehouses and walls) which helped to prevent theft. Later, mechanization governed the pace of production, and also the start and finish times of shifts, which required a strict control over workers' time, and punishments were imposed on those who 'wasted' their employer's time by talking to neighbours, and so on (see Ashton, 1955; Thompson, 1967). Some employers also attempted to control their workers' time outside of work by establishing factory sports teams or providing workers' outings in order to foster community spirit, but also to emphasize morality, punctuality and sobriety.

The factory established rigidly organized hierarchies of surveillance, and numerous sets of rules for workers to abide by, together with a list of punishments for those that ignored the rules (see the rules of Calderdale Mill and Stansfield Mill in Godfrey and Lawrence, 2005). Factory rules governing the use of time and space within the factory were comprehensive, but they would be little more than rhetorical if there was no-one to enforce them. The overlookers, overseers and foremen who policed the factory were organized within a system of delegated authority, and had the ability to mete out informal and formal punishment, thereby taking up a crucial role in the disciplining of labour.

For those that were caught by the foreman breaking the factory rules, there were three informal punishments: a fine (some mills were imposing fines on up to 600 workers a week); physical punishments; or dismissal from employment. Alternatively he could take the offender to the Worsted Inspector for prosecution either in the civil court (where financial damages could be claimed by the employer), or the criminal courts where the offender could receive a month in prison under the Worsted Acts, or even a capital sentence under the larceny acts (Godfrey, 1997; Locker and Godfrey, 2006).

The criminal law was clearly an important weapon in the employers' armoury, but some believe that it was changes in the organization of the workplace which had the greatest impact on levels of workplace appropriation. Indeed some have suggested that the factory can be ranked alongside the prison, the asylum, and the barracks, as a 'total institution' (see Foucault, 1977; Ignatieff, 1983). A number of commentators have debated the existence of 'total institutions' (which controlled most aspects of their inhabitants' lives) in the eighteenth and nineteenth century, and have drawn out the similarities between the factory and the prison (Melossi and Pavarini, 1981). Marxist historians of management and workplace organization have agreed with this position. For example, the development of the factory accomplished four aims in Dickson's (1989) opinion: first, the suppression of 'embezzlement'; second, control over the pace of production; third, the centralization of labour which both facilitated machine technology, and allowed the control of the worker's adverse reaction to new machinery; and lastly, it made capitalists indispensable to production because the factories needed large and frequent capital investments. Although the first two aims were explicitly concerned with labour control, Dickson, rightly, saw the other aims as also being primarily work discipline measures. The origins of the factory were therefore embedded in the desire to control labour, and this desire inevitably spawned supervisors and surveillance techniques in the workplace. Marglin (1976 and 1984) asserts that this explains why factories were established with the kind of technology already in place in much of the cottage textile industry, and also why many factories did not mechanize until years after their establishment. After all, Gott's mill in Leeds, a huge and highly developed complex, was managed for 25 years without mechanization taking place in any key area of production.

The assumption that centralization, and the concomitant surveillance systems, were successful in controlling the workers and eradicating workplace theft must be questioned, firstly, since the criminal law continued to be used until the mid-twentieth century, well beyond the point when the factory was supposed to have made the law redundant and informal internal disciplines the norm. Secondly, we have evidence that workplace theft, although no longer considered a customary right, was still practised well into the twentieth century. For example, a publicity leaflet for the Worsted Inspectorate issued in 1934 gave details of nine girls employed in Wakefield who were imprisoned for a month for taking home waste; a rag and waste dealer was fined £50 for receiving waste from an employee; three women employed in a mill at Bradford were imprisoned for 21 days for stealing yarn; and lastly a weaver was convicted of purloining botany weft piece ends and spools and was fined £5 or 21 days' imprisonment in default.

These cases may be singular or extraordinary, or possibly the most serious cases and thought to deserve prosecution where other minor cases may not. Whatever the case, they do illustrate that the law was still being used to discipline offending workers (and that workers were still illegally removing goods from work) well into the 1950s as Godfrey and Lawrence (2005) demonstrated.

Traditional ideologies about crime focused predominantly upon the lower-class offender as the chief social problem, and although there was no great public debate about workplace theft, the poor weavers and factory labourers would also have been classed as common or garden criminals. However, by the mid-nineteenth century the Victorian public was becoming increasingly aware of breaches of financial trust associated with higher status employees, such as clerks and departmental supervisors. As Locker (2005) noted: 'Cases of fraudulence and dishonesty were seen with growing frequency both within the public and private arenas of Victorian England, bringing not only media attention but also higher levels of scrutiny and supervision in the business environment (see Emsley, 2006: 298; Wiener, 1990: 244–56).

Traditional family businesses controlled their small number of employees who had financial duties simply by working in the same physical space as them and developing personal ties (Anderson, 1976: 30; Hall, 1952; Robb, 1992; Fukuyama, 1996: 63–4). Where these social bonds between employers and employees were strong, opportunities and temptations to commit acts of fraud were reduced. But these subtle controls were removed in the large joint-stock companies that grew in the Victorian period (Cressey, 1971). Joint-stock companies were financed through shareholders, tended to be large and complex organizations employing large numbers of staff, and generated large amounts of revenue (Perkin, 1971: 179). The opportunities for fraud and embezzlement amongst the growing class of clerks and accountants grew alongside the joint stock companies. Charles Dickens, the author and social commentator, noted in 1860 that 'The leading delinquency of the present day, is the robbery of joint-stock companies by confidential servants' (Dickens, 1860a: 202). The employers responded by sacking or prosecuting offenders, making 'trusted' employees provide sureties to indemnify their employers against fraudulent losses, and increased levels of surveillance. By the end of the nineteenth century, Van Oss (1898: 734, quoted in Locker and Godfrey, 2006) commented:

> For better or for worse, the shareholder has for good supplanted the old private proprietor, and a permanent change has come over British business. It can scarcely be doubted that this change has, to put it mildly, been a change for the worse... Personal ownership has ceased to be the controlling power in trade; and when it left it took along with it that personal care, personal supervision, and personal responsibility which made our business great, and which so long kept it great... Instead of men who depend for their very living upon their zeal, their energy, and their judgment we have... men who depend for their living upon the salaries paid to them by companies. Instead of people who work for their business day and night we have people who as it were stand outside the business they govern, who take things easy, meet once a week or once a fortnight, and leave the rest to hirelings who, though they may do their best, must in the nature of things be less efficient than direct owners, and who must become commercially demoralised by the knowledge that they serve a concern which virtually has no supervising head, and which neither restrains by rigid discipline nor encourages with the prospect of gratitude... if [British business is] really deteriorating it deteriorates chiefly because the system of personal responsibility which made it, and which so long kept it great, is gone... A board of directors or a general manager cannot be in touch with employees in the same way as a master is with his men, and certainly cannot have the same influence.

Surveillance was therefore expanding to cover all areas of the business enterprise and all types of workers by the start of the twentieth century. If anything, however, it was even harder to watch over the activities of higher-grade staff than it was over the shop floor. The appointment of investigating accountants, internal auditors, and the regular checking of the books did not eradicate fraud, as Locker and Godfrey (2006: 985) demonstrated: 'As a continual stream of cases attested, throughout the nineteenth century inadequacies in the internal supervisory mechanisms of many companies enabled white-collar employees, with the opportunity and knowledge, to manipulate paper documents and appropriate company money, often remaining undetected over considerable periods of time'.[4]

Whilst some have interpreted the use of the criminal law against the higher staff echelons as evidence that the State did not bear down solely on the labouring classes, Lea has been quick to remind us that embezzling clerks can not be considered to be members of a managerial class (Lea, 2002: 58). In fact, one could even argue that surveillance helped to lower the status of clerks in a sense, reducing them to the same level as shop-floor workers. However, we should not be too quick to see the State's hand here *at all*. The victim-led prosecution system had been declining in importance throughout the late nineteenth-century (see Kearon and Godfrey, 2007), but the State had never been enthusiastic about governing private workspaces, with the prosecution of both higher- and lower-grade workers being left with the victimized business owners. For example, between 1777 and 1880, the police routinely left cases of workplace appropriation to private security agencies (mainly the Worsted Inspectorate). In the mid-twentieth century, the Crime Prevention Department of the city of London Police Force issued a booklet also emphasizing that the security of the office workspace was not primarily a police responsibility. The message was reinforced by the booklet featuring advertisements for Chubb safes and locks, the Burgot Burglar Alarm, the British Insurance offices and Securicor.

The organization of discipline and surveillance in the factory clearly had great symbolic importance (to contemporaries and to modern theorists), and was arguably effective in combating time-wasting and helping to shape a factory culture in which work indiscipline was increasingly disapproved of by workers and employers alike. Nevertheless, workplace appropriation remained, and ebbed and flowed with economic conditions. It seems clear that the factory system is not, and has never been, sufficient by itself to eradicate workplace 'theft'. It is a similar story with higher-grade workers and fraudulent accounting practices. The new controls and more rigorous checks on clerks and foremen, and the investigating accounting departments, did not eradicate embezzlement and financial fraud. Until at least the 1950s, employers still used the criminal law to punish workplace offenders. By that date, the factory environment, particularly in the USA, had been altered in accordance with Fordist styles of labour organization which appeared to offer new and even more dominant techniques of surveillance. However, even production line work organization, with dedicated workers forming a continual process of production from raw material to finished product, was rife with 'fiddling'. Moreover, Henry (1978), Mars (1982), and

Ditton (1995) all found that underlying notions of customary entitlement persisted well into the twentieth century. Whether inside the factory system, or in less-supervised areas of work, some – maybe many – employees continued to cheerfully appropriate their employer's property.

In the twenty-first century, a reformation of work organization has again brought new disciplines and new techniques of surveillance over employees – for example, call centre workers have their interactions with customers recorded, timed and examined (Hamerlink, 2000; Jewkes, 2003), and Jewkes (2003: 196) states that, the 'information-gathering net' is constantly expanding to encompass aspects of workers' private lives, personal characteristics, appearance, and so on. Genetic testing and screening are being introduced into the workplace to allow employers to assess the behavioural dispositions of potential employees and their propensities to certain illnesses'. It is possible that workplace supervision could be refined, by innovations such as these amongst others, to a point where it completely eradicates workplace 'theft', but it does appear that all attempts at this have hitherto been incomplete, inadequate and ill-founded.

The history of surveillance of the workplace, especially for the late twentieth century, is beginning to be well-documented in criminological texts. In general, however, it was not the surveillance of workplaces that attracted media attention. The growing surveillance over public areas has prompted more comment, and latterly, anxiety. The following section asks how surveillance of the streets came to be so embedded in daily life – and to what extent the workplace was the model for that extension of surveillance into the public sphere.

The growth of a Big Brother state, 1829–2005?

Whilst historians have debated the efficiency of Parish Watches and private forces, generally the introduction of the New Police in 1829 has been seen as the moment when the State achieved the possibility of maintaining public order (see Godfrey and Lawrence 2005, and Chapter 4). Indeed, for Williams, 'the beat policeman was designed as, amongst other things, a machine for surveillance. He was to monitor a defined area, bringing it under his view, and reporting what went on to his superior officers' (Williams 2003: 9), but his attention was not solely on criminal acts. Robert Storch (1976: 481) argued that policemen did far more than prevent and fight crime. He argued that the wider mission was 'to act as an all-purpose lever of urban discipline... to mould a labouring class amenable to new disciplines of both work and leisure'. The uniformed 'domestic missionary' would thereby reform behaviour and instill middle-class moral codes into the working classes. If that was the intention, then surveillance

forms and technologies of surveillance. CCTV merely refines policing practices albeit in indirect ways and without using police personnel, whilst Marx focuses on more subtle forms of information-gathering which is designed for other purposes. Others have alleged that the passive-intrusive gaze of CCTV has allowed police to be successively removed from the community they are protecting, and reduced the relationship between the police and ordinary people (Crawford, 1998).[5]

Nevertheless, increasingly, police forces, local authorities and residents' associations are placing camera systems into housing estates and areas where prostitution or 'street violence' is concentrated. Tens of thousands of cameras operate in public places, in phone booths, vending machines, buses, trains, taxis, alongside roads and particularly motorways, inside Cashpoints (Automatic Teller Machines) and in a host of public areas.[6] Many town and city centres in Britain are now covered by remote surveillance camera systems involving a linked system of cameras with full pan, tilt, zoom and infrared capacity. Their use on private property is also becoming popular. CCTV surveillance has the potential to creep inside the home, with many products offering to survey and protect the area around the house from troublesome teenagers and cold callers. Andrew May, Assistant Chief Constable of South Wales, has urged victims of domestic violence to conceal video cameras in their homes to collect evidence, and technology is already being used in hospitals in Staffordshire to support covert surveillance of parents suspected of abusing their children. According to the Home Office booklet, 'CCTV: Looking out for you' (1994), the technology can be a solution for problems such as vandalism, drug use, drunkenness, racial harassment, sexual harassment, loitering and disorderly behaviour (see Garland, 2002; Lea, 2002; Honess and Charman, 1992). Advocates of CCTV now champion it as a weapon in the fight against terrorism. The Terrorism Act (2006) contains a comprehensive package of measures designed to ensure that the police, intelligence agencies and courts have all the tools they require to tackle terrorism and bring perpetrators to justice.[7] As Jewkes (2005: 185) stated 'As communications intelligence has moved its operations from narcotics trafficking, money laundering and terrorism to intercept "ordinary" citizens' personal and commercial telex messages, mobile phone communications, e-mails and Internet traffic, notions of what is "acceptable" in the interests of security are once again coming under scrutiny.' As in the nineteenth-century context, surveillance is not neutral, but falls disproportionately on Muslim, Asian or even just 'foreign looking' suspects (See Lyon, 2001; and essays in Zureik and Salter, 2005).

Despite the claims made for CCTV in the realm of crime and terrorism control, however, its successes have been limited. It may have had some success in reducing fear of crime (although not even this is certain, since the presence of CCTV cameras often provoked unease that one is entering an area 'where crime happens'); and it may have reduced or at least displaced car crime and prostitution.

It has helped to convict defendants who were caught on camera. But these successes were not on the scale envisaged by champions of CCTV. The introduction of CCTV has not reduced crime or deterred criminal behaviour on a large scale; they have displaced rather than reduced crime; they have been expensive; and they have not engendered a *general increase in surveillance* but an *increase in general surveillance*. The CCTV camera has become a totemic symbol of surveillance, but is one of the least subtle and least effective methods of surveillance. Moreover, as Norris and Armstrong (1999) have also pointed out, CCTV cameras have an inability to provide 'coverage' and terrorists have planted explosives out of camera-shot with relative ease. Not surprisingly, many commentators (from both sides of the political spectrum) have questioned the nature and efficiency of surveillance in the UK and the direction it is taking.

Dystopian futures?

For Lyon (1994) and Dandaker (1990), there has been a growing sophistication of surveillance techniques since the crude attempts to oversee **factory** labour. Indeed these authors chart a long history of surveillance. In the modern period, patronage and personal favour as a form of control was largely replaced with impersonal bureaucratic power; the nation states formed not only armies to guard their borders, but also domestic forces of control to watch over their subjects; the processes of manufacture required the collecting together of thousands of workers, controlled with a hierarchy of supervisors; the protection of citizens from harm required the new sciences of psychology and criminology to categorize and identify the potentially dangerous; electronic technology enabled massive amounts of information not only to be stored, but also quickly processed and shared between the powerful bureaucracies; and the information age which defines modernity is born, or as Lyon said:

> organizations of many kinds know us only as coded sequences of numbers and letters. This was once worked out on pieces of paper collated in folders and kept in filing cabinets, but now the same tasks – and many others, unimaginable to a Victorian clerk – are performed by computer. Precise details of our personal lives are collected, stored, retrieved and processed every day within huge computer databases belonging to big corporations and government departments. This is 'surveillance society'. (Lyon, 1994: 3)

Few would doubt that the capacity of the government and private enterprise to know more about 'us' has increased, and that those agencies do regularly take advantage of this capacity. But perhaps the routine transfer of information from the citizen to the state is part of participatory democracy. For example, many agree that a certain level of personal freedom must be sacrificed in dangerous times, and with the justification of avoiding terrorist outrages, governments across the Western world now feel able to claim more and more information about the daily activities of ordinary people. Moreover, the ease with which people give over personal information could be taken as a demonstration of increased trust in society, not fear (though many would dispute this).

But Lianos asks how it is possible to have total surveillance in a society with pluralistic sources of power and authority – where are the Big Brothers in our society who could combine to produce a totalitarian surveillance? 'The organization and the nature of power cannot remain immutable and subject to atemporal criteria whilst sociality transforms itself in a radical way. Once the dynamics of the social universe are disregarded, it is easy to produce dark visions by simply focusing on the likely operation of future technological systems, which will presumably become more complex and accurate in their interaction with human behaviour, social, private or intimate' (Lianos, 2003: 418). This was a line that can be traced back to a seminal article by Philp Stenning and Clifford Shearing: 'Surveillance is pervasive but it is the antithesis of the blatant control of the Orwellian state: its source is not government and its vehicle is not Big Bother. The order of instrumental discipline is not the unitary order of a central state but diffuse and separate orders defined by private authorities responsible for the feudal-like domains of Disney World, condominium estates, commercial complexes and the like' (Shearing and Stenning, 1996:). However, whether the central control of the surveillance enterprise is one embedded in State control or a pluralistic and diffuse network of interlinked private and commercial agendas, this chapter has demonstrated that the demand for information on the powerless by the powerful is not new. The historical road from the factory foreman in private businesses to the anonymous controller of CCTV cameras on public streets has been a long and uncomfortable one. Moreover the progress of surveillance recalls historical concerns, theories and practices which have hitherto been thought dormant. For example, John Lea recently commented that the 'reliance by police agencies on technological surveillance rather than public communication' and the proclivity and ability of private persons (the propertied) to install private surveillance around their homes and businesses suggests that society is returned to earlier forms of privatized public protection – to a time before the New Police were formed (Lea, 2002: 184). The categorization of personal – bodily – information, i.e. retinal scans, fingerprints, facial video recognition, and so on, in modern times also restates the anthropomorphic-centred criminology of the nineteenth-century Lombrosian School, again placing the body at the centre of police attention. Modern surveillance therefore recalls nineteenth-century theorists, equals their ambition, but fails to complete their project. Is it time to also revisit the Panopticon as a model for the surveillance society?

The Panopticon revisited

> The panopticon is now considerably more than a brick and mortar edifice, but is also easily the leading scholarly model or metaphor for analyzing surveillance. In this latter role the panopticon has also become oppressive. The sheer number of works that invoke the panopticon is overwhelming...
> (Haggerty, 2006)

Yar (2003: 254–5) has usefully categorized some of the studies that Haggerty may have been thinking of. He sketches out the ideas of those who broadly support the extension of panopticism into society (Norris and Armstrong, 1998, 1999; McCahill, 2002); those that believe it was a historically located moment which has given way to more sophisticated logics of control (Deleuze, 1995; Rose, 1999, 2000). Lastly, there are those who have posited super-panopticism (Poster, 1990). These theorists are only some of the large number of researchers revisiting Fouaultian theories, and by extension therefore revisiting Bentham's original views of a Panoptic prison. Why has Bentham's Panopticon been so useful and malleable to criminological theory, how did the Panopticon develop outside of theoretical constructs (in bricks and mortar), and is the concept still useful to describe the Surveillance State?

Jeremy Bentham (1748–1832), was an English philosopher, non-practising lawyer, jurist, and political theorist. His major work, an *Introduction to the Principles of Morals and Legislation* published in 1789, applied utilitarian theory to morality and the pursuit of the greatest level of happiness for the greatest number of people. He devised a kind of moral arithmetic for judging the value of a pleasure or a pain. He argued that self-interests, properly understood, are harmonious and that the general welfare is bound up with personal happiness. He also wrote tracts on prison reform, the codification of the laws, and extension of political franchise, but it was his proposal for a new model prison published in 1787 that has been the subject of most attention, especially for social policy theorists:

> **Panopticon**: or the inspection-house: containing the idea of a new principle of construction applicable to any sort of establishment, in which persons of any description are to be kept under inspection; and in particular to penitentiary-houses, prisons, houses of industry, work-houses, poor-houses, lazarettos, manufactures, hospitals, mad-houses, and schools: with **a plan of management** adapted to the principle: in a series of letters, written in the year 1787, from crecheff in white russia. to a friend in england by jeremy bentham, of lincoln's inn, esquire.

> The building is circular. The apartments of the prisoners occupy the circumference. You may call them, if you please, the cells. These cells are divided

from one another, and the prisoners by that means secluded from all communication with each other, by partitions in the form of radii issuing from the circumference towards the centre, and extending as many feet as shall be thought necessary to form the largest dimension of the cell. The apartment of the inspector occupies the centre; you may call it if you please the inspector's lodge... Each cell has in the outward circumference, a window, large enough, not only to light the cell, but, through the cell, to afford light enough to the correspondent part of the lodge. The inner circumference of the cell is formed by an iron grating, so light as not to screen any part of the cell from the inspector's view. Of this grating, a part sufficiently large opens, in form of a door, to admit the prisoner at his first entrance; and to give admission at any time to the inspector or any of his attendants. To cut off from each prisoner the view of every other, the partitions are carried on a few feet beyond the grating into the intermediate area: such projecting parts I call the protracted partitions... To the windows of the lodge there are blinds, as high up as the eyes of the prisoners in their cells can, by any means they can employ, be made to reach. To prevent thorough light, whereby, notwithstanding the blinds, the prisoners would see from the cells whether or not any person was in the lodge, that apartment is divided into quarters, by partitions formed by two diameters to the circle, crossing each other at right angles. For these partitions the thinnest materials might serve; and they might be made removeable at pleasure; their height, sufficient to prevent the prisoners seeing over them from the cells... To save the troublesome exertion of voice that might otherwise be necessary, and to prevent one prisoner from knowing that the inspector was occupied by another prisoner at a distance, a small tin tube might reach from each cell to the inspector's lodge, passing across the area, and so in at the side of the correspondent window of the lodge. By means of this implement, the slightest whisper of the one might be heard by the other...

These proposals were taken by Michel Foucault to epitomize the movement in disciplinary power from the punishment of the body to the punishment of the mind (or soul). What interested Foucault primarily was the fact that the centre of the Panopticon, where surveillance of each cell was possible, need not contain a human element. Inmates felt that they may be being watched, but never knew whether this was actually the case. This 'internalization' of the perception of being watched was taken to have a profound and coercive effect on human behaviour. The idea of the disembodied anonymous operation of surveillant power infused much of Foucault's work, and has become a theoretical paradigm in modern criminology.

Hence the major effect of the Panopticon: to induce in the inmate a state of conscious and permanent visibility that assures the automatic functioning of power. So to arrange things that the surveillance is permanent in its effects, even if it is discontinuous in its action; that the perfection of power should tend to render its actual exercise unnecessary; that this architectural apparatus should be a machine for creating and sustaining a power relation independent of the person who exercises it; in short, that the inmates should be caught up in a power situation of which they are themselves the bearers. To achieve this, it is at once too much and too little that the prisoner should be constantly observed by an inspector: too little, for what matters is that he knows himself to be observed; too much, because he has no need in fact of being so. In view of this, Bentham laid down the principle that power should be visible and unverifiable. Visible: the inmate will constantly have before his eyes the tall outline of the central tower from which he is spied upon. Unverifiable: the inmate must never know whether he is being looked at at any one moment; but he must be sure that he may always be so. In order to make the presence or absence of the inspector unverifiable, so that the prisoners, in their cells, cannot even see a shadow, Bentham envisaged not only venetian blinds on the windows of the central observation hall, but, on the inside, partitions that intersected the hall at right angles and, in order to pass from one quarter to the other, not doors but zig-zag openings; for the slightest noise, a gleam of light, a brightness in a half-opened door would betray the presence of the guardian. The Panopticon is a machine for dissociating the see/being seen dyad: in the peripheric ring, one is totally seen, without ever seeing; in the central tower, one sees everything without ever being seen. (Foucault, 1977: 195–228)

A very limited number of prisons actually adopted and adapted panoptic ideals, and only then to a limited extent. These include Joliet in Illinois and the Twin Towers Facility in Los Angeles. However, in fact, British textile factories were the first (and really the only true) structures to be built on panoptic principles. For example, Belper Round Mill was built in 1813 by William Strutt, a member of the Lunar Society – a group of manufacturers and writers who met monthly to discuss philosophy, mathematics, architecture and social issues. The **factory** incorporated many panoptic features to facilitate the constant supervision of workers, but was later replaced by mill buildings which were more suited to mechanized production than the Round Mill. The panoptic gaze, whether incorporated directly into commercial architecture or not, seemed to bore into the soul of workers, prisoners, and the ordinary citizen, in a way which disciplined the general population into routines of self-regulation and self-governmentality which suited mature capitalist enterprises (Haggerty and Ericson, 2000). The Panopticon design did not perfect supervision, of prisoners or workers, but as an idea has dominated academic discourse on surveillance and the information-ordering of society. It has come to epitomize public fears about the apparent constant extension of police and governmental scrutiny, but have those fears really been realized?

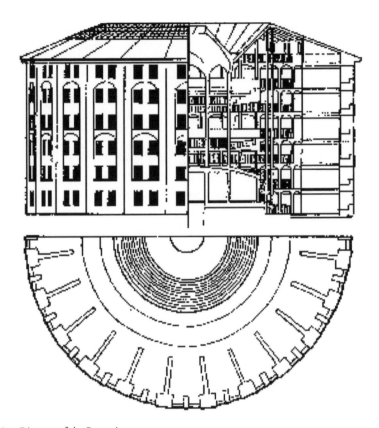

Figure 7.1   *Diagram of the Panopticon*

Summary

So, in conclusion, it is certainly possible to write a history of progressive surveillance of the powerful over the less powerful; and the processes and technologies of surveillance seem to be advancing as evidence presented in this chapter has shown. One can list a number of surveillance technologies ranging from the important (preventative policing, CCTV, habitual and later sex offender registers, and so on) to the seemingly trivial (the placing of cameras in dustbins to assess the scale of recycling waste materials). All speak to the greater regulation of society. But some speak softly, and most are inadequate, incomplete or plain daft. The subjects of surveillance – which at first were the criminal and the lunatic, then the factory worker, and now the general public – are increasingly vocal in their resistance to new forms of surveillance. They seem to have a greater distrust of government to collect information accurately and to use it wisely. Not least this is because the loose web of different forms of surveillance seem incapable of protecting society – people still fear violent attacks on the street, commuters and shoppers still anticipate terrorist attacks. One could contentiously suggest that the public need to decide whether they should rail against the increase in surveillance or against the fact that there isn't enough of it.

The conclusion to this chapter must be that the panoptic project, if it is even possible to speak of it in those terms, is incomplete. Moreover, it is incoherent. For much of its history, surveillance technology has been in search of an agenda to serve; if stopping street crime has not served that purpose then the War against Terror may well do, for the very incoherence and impossibility of that aim seems to give surveillance-mindedness free reign. It may well be that 50 years hence we are looking back to the early twenty-first century as the halcyon days of freedom compared to the surveillance society that may then be in place. However, the likelihood is that surveillance *will* increase, *but* that it will also continue to fail to deliver what it promises – or threatens.

STUDY QUESTIONS

1 How did surveillance operate in private spaces such as the nineteenth-century textile factories?
2 How were the possibilities of surveillance over public space increased by the extension of a national police system from 1829 to the introduction of CCTV cameras in the twentieth century?
3 What are the purposes of general surveillance, and how successful has surveillance been in achieving those aims?
4 Is Bentham's Panopticon a relevant analogy for today's situation?

FURTHER READING

Dandaker, C. (1990) *Surveillance, Power and Modernity. Bureaucracy and discipline from 1700 to the present day*, Polity Press: Cambridge.

Lyon, D. (1994) *The Electronic Eye. The Rise of Surveillance Society*, Polity Press: Cambridge.

Lyon, D. (2001) *Surveillance Society: Monitoring Everyday Life*, Open University Press: Buckingham.

Lyon, D. (2006) 'The search for surveillance theories', in D. Lyon (ed.) *Theorizing Surveillance. The Panopticon and beyond*, Willan Publishing: Cullompton.

Notes

1 This section of the chapter draws on Godfrey (1999) and Godfrey and Lawrence (2005).

2 The taking home of workplace materials by employees has had various labels attached to it – some refer to the practice as workplace appropriation, pilfering, 'fiddling', or 'embezzlement'. The multiplicity of terms for this activity reflects the conceptual differences between customary rights established by tradition, and theft (see Hobsbawm, 1968).

3 Moreover, by adapting their detective methods to the context of factory production, they continued as the most important employers' policing/prosecution agency for approximately 200 years (for a history of this organization see Soderlund, 1998 and Godfrey, 2002).

4 For a discussion of the historical dimensions of white-collar crime see Locker and Godfrey, 2006; see also seminal works by Sutherland (1940, 1941, 1945, 1949); and modern studies by Cressey (1971); for discussion of middle-class crime and how it has been conceived by historians, see Sindall (1983), Johnston (1998), Jenkins (1987). It would also be worthwhile looking at the development of trust within the business and commercial environment in Fukuyama (1996).

5 Wells alleges that, along with other factors, automatic detection of speeding motorists has also brought about a crisis of legitimacy for modern policing (Wells, 2005).

6 The use of these camera is controlled by the Data Protection Act 1998 which in the United Kingdom led to legal restrictions being imposed on the use to which CCTV footage can be put, and also mandated their registration with the Data Protection Agency (DPA). The successor to the DPA, the Information Commissioner in 2004 clarified that this required registration of all CCTV systems with the Commissioner, and prompt deletion of archived footage. However subsequent case law (Durant vs FSA) has limited the scope of the legal protection provided by this law, and not all CCTV systems are currently regulated.

7 Covert surveillance, as used by Public authorities under Part II of the Regulation of Investigatory Powers Act 2000, falls within two categories: directed surveillance or intrusive surveillance. Directed surveillance is defined in section 26(2) of the 2000 Act as surveillance which is covert, but not intrusive, and undertaken for the purposes of a specific investigation or specific operation in such a manner as is likely to result in the obtaining of private information about a person (whether or not one specifically identified for the purposes of the investigation or operation) otherwise than by way of an immediate response to events or circumstances the nature of which is such that it would not be reasonably practicable for an authorisation under Part II of the 2000 Act to be sought for the carrying out of the surveillance. Directed surveillance investigations or operations can only be carried out by those public authorities who are listed in or added to Part I and Part II of schedule 1 of the 2000 Act. The definition of intrusive surveillance is defined in section 26(3) of the 2000 Act as covert surveillance that is carried out in relation to anything taking place on any residential premises or in any private vehicle involving the presence of an individual on the premises or in the vehicle or is carried out by means of a surveillance device. Applications to carry out intrusive surveillance can only be made by the senior authorizing officer of those public authorities listed in or added to section 32(6) of the 2000 Act or by a member or official of those public authorities listed in or added to section 41(1). See http://security.homeoffice.gov.uk/counter-terrorism-strategy/legislation/terrorism-act-2006.

8

Incarceration and Decarceration

Chapter Contents

OVERVIEW

Chapter 8:

- Discusses the aims of punishment – deterrence, rehabilitation, capacitation and retribution – and how these have developed over time.

- Explores the promise of the penitentiary and the reformatory, the use of the death penalty, corporal punishment, transportation, and the longstanding debate about prison conditions.

- Asks: What about punishment today? If the nineteenth century can be described as the era of mass imprisonment, and the late twentieth century saw record numbers of prisoners in the UK, will the twenty-first century be the period of decarceration? This and other questions are considered in the conclusion to this chapter.

KEY TERMS

| mass imprisonment | punishment | incapacitation | decarceration |

Historians of criminal justice have long been fascinated with punishment. This is largely due to the central role in the theorization of the topic that was played by the French philosopher Michel Foucault. His classic work *Discipline and Punish: the Birth of the Prison* was first published in 1975 as *Surveiller et Punir*, and translated into English in 1977 (see Chapter 7). In it, Foucault turned the history of the prison on its head. Gone was the largely positive account that celebrated the history of the prison as a progressive triumph over the old corrupt and inefficient penal system, in which a few far-sighted humanitarians overcame vested interests to produce the efficient, modern and humane system of the present. Instead, he argued that in the modern system, power was far more ubiquitous and oppressive than it had previously been, and that whole systems of science and technology were now devoted to making the prisoner more of a totally controlled subject. His book involved a series of memorable images and sweeping pronouncements. *Discipline and Punish* begins with two detailed pictures of the changing face of punishment. The first, intended to illustrate the pre-modern tendency to punish the body, is the horrific execution in 1757 of the French criminal Damiens, convicted of attempting to kill the King. He was torn apart by horses, while the flesh was ripped from his body and red-hot metal poured into the wounds. The next is the daily routine at a reformatory school for young offenders in 1837. The schedule is so detailed that every minute of the day is controlled, and each inmate is under constant surveillance. The mind, not the body, was now being punished.

Over the last 25 years, Foucault's views about the role that power, knowledge, and surveillance play in modern society have proved to be very influential in the way that theorists and historians have seen the world, but the irony is that although they inspired much research into the history of punishment, most of this ended up by pointing out the flaws in his analysis (Ignatieff, 1983; Brown, 2003: 7). The most important of these is that although Foucault documented the changing intentions behind the punishment system, he did not check to see what happened in practice. Everywhere, this reveals a picture of continuity rather than abrupt change, and one where complex blueprints for action tended to break down in practice when matched with limited budgets, conservative staff and unco-operative prisoners. The visionaries were just one group of 'stake-holders' in the prison reform process, and although they might have wanted to create a new type of 'total institution', other stakeholders, notably those who were asked to pay for systems of non-stop secure supervision, tended to oppose such grandiose visions, to such an extent that it was only very rarely that they were allowed free rein. This understanding has meant that broad-brush approaches to the history of the prison, such as that of Foucault (1977), or of Michael Ignatieff (1979) are now less in favour. More detailed research however has picked out a number of common themes, and allows us to give much useful context to attempts to explain and theorize punishment in the present day.

There are now two main approaches to historical research into punishment: what were the new visions that each era came up with, and what happened in practice when the authorities tried to put the ideas into practice? The vision is much easier to assess and to comment on. It is also relevant even if we know that it was never put into practice (i.e. Bentham's Panopticon, see Chapter 7). The type of punishment that an era thinks ought to be carried out usually gives a very good indication of the way that it sees the problem of crime, and the proper role of the criminal justice system. Indeed, this kind of analysis can take us even further, into understanding how they saw the personality: what made people act in correct and deviant ways, and what steps could be taken to change their behaviour? The practical aspects of punishment regimes are also worth studying: they allow us to make judgements about which factors commonly act to impede the imposition of the vision. Perhaps the most significant of these is the hardest to eliminate: the role of society outside the prison, which can never be wholly removed, no matter how much effort is put into the process. As ever, therefore, a historical perspective can tell us what (if anything) about crime and punishment can be attributed to an unchanging 'human nature' and what or (if anything) to changing economic, social and political realities.

Punishment is usually seen by modern theorists of the prison as containing a number of different elements. These are most often broken down into deterrence, rehabilitation, incapacitation and retribution. *Deterrence* refers to the effect that the prospect of punishment has on those who might commit crimes: they will assess the unpleasantness of the punishment, divide it by the likelihood of getting caught, and decide not to commit the crime. It assumes that the potential criminal is a rational actor with a realistic understanding of the criminal justice system. *Rehabilitation* (or reformation) is the process whereby during punishment, the criminal is brought to face up to his/her crimes, and adjusts his/her personality in such a way as to make it less likely that they will reoffend. *Incapacitation* refers to the extent that a punishment prevents the criminal from committing more crimes: the ultimately incapacitating punishments are death and banishment, but secure imprisonment also temporarily incapacitates. *Retribution* (or punishment) refers to the pain of punishment that is delivered to the prisoner. This is best explicable as a message not to potential miscreants but to the community at large, to announce the fact that the criminal justice system delivers a just measure of pain to those who break the law.

Ways of looking at punishment

Punishment has been theorized for hundreds of years. For example, in the sixteenth century, in both England and the Netherlands, monotonous labour was seen both as a punishment in itself, and as a way of re-integrating anti-social individuals, such as prostitutes and vagrants, back into society. Giving them compulsory work in a **'House of Correction'** such as London's **Bridewell** or Amsterdam's *Tuchthuis* was intended to make them used to working in the world outside, and hence prevent them from being a burden on the wider society on their release. It was largely, therefore, presented and justified as a form of rehabilitation. It tended to be applied not to those who had committed a single serious identifiable crime, but instead to individuals whose lifestyle was judged to be immoral in some way, usually because of idleness. There is another reason why it was used however. It reinforced the values of the wider society, which stressed that all should work, and should also all fit in to social hierarchies, largely contained within households, which provided the basic structure of authority in early modern society. Bridewell was a substitute family for those who had none, and performed the important role of the household in giving all men and women an identifiable master, who was responsible for moulding and guiding their behaviour. Thus in European prison workhouses, there were officials whose job titles were 'father' and 'mother' (Spierenburg, 1995: 68–9). Punishment was never just a random activity, but always one which fitted into the society of which it was a part, and there is often evidence from contemporaries that they recognized how and why it fitted in, and tried to justify it accordingly.

A specific criminology of punishment, with claims to scientific understa̶n̶ ̶ ̶
and a view of the way that things ought to be, first developed in the late eighteenth century. In punishment as in policing, the Italian philosopher Beccaria
made a major impact (see Chapter 2). His work, *On Crimes and Punishments –*
written in Italian in 1764 and available in English by 1767 – advocated a move
away from a system based on very harsh punishments which were usually
evaded for one reason or another, towards one based on better policing, and the
greater certainty of punishment, which would allow for each individual punishment to be less harsh. Many of the proposals that he made had already been
advocated in Britain, but his was the first work to bring them together into a
coherent system (Dunthorne, 1999). Beccaria pointed to parts of Europe which,
in his opinion, already exhibited the innovations that he wanted to see put into
practice, and this was also a feature of the first British 'prison reformers'. When
the Bedfordshire Christian gentleman John Howard wrote his work *The State of
the Prisons*, he set out a vision for humane punishment that was in part derived
from overseas experience, and in subsequent editions of the book, published
from 1791 regularly up to his death (of a disease contracted in a Russian prison),
he included more and more material gleaned from visits to prisons around
Europe. In Randall McGowen's words 'Howard introduced the idea that a proper
prison regime already existed, only somewhere else' (McGowen, 1995: 87).

This idea was immensely powerful through the nineteenth century, and it is
impossible to consider the process of prison development without taking into
account the growth and influence of international examples. This was not limited to Europe. Reformers in Britain and the United States collaborated in developments that led to the creation of the discipline of penology, which saw itself
as creating a science of punishment. Between 1775 and 1820, exchange of ideas
between the US and Britain helped to define a body of professional penological
knowledge:

> By initially utilising their ready-made networks, and then extending these in
> the formation of specialist groups, the early penal reformers found effec-
> tive ways to inform themselves and others. But they also sought to justify
> their calls for penal reform by reference to a respectable branch of scien-
> tific knowledge (both empirical and philosophical). ... Penology, then, was
> a discipline in the making, and knowledge and expertise were essential to
> its development. (Burgoyne, 1997: 195)

Bilateral contacts and individual research expeditions such as Howard's developed into an international infrastructure. An international Prison Reform Congress
was held in Frankfurt in 1846, and, by 1910, ten further international penal and
prison congresses had been held in Europe and the United States. These acted as
a forcing-house for theories of crime and criminology, and in many cases, the
example of 'more progressive countries' was invoked by prison reformers in their

home states in order to obtain political backing for innovations that they wished to carry out. Penology was one of the earliest components of the discipline later described as criminology to organize itself (see Chapter 2).

Many of these penologists formed themselves into organizations to study prison conditions and lobby for a more rational and efficient approach to punishment. The most important such group in Britain is the Howard League (named after the prison reformer John Howard). Since the late twentieth century the Howard League has generally been seen as an organization that points out injustices against prisoners and works to secure their rights, but this has not always been the case: in the late nineteenth century its spokesman and organizer was a frequent correspondent to the newspapers, arguing that it was important to keep prison conditions harsh enough to act as a deterrent.

The dominance of a progressive and scientific view of the penal enterprise led to a view of the history of the prison that saw it as an inevitable progress towards a more humane, rational and effective system. This view placed reformers such as Howard at the centre of the picture, and accepted without question their views of what constituted the best model of punishment. Research over the last 30 years, inspired by writers such as Foucault, has tended to paint a much less cosy and simplistic view of the history of the prison. In association with this, the modern era has focused more on the victim of crime as an identifiable individual whose needs have to be met by more than just an abstract accounting between the perpetrator of crime and the state. Although the entire period of prison reform has been subjected to a powerful conservative critique which argues that the balance has been tilted too far towards the perpetrator, the modern identification of the victim was not performed by this group. Instead, it came from the liberal wing of the penal law reform movement, in the shape of Margery Fry, a prominent Quaker campaigner for prisoners' rights, who launched a campaign in the 1950s entitled 'What about the victim?'. It was this which prompted the creation of the modern system of criminal injury compensation, whereby the state elects to pay compensation to people who have been the victims of crime. The liberal reformers who backed Fry's campaign, though, did so for two reasons. In the words of one of Fry's supporters, eminent lawyer Hartley Shawcross, this was because they realized 'that the absence of any provision for compensation to the victim tended to accentuate the public's desire for vengeance against the criminal, and so stood in the way of a more efficient system of punishment' ('FD', 1958).

The pre-reform system of punishment

What was the prison that so revolted John Howard and other reformers? In the eighteenth century, prisons were not the highly controlled places that we know today. The great London prisons such as Newgate, Marshalsea, the Fleet and the Clink functioned mainly as compounds to secure malefactors. Inside them, prisoners were expected to make their own arrangements for food, and superior accommodation could be obtained by paying off the gaoler. Alcohol, sex and gambling were all apparent. It was during this century that a number of prison reformers, the most famous of whom is the evangelical Christian John Howard, began to complain about practices such as this, but we must not project their outrage on to our understanding of the past, nor judge it by our standards. Prison practice in the pre-reform era looks like something that we would call 'corrupt', but a fee-based system, in which the gaoler was a contractor who purchased the post as a franchise, was standard practice for the eighteenth century, and ought not to be dismissed as corruption. One of the factors that most offended the reformer was that various different categories of prisoner were mixed together. Not only were juveniles and adults mixed together, but so were those convicted of serious and trivial offences, as were prisoners awaiting trial with those who had already been sentenced. In addition, a large number of prisoners were debtors: people who had got into debt and been placed in prison by those to whom they owed money as an incentive to pay. Obviously, imprisonment did not make repayment easier, but this treatment was justified as a deterrent: it kept people honest in their business dealings, since, if they were afraid of being sent to prison, they would in theory be much less likely to trade while insolvent. Despite what we might think of as a lax regime, these prisons were not popular places with Londoners, and during the Gordon riots of 1780 many were burned down by the rioters. Whereas today the vast majority of the prison population have been sentenced to spend a certain period of time confined in prison as a punishment, this was not the case in the eighteenth century. Prisons were largely used as convenient places where offenders could be held until it was possible to try them, or while they were waiting to have their sentence carried out, with only a minority being imprisoned there as a punishment in itself.

The most overt punishment in England, as in the rest of Europe, was the death penalty. This was the punishment for scores of different offences in the eighteenth century (the so called 'Bloody Code'). The vast majority of these offences were obscure and often claimed no lives at all. The vast majority of those who faced the death penalty were charged with one of a few Common Law offences: murder, rape, burglary, robbery, forgery, coining (issuing counterfeit coins), and above all 'felony theft'. The latter accounted for the largest proportion of offenders. It encompassed non-violent theft of goods worth more than one shilling. This wide ranging scope of capital offences (ones carrying the death penalty) has been called 'Draconian'. To do so is to miss the point of it – Draco was an Athenian tyrant who was famous for a harsh penal code which was ruthlessly and remorselessly applied to all malefactors. The death penalty had no such reach. Barring those charged with a couple of offences (murder and forgery), the vast majority of offenders who faced the death penalty had it remitted to transportation for life, either by the judge at the time that sentence was passed, or afterwards by the King following a plea for mercy. The old legal concept of 'benefit of clergy' was used to give all non-violent thieves (the vast majority of the total) immunity from prosecution for their first offence – although they were branded on the hand in order to make clear their status if caught again. Juries were reluctant to convict if they thought that the offender did not deserve the death penalty, or else they ignored the true value of stolen items and instead judged them to be worth less than one shilling, thus removing the crime from the death penalty. Judges were perfectly happy to free the accused if there had been any error in the prosecution document, however minor. If we must have a classical word to describe the system, then 'Damoclean' is probably better. In Greek myth, the sword of Damocles hung over the hero's head on a thread, always threatening to fall on him. This is a far better description of the way that the death penalty worked in England: often threatened, but rarely carried out, its existence was intended to produce a feeling of dread in the minds of criminals. It also, in a direct way, showed them that the law was dominant, and that the best way to get clemency was to plead loyalty to those in power (Hay, 1975).

Those who escaped the gallows but were convicted of a capital crime faced the prospect of transportation. This was to the eastern shore of the American colonies, chiefly to the colonies of Maryland and Delaware on Chesapeake Bay. There, convicts were sold as indentured servants, to work for a master, usually for around seven years, before gaining their freedom, although in theory they remained banned from Britain. Between 1718, when the Transportation Act made this process much easier, and 1776, when transportation was ended by the **American War**, this involved significant numbers of people – between 1771 and 1775, one county in Maryland received 849 convicts (Ekirch, 1987: 50). Transportation was unlike the rest of the eighteenth-century criminal justice system in the important respect that it was not a public punishment. Prisons were not shut away, but porous institutions whose inmates could be inspected. Executions were carried out in public, as were corporal punishments such as whipping or exhibition in the pillory. Thus the public theatre of punishment was very important, stressing the deterrent function: reformers argued that this was at the expense of rehabilitation and incapacitation.

The promise of the penitentiary and the reformatory

In penology as in policing, the period between about 1770 and about 1840 laid the foundations for the institutions that were still in existence in the late twentieth century. As with policing, the great spur to these changes was the period of industrialization and population growth which saw the basic form of British society change greatly over this period. The Industrial Revolution was not the only influence on these developments, though, and other factors – notably the autonomous role of legal and penological thought – cannot be ignored if we are to explain what happened, when and why.

The first national initiative in Britain to set up a recognizably modern system of prisons came with the Penitentiary Act of 1779. This was introduced at a time when transportation of convicts outside the country was in a hiatus, owing to the outbreak of the American revolt. As the title suggests, it was intended to set up an institution designed to produce 'penitence' – the recognition by sinners that they have done wrong, and the desire for forgiveness and re-integration. It is important to note the central role played by religion in the conceptualization of punishment in the adult prison system right up to the mid-twentieth century and even later (though in less overt terms) in the juvenile punishment and treatment sector through the work of Christian charities such as the Rainer Foundation. In an era where questions of right and wrong were largely (though not exclusively) defined in religious terms, this is unsurprising.

There were several factors behind the Act. One was an increasing tendency of magistrates and judges to use longer prison sentences as a punishment in themselves (Beattie, 1986: 538–40). This pre-dated the arrival of Beccaria's work into Britain, and thus appears to suggest that one reason this was so popular was that it justified and described policies which were already in being. The precipitating event was the interruption of transportation owing to the American War, which gave penal reformers in the government the opportunity to put their plans into practice (Deveraux, 1999). The Act provided for two new prisons, devoted to hard labour, to be built in or near London. The internal regime was described in detail: inmates were to be housed at night in cells, and during the day set to labour which would involve as little association as possible. As well as being divided by background, they were to be allocated to three different classes, depending on their behaviour; those of the highest class could even be trusted with some supervisory duties. Systems of different class of inmate, who could earn more privileges via good behaviour; or lose them for misbehaviour, remained a feature of most British prison regimes: sometimes they involved a highly complex accounting of 'marks' which could be earned or forfeited, and could result in remission of sentence.

The Act marked the arrival of the penitentiary ideal into Britain, but the prisons it described were never built, chiefly because of the great sums of money that would have been required to complete them. Yet it provided a blueprint through which local prisons reformed themselves. These were paid for and directed at the county level, and in the last third of the eighteenth century, often under the influence of Howard and his followers, many were re-modelled to incorporate the penitentiary ideal and its goal of rehabilitation. Fees were ended, uniforms introduced, and new and expensive buildings were constructed, so that various categories of prisoner could be kept segregated from one another. One influential figure in this development was a follower of Howard, the architect William Blackburn, who designed 19 prisons before his death in 1790. In Randall McGowen's view:

> Blackburn expressed the ambition to use space and stone to shape human nature. His design revealed the implicit belief that architecture could promote the goals of confinement. Geometry and symmetry triumphed in these designs, which pursued health, order and more equal conditions. A rationally organized space, he believed, would foster the development of reason and self-regulation in its inmates. His plans also sought to strengthen the position of the jailer within the prison by promoting inspection. Above all Blackburn sought to secure classification and separation; he set the main task of prison architecture as the regulation of human sociability. (McGowen, 1995: 91)

Separation was the key to rehabilitation in this view.

In the atmosphere of enthusiasm for prison reform, many systems of incarceration were advocated. Perhaps the most famous was Bentham's Panopticon (described in Chapter 7). In brief, the Panopticon prison was designed as a four to six storey building that took the form of an upright cylinder. The cells were on the inside, accessed by walkways that ran along the inside, and with their interior walls entirely formed from bars, looking inwards to the central courtyard. At the centre of this space, on the axis of the cylinder, stood a tower which rose to the same height as the prison cells. This was occupied by the prison warders, who could arrange shutters and blinds within the tower so that the inmates were not aware whether or not they were being watched at that moment. There was a practical point to this design: it allowed a small number of employees to watch a large number of prisoners at the same time, thus saving money. But there was also a broader point. The prisoner knew that at any time he might be under observation, but he had no way of telling whether or not he was being watched at that time. Thus there was every chance that he would act as if he was being watched all the time, and this change in his behaviour might outlast his term of imprisonment.

The Panopticon provided a compelling and intriguing vision of the possibilities of total surveillance, as Chapter 7 debates, but it was never built in Britain. Pentonville Prison, opened in 1842, incorporated some of the practical innovations of the Panopticon. Later in the nineteenth century, under the influence of the international penological congresses mentioned above, some prisons were built on this model in the United States and elsewhere.

The death penalty, corporal punishment and transportation

As alluded to in the introduction, the birth of the prison in Britain was accompanied by innovations in other forms of punishment. Again, these were the focus of arguments about the proper way to punish, and again, they went through different stages of development.

The modern campaign to limit the death penalty in Britain dates from 1808, when the politician Samuel Romilly launched a campaign to limit its scope to the most serious crimes. He took exception to the fact that the decision to execute was generally taken as a matter of discretion by the judge. Like Bentham, he opposed random exemplary punishments, and instead advocated a mechanical and calculated punishment. They also took exception to the public nature of executions, which they thought served to harden the spectators and make them cruel as much as it impressed them about the power of the law (McGowen, 1995: 93). In addition, executions were disorderly spectacles, and the prospect of large, unruly and uncontrolled crowds was not welcome to the reformers.

The process of abolition of the death penalty for property crimes lasted from 1808 to 1837. By 1830, it was retained for murder, but the vast bulk of death sentences for property crimes had been replaced by sentences of transportation to the Australian colonies. The organization of the convict system in Australia went through a number of stages, driven both by the needs of the colony and by changing fashions in punishment, but some features were constant. They constituted a vast open prison: outside a very few penal institutions where convicts who committed further serious crimes were held, the penal colonies were a labour camp where, if they behaved themselves, the freedom of the convicts was gradually extended until, at the expiration of their period of transportation, they were once again free. Many spent the majority of their sentences on a 'ticket-of-leave': given freedom from close control so long as they resided in a certain area and kept out of trouble. Others were indentured to employers; a situation which led to some abuses, but in the main was not significantly worse than that of many servants in Britain.

In Australia, as in the UK, the punishment for most convicts who committed additional offences was a flogging: being beaten with a whip made of heavy knotted cords, which inflicted permanent (sometimes fatal) damage as well as pain to the victim. Corporal punishment was a prominent part of the judicial arsenal in eighteenth-century Britain, as well, but fell out of use, and was abolished in 1861, only to be reinstated following a panic over street theft in 1863, and finally struck off the statute book in 1948. That year also saw the abolition of corporal punishment for juveniles, who were struck by a birch, which was a considerably less damaging punishment than flogging.

The paradox of transportation (at least in the British context) is the extraordinary success that it made of rehabilitation. While a hard core of transportees maintained their criminal ways after transportation, the majority of the 160,000 transported to Australia between 1788 and 1869 earned their freedom, and indeed formed the core of a law-abiding society. In an era when the prison was becoming the centrepiece of the new science of penology, a colony that resisted attempts to turn it into a prison was a remarkably successful aberration. As Hirst puts it:

> a society peopled so largely by convicts nevertheless maintained the rule of law for all, imposed no disability on ex-convicts, and gave them the opportunity for economic success through employment of convict labor. It is a society without parallel, a strange, late flowering of the *ancien régime* in crime and punishment. (Hirst, 1995: 294)

The 1860s, which saw the end of transportation, also saw the end of public execution (in 1868). Abolitionists had long put effort into singling out the public nature of execution as one of its drawbacks; this tactic backfired when it was moved within the walls of the prison, where it stayed for nearly 100 years until its final abolition.

Reformatory philosophies and their roots

The cellular prison, as created in the early nineteenth century, was no more than a secure box; the exact plan of regime of punishment and rehabilitation to be followed within it became the focus of an argument about government policy. It is worth looking at this argument in detail, as an example of how rival penal policies, which looked similar on the surface, actually expressed very different world-views. In the 1830s the two main schools of thought were the 'separate system' and the 'silent system'.

The separate system was built around the widespread use of solitary confinement, and was explicitly designed to lead the inmates to a religious rebirth. Prisoners were to be left on their own in a cell for months at a time, save for regular visits from the prison chaplain to discuss religious matters. This was intended to allow them to consider the error of their ways and brood upon the mistakes that they had made and the sins that they had committed. The intention was that they would then be glad of the opportunity to attend church and perform labour; the threat of a return to solitary confinement would also render them tractable. The greatest triumph of the advocates of the separate system was the opening of Pentonville Prison in 1842. As McGowen puts it:

> The prison was a monument to faith in an ideal. It became the model for the construction of many local prisons in the decades that followed and attracted worldwide attention. The prison held 250 prisoners in separate cells. Four wings radiated out from a central point, from which one could observe each cell door. The construction of the walls hindered communication between prisoners, and even the guards wore padded shoes so that they would not disturb the silence. The guards were as strictly controlled as the prisoners, forbidden to talk to the convicts and kept to a steady patrol by a system of time clocks. ... For a regime that was intended to individualise punishment, it did its best to erase any trace of individuality. Prisoners wore hoods when they emerged from their cells. Their names were replaced by numbers. They had separate stalls in the chapel as well as separate exercise yards. Pentonville represented the apotheosis of the idea that a totally controlled environment would produce a reformed and autonomous individual. (McGowen, 1995: 101)

The separate system's advocates were mainly evangelical Christians. Advocates of other schemes often pointed out that one common outcome of prolonged solitary confinement was insanity.

The silent system, on the other hand, was promoted by men who had more experience with prisons, and tended to stress its deterrence aspects at the expense of its ability to reform, although they never rejected this ability outright. They based their plans on the foundation of 'associationism', a school of thought which held that a man's associations during his life combined to create his personality. Prominent associationists included materialist philosophers like Bentham and Mill, and many for whom religion was not the sole source of inspiration, although the silent system was not explicitly anti-religious. In the silent system, inmates would be prevented from interacting with one another, not as a means to reformation, but strictly as a punishment, and to prevent further contamination. Its very strictness was designed to lead to breaches of discipline which would be swiftly and mercilessly punished. Prisoners would 'defy the system and for perhaps the first time in their lives would encounter immediate pain as a result of prison punishment for breaking the silence' (Forsythe, 1987: 32). This process was designed to force them to the conclusion that obedience was the only policy. Advocates of the silent system saw prison as a place largely of punishment and deterrence, where the personality was altered not through a sudden religious conversion deriving from within an individual, but through the activity of a carefully thought-out system of punishments and rewards. In Bentham's plan:

> The individual tendencies of prisoners would need to be taken into account and the regime tailored for each. Staff would need to inspect closely the progress of each prisoner's reformation and new skills would need to be taught to them so that the newly acquired attitude to work, for example,

would bear fruit after release. Certain groups were deemed easier to reform than others, in particular the young, whose experience of crime as pleasurable was seen as smaller than that of older offenders. (Forsythe, 1987: 13)

If reformation in these institutions failed, then Bentham advocated incapacitation: the prisoner would be held for life.

In *Discipline and Punish*, Foucault argued that the main shift in punishment in the modern era was from punishing the body to punishing the mind. The 'model' prisons of the nineteenth century, with their treadmills and brutally inadequate diets, certainly continued to punish the body, but we can see from both the silent and (especially) the separate systems that they certainly attempted to punish the mind. Prisons in the eighteenth century may have been places of ill-health and corruption, but they allowed the inmates to interact and to maintain a sort of human society, with an often surprising degree of integration with the world outside the prison. The nineteenth century changed this, and set the pattern which persists today, of the prison as a place where the authorities claim the right (even though they do not always exercise it) to control every aspect of the prisoner's life.

The ongoing public debate about prison conditions

For more than 200 years – since before the publication of the pamphlet 'Hanging Not Punishment Enough' in London in 1701 – the public have been divided in their response to prison conditions. Although reformers like John Howard, usually motivated by religious belief in universal human worth, criticized the harshness of prison conditions, and obtained a significant degree of public support for their position, many other commentators have expressed disquiet about the perceived leniency of these conditions. One way to think about this was provided by the pioneering French sociologist Emille Durkheim at the end of the nineteenth century. Durkheim described the criminal justice system as a way of enforcing the norms of the community against those who would break them. He believed that prison and punishments, therefore, had to have a certain level of harshness in order to be effective at protecting society as a whole. Given this, it is unsurprising that there has been an almost constant refrain from many politicians that prison is too lenient to give the necessary deterrent message to potential law-breakers, that the chief culprits in this situation are the penal reformers, and that the chief victims are the public at large who are the victims of crime. This view is remarkably constant, despite the fact that it usually expresses itself in dynamic terms, involving an ongoing slide in morals and standards of behaviour. This was examined by Geoff Pearson in his 1983 book *Hooligan: a History of Respectable Fears*, which summed up the debate in England following the end of transportation in the 1860s thus:

> At the moment of its inception, however, the reformed system of criminal justice was greeted with howling disapproval...Respectable England was haunted by the fear that the 'safety of society would soon be at an end' and that the 'dangerous classes' were gaining the upper hand because of the weakened authority of the law. It was immediately much regretted that the death penalty could not be applied to burglars and footpads, and the prison system was the object of particularly fierce criticism. *Punch* [the satirical magazine] regularly indicated the mildness of magistrates and the 'luxurious' convenience of a 'snug cell in prison' which...'unless the Government interfere to make the living less luxurious...will be popularly looked upon as one of the most comfortable ways of spending life.' 'The present gaols are really beautiful penal toys', wrote a complaining correspondent to *The Times* in 1863 , 'the perfection of lodging-houses-for-single-men architecture...in a better situation [location] Pentonville would sell well as 'chambers' for Bank clerks and MPs of limited income.'
>
> The moral vocabulary of these accusations against sentimentality, leniency and crinolined philanthropy that unfolded in the wake of the great legislative transformations of this era is one which we would find entirely familiar in our own historical time, and which has rolled down to us virtually unchanged across more than a century of resistance to penal reform. (Pearson, 1983: 127–8)

This matter has always been linked to the provision of state welfare to the poor in general. In Britain, first the Poor Laws, and then the welfare state, guaranteed that everybody would be kept alive by the state – although the able-bodied poor might be forced to work for their keep. Under the New Poor Law, which was in existence for a century after 1835, those who could not support themselves were usually taken into a workhouse as a condition of support. Workhouses, many of which enforced separation of families, were seen as a place of oppression by members of the working classes, at the same time that local ratepayers, who had to finance them, were concerned lest their taxes were being used to unnecessarily coddle the poor. Thus workhouse conditions were kept spartan, and the diet was cut to the minimum necessary to support life. The conditions in the workhouse immediately gave a baseline of provision; if prisons offered conditions which were (or were seen to be) better than those on offer to the law-abiding poor, they came under criticism on two grounds. Firstly, that this was an injustice in itself to society in general, the wronged party who were financing the prisoner's punishment and hence lifestyle. Secondly, that in itself this acted as a magnet for crime, for which working person would meekly submit to an inferior diet in the workhouse when the worst reward of crime would be a better standard of living? This latter argument, of course, implied that there was no stigma attached to imprisonment for the lower classes, and that the only punishment whose effects could be relied upon was the harshness of physical conditions in the prison.

Diet was a punishment in itself: the nineteenth-century British prison diet was pared down to such an extent that it was barely able to keep inmates alive. Convicts working on forced labour were generally not given enough to sustain them over the long term. For example, Alyson Brown has found that among those convicts sentenced to dig out the naval base at Chatham in the 1860s:

> One indication of the severity of penal servitude in this period is the evidence of persistent conflicts over food. Several references were made by convict prison medical officers and discharged convicts to the items that hunger induced the convicts to eat: these included dead shellfish found on the works, candles, and worms. (Brown, 2003: 92)

Yet although conditions of such hardship were routine in convict prisons (those run by the central government, which housed serious offenders), they were not much known outside, and public pressure for harsher punishments in the face of perceived crime waves remained high in the 1860s.

This was caused, to a large extent, by the final ending of transportation to Australia. Transportation had served to remove the most serious offenders from the United Kingdom, and although by the 1860s the numbers of convicts transported had fallen, it still had an important symbolic role to play in the criminal justice system. It was replaced by the sentence of 'penal servitude' in a convict prison. The first third of this was to be spent in solitary confinement, the next carrying out hard labour, and the third released on a ticket-of-leave, earned by good behaviour in prison. When London was struck by a number of (heavily reported) violent robberies which became known as 'garottings', the ticket-of-leave system became the focus for public anxiety about crime, and 'ticket-of-leave men' were blamed for many outbreaks of crime and disorder. This perceived crisis in punishment also led to further centralization of the prison system, and in 1877 this was nationalized: the local prisons, which held the vast majority of offenders, were put under the control of the Home Office's Prison Commission, which until then had been responsible only for the convict prisons. This had the effect of worsening the conditions in local prisons, in an effort both to save money and to produce a uniform deterrent effect throughout the country. It was also a consequence of the assumptions underlying the philosophy of punishment, which stressed that uniformity of treatment was the best way to reform prisoners:

To a behaviourist, good punishment was that which was most deterrent, and the most deterrent was likely to be as severe as public sentiment and political opinion would tolerate. The move from locally administered local prisons to nationally administered local prisons was therefore bound to mean an overall increase in severity. (McConville, 1995: 146)

In the 1880s, the prison establishment in the UK became as tough as it has ever been.

Punishing the criminal or punishing the crime

The notion of equality under the law suggests that the punishment should fit the crime; that everyone who carries out a similar crime should receive a similar sentence. Opposed to this is the notion that the punishment should instead fit the criminal: that it should be tailored to provide the maximum deterrent effect. At one end of the spectrum this can be seen if the prisoner's previous record of good behaviour or earlier convictions influences the length of their sentence. At the other end, this is manifest in laws which prescribe long prison sentences for repeat offenders, no matter what the seriousness of the crime that precipitated the sentence, or even in sentences of preventive detention which could be indefinite, and were ended (or suspended) only when the offender was deemed no longer a threat to the public.

The first step in establishing such a regime was to identify the habitual criminal. The 1869 Habitual Criminal Act created a national register of all those imprisoned for a serious offence, which included a list of their known aliases and distinguishing marks. This tracking process was intended to identify habitual offenders, who would be forced to register with the police after they were released from prison. Thus the reach of the criminal justice system was extended outside the prison system itself. In practice, this register was too unwieldy to serve to track ex-offenders, and would remain so until the introduction of a successful fingerprint index at the start of the twentieth century. Fingerprints were only moderately useful for detection of crimes, but for the first time they offered a reliable means of tracking an individual offender through the criminal justice system, and being able to overcome the widespread use of aliases by criminals.

The 1908 Prevention of Crimes Act allowed for up to five years to be added to the sentence of those repeat offenders who were judged to be 'habitual criminals'. This type of sentence was devoted entirely to *incapacitation*: to protecting the public from a repeat offender. Prisoners jailed under it actually received (or were supposed in theory to receive) better treatment than others, on the grounds that the deterrent and retribution portions of their sentence had already been served. No effort was made to rehabilitate them: their designation as habitual criminals implied that this would have a low chance of succeeding. This class of sentence was attacked, and rendered less popular, by Winston Churchill when he became Home Secretary in 1910. Churchill was pointedly in favour of civil liberties and equality under the law for all, including convicted criminals, and he was concerned that this system of preventive detention was contrary to traditional English ideas of freedom. He famously told the House of Commons in 1910, 'The mood and temper of the public in regard to the treatment of crime and criminals is one of the most unfailing tests of civilisation in any country.' By pointing out a number of anomalous cases where petty criminals received long sentences for minor offences, Churchill helped to reduce the frequency that the 1908 Act was used to just 31 cases per year in the 1920s. (McConville, 1995: 165, 156).

The British penal system reached a peak of uniformity around 1880: all prisons were run according to standardized rules, with the object being the maximum conformity, and the greatest severity of punishment that was consistent with the minimum of health of the prisoner. This state of affairs, though, was gradually challenged, and the prison system was subject to a number of influences that led towards **decarceration** – the process whereby fewer inmates are sent to prison. One of them was the identification of the core group of habitual recidivists: as the assumed characteristics of this group became more closely defined, and it became labelled as a criminal residuum, offenders who did not fit into it began to stand out further. During this period, a number of offenders who did not fit into this category began to go public about their experiences in prison. More and more white-collar offenders were receiving prison sentences for fraud and other 'middle-class' crimes, and these men were articulate and literate. Several of them published memoirs which outlined the brutal arbitrariness of the system, and although most of these drew the conclusion that it was correct to apply this to brutalize convicts, they exposed its contradictions and petty cruelties to public attention. Other groups of prison memorialists saw themselves as political prisoners, and mounted sustained political campaigns against the abuses of the prison system. These included Irish Nationalists, whose political party had a significant presence in Parliament, as well as prisoners of conscience who had deliberately put themselves in prison rather than co-operate with what they saw as unjust laws. These groups included members of the Salvation Army arrested for obstruction, as well as anti-vaccination campaigners, and radical left activists. All these voices added up to a potent lobby which rejected the notion that everyone in prison was a hardened criminal who deserved all that they got; instead they drew attention to the fact that the pain and degradation inflicted in the prison system might harm the offender, but it seemed to do little to deter, and nothing to reform, him or her. Beyond the activities of the specific anti-incarceration lobby, a generally increasing humanitarian sensibility objected to the systematic infliction of pain, even in cases where the behaviour of the offender appeared to justify this. By the end of the century, even Home Office officials were ready to recognize that there was a distinction between 'criminals', who were professionals devoted to a life of crime and as such fit subjects for deterrence and punishment, and 'offenders', whose law-breaking activity was not serious enough to justify this degree of harsh treatment (Wiener, 1990: 328–36).

In the middle of the nineteenth century, the uniformity of the British prison system had been presented as its chief virtue and justification; by the end, even its defenders were acknowledging that it was a drawback: 'punishing the crime' without regard to the condition of the criminal was becoming less popular, in favour of 'punishing the criminal'.

A greater focus on the offender, and a less insistent one on the crime, led to a new innovation in punishment in the early twentieth century: probation. Like many other innovations, this grew out of an informal practice, which was intended to prevent the alleged 'contamination' of first-time offenders by imprisonment, and the First Offenders Act of 1887 which was designed to divert many from a period of imprisonment. Magistrates in London, wary of sending minor criminals to prisons which they regarded simply as nurseries of crime, released them instead into the care of the London Police Court Mission, whose missionaries' job was to supervise them for a set period in order to help them to get, and keep, gainful employment and hence stay out of trouble. From 1907, courts were given the power to employ probation officers, thus converting the informal practice into a legal and institutional one. In numerical terms, its impact was relatively minor until the 1920s and 1930s, when the probation service was expanded. Probation helped to divert thousands of offenders from prison, but like a number of secondary punishments, from transportation to reformatory schools, it provided an additional punishment for petty offenders, who may well have otherwise escaped punishment altogether. Thus the net of the criminal justice system was widened.

Increasingly in the twentieth century, the criminal justice system re-oriented itself towards the concept of 'penal welfare'. Prison was treated as a last resort for the most serious offenders, while an increasing use was made of special prisons and reformatories for juveniles. Psychiatric treatment was also used in prisons and in special hospitals: the inmate was at once an offender and also a medical subject, whose welfare the system was responsible for. Intertwined with this focus on welfare, though, was the continuing belief that all aspects of the prisoner's life were in the power of the penal authorities.

The role of punishment in the late twentieth century

Prisons are expensive buildings, and their design is often a practical and (literally) concrete expression of a particular penal philosophy. Thus the bricks and mortar of an earlier age can frustrate the prison reformers who inherit buildings which are inherently difficult to run in ways that the designer did not intend. One example of this issue in practice is the predominance in late twentieth-century Britain of an inherited Victorian prison estate which was built on the basis that confinement in cells was the central point of prison practice (McConville, 1995: 154). This made it difficult to put into use rehabilitation practices that relied on allowing prisoners to socialise. Yet despite the ever-changing sociological and psychological theories of what creates criminal behaviour and what can be done to change it, rates of re-offending remained stubbornly high. By the 1970s, a new wave of criminological theory was even reduced (largely on the basis of re-offending research) to conclude that 'nothing works' (Sullivan, 2000: 30). Prison was not deterring, but it did not seem to be rehabilitating either. This orthodoxy was best expressed by a Conservative Home Secretary in the 1980s, who claimed that without a workable programme for rehabilitation, prison was merely 'an expensive way of making bad people worse'. Nevertheless, a few years later, another Home Secretary from the same party felt able to claim that 'prison works', yet the substantive and credible claims that he made for it involved only incapacitation – a far cry from the promise of the penitentiary.

Reviewing changing modes of punishment

By reviewing the aims of punishment through documentary sources, we can see that historically situated ideas about deterrence, rehabilitation, retribution and incapacitation have influenced all forms of punishment throughout history. Yet as we have seen, these themes are not constants; some forms of punishment attempt to combine them all, but others merely stress one or the other, as can be seen from the following extracts.

Jonas Hanway (1712–86) was a London merchant who took a keen interest in the social development of his city. In 1756 he founded the Marine Society, a charity which educated orphan or poor boys and trained them for careers at sea. This passage refers to the Bridewell hospital in London, the original 'Bridewell'. In the eighteenth century, 'hospital' referred to any public residential institution, not merely one where ill people were treated. This extract immediately follows a reference to the recent rebuilding of some of the institution's accommodation. The Lord Mayor, Alderman, and Chamberlain of London all had judicial powers, and the Mayor also worked as the City's chief magistrate during the year of his term of office.

Jonas Hanway (1775) *The defects of police the cause of immorality,* **London, p. 35.**

I hope that sufficient room is left for the more essential purposes, of providing for the due correction of offenders, and what else belongs to the peace of the city and the common safety; which it may be also presumed, will be hereafter regarded with the tender circumspective eyes of good magistrates and faithful citizens.

The purpose for which the governors profess to employ the Hospital, is for the correction of harlots, night-walkers, pick-pockets, vagrants, disobedient servants, and such as are not to be reformed by the ordinary means of authority of parents and masters. These are committed by the Lord Mayor or Alderman. Apprentices are also sent by the Chamberlain of London. By the standing regulation the prisoners are obliged to beat hemp; and, supposing the nature of the offence to require it, they are whipped. –When I made the Hospital a visit, I did not discover that such rigid discipline was in use, except on extraordinary occasions. In more early days it might be presumed, that where labour began, vice ended.

The ancient mansion is spacious, but the labour done in it contributes so little to reformation, the objects sent out from their imprisonment are generally reputed to be much less moral than when they came into it.

The next extract was written about half a century after Hanway's, and was part of the evidence given to a Select Committee – a Parliamentary inquiry into a policy area. The format of these sources is that the question which follows the number was spoken by a member of the committee, and the text after the question mark repeats the answer from the witness, in this case Governor George Arthur, who was the recently retired Governor of the penal colony of Van Diemen's Land (now Tasmania) in Australia. As the numbers imply, the responses given below are from two different lines of questioning, but both from the same day.

Colonel George Arthur, Governor of Van Diemen's Land [Tasmania] 1823–36, from evidence to 1837 Select Committee on Transportation, pp. 289, 304 and 305.

4308. Then, according to your account, although a considerable degree of suffering is experienced in the colony, yet hardly any terror is produced in England by it?- I do not know what the effect is in England; I have seen the effect from those letters [from convicts, alluded to earlier in Arthur's evidence], but how far it has produced any further effect I do not know.

4309. Do you conceive that there was any apprehension in the minds of the criminals before they were fully informed of the system in Van Diemen's Land?- It always appeared to me, when they were liable; it always appeared to me to impress them in a very striking manner, and therefore I infer from that circumstance that they could not have been sensible of the extent of the punishment they would be liable to when they embarked.

4310. Then, according to your notion, they had no idea, or even a vague impression of the amount of suffering which might be inflicted upon them when they arrived in the colony?- I do not think they had the least conception of it.

4311. By the least conception, do you mean that they thought it less than it was in reality?- My opinion is, that that body of persons have very little reflection at all; they have a notion that they are going out to a colony, and that they are going to be assigned as servants, where they will get food and clothing.

4312. But if they are a set of people who have not any reflection at all, would it not be difficult to make any system of transportation so terrifying as to cause them to reflect?- I would answer that generally by saying, if the real state of convicts and the punishment to which they were liable were well known in this country, I think it would have as much effect in deterring men from committing crime as any punishment ever will have.

… 4466. You never contemplated the practicability of anything like complete separation in the colony?- Yes my Lord, I have tried the effect at Hobart Town of punishing men who have been sentenced to solitary confinement and hard labour on the tread-wheel. In the first place, they were sentenced to solitary confinement; that I found, after trying it some considerable time, to be almost wholly inoperative, the man appeared to me to adapt himself after a few days to his situation, and I do not think he felt the punishment of solitary confinement, neither did solitary confinement strictly operate bene-ficially as an example to others; they knew not what passed within the cell.

4479. Do you think in order to carry on a good system of road parties, that communication between the men should be cut off?- As far as possible; I would not say they should be placed in solitary confinement.

4480. That they should be prevented communicating with each other by words or signs?- Probably that is carried rather too far; I do not know that any advantage is derived from total silence; I think the contrary.

In the first extract, Hanway discusses the Bridewell in London. It is notable that the Bridewell is practising imprisonment largely for those who are convicted of less serious offences, whose main problem is seen to be a disorderly lifestyle, and who are out of control of the traditional sources of authority in eighteenth-century England: heads of household or employers. Clearly, the institution is sup-posed to be devoted to the *reformation* of prisoners through manual labour, and also in some cases to their *punishment* through whipping. The labour in question – pounding hemp plants with hammers – was remarkably monotonous work, which would not train the inmates in any useful skills. It is perhaps this factor, or maybe the lack of discipline that Hanway complained his work revealed, that makes him pessimistic about the Bridewell's ability to reform its inmates. Although he does not make this clear, it is likely that he thinks that the reason the released inmates are less moral than those who enter is because of the idleness they experience there, which gives them time to educate and socialize one another in criminal ways: the concept of 'contagion' which John Howard referred to in his 1777 work *The State of the Prisons*.

In the second extract, two of the themes are present. In the first part reproduced here (4308–4312) Arthur is responding to questions about the extent to which transportation of convicts could function as a *deterrent*, given that however harsh its conditions were, it was so far away from the United Kingdom that there was very little chance of the population having objective knowledge of the conditions. In the second half (4466–4480) Arthur is referring to the function of *rehabilitation*, through both the separate and the silent systems, which were designed to be imposed inside a prison rather than in a penal colony, and stating that he is not in favour of either. In both parts, the practicalities of transportation are interfering with the realization of the objects of punishment. In the first case, by its very nature transportation does not deter well, since any punishment is shrouded in mystery and occurs far away. In the second, Arthur appears to think that neither of the two penitentiary systems could be practically combined with penal labour.

Summary

In the early years of the twenty-first century, we can see two apparently contradictory trends – a fast-rising prison population leading to the largest total number of prisoners (nearly 80,000 in 2007); and the growth of a wide range of alternatives to custodial sentences. Anne Worrall, a leading authority on community sentences, has a pessimistic view of these developments:

> Our conceptual analysis of non-incarcerative sanctions was impoverished by our inability to think of them [community penalties] as anything other than 'alternatives' to prison... on the contrary, to the extent that they blur the boundaries between freedom and captivity, they cease to be genuine 'alternatives' and are merely poor substitutes for the 'real thing'. Life for many offenders at the end of the [twentieth] century is not so good that we can make limitless demands on them in the belief that they will endure anything to avoid prison. And we must stop pretending that the criminal justice system can find the answer to crime. (Worrall, 1997: 150)

If Worrall is correct in her analysis, and there does indeed need to be a wholesale reappraisal of the role of prison and of punishment in society, a starting point must be to re-visit some of the classic debates from our punitive past that this chapter has described.

STUDY QUESTIONS

1   How have the sometimes conflicting aims and principles of deterrence, rehabilitation, incapacitation and retribution been developed over time?

2   How and why have there been changes in the format and operation of punishment, i.e. penitentiaries, reformatories, the death penalty, corporal punishment and transportation?

3   How was penal-welfarism established, and what are its successes and failures?

FURTHER READING

Brown, A. (2003) *English Society and the Prison: Time, Culture and Politics in the Development of the Modern Prison, 1850–1920*, Woodbridge: Boydell.

Foucault, M. (1977) *Discipline and Punish: the birth of the prison*, Penguin: Harmondsworth [tr. Alan Sheridan].

Ignatieff, M. (1978) *A Just Measure of Pain: The Penitentiary in the Industrial Revolution 1750–1850*, Macmillan: London.

Spierenburg, P. (1995) 'The Body and the State', in N. Morris and D. J. Rothman (eds) *The Oxford History of the Prison: The Practice of Punishment in Western Society*, Oxford University Press: New York, pp. 49–78.

Weiner, M. (1990) *Reconstructing the Criminal: Culture, Law and Policy in England, 1830–1914*, Cambridge University Press: Cambridge.

Glossary

American War (1775–83) – Also known as the American Revolutionary War or the American War of Independence, this was a war between Great Britain and 13 settler colonies which declared themselves independent from the mother country and founded the United States of America in 1776.

Bentham, Jeremy (1748–1832) – As one of the most influential exponents of Utilitarianism, Jeremy Bentham had maintained that social organization had to be adjusted in such a way as to maximize human happiness, and that the best way to effect this was via a series of specialized government departments, controlling public administration from Whitehall. He was the designer of what might be termed the ideal surveillance prison – the Panopticon – which, for a variety of reasons, was never constructed.

Big Brother – originally coined by George Orwell in his novel *1984* (published in 1948), this term has come to symbolize anonymous surveillance, as in 'Big Brother is Watching You'. The Big Brother of the book watched citizens through a television set in each room of the house, although it was never clear whether there was actually anyone watching or not – therefore evoking the Panopticon. Many who use this term have now forgotten its origins, and yet it remains a powerful and critical comment on state powers of surveillance.

Borough – An administrative division used in England, generally denoting a self-governing town or city. Boroughs also usually had the right to elect a member of parliament. As part of a large reform of local government in 1974, boroughs were replaced by district councils.

City of London – The City of London is the historic core of the larger city of London itself. The boundaries of the City have remained the same since the Middle Ages, and hence it is now only a tiny part of the metropolis. Often also referred to as 'the City' or the 'Square Mile' (it is about that size). The City of London still maintains its own police force, as distinct from the Metropolitan Police serving the rest of the city.

Crank – A machine used in nineteenth-century prisons. Consisting of a wheel with a counting device fitted into a box of gravel, prisoners were required to turn the handle for a set number of rotations, moving the gravel around the box.

This had no useful function, but prisoners were often denied food or drink until a set number of rotations had been completed.

Decarceration – Literally, the opposite of incarceration. This term refers to the (often conscious) process of turning away from imprisonment towards different forms of punishment – including fines and correction in the community. At various points during the twentieth century (1908–39 in the UK, 1950–75 in the Netherlands, the 1980s in West Germany) prison populations have fallen significantly, despite the overall crime rate increasing.

Degeneration theory – Popular towards the end of the nineteenth century, this theory suggested that, just as Darwin had proposed that species evolved into more sophisticated forms over time, it was also possible that some people were degenerating into lower, more animalistic forms of being. Typically, the criminal element of the working class was identified as degenerate, due to a combination of inherited characteristics and the effects of unhealthy slum living.

Disciplines and sub-disciplines – Academic disciplines are branches of knowledge or fields of study which are found on university syllabuses at either undergraduate or post-graduate level. Disciplines are defined by the practitioners within it, the academic journals in which research is published, and usually, though not always, through the development of learned societies. Disciplines usually claim a particular and distinctive form of working or methodology, and comprise sub-disciplines or branches. For example, history contains ancient history, mediaeval history, modern history, and so on. Many see criminology as a sub-discipline of sociology (which others do not even recognize as a discipline). The boundaries between sub-disciplines are not fixed, and often seem difficult to locate. The disciplinary or sub-disciplinary boundaries between crime history and historical criminology are a case in point.

Eugenics – The term 'eugenics', first coined in 1883 by Francis Galton, was inspired by discoveries in biological sciences which suggested that behavioural traits could be traced to the genetic make-up of individuals, or families of individuals. A very influential theory which developed in many branches of natural and social sciences, it suggested that the human race could and should be improved through the breeding out of deficiencies such as mental retardation and inheritable diseases – including indolence, alcoholism, sexual deviance (including the urge to prostitution) and criminality. Taken up by the Nazis in Germany, it was part of the justification for the concentration camps, and for that reason the theory is rightly denounced. What has been largely forgotten is that eugenic theory was championed by many influential thinkers across Europe up to (and even after) the Second World War. If one looks carefully, eugenic theory can be seen in the background to many modern debates on the underclass and on the 'criminal gene'.

Factory – an abbreviation for manufactory or place where manufacturing takes place. The term is most commonly used to describe the huge textile mills created in Lancashire and Yorkshire in the 1820s and 1830s. These centralized labour, complete with supervisory system, behind walls in enclosed compounds. As factories developed they contained a linked system of steam-driven machines, and, in their highest form, a production line system with specialized workers employed on each stage of the manufacturing process. The factory remained the dominant form of industrial organization until the middle of the twentieth century, at least in the UK. Since the 1980s there has been an accelerating de-industrialization process, and nowadays factories and textile mills are no longer held to be the model for industrial progress.

Foucault, Michel (1926–84) – Foucault taught philosophy in Paris at the time of the 1968 student revolts, which influenced him to some extent. That year he joined with other intellectuals to form the Prison Information Group, an organization which attempted to provide prisoners with a means of communicating about their concerns as prisoners. In the following year he published the *Archaeology of Knowledge*. Like his later work, this book historically and theoretically analysed discourses within the context of specific historical practices. *Discipline and Punish: The origin of the prison*, his most influential book, was published in 1975 (translated into English in 1977). With this book, his work begins to focus on the technology of power. He examined power in relationship to both knowledge and the corporeal/physical body, focusing on what he sees as the coercive technologies of control over it. He argued that the modern prisons in the nineteenth century, like the army, the factory and the school, were mechanisms/technologies that used surveillance techniques that could be either real or merely assumed to exist (using Bentham's Panopticon as an example).

French Revolution – Taking place in 1789, the French Revolution marked the end of the *ancien regime* (the monarchy) in France and the birth of the Republic. Now, ostensibly at least, 'the people' were in charge of the nation, rather than a privileged ruler. Many of the nobility were executed publicly, and this caused a frisson of fear across Europe that similar events might unfold in other countries.

House of Correction – The first Houses of Correction date from the Tudor period. Also known as 'Bridewells', they continued in use until well into the nineteenth century. Over the centuries, however, their role changed from a place to contain and train vagrants and the idle, to a lock-up for petty criminals who the state were unwilling to expose to more hardened prisoners in gaol.

Industrial Revolution – During the late eighteenth and early nineteenth century, a series of technological advances meant that the British economy shifted from one based on agriculture and manual labour to one based on manufacture and machinery. This process had huge socio-economic and cultural effects for both Britain and the wider world.

Inquest jury – Coroners are independent judicial officers (usually lawyers but sometimes doctors). When a death is sudden, unexpected, or unnatural, a coroner will look into the matter and an inquest (an investigation into the death) may be held. Many inquests are held without a jury but in some circumstances one will be appointed. In these instances, it is the inquest jury rather than the coroner which makes the final decision (i.e. returns the verdict).

Inspectorate, HMI – There are three independent Home Office inspectorates relating to the criminal justice sphere – prisons, constabulary and probation. All are charged with ensuring the efficiency and cost-effectiveness of their area of jurisdiction. HMI Constabulary was set up in 1856, HMI Probation in 1936 and HMI Prisons in 1980.

Jurisdiction – Deriving from the Latin *ius/iuris* (meaning law) and *dicere* (meaning to speak), this is the formal authority given to a legal body to administer justice within a defined area or responsibility.

Justice of the Peace – the official title of a magistrate. These officials were (and indeed are) unpaid volunteers from the local community who serve in the lower criminal courts. Prior to the twentieth century, JPs tended to be prominent local landowners or industrialists, and were also likely to be heavily involved in local government.

Magistrate – see *Justice of the Peace*.

Night watch – An urban force, initially of householders but later composed of poorly-paid employees. It was the job of the night watch to guard the streets of the town or city at night, stop suspicious characters and enforce any curfews. They did not have the same legal powers as constables, and from the early nineteenth century were replaced by the new police forces.

Parish – An administrative subdivision. Originally deriving from the organization of the church, English parishes also undertook civil local government duties.

Parish constable – Before about 1800, parish constables were mainly householders who worked at the job part-time. From then on, more and more were semi-professional substitutes who held the office for a number of year in succession

Poor Law – Dating from 1601, the Poor Law Act specified community responsibility for the poor. Each parish had to appoint an overseer responsible for disbursing funds for the relief of the sick and elderly. The 1622 Act of Settlement allowed parishes to return paupers to their place of birth after 40 days. In 1834 the Poor Law Amendment Act was passed, requiring parishes to amalgamate into Unions and set up residential workhouses.

Quarter sessions – A court sitting four or six times a year, often moving around the county. Any member of the county bench of Justices of the Peace could sit on quarter sessions, whose members tried offences and dispensed punishment without a jury.

Recidivist – A repeat offender.

Residuum – A term which originated in the last third of the nineteenth century, the 'residuum' were the layer of society that contemporaries thought were, by virtue of their inability to adapt to the realities of mature industrial capitalism, confined to poor housing, poor education, the workhouse and ultimately the prison. Although causing widespread concern and anxiety, this putative group was not creating a rising tide of crime that could engulf respectable society, or challenge the authority of the state, but was considered by some commentators to be a persistent nuisance and drain on national resources. The term lost currency with the professionalization of welfare services and an increasing belief in the efficacy of medical treatment and social rehabilitation.

Select Committee – A committee made up of a small number of parliamentary members (either elected MPs or members of the House of Lords), appointed specifically to investigate and make recommendations on a particular issue. House of Commons Select Committees tend to consider matters relevant to government departments or agencies while those composed of members from the House of Lords consider more general topics. A Joint Committee is a Select Committee with members drawn from both houses. A Standing Committee (from 2006, Public Bill Committee) is one constituted to consider a specific Bill before Parliament.

Siege of Sydney Street – An infamous criminal case of 1911. Following the robbery of a jewellers and the murder of three police officers, the three Eastern European suspects were laid under siege in Sydney Street (East London). Winston Churchill as Home Secretary ordered in the Scots Guard in full battle regalia. The bodies of two of the criminals were found after the house was set on fire, but the third was never traced.

Standing Joint Committee – A county police authority, created by the 1888 Local Government Act. This took almost all local government functions in the countries of England and Wales out of the hands of the magistrates, and gave them to elected councillors. The exception was policing: the SJC was formed half from elected councillors and half from appointed magistrates.

Temperance – Temperance is the virtue of moderation. During the early part of the nineteenth century, when concern over the alcohol consumption of the working class was prevalent, a temperance movement arose advocating reducing or eliminating the consumption of alcoholic drinks.

'Ticket of Leave' system – An early form of probation, introduced by the Penal Servitude Act of 1853. Tickets were issued to convicts on release, allowing them free movement but only within set terms. For example, the 'ticket' might specify that they had to travel home from prison by a particular route, or within a certain period. Ticket-of-leave men were often suspected of committing crimes as soon as they were released.

Treadmill – A machine used in nineteenth-century prisons. Consisting of a revolving cylinder and a set of iron steps, prisoners could be required to walk the treadmill for up to six hours a day. This had no useful function but it was believed in the early part of the century that hard labour had reformative value.

Utilitarianism – A school of thought proposed by Jeremy Bentham and championed by later thinkers such as James and John Stuart Mill. Utilitarians believed that public policy should be determined by the 'principle of greatest happiness', and that this was the sole criterion of moral worth. In other words, whatever course of action resulted in a desired outcome for the largest number of people was the one which should be pursued.

Watch Committee – Elected from the members of a borough council, the Watch Committee was responsible for the oversight and direction of the city's police force.

Whig history – In formal terms, 'Whig' derives from the eighteenth-century British Whigs, who advocated the power of Parliament, as opposed to the autocratic power of the King and the aristocracy. The writers who described British constitutional history as a continual development of justice, harmony and civilization therefore became known as Whig historians. Today, it is associated with a type of historical writing which teleologically describes the past in terms of an inevitable progression towards the present. The past is therefore usually pejoratively described in comparison to a better present. For that reason, and others, Whiggish historians are now disparaged as lacking critical awareness (and often receive disproportionately harsh criticism). In crime history, the term is most often used in connection with historians of policing and prisons writing in the 1960s. The story of progress they described jarred with those experiencing the political turmoil of the late 1970s and 1980s. Whig history became the antithesis of the critical histories that used Marxist theory to explain the part the police and courts played in supporting traditional authority in the nineteenth century (and by implication the twentieth century).

Whitehall – A road in Westminster, London (running from Parliament to Charing Cross). Lined with ministries and other government departments, the term is used as a shorthand for government administration, as well as being the name of the surrounding geographical area.

Workplace appropriation – This is a contentious term, called a customary perk (perquisite) by some, and employee theft by others. The practice involves the taking home of workplace material by employees, and was increasingly criminalized in the eighteenth and nineteenth centuries. The factory introduced a supervisory and surveillance system partly in order to try to combat workplace appropriation.

Bibliography

Anderson, G. (1952) *Victorian Clerks*, Manchester: Manchester University Press.

Anon. (1994) *Looking out for you*, Home Office publication, HMSO: London.

Ashton, T. (1955) *An Economic History of England. The Eighteenth-Century*, Methuen: London.

Auletta, K. (1981) 'Underclass I', The New Yorker, Nov 16, pp. 63–161.

Auletta, K. (1982) *The Underclass*, Random House: New York.

Bagguley P. and Mann K. (1992) 'Idle thieving bastards?: scholarly representations of the "underclass"', *Work, Employment and Society*, 6(1): 113–26.

Bailey, V. (1993) 'The Fabrication of Deviance: "Dangerous Classes" and "Criminal Classes" in Victorian England', in J. Rule and R. Malcomson (eds) *Protest and Survival: The Historical Experience. Essays for E.P. Thompson*, London: Merlin Press, pp. 221–56.

Bartrip, P. (1981) 'Public Opinion and Law Enforcement: The Ticket-of-Leave Scares in mid-Victorian Britain', in V. Bailey (ed.) *Policing and Punishment in Nineteenth-Century Britain*, Rutgers University Press: New Brunswick.

Beattie, J.M. (1986) *Crime and the courts in England*, Princeton, NJ: Princeton University Press.

Benyon, J. and Solomos, J. (1990) 'Race, Injustice and Disorder' in S. Macgregor and B. Pimlott, *Tackling the Inner Cities. The 1980s Reviewed, Prospects for the 1990s*, Clarendon: Oxford.

Birmingham Journal (1840) 'Returns from Birmingham Police for June 23–30', July 4th Birmingham Local Studies Library: Birmingham.

Bittner, E. (1975) *The Functions of the Police in Modern Society: a review of background factors, current practices, and possible role models*, Aronson: New York.

Bottomley, A.K. and Pease, K. (1986) *Crime and Punishment: Interpreting the Data*, Open University Press: Milton Keynes.

Bourke, J. (2005) *Fear. A Cultural History*, Virago: London.

Brogden, M. (1982) *The Police: Autonomy and Consent*, Academic Press: London.

Brogden, M. (1991) *On the Mersey Beat: Policing Liverpool between the Wars*, Oxford University Press: Oxford.

Brown, A. (2003) *English Society and the Prison: Time, Culture and Politics in the Development of the Modern Prison, 1850-1920*, Woodbridge: Boydell.

Brown, A. and Barratt, D. (2002) *Knowledge of Evil: Child prostitution and child sexual abuse in twentieth century England*, Willan Publishing: Cullompton.

Burgoyne, C. (1997) '"Imprisonment the best punishment" The transatlantic exchange and communication of ideas in the field of penology, 1750-1820', Unpublished PhD thesis, University of Sunderland.

Burke, P. (1992) *History and Social Theory*, Polity: London.

Clancy, A., Hough, M., Aust, R. and Kershaw, C. (2001) 'Crime, Policing and Justice: the Experience of Ethnic Minorities - Findings from the 2000 British Crime Survey', *Home Office Research Study* 223, Home Office: London.

Clay, Revd. J. (1853) *Chaplain's Report on the Preston House of Correction*, Preston.

Clouston, T.S. (1906) *The Hygiene of Mind*, Methuen: London.

Cockett, R. (1994) *Thinking the Unthinkable. Think-Tanks and the Economic Counter-Revolution, 1931-83*, Harper Collins: London.

Cohen, S. (2002) *Folk Devils and Moral Panics: The Creation of Mods and Rockers*, Routledge: London.

Coleman, R. (2004) *Reclaiming the streets; surveillance, social control and the city*, Willan Publishing: Cullompton.

Coleman and Sim (2000) '"You'll never walk alone": CCTV surveillance, order and neo-liberal rule in Liverpool city centre', *British Journal of Criminology*, December, 51(4).

Colquhoun, P. (1800) *A Treatise on the Police of the Metropolis*, London.

Conley, C. (2005) 'War among Savages: Homicide and Ethnicity in the Victorian United Kingdom', *Journal of British Studies*, 44(4): 775-95.

Crawford, A. (1998) *Crime Prevention and Community Safety: Politics, policies and practices*, Longman: London.

Cressey, D. (1971) *Other People's Money: A Study in the Social Psychology of Embezzlement*, Belmont: Wadsworth.

Cretney, A. and Davis, G. (1995) *Punishing Violence*, Routledge: London.

Critchley, T.A. (1967) *A History of Police in England and Wales, 1900-1966*, Constable: London.

Critchley, T.A. (1970) *The Conquest of Violence. Order and Liberty in Britain*, Constable: London.

Dandaker, C. (1990) *Surveillance, Power and Modernity. Bureaucracy and discipline from 1700 to the present day*, Polity Press: Cambridge.

Daniel, W. (1968) *Racial Discrimination in England*, Penguin: Harmondsworth.

Davies, A. (1998) 'Youth gangs, masculinity and violence in late Victorian Manchester and Salford', *Journal of Social History*, 32(2): 349-69.

Davis, J. (1980) 'The London Garotting Panic of 1862: A Moral Panic and the Creation of a Criminal Class in mid-Victorian England', in V.A.C. Gatrell, B. Lenman and G. Parker (eds) *Crime and the Law. The Social History of Crime in Western Europe since 1500*, Europa: London.

Davis, J. (1987) 'The thief non-professional: Workplace appropriation in nineteenth-century London' (summary of paper), *Bulletin of the Society for the Study of Labour History*, 52.

Davis, J. (1989) 'Prosecutions and their Context: The use of the criminal law in later nineteenth-century London', in D. Hay and F. Snyder (eds) *Policing and Prosecution in Britain, 1750-1850*, Clarendon: Oxford. pp. 397-426.

Davies, S. (1996) *Big Brother: Britain's web of surveillance and the new technological order*, Pan Books: London.

D'Cruze, S. (1998) *Crimes of Outrage. Sex, violence and Victorian working women*, UCL Press: London.

Deflem, M. (2002) 'Technology and the internationalization of policing: A comparative-historical perspective', *Justice Quarterly*, 19(3): 453-75.

Deleuze, G. (1995) 'Postscript on the societies of control', *Negotiations*, Columbia University Press: New York.

Deveraux, S. (1999) 'The Making of the Penitentiary Act, 1775-1779', *The Historical Journal*, 42(2): 405-33.

Dickson, D. *Alternative Technologies*, Fontana: London.

Ditton, J. (1995) *Natural Criminology: An essay on the Fiddle*, Press Gang: Glasgow.

Dunbabin, J.P. (1963) 'The Politics of the Establishment of County Councils', in *The Historical Journal*, 6:2, 226-52.

Dunthorne, H. (1999) 'Beccaria and Britain', in D. Howell and K. Morgan (eds) *Crime, Protest and Police in Modern British Society: Essays in Memory of David J.V. Jones*, University of Wales Press: Cardiff.

Edwards, S. (1989) *Policing 'domestic' violence*, Sage: London.

Ekirch, R.A. (1987) *Bound for America: the transportation of British convicts to the colonies, 1718-1775*, Clarendon Press: Oxford.

Emsley, C. (1993) '"Mother, what did police do when there weren't any motors?". The law, police and the regulation of motor traffic in England, 1900-1939', *The Historical Journal*, 36, 357-82.

Emsley, C. (1996) *The English Police: A Political and Social History*, 2nd edition, Longman: Harlow.

Emsley, C. (2005) *Crime and Society in England, 1750-1900*, 3rd edition, Longman: Harlow.

Fattah, E. (1997) *Criminology. Past, present and future*, Macmillan: London.

'FD', 'Miss Margery Fry' (1958) *The Times*, 30 April.

Field, F. (1989) *Losing Out: The emergence of Britain's underclass*, Blackwell: Oxford.

Fielding, H. (1751) *An Enquiry into the Causes of the Late Increase of Robbers*, London.

Finnegan, F. (1982) *Poverty and Prejudice: A Study of Irish Immigrants in York, 1840-1875*, Cork University Press: Cork.

Forsythe, W.J. (1987) *The Reform of Prisoners, 1830-1900*, Croom Helm: London.

Foucault, M. (1977/1991 translated by Alan Sheridan) *Discipline and Punish. The Birth of the Prison*, Penguin: Harmondsworth.

Fukuyama, F. (1996) *Trust: The Social Virtues and the Creation of Prosperity*, Penguin: London.

Garland, D. (1985) 'The Criminal and His Science. A Critical Account of the Formation of Criminology at the End of the Nineteenth Century', *British Journal of Criminology*, 25(2): 109-37.

Garland, D. (1985) *Punishment and Welfare. A History of Penal Strategies*, Gower: Aldershot.

Garland, D. (1996) 'The Limits of the Sovereign State. Strategies of Crime Control in Contemporary Society', *The British Journal of Criminology*, 36(4): 445-71.

Garland, D. (2002) *The Culture of Control*, University of Chicago Press: Chicago.

Garland, D. (2002) 'Of Crimes and Criminals: The development of criminology in Britain', 3rd edition, in M. Maguire, R. Morgan and R. Reiner (eds) *The Oxford Handbook of Criminology*, pp. 7-50.

Gatrell, V.A.C. (1980) 'The decline of theft and violence in Victorian and Edwardian England' in V.A.C. Gatrell, B. Lenman and G. Parker (eds) *Crime and the Law: the social history of crime in early modern Europe*, Europa: London. pp. 238-337.

Gatrell, V.A.C. (1990) 'Crime, authority and the policeman-state' in F.M.L. Thompson (ed.) *The Cambridge Social History of Britain 1750-1950: Vol. 3 Social agencies and institutions*, Cambridge University Press: Cambridge, pp. 243-310.

Gatrell, V.A.C. and Hadden, T. (1972) 'Criminal statistics and their interpretation in E.A. Wrigley (ed.) *Nineteenth century social history: essays in the use of quantitative methods for the study of social data*, Cambridge University Press: London.

Gerzina, G. (1995) *Black England. Life Before Emancipation*, John Murray: London.

Gibson, M. (2002) *Born to Crime: Cesare Lombroso and the Origins of Biological Criminology*, Greenwood Press: Connecticut.

Giddens, A. (1995) *A Contemporary Critique of Historical Materialism*, 2nd edition, Macmillan: London.

Gilroy, P. (1987) *There Ain't no Black in the Union Jack*, Routledge: London.

Godfrey (1997) 'Policing the Factory, 1840-80', unpublished Ph.D thesis, Leicester University.

Godfrey, B. (1999) 'The Impact of the Factory on Workplace Appropriation in the Nineteenth Century', *British Journal of Criminology*, 39(1): 56-71.

Godfrey, B. (2002) 'Private Policing and the Workplace: The Worsted Committee and the Policing of Labour in Northern England, 1840-80', *Criminal Justice History Special Issue: Policing and War in Europe*, 16: 87-107.

Godfrey, B. (2003) 'Counting and accounting for the decline in non-lethal violence in England, Australia and New Zealand, 1880-1920', *British Journal of Criminology*, 43, 340-353.

Godfrey, B., Cox, D. and Farrall, S. (2007) *Criminal Lives: Family, Employment and Offending*, Clarendon Series in Criminology, Oxford University Press: Oxford.

Godfrey, B. and Lawrence, P. (2005) *Crime and Justice 1750-1950*, Cullompton: Willan Publishing.

Godfrey, B.S. and Locker, J.P. (2001) 'The Nineteenth-Century Decline of Custom, and its Impact on Theories of Workplace Theft and White-Collar Crime', *Northern History*, 38(2): 261-73.

Gottfredson, M. and Hirschi, T. (1990) *A General Theory of Crime*, Stanford University Press: Stanford.

Haggerty, K. (2006) 'Tear down the walls: on demolishing the panopticon', in D. Lyon (ed.) *Theorizing Surveillance. The panopticon and beyond*, Willan Publishing: Cullompton.

Haggerty, K. and Ericson, R. (2000) 'The surveillant assemblage', *British Journal of Sociology*, 51(4).

Hall, J. *Theft, Law and Society*, Bobbs-Merrill: Indianapolis.

Hall, S., Crichter, C., Jefferson, J.C., Robert, B. (1978) *Policing the Crisis: Mugging, the State and Law and Order*, Palgrave Macmillan: Basingstoke.

Hampton, M. (2004) *Visions of the Press in Britain, 1850-1950*, University of Illinois Press: Chicago.

Harris, J. (1995) 'Between civic virtue and Social Darwinism: the concept of the residuum', in D. Englander and R. O'Day (eds) *Retrieved Riches*, Scolar Press: Aldershot.

Hay, D. (1975) 'Property, Authority and the Criminal Law', in D. Hay, P. Linebaugh and J. Rule *Albion's Fatal Tree. Crime and Society in Eighteenth-Century England*, Allen Lane: London, pp. 17-63.

Hay, D. (1980) 'Crime and Justice in Eighteenth and Nineteenth Century England', *Crime and Justice*, 2: 45-84.

Hay, D. (1983) 'Manufacturers and the criminal law in the later eighteenth century', *Past and Present*, Colloquium on Policing, special issue.

Hay, D. and Snyder, F. (1989) 'Using the Criminal Law, 1750-1850: Policing, Private Prosecution, and the State', in D. Hay and F. Snyder, *Policing and Prosecution in Britain, 1750-1850*, Clarendon: Oxford.

Henderson, W. (1967) (ed.) *Engels. Selected Writings*, Penguin: London.

Henry, S. (1978) *The Hidden Economy: The context and control of borderline crime*, Martin Robertson: London.

Himmelfarb, G. (1984) *The Idea of Poverty. England in the Early Industrial Age*, Alfred Knopf: New York.

Hirst, J. (1994) 'The Australian Experience: the convict colony', in N. Morris and D.J. Rothman (eds) *The Oxford History of the Prison: The Practice of Punishment in Western Society*, New York: New York, Oxford University Press: pp. 263-96.

Hitchens, P. (2003) *A Brief History of Crime*, Atlantic Books: London.

Hobsbawm, E. (1968) 'Customs, wages and workload' in E. Hobsbawm, *Labouring Men, Studies in Labour History*, Weidenfield and Nicolson: London.

HMSO (1894) *Board of Trade Reports on the Volume and Effects of Recent Immigration from Eastern Europe*, HMSO: London.

Holdaway, S. (1996) *The Racialisation of British Policing*, Macmillan: London and New York.

Holmes, C. (1988) *John Bull's Island. Immigration and British Society, 1871-1971*, Macmillan: London.

Holmes, T. (1912) *London's Underworld*, Methuen: London.

Home Office (1909) *Judicial Statistics, England and Wales 1907, Part One-Criminal Statistics*, HMSO: London.

Honess T, and Charman E. (1992) 'Closed Circuit Television in public places', *Crime Prevention Unit*, 35, HMSO: London.

Hoppit, J. (1996) 'Political Arithmetic in Eighteenth-Century England', *Economic History Review*, 49: 3, 516-40.

Horn, D. (2003) *The Criminal Body: Lombroso and the Anatomy of Deviance*, Routledge: London.

Ignatieff, M. (1979), *A Just Measure of Pain. The Penitentiary and the Industrial Revolution*, Macmillan: London.

Ignatieff, M. (1983) 'State, civil society and total institutions', in S. Cohen and A. Scull (eds) *Social control and the state*, Oxford: Oxford University Press. pp. 75-106.

Innes, M. (2003) *Investigating murder: detective work and the police response to criminal homicide*, Oxford University Press: Oxford.

Ireland, R. (2004) 'The Angel and the Photocopier', *Criminal Justice History Special Issue: Policing and War in Europe*, 16.

Jackson, L. (2000) *Child Sexual Abuse in Victorian England*, Routledge: London.

Jackson, L. (2006) *Women Police: gender, welfare and survelliance in the twentieth century*, Manchester University Press: Manchester.

Jenkins, P. (1987) 'Into the upperworld? Law, crime and punishment in English society', *Social History*, 12.

Jewkes, Y. (2004) *Media and Crime*, Sage Publications: London.

Jewkes (2005)

Johnston, L. and Shearing, C. (2003) *Governing Security: Explorations in Policing and Justice*, Routledge: London.

Johnston, P. (1998) 'Serious white collar fraud: Historical and contemporary perspectives', *Crime, Law and Social Change*, 30(2).

Jones, D.J.V. (1992) *Crime in nineteenth-century Wales*, University of Wales Press: Cardiff.

Jones, M. (1993) 'Wedded to Welfare', *Sunday Times*, 11 July.

Kearon, T. and Godfrey, B. (2007) 'Setting the scene: A question of history', in S. Walklate (ed.) *Handbook of Victims and Victimology*, Cullompton: Willan.

Kershen, A. (2005) 'The 1905 Aliens Act', *History Today*, 55(3): 13–19.

King, P.J.R. (1999) 'Locating Histories of Crime', *Histories of Crime and Modernity: Special edition of the British Journal of Criminology*, 39(1): 161–74.

King, P. (2000), *Crime, Justice and Discretion in England 1740-1820*, Oxford University Press: Oxford.

Lafree, G. (2007) 'Expanding criminology's domain: The American Society of Criminology 2006 Presidential Address', *Criminology*, 45(1): 1–31.

Lawrence, P. (2000) 'Images of Poverty and Crime. Police Memoirs in England and France at the end of the Nineteenth Century', *Crime, Histoire & Sociétés/Crime, History and Societies*, 4(1): 63–82.

Lea, J. (2002) *Crime & Modernity: continuities in left realist criminology*, Sage Publications: London.

Lees, A. (1985) *Cities Perceived. Urban Society in European and American Thought, 1820-1940*, Manchester University Press: Manchester.

Leps, M-C. (1992) *Apprehending the Criminal: The production of deviance in nineteenth-century discourse*, Duke University Press: Durham/London.

Lianos, M. (2003) 'Social control after Foucault', *Surveillance and Society*, 1(3): 412–30.

Linebaugh, P. (1991) *The London Hanged. Crime and Civil Society in the Eighteenth Century*, Cambridge University Press: Cambridge.

Loader, I. and A. Mulcahy (2003) *Policing and the Condition of England: Memory, politics and culture*, Oxford University Press: Oxford.

Locker, J.P. (2005) '"Quiet thieves, quiet punishment": private responses to the "respectable" offender, c.1850-1930', *Crime, Histoire et societies/Crime, History and Societies*, 9(1): 9–31.

Locker, J. and Godfrey, B. (2006) 'Ontological boundaries and temporal watersheds in the development of white collar crime', in Godfrey, Karstedt and Levi '*Markets*, Risk and 'White-collar' Crimes: Moral Economies from Victorian times to Enron', *Special Edition, British Journal of Criminology*, 46(6).

Lombroso C. (1896) *L'uomo Delinquente*, Bocca: Torino, Italy.

Loveday, B. (2001) *Going Local: who should run Britian's police?* Policy Exchange: London.

Lyon, D. (1994), *The Electronic Eye. The Rise of Surveillance Society*, Polity Press: Cambridge.

Lyon, D. (2001) *Surveillance Society: Monitoring Everyday Life*, Open University Press: Buckingham.

Lyon, D. (2006) 'The search for surveillance theories', in D. Lyon (ed.) *Theorizing Surveillance. The panopticon and beyond*, Willan Publishing: Cullompton.

Macnicol, J. (1987) 'In Pursuit of the Underclass', *Journal of Social Policy*, 16(3): 293–318.

Mann, K. (1994) 'Watching the Defectives: Observers of the underclass in the USA, Britain and Australia', *Critical Social Policy*, 41: 79–99.

Mannheim, H. (1960) *Pioneers in Criminology*, Stevens: London.

Marglin, S. (1976), '"What do bosses do?" The Origins and Function of Hierarchy in Capitalist Production', in A. Gorz (ed.) *The Division of Labour: The labour process and class struggle in modern capitalism*, Allen Lane: Brighton.

Marglin, S. (1984) 'Knowledge and Power', in F. Stephen (ed.) *Firms, Organization and Labour, Approaches to the Economics of Work Organization*, Palgrave Macmillan: Basingstoke.

Mars, G. (1982) *Cheats at Work: An Anthology of Workplace Crime*, Allen & Unwin: London.

Marx, G. (2002) 'What's new about the "New Surveillance"? Classifying Change and Continuity', *Surveillance and Society*, 1(1): 9–29.

Maudsley, H. (1873) *Body and Mind*, Macmillan: London.

Mayhew, H. ([1851] 1861) *London Labour and the London poor. Vol 4, A cyclopaedia of the condition and earnings of those that will work, those that cannot work and those that will not work: Those that will not work; comprising prostitutes, thieves, swindlers, beggars... with introductory essay by W. Tuckniss*, Griffiths: London.

Mayhew, H. and Binney, J. (1862) *The Criminal Prisons of London*, London.

McCahill, M. (2002) 'On the threshold of the Panopticon? Analysing the employment of CCTV in European Cities and assessing its social and political impacts', *Urban Eye*, 1-28.

McCahill, M. (2002) *The surveillance web: the rise of CCTV in an English city*, Willan Publishing: Cullompton.

McConville, S. (1995) 'The Victorian Prison' in N. Morris and D.J. Rothman (eds) *The Oxford History of the Prison: The Practice of Punishment in Western Society*, Oxford University Press: New York, pp. 131-68.

McGowen, R. (1990) 'Getting to Know the Criminal Class in Nineteenth-Century England', *Nineteenth-Century Contexts*, 14(1): 33-54.

McGowen, R. (1995) 'The well-ordered prison: England 1780-1865' in N. Morris and D. Rothman (eds) *The Oxford History of the Prison: the practice of punishment in western society*, Oxford University Press: Oxford. pp. 71-99.

Melossi, D. (2000) 'Changing Representations of the Criminal', *British Journal of Criminology*, 40: 296-320.

Melossi, D. and Pavarini, M. (1981), *The Prison and the Factory. The Origins of the Penitentiary System*, Macmillan: London.

Mhlanga, B. (1997) *The Colour of English Justice*, Aldershot: Avebury

Modood, T., Berthoud, R., Lakey, K., Nazroo, J., Smith, P., Virdee, S. and Beishon, S. (1997) *Ethnic Minorities in Britain: Diversity and Disadvantage*, Policy Studies Institute: London.

Morris, L. (1994) *Dangerous Classes. The Underclass and Social Citizenship*, Routledge: London.

Morrison, W. (1896) *Juvenile Offenders*, Allen: London.

Murray, C. (1984) *Losing Ground: American Social Policy 1950-1980*, Basic Books: New York.

Murray, C. (1989) 'The Emerging British Underclass', *Sunday Times Magazine* November.

Murray, C. (1994) 'Underclass: The Crisis Deepens', *Sunday Times Magazine*, May.

Murray, C. (1999) *Charles Murray and the Underclass. The Developing Debate*, Institute of Economic Affairs: London.

Myers, N. (1996) *Reconstructing the Black Past. Blacks in Britain, c.1780-1830*, Frank Cass: London.

Newburn, T., Shiner, M. and Hayman, S. (2004) 'Race, Crime and Injustice? Strip Search and Treatment of Suspects in Custody', *British Journal of Criminology*, 44: 677-94.

Norris, C. and Armstrong, G. (1999) *The Maximum Surveillance Society: The rise of CCTV*, Berg: Oxford.

Norris, C. and Armstrong, G. (2002) 'To CCTV or not to CCTV. A review into the effectiveness of CCTV in reducing crime', Community Safety Practice Briefing, May, pp. 1-8.

Nott-Bower, Sir William (1926) *Fifty-two years a policeman*, Edward Arnold: London.

O'Leary, P. (2002) *Immigration and Integration. The Irish in Wales 1798-1922*, University of Wales Press: Cardiff.

Orwell, G. (1984) (originally written in 1948, but reprinted in many editions to the present day, and the full text is now available online at http://www.online-literature.com/orwell/1984/).

Paley, Ruth, (1998) *Before the Bobbies: The Night Watch and Police Reform in Metropolitan London, 1720-1830*, Stanford University Press: Stanford, California.

Parenti, C. (1999) *Lockdown America: Police and Prisons in the Age of Crisis*, Verso: London & New York.

Pearson, G. (1983) *Hooligan: a history of respectable fears*, Macmillan: London.

Peek, F. (1883) *Social Wreckage - A Review of the Laws of England as they Affect the Poor*, London.

Perkins, H. (1971) *The Age of the Railway*, Newton Abbot, David and Charles; and Dickens, 'Convict Capitalists', All the Year Round, no.3.

Philips, D. (1977) *Crime and Authority in Victorian England: the Black Country 1835-1860*, Croom Helm: London.

Philips, D. (1993) 'Crime, law and punishment in the Industrial Revolution', in P. O'Brien and R. Quinault (eds) *The Industrial Revolution and British Society*, Cambridge University Press: Cambridge.

Philips, D. (2001) *William Augustus Miles. Crime, Policing and Moral Entrepreneurship in England and Australia*, University of Melbourne: Melbourne.

Philips, D. (2003) 'Three "moral entrepreneurs" and the creation of a "criminal class" in England, c.1790s-1840s', *Crime, Histoire & Sociétés/Crime, History and Societies*, 7(1): 79-107.

Phillips, C. and Bowling, B. (2002) 'Racism, Ethnicity, Crime and Criminal Justice', in M. Maguire, R. Morgan and R. Reiner, *The Oxford Handbook of Criminology*, 3rd edition, Oxford University Press: Oxford.

Pick, D. (1989) *Faces of Degeneration. A European Disorder, c.1848-1918*, Cambridge University Press: Cambridge.

Pike, L.O. (1875/1968) *A History of Crime in England, Illustrating the Changes of the Laws in Progress of Civilization*, Smith, Elder and Co.: London (reprinted by Patterson Smith: London).

Plint, T. (1851) *Crime in England: its relation, character and extent as developed from 1801 to 1848*. London.

Porter, T. (1981) 'The Calculus of Liberalism: The Development of Statistical Thinking in the Social and Natural Sciences in the Nineteenth Century'. Ph.D. dissertation, Princeton University.

Poster, M. (1990) *The Mode of Information*, Polity: Cambridge.

Poynter, J.R. (1969) *Society and Pauperism. English Ideas on Poor Relief, 1795-1834*, Routledge and Kegan Paul: London.

Pratt, J. (1997) *Governing the Dangerous. Dangerousness, law and social change*, The Federation Press: Sydney.

Quetelet, L. (1831) 'Recherches sur le Penchant au Crime aux Différent Agres' in *Nouvaux Mémoires de l' Académic*, 1, 80-1.

Radzinowicz, Sir Leon (1948) *A History of English Criminal Law and its Administration Since 1750, Vol. 1: The Movement for Reform*, Pilgrim Trust, Stevens and Sons Ltd: London.

Radzinowicz, Sir Leon (1965) 'Ideology and Crime: The Deterministic Position', *Columbia Law Review*, 65:6, 1047-60.

Rafter, N-H. (1997) *Creating Born Criminals*, University of Illinois Press: Chicago.

Rawlings, P. (1999) *Crime and Power. A History of Criminal Justice 1688-1998*, Longman: London.

Reiner, R. (1990) 'Crime and Policing', in A. Macgregor and B. Pimlott (eds) *Tackling the Inner Cities. The 1980s Reviewed, Prospects for the 1990s*, Clarendon Press: Oxford.

Reiner, R. (1991) *Chief Constables: bobbies, bosses or bureaucrats?* Oxford University Press: Oxford.

Reith, C. (1943) *British Police and the Democratic Ideal*, Oxford University Press: London.

Reynolds E.A. (1998) *Before the Bobbies: The Night Watch and Police Reform in Metropolitan London, 1720-1830*, Macmillan: Basingstoke.

Richardson, C. (1976) 'The Irish in Victorian Bradford', *The Bradford Antiquary*, ix: 294-316.

Robb, G. (1992) *White-Collar Crime in Modern England: Financial Fraud and Business Morality, 1845-1929*, Cambridge University Press: Cambridge.

Rock, P. (2003) 'Sociological theories of crime', in M. Maguire, R. Morgan and R. Reiner, *The Oxford Handbook of Criminology*, 3rd edition, Oxford University Press: Oxford, pp. 51-83.

Rose, N. (1999) *Powers of Freedom. Reframing Political Thought*, Cambridge University Press: Cambridge.

Rose, N. (2000) 'Government and control', *British Journal of Criminology*, 40: 321-39.

Rule, J. (1981) *The Experiences of Labour in Eighteenth-Century Industry*, Croom Helm: London, pp. 124-46.

Rule, J. (1986) *The Labouring Classes in Early Industrial England, 1750-1850*, Longman: London, pp. 107-38.

Rylands, L.G. (1889) *Crime: Its Causes and Remedy*, T. Fisher Unwin: London.

Samuel, R. (1981) *People's History and Socialist Theory*, Routledge: London.

Sharpe, J.A. (1999) *Crime in Early Modern England, 1550-1750*, 2nd edition, Longman: London.

Shearing C. and Stenning, P. (1996) 'From the Panopticon to Disney World: The Development of Discipline' reprinted in J. Muncie, E. MacLaughlin and M. Langan *Criminological Perspectives: A Reader*, Sage Publications: London.

Sheffield Watch Committee (1855) *Sheffield Watch Committee Minutes*, [unpub.] City Archives: Sheffield.

Shore, H. (1999) *Artful Dodgers. Youth and crime in early 19th century London*, The Boydell Press: Woodbridge.

Sim, J. (1990) *Medical Power in Prisons. The prison medical service in England 1774-1989*, Open University Press: Buckingham.

Simon, B. (2003) 'The return of Panopticism: Supervision, subjection and the new surveillance', *Surveillance and Society*, 1(3): 1-20.

Sindall, R. (1983) 'Middle-Class Crime in Nineteenth-Century England', *Criminal Justice History. An International Annual*, 4: 23-40.

Sindall, R. (1987) 'The London Garotting Panics of 1856 and 1862', *Social History*, 12: 351-9.

Sindall, R. (1990) *Street violence in the nineteenth century: media panic or real danger?* Leicester University Press: Leicester.

Skocpol, T. (1984) 'Sociology's Historical Imagination', in T. Scocpol (eds) *Vision and Method in Historical Sociology*, Cambridge University Press: Cambridge.

Smith, D. (1992) 'Race, Crime and Criminal Justice', in M. Maguire, R. Morgan and R. Reiner, *The Oxford Handbook of Criminology*, 1st edition, Oxford University Press: Oxford

Smith, D. (1997) 'Ethnic Origins, Crime, and Criminal Justice', in M. Maguire, R. Morgan and R. Reiner, *The Oxford Handbook of Criminology*, 2nd edition, Oxford University Press: Oxford.

Soderlund, R. (1998) '"Intended as a Terror to the Idle and the Profligate": Embezzlement and the Origins of Policing in the Yorkshire Worsted Industry, c.1750-1777', *Journal of Social History*, 31(3).

Spierenburg, P. (1995) 'The Body and the State' in N. Morris and D.J. Rothman (eds) *The Oxford History of the Prison: The Practice of Punishment in Western Society*, Oxford University Press: New York, pp. 49-78.

Stedman Jones, G. (1976) *Outcast London*, Penguin: London.

Stedman Jones, G. (2002) *Outcast London. A study in the relationship between classes in Victorian Society*, Open University Press: Milton Keynes.

Steedman, C. (1984) *Policing the Victorian Community: the formation of English provincial police forces, 1856-80*, Routledge and Kegan Paul: London.

Stone, D. (2001) 'Race in British Eugenics', *European History Quarterly*, 31, 3, pp. 397-425.

Storch, R. (1975) 'The plague of the blue locusts: police reform and popular resistance in northern England, 1840-57', *International Review of Social History*, 20, 61-89.

Storch, R. (1976) 'The Policeman as Domestic Missionary; Urban Discipline and Popular Culture in Northern England, 1850-80', *Journal of Social History*, IX: 481-509.

Storch, R.D. and Philips, D. (1998) *Policing Provincial England, 1829-1856: The Politics of Reform*, Leicester University Press, London.

Styles, J. (1983) 'Embezzlement, Industry and the Law in England, 1500-1800', in M. Berg et al., *Manufacture in Town and Country before the Factory*, Cambridge University Press: Cambridge.

Sullivan, R. (2000) *Liberalism and Crime: the British Experience*, Lexington Books: Lanham.

Sutherland, E.H. (1940) 'White Collar Criminality', *American Sociological Review*, 5(1).

Sutherland, E.H. (1941) 'Crime and Business', *Annals of the American Academy of Political and Social Science*, 217.

Sutherland, E.H. (1945) 'Is "White Collar Crime" Crime?', *American Sociological Review*, 10.

Sutherland, E.H. (1949) *White Collar Crime*, Holt, Rinehart & Winston: New York.

Sutherland, E. and Cressey, D. (1955) *Principles of Criminology*, 5th edition, Lippencott: Chicago.

Swift, R. (1984) 'Another Stafford Street Row: Law, Order and the Irish presence in mid-Victorian Wolverhampton', *Immigrants and Minorities*, 3(1): 5-29.

Swift, R. and Gilley, S. (eds) (1989) *The Irish in Britain 1815-1931*, Barnes and Noble: London.

Taylor, D. (1998) *Crime, Policing and Punishment in England, 1750-1914*, Macmillan: Basingstoke.

Taylor, D. (2002) *Policing the Victorian Town. The development of the police in Middlesbrough c.1840-1914*, Palgrave Macmillan: Basingstoke.

Thompson, E.P. (1967) 'Time, work-discipline and industrial capitalism', *Past and Present*, 38: 56-97.

Thompson, E.P. (1975) *Whigs and Hunters: The Origins of the Black Act*, Allen Lane: London.

Tobias, J. (1967) *Crime and Industrial Society in the Nineteenth Century*, Penguin: Harmondsworth.

Van Oss, S.F. (1898) 'The "Limited-Company" Craze', *The Nineteenth Century*, 43.

Waddington, P.A.J. (1994) *Liberty and order: Public order policing in a capital city*, UCL Press: London.

Wade, J. (1829) *Treatise on the Police and Crimes of the Metropolis*, London.

Walvin, J. (1973) *Black and White. The Negro and British Society 1555-1945*, Allen Lane: London.

Weaver, M. (1994) 'The new science of policing: crime and the Birmingham police force, 1839-1842', *Albion*, 26: 289-308.

Wells, H. (2005) 'The fast and the furious', paper to the British Criminology Conference, Leeds.

Welshman, J. (2006a) 'The concept of the unemployable', *Economic History Review*, LIX(3): 578-606.

Welshman, J. (2006b) *Underclass. A History of the Excluded, 1880-2000*, Hambledon: London.

Westmarland, L. (2001) *Gender and Policing. Sex, Power and Police Culture*, Willan Publishing: Cullompton.

Whitfield, J. (2004) *Unhappy Dialogue. The Metropolitan Police and black Londoners in post-war Britain*, Willan Publishing: Cullompton.

Wiener, M. (1990) *Reconstructing the Criminal: Culture, Law and Policy in England, 1830-1914*, Cambridge University Press: Cambridge.

Williams, C.A. (1998) 'Police and Crime in Sheffield, 1818-1873', Unpublished PhD thesis, University of Sheffield.

Williams, C.A. (2000) 'Expediency, authority and duplicity: reforming Sheffield's police 1832-1840' in R. Trainor and R. Morris (eds) *Urban Governance: Britain and Beyond since 1750*, Ashgate: Aldershot, pp. 115-27.

Williams, C.A. (2003) 'Police surveillance and the emergence of CCTV in the 1960s', *Crime Prevention and Community Safety: An International Journal*, 5(3): 27-37.

Williams, C.A. (2004) 'The Sheffield Democrats' critique of criminal justice in the 1850s' in R. Colls and R. Rodger (eds) *Cities of Ideas: Civil Society and Urban Governance in Britain 1800-2000*, Ashgate: Aldershot, pp. 96-120.

Wilson, W.J. (1987) *The Truly Disadvantaged*, University of Chicago Press: Chicago.

Winder, R. (2005) *Bloody Foreigners. The Story of Immigration to Britain*, Abacus: London.

Wood, J.C. (2004) *Violence and Crime in Nineteenth Century England: The shadow of our refinement*, Routledge: London.

Worrall, A. (1997) Punishment in the community: the future of criminal *justice*, Longman: London.

Wright Mills, C. (1959) *The Sociological Imagination*, Oxford University Press: New York.

Yar, M. (2003) 'Panoptic power and the pathologisation of vision: Critical reflections on the Foucauldian thesis', *Surveillance and Society*, 1(3): 254-71.

Young, J. (1999) *The Exclusive Society. Social exclusion, crime and difference in late modernity*, Sage Publications: London.

Young, J. (2002) 'Crime and Social Exclusion', in M. Maguire, R. Morgan and R. Reiner (eds) *The Oxford Handbook of Criminology*, 3rd edition, Oxford University Press: Oxford.

Young, M. (1991) *An Inside Job: Policing and Police Culture in Britian*, Clarendon Press: Oxford.

Zureik, E. and Salter, M. (eds) (2005) *Who and What Goes Where: Global Policing and Surveillance*, Willan Publishing: Cullompton.

Index

NOTE: Page numbers in **bold** type refer to glossary entries, page numbers followed by 'n.' refer to notes.

Contents

About the Author

Phillip C. Shon is an Associate Professor of Criminology at the University of Ontario Institute of Technology. He holds a bachelor's degree in philosophy, a master's degree in linguistics, and a PhD in criminal justice. His research examines the sociolinguistic organization of police–citizen encounters and nineteenth-century American parricides. His works have appeared in journals such as the *International Roundtable for the Semiotics of Law, Discourse & Society, Punishment & Society, International Journal of Law and Psychiatry, International Journal of Offender Therapy and Comparative Criminology, Journal of Investigative Psychology and Offender Profiling,* and the *Journal for the Psychoanalysis of Culture and Society.* For fun, he lifts weights and watches Asian gangster movies (not at the same time). He still has aspirations of becoming a professional wrestler someday.

Acknowledgements

In another work, I stated that acknowledgements and citations are the currency with which intellectual debts are paid. Since then, I have made a small down payment, but now find that I have incurred additional debts. I'm not sure if I can pay them back. This state of being in perpetual debt, it seems, is not atypical; rather, it is an unavoidable feature of life in the academy. Luckily, I happen to be surrounded by good people who do not mind being creditors. Here, again, I would like to thank those who have helped me shape the ideas in this book.

I am much indebted to Dr Brian Cutler for providing me with the initial impetus to write a book about this topic. Otherwise, this book might not have materialized. Of course, recognizing potential in its nascent form is possible precisely because that template has already been forged and refined from years of experience and unparalleled achievements as a distinguished scholar. I am grateful to Dr Steven Downing for reading and providing helpful comments and feedback on earlier drafts. I am also heavily indebted to Dr Kimberley Clow for providing obsessively helpful comments and feedback on several chapters; she also helped me to navigate the complexities and subtleties of psychology journal articles. To my aforementioned colleagues at the University of Ontario Institute of Technology, thank you. To my partner-in-crime "Stonecold" Rick, thanks for the "So what?" And to my most trusted friend, colleague, and confidant, CWW, thanks – for everything. You know who you are.

Thanks to the wonderful students in Canada and at the University of Ontario Institute of Technology for being so receptive and open to the idea of the reading code. I know it was painful reading with a ruler, a highlighter, and a pen. I understand. For that, I am grateful to the students in SSCI 4099U (Winter 2010, 2011) and SSCI 5020G (Fall 2010) for their patience.

Although my teachers at Northeastern Illinois University will not – nor care to – remember me, I have not forgotten my professors who tried to teach me to be a critical thinker and a reader. I am quite certain that that was not an easy task, and I am not entirely sure that they succeeded. But that fault is mine. In particular, Dr Roger Gilman, Dr Sarah Hoagland, and Dr Stanley Kerr taught me to love and pursue wisdom for intrinsic ends. They may not know – and they may not even care – that they altered the course of my life, but I will now say what I could not have said 20 years ago: thank you for molding me into the form of a scholar. I am stumbling along, but hope to be able to walk on my own someday.

Dr Kerr passed away when I was away from home. I didn't get a chance to say my final farewell. I want you to know that my heart still shakes when I read Nietzsche, and that I still can't turn a page of *Will to Power* without thinking of you. *Let the world perish, but let there be philosophy, the philosopher, you.*

Phillip C. Shon

Introduction

Previous works that provide tips on how to successfully write research papers, theses, dissertations, and journal articles have emphasized that writing is like any other skill: it has to be developed, taught, and practiced daily (Cone & Foster, 2006; Glatthorn & Joyner, 2005; Miller, 2009; Rudestam & Newton, 2001; Silvia, 2007). Although graduate students are taught how to teach during their graduate education, through seminars and by working as teaching assistants, Silvia (2007, p. 6) laments that they are not taught how to write: "the most common model of training is to presume that graduate students will learn about writing from their advisors." The same argument could be made about reading.

In previous works, readers are taught how to structure their time to facilitate writing, how to outline their thoughts to prepare to write, how to structure a paper to submit to a journal, and how to conceptualize any "action that is instrumental in completing a writing project" as writing (Silvia, 2007, p. 19). Professional academic writing, Paul Silvia writes, is serious business that entails tremendous complexity, as the literature on a given topic must be extensively covered, data carefully analyzed, and the descriptions of research methods precisely worded (see Landrum, 2008; Noland, 1970). To do so, Silvia writes that we may even have to read scientific journal articles we do not particularly like. The act of reading, again, is treated as a tertiary activity, necessarily subservient to and less consequential than writing.

This book is necessary because reading is often a blindly assumed and unexamined part of the writing – and graduate education – process. If writing is learned throughout graduate school, as part of the thesis, dissertation, and journal-writing process, then, to my knowledge, no such formal and systematic training exists for reading in the social sciences; instead, students bring to graduate school the reading habits and techniques they acquired in high school. With the possible exception of philosophy and literary criticism, where careful reading is taught to students at the graduate level, disciplines in the social sciences tacitly expect students to already be competent readers.

With such an unexamined assumption in place, it is not surprising that advanced undergraduates and graduate students have trouble reading critically in order to write research papers and theses. Rather than assuming that students already possess the skills necessary to be a critical reader, this book teaches students – advanced undergraduate students writing honors' theses and graduate students writing theses – how to read so that they are able to maximize their output in the writing process.

This book illuminates the steps in the prewriting process that scholars in the field have uncritically presupposed in the practice (not theory) of writing and reading. For example, I am sure that students, at one time or another throughout their career, have heard the directive, "You have to read critically" from their professors. The problem with that benign advice is that telling someone to do something is meaningless unless how to do that something is actually taught. The numerous how-to books on the market do little better. That is, in such books, readers are given general and vague instructions on how to read critically; they are told that a good critique of the literature is developed from "careful readings." Others advise that readers need to maintain a "critical perspective." The problem common to all such benign prescriptions is that no one has explicitly unpacked what it means to read "critically." Again, the travel destination is told, but the map is not provided.

According to others who have written on this topic, "critical" reading is important because it allows readers to develop new ideas, claims, and unique "spins" if they don't have new ideas of their own. Research articles in social science journals, however, are necessarily full of new and yet-to-be-developed ideas. A gap or a deficiency in the literature – absence of new ideas – is the reason why scholars write journal articles; that's why authors discuss limitations of their research and recommendations for future works in the papers they are writing – as a tacit way of setting up the work they will do in the future or providing an itinerary for others who may want to remedy that gap in the literature. Simply put, critiques are embedded in bits and pieces in journal articles; readers just have to be taught how to decipher them in the text. Writers have difficulty developing new ideas because they have not learned the art of textual criticism and critical reading – not because new ideas do not exist. Using my reading code sheet (see Figure 1), this book teaches students how to approach social science journal articles as texts that can be deciphered structurally, mechanically, and grammatically. This book thus fills in the content of general advice such as "read critically" by teaching students the techniques of critical reading.

Code Location in Text	CODE	MEANING
Intro/Lit Review	WTD	**What They Do**: what the author(s) purport to do in a paper/book; this code captures the main research question that the author is posing in the text.
Lit Review	SPL	**Summary of Previous Literature**: this sentence, paragraph, or page describes a simple summary of the results from prior studies. This process entails a tremendous amount of condensation, taking complex ideas and reducing them into paragraphs, sentences, and if the author is brilliant, one word.
Lit Review	CPL	**Critique of Previous Literature**: the author is providing a critique and a limitation of the previous and existing scholarly works. CPL is conceptually related to POC, GAP, and SPL since the deficiencies in the existing works provide a theoretical, methodological, and analytical justification as to why the current work is warranted. CPL usually follows SPL since the author has to first proffer a body of ideas before it can be criticized.
Lit Review	GAP	**Gap**: the author is (probably in some systematic way) pointing out the missing elements in current literature. When GAP and CPL are done properly, a reader should be able to anticipate the RAT even before the author declares it.
Lit Review	RAT	**Rationale**: the author is providing the justification of why the work is necessary and warranted. RAT should be deduced and logically follow if the author has CPLed and GAPed previous literature.
Results/ Discussion	ROF	**Results of Findings**: describes the primary results of the current article. This code is usually found in the abstract, results section, and conclusion since this point must be hammered at least three times in most social scientific journals.
Discussion	RCL	**Results Consistent with Literature**: describes the findings of the current work that are consistent with the existing literature. That is, the author's own work supports the work that others have done.
Discussion	RTC	**Results To the Contrary**: describes the findings of the current work that are inconsistent with the existing literature. That is, the author's own work does not support the work that others have done.
Conclusion	WTDD	**What They Did**: what the author(s) have done in a paper/book; a logical and sequential cognate of WTD. This code captures the main research question that the author has answered and contributed to the body of literature on the chosen topic.
Conclusion	RFW	**Recommendations for Future Works**: the current work is not complete; the author is providing a map of what is still lacking (GAP) in the literature and recommending that others do in future work.
		Reading Strategies
	POC	**Point of Critique**: a deficiency in the current article or literature that YOU (the student author) could critique and exploit as a way of remedying the gap in the literature for a future paper.
	MOP	**Missed Obvious Point**: the author that you are reading has missed an obvious theoretical, conceptual, and analytical connection to earlier works. (MOP usually occurs when the article's author has not read sufficiently or widely.)
	RPP	**Relevant Point to Pursue**: and mine in another paper. Although this code does not point out any limitations and gaps in the current work, the stated point could be used as a POC in a future paper. Obviously, RPP entails MOP and GAP.
	WIL	**Will** this theoretical and conceptual connection be logically teased out to its conclusion to reconcile a text that is fraught with tension and needs resolving?

FIGURE 1   Dr Phil's Reading Code Sheet for Social Science Journal Articles

Another significant problem that is not adequately addressed in previous work is one of management. Let's suppose that a beginning graduate student is writing a thesis on a chosen topic, and has identified 50 peer-reviewed journal articles that have been published within the past 15 years. Is there a way to read the articles that will enhance the writing process by organizing the themes and patterns in the literature as well as their critiques? Most how-to books recommend the use of 3 × 5 index cards as a way of organizing and collating relevant information to be used during the reading, outlining, and writing process. To be able to even come up with a rough outline, however, the student will have to have digested and organized the readings in a particular way; and unless that student sat down with a blank sheet of paper and kept track of recurring themes, patterns, and gaps in the literature, the critique of the literature that should have emerged is apt to get lost in the unstructured reading.

The reading code sheet that I have developed systematizes the reading, note-taking, and organizing of voluminous amounts of information in an easily identifiable and retrievable format.

My proposed book on reading explains how to use ten (10) codes directly related to "critical" reading of social science journal articles that others have presupposed but left unexplored (e.g., SPL, CPL, GAP, RAT, RCL), and four (4) strategic reading codes necessary to critique and cultivate a reader's new ideas and claims (e.g., POC, MOP, WIL). By illuminating and elaborating on the previously assumed aspects of "critical" reading, this book attempts to teach students how to read so that the major conceptual divisions and subdivisions of research papers and theses can be logically organized during the act of reading.

There are other books that teach students how to understand and digest existing research. Most of the how-to books in academia, with the possible exception of Paul Silvia's (2007) *How to Write a Lot*, suffer from a major shortcoming: they are unwieldy. For example, *Reading and Understanding Research* (Locke et al., 2010) is 312 pages long; *How to Write a Master's Thesis* (Bui, 2009) is 320 pages; *Surviving Your Dissertation: A Comprehensive Guide to Content and Process* (Rudestam, 2007) is 328 pages; even *Conducting Research Literature Reviews: From the Internet to Paper* (Fink, 2010) is a whopping 272 pages. A book that teaches students how to read cannot be long and cumbersome; it needs to be succinct, concise, and operational – not long-winded and theoretical. *How to Read Journal Articles in the Social Sciences* meets that goal.

This book is directed at graduate students and upper-level undergraduates. This book's primary aim is to be used as a supplementary text in first-year professional seminars for graduate students, and as a supplementary text that undergraduate honor's thesis supervisors, and directors of teaching and learning centers in colleges and universities can recommend to their students.

How to Read Journal Articles in the Social Sciences will be relevant and helpful in preparing their students to write original research papers, literature reviews, and theoretically-oriented essays in undergraduate writing courses.

A book like *How to Read Journal Articles in the Social Sciences* will be particularly useful as preparatory reading material to international students who are preparing to go abroad to North America, the United Kingdom, and Australia for their studies, particularly students from Asia. First, China, India, and Korea comprise the largest share of international students who come to North America for undergraduate and graduate education. Second, even native speakers of English experience difficulty reading and writing social science texts when they enter graduate school. That's because they have not been taught how to do so.

International students who speak English as a second language therefore have to shoulder a double burden: (1) they have to acquire sociolinguistic competence as second-language speakers in order to function in their new social milieu; (2) they have to acquire vocabulary competence in their respective disciplines and in academic writing. Rather than trying to comprehend and act on vague instructions from their professors and thesis advisors about "reading critically" and "synthesizing the literature" during the writing process, my book will teach students how to read so that they can organize information during their reading to be able to write more effectively. Being prepared to read critically during their studies will help international students overcome burden #2 before they encounter it.

Organization of the book

Chapter 1: Serial Killers and Book Reports: This chapter provides an anecdotal account of a commonly occurring scenario in criminology and criminal justice courses, perhaps in other academic disciplines as well: students wanting to write "research papers" on serial killers. Using the author's experiences with undergraduate students who write book reports – not research papers or review articles – on serial killers, this chapter introduces readers to the origins of the reading code sheet.

Chapter 2: Trying to Fix Mechanical and Structural Writing Problems with Abstract Tools: This chapter begins with one of the most perplexing and mysterious aspects of paper writing in colleges and universities – how professors arrive at the grades they assign to students' papers. In elaborating on the exigencies that untenured assistant professors face, I describe the necessity and the origins of the grading code sheet that preceded the reading code sheet. I relate the failures I encountered trying to teach students how to write research papers and theses using the grading code sheet.

Chapter 3: Three Types of Stains and False Assumptions about Writing: Using Barbara Ehrenreich's (2001) descriptive account of her stint as a maid cleaning toilets, this chapter challenges a fundamentally false assumption about writing that some authors make in their works – the difference between performance of an activity and its description. Rather than explaining writer's block as one attributable to motivation, this chapter argues that writer's blocks are attributable to one of poor reading technique and information management.

Chapter 4: Should I Even Read This? How to Read the Abstract, General Introduction, and Methods Section: This chapter teaches students how they ought to read the abstract, introduction, and the methods section using the reading code sheet. By learning how to read the abstract, this chapter attempts to show students how to mine for the pertinent information necessary to determine if an article should be included in their literature review without actually reading the entire paper. By learning how to critically read introductions, the practice of anticipatory reading is demonstrated, whereby students use the elements contained in it to rehearse and anticipate the shape of the more complex arguments to emerge in the rest of the text. Students are also taught how to use one particular reading code, Point of Critique (POC), in their reading of the data and methods section to cultivate a methodological critique of previous studies along with a rationale for their own proposed works. This chapter will select excerpts from social science journals in sociology, criminology, communication, and psychology to demonstrate the applicability of the reading code sheet to the social sciences.

Chapter 5: So What? How to Read the General Literature Review, Psychology Introductions, and Results Section: This chapter teaches students how they ought to read the literature review using the reading code sheet. Students will learn the rudiments of structural and grammar-based reading to anticipate emergent critiques, hypothesis generation, and rationale for a study – hence answering the "so what?" question. Students are also taught how to make the transition from the act of reading the results (ROF) section to organizing summaries (SPL) as part of their own writing process. This chapter will select excerpts from social science journals in sociology, criminology, communication, and psychology to demonstrate the applicability of the reading code sheet to the social sciences.

Chapter 6: Becoming a Part of the Scholarly Community: How to Read the Discussion and Conclusion: This chapter teaches students how they ought to read the discussion and conclusion using the reading code sheet. Students will learn how key words in both sections of journal articles tether our work to those of previous researchers. This chapter will select excerpts from social science journals in sociology, criminology, communication, and psychology to demonstrate the applicability of the reading code sheet to the social sciences.

Chapter 7: Highlighting and Organizing the ROF, SPL, CPL, GAP, RFW, and POC: This chapter provides practical tips for using the accoutrements of reading: ruler, pen, and highlighter. I demonstrate how these essential tools of reading are to be used to slow down the act of reading and to "do" the act of critical reading that others have advised but never taught. In addition to reading, this chapter provides concrete suggestions about how to organize the information gathered through the reading codes to maximize organization, management, and retrieval of information necessary for paper writing. After students are introduced to the Reading Code Organization Sheet (RCOS) as a way of collecting, organizing, and managing information, they are taught how to create an outline using RCOS before writing that first professional-quality research paper.

Chapter 8: Will the Reading Code Sheet Work on Non-Social Science Texts? This chapter tests the applicability of the reading code sheet to non-social science texts. In particular, classic philosophical works are used as examples to determine the generalizability of the reading code sheet to book-length texts and journal articles in philosophy, arguably, one of the more abstract and abstruse disciplines in academia. This chapter argues that the ideas foundational to the reading codes are applicable across various types of academic texts and disciplines.

Chapter 9: Concluding Remarks: This chapter argues that reading and writing are inextricably related acts. That is, despite the solitary character of both academic activities, they are fundamentally social and intersubjective acts, inaugurating readers and writers into socio-moral order of the scholarly community.

1

Serial Killers and Book Reports

Serial killers are nightmares for police departments. Investigating serial homicide offenders requires a tremendous amount of resources: multi-jurisdictional task forces have to be formed; tips that come into the task force office have to be recorded, investigated, filed, and retrieved (Keppel & Birnes, 2003); interagency rivalry usually develops if the task force involves a federal agency (e.g., Federal Bureau of Investigation); the lead investigator must manage the ongoing investigation, keep his/her supervisor (Police Chief, mayor) apprised of promising leads, suspects, and activities, and communicate with members of the media through daily briefings – without giving away too much information to the suspect, who is most likely watching the news daily to determine how much the police know (Keppel & Birnes, 1995). Detectives have to be reassigned from their normal caseload to the serial killer investigation; their family life and morale suffer because their routine life has been put on hold; and if a task force can't produce the killer in a reasonable amount of time, all the resources that were put in get taken away (Reichhart, 2004).

But even before the initial investigation can begin, someone must conclude that the series of victims are connected to one killer. Low-ranking members of police departments who insist that the victim series is attributable to a solitary killer often face banishment, mockery, and punishment from fellow officers and supervisors. In the 1970s when Ted Bundy stealthily rampaged across the Pacific Northwest, killing victim after victim, the idea and the word "serial killer" did not even exist. The lead detective in the Bundy investigation, Robert Keppel, had to convince his fellow detectives that the victims were attributable to the work of one offender.

Similarly, Kim Rossmo, a Detective Inspector with the Vancouver Police Department (VPD), tried to show using geographical profiling techniques that the numerous disappearances of women in the Vancouver area were the work of a single serial killer. Detective Inspector Rossmo presented his findings to the chief homicide inspector at the time. Rather than praising the Detective Inspector and his innovative work, his bosses berated him and refused to acknowledge or support his work. Had the senior supervisors at VPD acknowledged Rossmo's findings, they most certainly would have concentrated their resources into the investigation of Robert Pickton, a pig farmer who was later convicted of killing prostitutes and feeding their remains to pigs (see Mickleburgh, 2010).

Sometimes, the person who points out that obvious fact does not come from the ranks of police organizations. Usually, victims' families or close acquaintances bring to a journalist's attention the obvious connections between the missing persons' reports and victims who turn up dead; sometimes, curious journalists stumble across the patterns of homicide in a particular geographical area where the bodies were recovered, where victims were last seen, and the way they were murdered. Sometimes, a pimp finds the person who last "dated" his girl before she went missing, and leads the police to the killer (Reichart, 2004). Such cases are exceptions to the rule. For victims, their families, and detectives who work such cases, serials killers are a nightmare.

But female undergraduate English majors love them – they can't get enough of Ted "the necrophiliac" Bundy, Gary "Green River" Ridgeway, Jeffrey "the cannibal" Dahmer, Jack the Ripper, and others like them. English majors are usually required to pick a topic, and instructed to write a "research paper" about it in one of their general composition courses. Since general composition courses have no specific content (e.g., nineteenth-century American Literature, Chaucer, Shakespeare) except to improve their writing skills, students are allowed to pick whatever topic that interests them. In my seven years of teaching a course entitled "Murder in America" I have never had sociology, philosophy, and linguistics majors sign up for a class on homicide as a result of their infatuation with serial killers. But for some odd reason, female undergraduate English majors love that topic, much like the way that a necrophiliac loves a corpse.

When asked to describe the papers they wrote on serial killers, those students would usually name their favorite serial killer, much like the way any Canadian male could name a favorite hockey player or a true Chicagoan can name a favorite player from the 1985 Chicago *Bears*; and then they would describe the true-crime books that they had read (all three of them), and how the killers' poor and miserable childhood spent at the hands of a domineering mother had "caused" their violent propensities. I would then ask, "Well, how did your paper contribute to the literature on serial homicides?" "What do you mean?" students would ask. "I mean, does your work on serial murder support or refute existing research on serial killers? If your findings on or understanding of serial murder are different from the ones described by scholars in the field, how do they differ?" "My paper was a case analysis" or its variations would often follow. I would then bang my head against the office wall in frustration after the student left.

After about five years of conversations like that, semester after semester, I realized that undergraduates, especially English majors, did not know what a social science research paper was. They were confusing a research paper with a book report. Students who had written 10–12 pages of double spaced text, it seemed, concluded that they had written a "research paper." That is, students had defined a research paper on length rather than its structure, form, and logic. Ten to twelve pages of simple summaries of others' work may be a lot of things, but they are not research papers.

Landrum (2008) refers to such papers as "term papers" – papers that provide summaries of others' research findings. In psychology alone, Landrum (2008) notes, there are 12 different types of writing assignment, from progressive papers to reaction papers. At best, papers that only summarize the work of others might be described as a review paper; but as Silvia (2007) notes, "a review article's most common flaw is the absence of an original point. Some authors rehash research without drawing a conclusion, while other authors describe competing theories without offering a resolution." A "research paper" on serial killers that simply rehashes existing works and theories of serial murder without a resolution of some sort is best described as a book report on steroids. Two explanations are generally proffered for the common aforementioned writing error: (1) the absence of new ideas even after having read through the previous works of others in the field; (2) the failure to outline: "complex project requires a strong outline – without one, your original point will be eclipsed by the mass of past research" (Silvia, 2007, p. 106).

The aforesaid assertions are certainly accurate. Writing a research paper is not like writing a novel: we do not "develop" characters; we do not create conflicts between characters or within them. Instead, research papers resolve "preexisting conflicts between previous literature and current findings" (Landrum, 2008, p. 14). That is, the literature has already been reviewed, the data have been analyzed, and we already know how the paper will turn out; we know if our results support or contradict the work others have done. Yet, there are certain steps in the writing – prewriting – process that have been overlooked in previous research, and blindly presupposed in order for the preceding explanations to work. The first incorrect assumption is that writers cannot develop new ideas if they don't have new ideas. Research articles in social science journals are necessarily full of new ideas that have not been addressed in the current paper. There are always gaps or deficiencies in the literature. That's why authors discuss limitations of their research and recommendations for future works – as a tacit way of setting up the work they will do in the future or providing an itinerary for others who may want to do the work that was not done in the current paper. Writers are not able to develop new ideas because they have not learned to read critically.

The second flaw arises from a major omission in the accounting sequence. Let's say that a master's-level graduate student is writing a thesis on serial killers, and she has identified 50 peer-reviewed journal articles that have been published within the past 15 years – and she has read them. Then what? To be able to "grimly describe each study" requires a tremendous amount of work and effort. To be able to even come up with a rough outline, the student will necessarily have had to process the literature in a particular way; and unless that student sat down with a blank sheet of paper and kept track of recurring themes, patterns, and deficiencies in the literature, the "new idea" that should have emerged is apt to get overlooked in such unguided reading. Thus, previous works fail to address a logistic issue related to writing that actually precedes it – how to read in a way that pro-motes development and cultivation of new ideas prior to the outline; and just as importantly, how to manage the information from the "mass of past research."

As master's-level students and then as doctoral-level students, most pro-fessors have all been there. I am sure they asked themselves, "How do I organize, classify, and retrieve the relevant information for my own pur-pose?" during the dissertation process. Perhaps we have been lucky enough to stumble through that process through trial and error, even without a cogent theory of the practice behind it. About six years into my teaching career, I realized that students may not know how to do that either. One reason that students may not know how to write social science research papers is that they have not been taught how to write them. In the US, most undergraduates take mandatory English composition courses as part of the general education curriculum; these courses are viewed as "something to get out of the way" before students take courses related to their major – the real stuff. Furthermore, people who teach the composition courses are trained in a discipline that is recognizably different from psychology, sociology, and criminology.

As a teacher, I struggled with reading and grading student papers. When handing back papers to students, I would deliberately not make eye contact with students when the papers they were receiving – and the comments on them – were marked in red. I would try to hand out the papers as quickly as I could because I hated passing negative judgments on students' work – even if the sea of red marks on their poorly-written papers were justified and warranted – and I hated even more the eye contact I made as I handed their papers back. I also found that the students were making the same types of error on most of the papers, so essentially, I had written similar comments on most of the papers. Such redundancy angered me because it made my work dull. That anger would morph into sadness, mild depression, and temporary hopelessness, which could only be alleviated by viewing mind-numbing television. I found it difficult to write good sentences after having read through hours of bad ones; I found it impossible to write after viewing hours of bad television – excuses, excuses, excuses.

To minimize the work that I had to do on student papers, and to make myself at least feel like a teacher, I found a way to reconcile the need to pass judgment on a student's written work; and to go through the motions of having acted like a teacher, I came up with a grading code sheet. Rather than writing out lengthy comments on each and every student's paper, I created codes of commonly occurring errors. That would save me from repetitive writing. All students would have to do to improve their writing was to look at the codes that appeared on their papers, and if they were sufficiently motivated, all they had to do was buy and consult specific pages and sections in Strunk and White's (1979) *Elements of Style* where the codes directed them.

2

Trying to Fix Mechanical and Structural Writing Problems with Abstract Tools

As undergraduate and graduate students, we have all experienced the magic acts that our professors practiced on us. That is, we hand in a paper at the end of the semester, and when we receive our papers back, there is an inexplicable grade that appears at the top of the first page or at the bottom of the last page. Sometimes, there are a few laudatory phrases peppered here and there, but no systematic accounting of how the professor arrived at the grade. I do not ever recall any of the professors correcting mechanical or stylistic errors on the papers I had submitted, except one; I am quite certain I must have had countless structural, logical, and mechanical errors on the papers I turned in. My best guess now is that they were probably overwhelmed by the sheer number of mistakes and just gave up trying to correct them.

Being on the other end of the lectern, I can now understand why my professors were reluctant to correct each and every grammatical mistake or fix awkward sentences. Such tasks are time-consuming, soul-draining, and nearly impossible to accomplish on every single paper. That is, I may begin a grading session with magnanimous and noble intentions, but such ideals vanish about an hour into the grading. Moreover, grading papers is marked by a sense of futility, if one assumes a pessimistic view of the world, and despair if one assumes an optimistic view of the world. If the professor is untenured and needs to write her own articles, even idealists turn into pragmatists.

Assistant professors also have to worry about student evaluations in their tenure dossier. This means that they can't tell students what they really think of the papers. They have to find a way to be tactful and diplomatic; moreover, they have to practice such skills while being cognizant of grade challenges from students. Students compare their grades (marks in Canada) with one another; students who are dissatisfied with their grades will want to know why Jane Doe received a higher grade; students who are still not satisfied take their complaints to the department chair, the Dean, the Ombudsman, and if motivated enough, the President of the University. To be able to withstand such bureaucratic scrutiny when challenged, I as an untenured assistant professor needed a way to justify the grade assigned on a paper. I needed to have an accounting system. I painfully learned this lesson during my first year of full-time teaching.

Of course, it is difficult to assign a quantitative value on a qualitative work. As instructors, we can instantly recognize an A+ paper when we read it (unless it was purchased at a paper mill, which was not discovered until the grade was turned in or another student handed in a similar paper the next semester). It is also easy to spot an F paper. Those papers are a "slam dunk" for professors. Students who write bad papers rarely have the energy, motivation, or the will to challenge their grades – and they usually know they have done shoddy work. The B, C, and D quality papers are a different story. Students who have received the grade of a B might challenge their grades because they erroneously believe that a slight adjustment in the professor's grading scheme or a vigorously argued point will upgrade their B to an A – especially if the student challenging the grade has been averaging A throughout the semester. Students who have written C quality papers might challenge their grades because such a grade in a major assignment will lead to the loss of a scholarship. Similarly, D papers might be challenged because students who have received such grades are on the precipice of an F and will do what is necessary to avoid failure.

I was observing that students were making similar types of errors on their papers; and because I needed to be able to provide a justification of the assigned grade, I initially created a grading code sheet. I noticed that students – undergraduate and graduate – were making recurring errors on their papers. For instance, they would write sentences that sounded awkward, so the code AWK was created. Students would assert a claim, but without citing or substantiating the source, so the code CITE was formed. Students would try to "BS" their way through some papers, so the code LMG (Largely Magnified Generalities) was created. Students would fail to use paragraphs (NP: New Paragraph) or write long-winded sentences that could be reduced to one succinct sentence (TLW: Too Long-Winded). Some assertions made in the paper were so incredulous and outlandish that the code JOK (Joke) was added. (In criminology, such I-can't-believe-s/he-said-that and are-you-kidding-me? paper comments are usually related to race and crime.)

After trying out the codes and seeing modest success, I wondered if it would be possible to teach grammar through such a system as well. I found that students needed concrete and specific advice on how to write better sentences, use correct punctuation marks, etc. So I began to collect information on student grammar errors. I discovered that most student errors could be corrected if they consulted Strunk and White's *Elements of Style*. The grading code sheet was expanded even more to include page and section references to Strunk and White (SSW).

Now, I could underline, circle, and highlight particular sentences, words, phrases and identify a problem to a student; I could also show students what needed to be fixed in their papers, and suggest concrete changes that needed to be made. Moreover, I could penalize points each and every time an error occurred to demonstrate how I arrived at the numerical grade that appeared on a student's paper. The value of the penalty points was entirely arbitrary and subjective. Thus, if a student made 15 errors in a ten page paper, and if each penalty was a 3-point deduction, the student could be penalized for a total of 45 points out of a possible total point value of 100. I began to notice that students' writings were improving little by little. Once students realized where they needed to fix the problems and how to go about fixing them, they did it. Penalty for each and every error was probably a highly-motivating factor, I presume. I never asked.

There were two principal reasons why I developed the grading code sheet. The first I have already mentioned: untenured, assistant professors cannot have too many grade challenges and appeals; once the chair of the department gets involved, there is a paper trail of the actions taken, if not formally, then informally in the form of whispers and hush-hush-chatter in personnel committee meetings. Those formal and informal assessments have the potential to come back and bite the assistant professor in the butt at tenure time, when the most trivial and inconsequential items become amplified and serve as fodder for denial of tenure. I wanted to minimize such occurrences.

Second, I was a teacher. That role and identity meant – means – a lot to me. If I didn't fix those writing problems, then who would? I could have defined out of the problem rather easily (Muir, 1977): I could have justified easy or minimal grading by stating my need to produce articles for tenure. I could have blamed the English teachers (college, high school, elementary school) who had failed to properly teach students the mechanics of writing. I could have blamed the moon and its pull on the ocean if I wanted to define out of my role as a teacher. But that would have been inconsistent with what my own teacher(s) had done, and it would have violated the code of professionalism.

For example, imagine a uniformed patrol officer who receives a radio dispatch about a citizen who needs assistance because intruders are breaking down her door. The officer thinks the call might be dangerous, so s/he decides to ignore the call. In my work with patrol officers, I found that whatever biases they harbored, whatever personal attitudes they held, they never let those personal beliefs interfere with the performance of their professional duties. I would often ask patrol officers why they did certain things, and the answer was almost always, "I'm the police. It's my job." That's the only justification they needed to perform their duties. Now, I am not trying to excuse cases where such self-justified ideologies go awry. This is not the place to argue about the causes and consequences of police misconduct. I am simply making the point that police officers I met and interacted with never let other conflicting ideologies or ambiguities confound their roles as professionals. Once I came to view my own work as a teacher along such lines, I found it difficult to define out of my professional duties and obligations.

There are two grading codes (EXQ and POC) that I want to elaborate on. These codes were developed because I saw similar recurring errors on graduate student literature review papers, non-thesis major papers, and theses. For example, I noticed that graduate students were excessively quoting (defined as more than two full lines in a submitted paper) an author if the author's main points were particularly abstruse or difficult to paraphrase; excessive quotes (EXQ) appeared on papers because students had not understood the author adequately – or the students were just being lazy. In essence, students were able to let the quoted author do the work of explaining a concept rather than doing the work for themselves. I also noticed that students would merely move from the concatenation of summaries of previous works to the data and methods section without adequately providing a critique of the literature (POC: point of critique), thereby providing an insufficient rationale of why the student's own paper was warranted. I then realized that graduate student papers needed a different type of guidance to complete their papers – more than what the grading code sheet could provide. Consequently, I began to mine their papers for patterns in their errors. Before I could remedy the problems, I first needed to figure out what the problems were.

One type of error immediately stood out, and I am sure most instructors of graduate classes have seen this type of error in the research papers and first drafts of theses that students submit. The error involves citing one author to death as part of a literature review. In the course of 1–3 paragraphs, rather than summarizing the work of previous researchers in some principled and methodical way, in a way that is logically and thematically connected, the student author will make several points with one author, in the process, citing the said author *ad nauseam*. Then the student will move on to make several other summaries using another author, citing the new author *ad nauseam*. I will refer to this as the "beating-one-horse-to-death" problem.

What was missing from the typical papers I received from first-year graduate students were critiques of the literature. Students were already good at summarizing previous works. After all, simple summaries – term papers – are just book reports on growth hormones. However, they had trouble figuring out how to critique what they were reading. I mistakenly believed that such problems could be remedied by working on their writing: I tried to develop codes to help students write better, but to no avail. Then in 2008 (after tenure) I began to think that one way of improving the structural organization of graduate student papers was to critically reexamine the reading process.

3

Three Types of Stains and False Assumptions about Writing

Barbara Ehrenreich (2001) in *Nickeled and Dimed* describes the three common types of stains that she encountered while temporarily working as a maid. The first type of stain runs down the insides of toilet bowls, or what Ehrenreich calls "landslides"; the second type is aptly described as "splashbacks," the liquid that most likely ricocheted off the toilet water by the sheer expulsive force of the excreta; the third type of stain refers to those that are caked onto the rims of toilets – the kind that eventually falls off when enough men urinate directly on it. She mentions the different types of stains because they all require different cleaning approaches, and she tells the readers that she became intimately familiar with the defecation habits of middle-class Americans by having to clean up after them.

I worked the nightshift as a gas station attendant throughout my undergraduate years and parts of my graduate student years so I too am familiar with the toilet stains of Americans, especially in public toilet facilities. In addition to selling gas as a "sales associate" (cashier), I had to pick up garbage from those huge garbage cans next to pumps (trash collector), and I had to clean the bathroom every night (janitor). Although what Ehrenreich describes is certainly true, she missed the other varieties of stains, primarily because she was cleaning toilets located in private homes. Stains in public toilets reek in a different way.

One evening, I entered the bathroom only to be immediately slapped in the face by an unmistakable odor. After recoiling from the initial olfactory shock, I opened the door further and scanned the walls of the restroom. Someone had smeared – actually smeared – brown stuff all over the walls of the restroom. I wasn't sure if the smearing was done with hand or with toilet paper; at that point, it really didn't matter, for I knew I would have to go in there and clean it up. I still remember gagging on its smell as it penetrated my nose and lungs; I must have dry heaved throughout the entire cleaning session, despite my noble attempts to hold my breath. I put on my red rubber gloves, grabbed a bucket full of hot water, bleach, and soap, and wiped down the stains until they were visible and malodorous no more.

I still remember that night vividly. I remember it because after I was done cleaning, and no one was around, I wept. I could not believe how pathetic my life had become: I was cleaning up someone else's crap at 2 a.m. in my first year of graduate school. As an undergraduate philosophy major, my cohorts and I would joke that we were going to ask our customers "Do you *really* want fries with that?" or "How do you *know* you want fries with that?" in our new jobs upon completion of our degrees in philosophy, but I never imagined that I'd be cleaning poop. That night, I promised myself that whatever I did in life, whatever career I chose, I would never clean up someone else's fecal stains. That night, after cleaning those stains smeared all over the bathroom wall in a gas station, I vowed to work harder in school, and made a conscious choice never to do that type of work again. Now, don't get me wrong. I am not look-ing down on people who clean toilets for a living; cleaning toilets is probably an unappreciated and underpaid form of work that unnecessarily leads to the experience of shame. I just did not want to be the one doing it.

The preceding turning point in my life and its description can be used to illustrate a flaw in the common assumptions people make about writing. Cleaning up other people's toilet stains is an activity. One does not theorize about cleaning up poop, nor does one even argue about its ethics. One might, however, debate the methods of cleaning to maximize cleanliness and mini-mize the lingering odor afterwards. Engaging in an activity requires no mediation between the doer (e.g., maid, janitor) and the deed (e.g., cleaning). There is no filter or representation. Cleaning poop is uncomfortably raw. Writing about cleaning poop, as I am doing now, involves a representation, and is filtered by an additional barrier; that is, describing the performance of an activity is not on the same plane as performing the activity, for there is dis-tance between the two: one is an unmediated act of doing (performance) while the other is an analytically mediated act of describing the doing (description).

The physical act of writing is a performance, much like the way we experi-ence emotions (e.g., I'm sad; I write). Writing about something (e.g., psychol-ogy experiment, likelihood of recidivism, cleaning up poop) is an analytical act, one that is necessarily different from the activity being described. For example, "I'm sad" is an agent's direct experience of an emotional state; in the sentence "I feel sad" the agent (I) makes the emotional state (sadness) the object of his/her analysis (feel). The two sentences and the two acts are not the same (see Lewis, 1955, pp. 217–219). And when Silvia (2007, p. 11) writes that "writing is a grim business, much like repairing a sewer or running a mortuary … although I have never dressed a corpse, I'm sure that it's easier to embalm the dead than to write an article about it," he conflates the two types of acts, performance and description. Now suppose Silvia substituted "dressing a corpse" with "cleaned up smeared feces from the walls of public restrooms"; imagine the intuitive plausibility of such a sentence:

> Although I have never cleaned up smeared feces from the walls of public restrooms, I'm sure that it's easier to clean up smeared feces from the walls of public restrooms than to write an article about it.

I would much rather write about cleaning up feces than to actually do it. I have done both, and I can unequivocally state that writing about cleaning feces is easier, cleaner, and more antiseptic than gagging on the stench while cleaning them; I don't have to worry about getting fecal matter on my hands and clothes when I am writing about cleaning.

That academics view writing as being on par with dressing up a corpse may be one reason that the working-class people frown on academics, and make bad inferences about people who sit in their offices and write; that's why the general public is likely to view academics as being disconnected from the real world, and reflect that disdain in the waning financial support of higher education (Fish, 2008). They can't even differentiate between the lesser of the two evils. As I have tried to argue by using the public bathroom example, writing is not that bad. It is far easier to write about something than to do that something, especially when that something involves excrement. And unless you are a necrophiliac-in-training, you ought not to have any desire to dress up a corpse or be around it in a funeral home, hospital, county morgue, or a cemetery (Burg, 1982; Rosman & Resnick, 1989). As academic writers who primarily write for other academics, we don't have to write sentences others will recall and talk about decades later. That is, we do not have to write sentences like, "*Happy families are all alike; every unhappy family is unhappy in its own way*"; or "*Maman died today. Or yesterday maybe, I don't know.*" We just have to write competent ones to persuade the editor and the anonymous reviewers.

But make no mistake. Writing is tough work. Its difficulty and arduousness are qualitatively different from cleaning poop, dealing with unruly customers in a retail store, lifting heavy objects all day, or trying to mediate a domestic dispute between two toothless drunks in a trailer park; the type of fatigue and stress that writing produces paralyzes the soul and damages self-esteem. When my own writing was not going well, there were days when I seriously thought about giving up academic life and trying something else (I don't know what). But then I recalled that night at the gas station, and I knew without a doubt that I did not want to clean poop again. I went back to writing in a day or two, after the sting of the painful rejection from a journal subsided. That's why the advice that general how-to books provide to treat writing like work is sound: we have to set schedules, "clock in," and do what the Nike commercials tell us we ought to do – just do it; by doing so we dignify our activity as work and reproduce the moral order of writing as work.

Imagine a bus driver, nurse, or a patrol officer who says things like, "I must be inspired to [drive, take care of patients, answer 911 calls]" or "I don't have the time to [drive, take care of patients, answer 911 calls]." People who harbored such thoughts and translated those hidden values into everyday behavior (as academics regularly do) would be out of a job yesterday. Only privileged academics can get away with talking such bovine scatology. Our job is to teach and write. If we treat reading and writing like the way ordinary people treat their work, then the idea of a psychological barrier to writing ought to be seen for what it is.

As others have noted, writing is more than just typing. It entails prewriting activities such as "reading, outlining, idea generation, and data analysis necessary for generating text" (Silvia, 2007, p. 18). Even prior to outlining, reading and note-taking may be just as implicative, if not more, than the actual writing, for it is during the act of reading that we decide what we might use in a paper (Landrum, 2008); it is during reading that we identify "main themes, strengths, and weaknesses" in the literature (Cone & Foster, 2006, p. 103). In fact, Cone and Foster (2006) instruct their readers to keep a record of observations while reading, in order to arrive at a major insight about a topic based on those observations. As can be seen, careful reading ought not to be treated as a secondary activity to writing; that proper reading may lead to insightful observations about a topic is already implied in the previous works. Students just have to learn how to read the literature in a way that cultivates insightful observations.

Framing blocks to writing as one of poor motivation is one way of diagnosing the problem. Writers who complain about "writer's block are writers who don't outline. … After trying to write blindly, they feel frustrated and complain about how hard it is to generate words. No surprise – you can't write an article if you don't know what to write … get your thoughts in order before you try to communicate them to the world of science" (Silvia, 2007, p. 79). That writing problems still get framed as one of motivation is a bit puzzling, for academics do not write blindly – without any idea about how the paper will begin and end. By the time we have reviewed the literature, justified the reason for our study, collected the data or synthesized the literature for a review article, and conducted the study and analyzed the results, we ought to know, unequivocally, what we want to say in our papers.

Academics – and first-year graduate students – do not know what to write or have trouble organizing their thoughts into papers because (1) they have

not read the literature sufficiently or (2) they have read the literature sufficiently but have not found a way to organize the information gathered from
their readings. Before one can put together an outline, s/he has to be familiar
with the contents that will occupy the outline. Both of these errors lead to the
type of writing problems that others have described. Both types of error occur
at the reading level and ought to be remedied there.

Readers in general how-to books are given general and vague instructions
on how to read critically; they are told that they can "develop a valid critique
only on the basis of a careful reading of the full text," that they must "read to
inquire" (Glatthorn & Joyner, 2005, pp. 92, 25). Vipond (1996, p. 39) states that
"knowledge claims" are developed "through careful, critical reading" of existing
works, and that an individual's unique spin or "take" occurs after such careful
readings. Similarly, Rudestam and Newton (2001, p. 60) assert that readers
"need to maintain a critical perspective" while reading previous works to discern the applicability of previous literature to the student's current paper.

Rudestam and Newton (2001) do offer a concrete list of questions to keep
in mind while reading as a way of cultivating critique and structuring reading; the list, however, is too cumbersome, hence, has little operational value.
If the list is translated into a reading code sheet, there would be a total of 21
reading codes – too unwieldy to implement and use. Thus, previous works fail
to address a logistic issue related to writing that actually precedes it – how
to read in a way that promotes development and cultivation of new ideas and
critiques in a succinct way; just as importantly, how to manage the volume
of information that is gleaned from reading previous works, aside from the
traditional use of index cards.

The reading code sheet that I have developed systematizes the reading, note-
taking, and organizing of voluminous amounts of information in an easily identifiable and retrievable format. This book explains how to use ten (10) reading
codes directly related to "critical" reading of social science journal articles that
others have presupposed but have not explored (e.g., SPL, CPL, GAP, RAT,
RCL), and four (4) codes necessary to critique and cultivate a reader's new ideas
and claims (e.g., POC, MOP, WIL). By illuminating and elaborating on the
previously assumed aspects of "critical" reading, this book attempts to teach
students how to read so that the major conceptual divisions and subdivisions of
research papers and theses can be logically organized during the act of reading.

This book presents an alternative way of diagnosing – hence resolving – a
writer's block, and frames it as one of poor reading technique, execution, and
management rather than motivation. Without adequate knowledge of the
work of previous researchers, it is impossible to organize our own thoughts
without appearing solipsistic or narcissistic. Without the right reading tools
and techniques, we fall into the trap of simple summaries rather than logical
critiques and anticipatable rationales – the big so what? – for our papers.

4

Should I Even Read This? How to Read the Abstract, General Introduction, and Methods Section

Let's assume that you – the student – have searched a database of some sort (e.g., PsycINFO, Social Science Citation Index) to check the number of articles that have been published within the past 20 years on your topic, and the results appear to be unwieldy. For the sake of illustration, let's assume that you get 200 "hits" from the topic words you searched. That is too many to manage, let alone read, so you narrow the search terms and now the results page indicates 70 hits. That's much more manageable. So you peruse the titles; some of the recent works definitely appear to be related to the topic you want to write about – the title is unmistakable. We'll say that 40 articles will be included in your literature review because the titles are relevant or because you are sufficiently familiar with the research area to know that certain scholars who have appeared on the list are always cited in relation to the topic you searched, and need to be included. Ten articles appear to be irrelevant to your topic, so they are excluded. You are not sure about the remaining 20 articles. From the title of the papers, they appear to be related to your topic, but you are not sure. What to do at this point? One, you could just go with the 40 articles that you found and ignore the remaining 20, and risk missing out on some important and relevant points – points that might have altered how you might frame your research. Or, you can read the abstract, and then determine if the article is worth including in your literature review or not.

An abstract is a very, very brief summary of a journal article. Most journal publications require an abstract of some sort, which range from 100 to 200 words. Reading through an abstract is less time consuming than reading the full-length article. An abstract contains enough essential information about the article to be able to assess its merit and relevance. In less than two minutes it takes to read through an abstract, you can discern and anticipate the logic of the author's argument before even reading through the full article. Even in medical and hard-science journals, the format of a research article is similar to a social science article: background, materials and method, results, discussion, and conclusion. In an abstract, those five components are covered in one way or another. And whether the student is reading the articles as part of the literature review or trying to decide if the article is pertinent enough to the chosen literature to be included, reading should begin with the abstract. While reading the abstract, the reading codes ought to be inserted where relevant at the right margins of the hard copies of articles. There is a reason why the codes should be inserted at the right margins. After the reading is completed, thematic codes will be inserted at the left margin as a way of classifying and organizing recurring patterns and themes in the literature. The right margin is therefore reserved for the reading codes while the left is reserved for thematic codes.

How to read the abstract

In the section below, the abstracts of four published articles from reputable journals have been reproduced. To describe the function of the words in the abstract, and for accessibility, clarity, and ease of reference, each sentence has been numbered consecutively.

The abstract in DiCataldo and Everett's (2008) article on "Distinguishing juvenile homicide from violent juvenile offending" is exactly 151 words. The abstract is composed of seven sentences. Now, consider the type of information that is contained in the abstract:

(1) Juvenile homicide is a social problem that has remained a central focus within juvenile justice research in recent years. (2) The term juvenile murderer describes a legal category, but it is purported to have significant scientific meaning. (3) Research has attempted to conceptualize adolescent murderers as a clinical category that can be reliably distinguished from their nonhomicidal counterparts. (4) This study examined 33 adolescents adjudicated delinquent or awaiting trial for murder and 38 adolescents who committed violent, nonhomicidal offenses to determine whether the two groups differed significantly on family history, early development, delinquency history, mental health, and weapon possession variables. (5) The nonhomicide group proved more problematic on many of these measures. (6) Two key factors did distinguish the homicide group: These adolescents

endorsed the greater availability of guns and substance abuse at the time of their commitment offenses. (7) The significance of this finding is discussed, and the implications for risk management and policy are reviewed.

Sentences #1–3 do the type of work that could be described as Summary of Previous Literature (SPL). This type of sentence provides a general background on the topic of discussion, and summarizes the results from previous studies. In the preceding abstract, the previous literature has been framed along the theme of (1) time, (2) definitions, (3) distinguishing characteristics. Sentences #2 and #3 tacitly hint at a Critique of Previous Literature (CPL), but those missing gaps (GAPs) are not explicitly stated. In CPL, the author you are reading is providing a critique and a limitation of the previous and existing works; GAP highlights missing elements, deficiencies, and limitations in the current state of knowledge in some systematic way.

Sentences like #4 in the abstract convey what the authors of the paper are doing. Those types of sentences in general are best represented by the reading code WTD: What They (authors) Do. This code captures the main research question that the authors pose and resolve in their text. In abstracts, WTDs describe not only the main problems the papers address, but also the material and method used for the study. Simply put, WTDs are what the article is about. WTD sentences usually begin with phrases like "This paper examines... In this paper... This paper attempts to..." WTDs generally appear in three places for most social science journal articles: abstract, introduction, and conclusion (WTDD: What They Did).

Sentences #5 and #6 present the Results of Findings (ROF). ROFs describe the primary results – main claims – of the journal article that you are reading. This code is usually found in three places in a social science journal article: abstract, results section, and the conclusion. There are two main ROFs that are noteworthy in the preceding article. The ROFs should tell you if the study is relevant to your own research topic or not. In scanning an article and reading through an abstract, the ROF should be the nugget that ought to be mined for, as this will tell you if the article is related to your own paper and topic. If the ROF suggests that the article you are reading is not pertinent to your topic and the paper you are writing, then that article probably should not be included in your literature review, and you should not read on any further. Sentence #7 discusses the implications of the findings. Readers are not told what the implications are, just that implications exist. Those implications are not revealed because the authors are constrained by space and word limits imposed on abstracts.

In reading through one 151 word abstract, we have at least a general idea of what the paper is about. The readers are introduced to the background (SPL), possible critiques (CPL/GAP), what the authors are doing in their

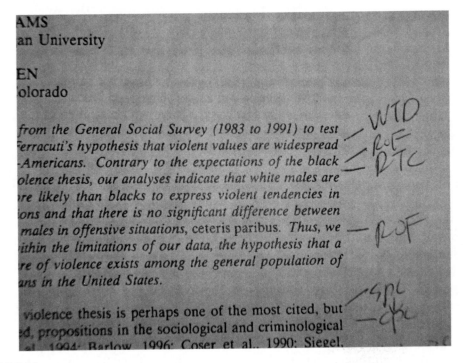

AMS
an University

EN
olorado

from the General Social Survey (1983 to 1991) to test *errracuti's hypothesis that violent values are widespread* *-Americans. Contrary to the expectations of the black* *olence thesis, our analyses indicate that white males are* *re likely than blacks to express violent tendencies in* *ions and that there is no significant difference between* *males in offensive situations,* ceteris paribus. *Thus, we* *ithin the limitations of our data, the hypothesis that a* *re of violence exists among the general population of* *ans in the United States.*

violence thesis is perhaps one of the most cited, but
d, propositions in the sociological and criminological
al 1994; Barlow 1996; Coser et al. 1990; Siegel,

FIGURE 2

work as a way of improving the gap in the literature (WTD), and the results of their findings (ROF). These reading codes ought to be marked on the right margin of the text, next to the sentences that exemplify that code. Therefore, sentences #1–3 should be bracketed and the code SPL ought to be inserted at the right margin. Next to sentence #4 the code WTD ought to be inserted; next to sentences #5 and #6 the code ROF ought to be inserted.

The abstract in Sampson's (1987) article on "Urban black violence: The effect of male joblessness and family disruption" is exactly 168 words. The abstract is composed of eight sentences. Again, consider the type of information that is contained in the abstract:

(1) This paper examines the relationships among employment, crime, and family disruption in the black "underclass." (2) The main hypothesis tested is that the effect of black adult male joblessness on black crime is mediated largely through its effect on family disruption. (3) The study examines race-specific rates of robbery and homicide by juveniles and adults in over 150 U.S. cities in 1980. (4) The results show that the scarcity of employed black men increases the prevalence of families headed by females in black communities. (5) In turn, black family disruption substantially increases the rates of black murder and robbery, especially by juveniles. (6) These effects are

26

independent of income, region, race and age composition, density, city size, and welfare benefits and are similar to the effects of white family disruption on white violence. (7) This paper concludes that there is nothing inherent in black culture that is conducive to crime. (8) Rather high rates of black crime appear to stem from the structural linkages among unemployment, economic deprivation, and family disruption in urban black communities.

Sentences #1–3 describe the main point of the article, along with the material and method. Next to those sentences, the code WTD ought to be inserted at the right margin. Sentences #4–8 all describe the ROF. Sentence #8 possibly hints at the implications of findings, especially for sociological and criminological theory, but readers are not explicitly told this. Therefore, only the code ROF ought to be inserted next to the preceding sentences. Notice what is absent from the preceding abstract: SPL and CPL. The abstract does not provide adequate background information for readers as to why the topic is important. If this component is missing in the abstract, it will be covered again in the introduction and then the literature review, for without the background, the rationale for the current paper will not work. The ROFs, however, tell the reader the main claims of the article – that the prevalence of unemployed black men results in family disruption, which, in turn, leads to crime. The student who reads this abstract should be able to determine if this article should be included in his/her review of the literature.

The abstract in Pritchard and Hughes' (1997) article on "Patterns of deviance in crime news" is exactly 133 words. Consider the work that the sentences in the abstract perform:

(1) Existing research has failed to develop a satisfactory theoretical explanation for journalists' decisions about which crimes to highlight and which to ignore. (2) We proposed that four forms of deviance (normative deviance, statistical deviance, status deviance, and cultural deviance) account for much of the variation in decisions about crime news. (3) To test deviance-based explanations for crime news, we conducted a comprehensive investigation of Milwaukee, WI, homicides and how two newspapers covered them. (4) We used content analysis and interviews with journalists. (5) The results showed that the newsworthiness of a homicide is enhanced when whites are suspects or victims, males are suspects, and victims are females, children, or senior citizens. (6) We concluded that status deviance and cultural deviance are important components of newsworthiness and that statistical deviance (unusualness) may be much less important than commonly assumed.

The presence of the word "failed" after "existing research" should be a clue that sentence #1 is pointing out a CPL/GAP of some sort; in the sentences that follow, that's what the readers are told. Sentence #1 is an example of

CPL/GAP. What is the missing element in the existing literature? A "satisfactory theoretical explanation" that explains why journalists highlight some crimes while ignoring others. Sentences #2–4 describe the WTD, for they describe the material and method as well as the main research questions being addressed in their study. Sentences #5–6 describe the ROF. The SPL is implicitly contained in the words "commonly assumed," but readers are not explicitly told what it is. The codes, CPL/GAP, WTD, and ROF ought to be entered in the right margin of the article next to the respective sentences. Again, even without adequate background knowledge of the literature or SPL, the ROFs ought to tell you – the reader – if the main claims made in the article are pertinent for your ends. Readers know that status deviance and cultural deviance constitute "important components of newsworthiness."

The abstract in Moffitt et al.'s (1996) article on "Childhood-onset versus adolescent-onset antisocial conduct problems in males: natural history from ages 3 to 18 years" is exactly 174 words. Again, notice the recurring pattern:

(1) We report data that support the distinction between childhood-onset and adolescent-onset type conduct problems. (2) Natural histories are described from a representative birth cohort of 457 males studied longitudinally from age 3 to 18 years. (3) Childhood- and adolescent-onset cases differed on temperament as early as age 3, but almost half of childhood-onset cases did not become seriously delinquent. (4) Type comparisons were consistent with our contention that males whose antisocial behavior follows a life-course-persistent path differ from males who follow an adolescence-limited path. (5) As adolescents, the two types differed on convictions for violent crime, personality profiles, school leaving, and bonds to family. (6) These differences can be attributed to developmental history because the two groups were well matched on measures of antisocial conduct at age 18 years: parent-reports, self reports, and adjudication records. (7) By age 18 years, many conduct-problem boys had encountered factors that could ensnare them in antisocial future: substance dependence, unsafe sex, dangerous driving habits, delinquent friends, delinquent perceptions, and employment. (8) Implications for theory, research design, prevention, and therapeutic treatment of conduct problems are highlighted.

Sentence #1 could function as SPL, for the current paper supports a distinction that has already been proposed in previous work. However, such claims have not been explicitly made. Sentence #2 describes the material and method for the current paper. Therefore, sentences #1–2 will be coded as WTD. Sentences #3–7 describe the ROF – the main claims the authors of the paper make. Sentence # 8 provides the implications of the findings. The three reading codes ought to be inserted at the right margin. Again, after reading the abstract, readers ought to be able to tell if the full paper is relevant to their own projects.

As one can observe, there is some variance in the way the abstracts are composed. Some abstracts provide SPL and CPL while others do not; some abstracts use two sentences to describe their ROFs while others expend five to do the work. And when students are not sure whether an article should be included in their literature review – and the title of the paper does not provide adequate clues about the paper's pertinence to one's chosen topic – the abstract should be read to discern if the primary findings (ROF) of the studies being read are consistent with the proposed topic and aim of the student's paper. Furthermore, even after an article has been deemed to be relevant for inclusion in one's literature review, the abstract should be read first so that the logic of the author's argument embedded in the article can be rehearsed and anticipated in the subsequent sections.

As stated earlier, certain components of an article will appear more than once throughout the article. For example, ROFs are found in the abstract, the results, and discussion and conclusion. Similarly, the rationale (RAT) for why a particular study is necessary and warranted cannot appear randomly and out of the blue. It has to follow a logical, linear, and anticipatable path of reasoning and argumentation (Jordan & Zanna, 1999). This logical "set-up" unfurls in the literature review section; its shadow is implicitly cast in the abstract.

The use of reading codes can also serve as a guide to students for how to construct an abstract. One sentence can describe the SPL, another the CPL. The SPL and the CPL ought to at least tacitly suggest a GAP, which logically leads to the WTD. One to two sentences can be used to describe the WTD, including the material and method. One to two sentences could be used to describe the ROF, with a final sentence for implications of results. With a minimum of five sentences, then, a student ought to be able to craft an abstract of her/his own, without wondering about the constitutive elements of an abstract.

By noting the primary function of words, sentences, and paragraphs in texts, readers are able to structure their reading so that the contents of what they have read can be organized and classified along predictable, anticipatable, and recurring patterns. In this section, I have shown students how to read abstracts. In subsequent sections and chapters, I will show how to read much longer blocks of text using the reading codes. Thus, rather than reading social science articles without boundaries (unstructured reading), the reading codes provide textual, cognitive, and conceptual boundaries so that readers do not engage in mindless and meandering reading. By actively engaging with the text (and the author), readers of social science articles should not ask, "What did I just read for the past 30 minutes?" Those types of questions arise either because texts are too difficult to decipher (e.g., Jacques Lacan, Immanuel Kant, Judith Butler) or because the mind has wandered away during the act of reading from an absence of structure to the reading.

By identifying the function of texts and inserting them into the right margin, readers achieve three objectives. (1) Slowing down the act of reading – the use of reading codes structures the mind toward a purposive task, thereby delineating cognitive boundaries. (2) Organizing the contents of the reading into recurring themes (e.g., SPL, CPL, GAP, ROF) that can be easily retrieved for writing purposes. (3) Identifying potential GAPs so that the reader can anticipate the RAT (see Chapter 5) from the given CPL and GAP for use in their own papers.

How to read the general introduction

An introduction, as the word denotes, appears at the beginning of something; it does not appear at the end, for that would make it a conclusion. An introduction in a social science journal article is like a blueprint and a map: it lays out the itinerary of an article's path of logical travel. Introductions are longer than abstracts but shorter than literature review sections. Introductions tend to be between two and four paragraphs; they are also organized and structured into predictable patterns. Consider the following introduction from Gruenewald, Pizarro, and Chermak's (2009) article on "Race, gender, and the newsworthiness of homicide incidents."

There are four paragraphs that make up the introduction. In the first paragraph, second sentence, the authors write, "Scholars have found that crime is generally a staple of news programming, comprising from 10 to 50 percent of all news stories [citations omitted]" (p. 262). Sentences like it summarize the state of the literature, so the code SPL ought to be inserted in the available margin. The first five sentences are written in a similar spirit, as a way of summarizing previous literature. Then in the last sentence of the first paragraph, the authors write, "Despite such increased attention, an empirical void remains in the literature regarding the factors that contribute to the decision-making process..." (p. 262). Sentences like the preceding one critique the previous literature (CPL) and identify a GAP in the knowledge base. In one paragraph, the authors have summarized the literature, and provided a critique of, and identified a gap in, the existing literature.

The first sentence of the second paragraph reads, "To date, few studies [citations omitted] have seriously considered how the gender and race of homicide victims and offenders, and their interaction, affect news media selection and prominence decisions, and whether these interactions supersede incident characteristics in increasing the newsworthiness of a particular homicide" (p. 262). Again, the sentence points to a critique of the existing literature and identifies a gap in it: few studies have examined how gender and race affect the decision-making process in the news. The rest of the sentences in the paragraph go on to provide other shortcomings in the literature (e.g., criteria used to assess newsworthiness; lack of Hispanics in previous study samples; lack of a specific examination of race and gender). Thus far, in the first paragraph, authors have provided a broad summary of the literature, ending it with a critique. In the second paragraph, the authors have put forth more GAPs that exist in the literature. So what? Why should these GAPs matter?

The authors answer that "The scholarly understanding of newsworthiness criteria is important for several reasons" (Gruenewald et al., 2009, p. 262). They list three. The answers to the "so what?" question constitute a rationale for the study (RAT): our proposed work is warranted and necessary because others have not addressed the GAPs. Every study and/or experiment has to be able to answer this question. After the three RATs are proffered, the WTD appears in the fourth paragraph: "This study examined the relationship between homicide participant and incident characteristics and news media decision-making in the city of Newark, New Jersey" (p. 262). Again, WTD tells readers what will be done in the paper. In the rest of the article, the authors will remedy the GAPs they have identified. The general introduction, very much similar to an abstract, provides a taste of the full-course meal to emerge in the rest of the article. In the preceding introduction, that initial "taste" is offered in the form of SPL→CPL→GAP→ RAT→WTD in four paragraphs.

In Pritchard and Hughes' (1997) article on "Patterns of deviance in crime news," six paragraphs make up the introduction. The first three paragraphs summarize the literature (SPL). The fourth paragraph begins with, "Our research tested the adequacy of deviance-based explanations for crime news decisions" (p. 50). That sentence and the entire paragraph would be an example of WTD – What They Do. After the WTD, the authors proffer a RAT of why their study is necessary, then go on to provide the data and materials used in their study. In six paragraphs, the authors have provided the reader with SPL→WTD→RAT→data and materials, in no particular logical order. The introduction, however, still contains the essential element – the WTD.

Shumaker and Prinz's (2000) review article on "Children who murder: A review" has four paragraphs that make up the introduction. The first sentence of the first paragraph begins with, "Though homicidal youth have received considerable attention in the media and in the social sciences, children under age 13 who committed homicide are understudied" (p. 97). That is, the authors provide a summary of the literature ("homicidal youth have received considerable attention in the media and in the social sciences") and a critique of the previous literature (but "children under age 13 who committed homicide are understudied"). Thus far, the sequence of the logic of ideas in the first paragraph of the introduction can be represented by the reading codes SPL→CPL→GAP.

If a GAP exists in the literature, so what? Why should that deficiency matter? Why should anyone care? Consider Shumaker and Prinz's (2000) answer to the "so what?" question: "Despite the low base rate, preteen offenders should be studied for several reasons" (p. 97). They list three reasons why the topic is important and should be studied: (1) young killers pose problems for the juvenile justice system; (2) juvenile homicide rates have doubled; and (3) for prevention purposes. These are the RATs for why their work is important. RAT, again, follows the GAP in the logical sequence of how ideas in introductions are structurally organized. Since Shumaker and Prinz (2000) are writing a review article in a psychology journal, the third paragraph elaborates on how the authors selected the published studies to be included in their review paper.

In the last paragraph of the introduction, the authors write, "The review examines classification schemes and typologies of youthful homicide, predictors of homicidal behavior in children, and how childhood behavioral characteristics of adult murderers, particularly adult serial-killers, might bear on the study of preteen homicide" (p. 98). The occurrence of the first three words of the paragraph, "the review examines," ought to signal that the sentence and/or paragraph will be related to what the paper is about – WTD. In four paragraphs, the authors have summarized the literature (SPL), critiqued it (CPL), and by doing so they have identified a shortcoming (GAP), which has served as a rationale (RAT) for why their paper is warranted – why someone should care. The last paragraph tells readers what the authors will do in the paper (WTD).

As can be seen, introductions, like abstracts, are not formless; they have a logical form and structure. As appetizers before the main course – the literature review, data and methods, and results – they provide an outline and a map of what's to come in the rest of the article. When students are reading social science journal articles, they should follow the logic and form that is already inherent in them. As shown here, abstracts are organized in a way that is predictable and anticipatable. The reading codes ought to be used as boundary markers so that students know what they're reading, page by page, paragraph by paragraph, line by line. Thus, the ideas contained in the abstract should appear in the introduction, and the ideas in the introduction elaborated to a greater extent in the literature review. And by using the reading codes, students should be able to anticipate the next item to appear in the article; if the reading codes are used during the act of reading, students should never have to ask "Where is this article going?" or "What's the author trying to do?" The answers to those questions should emerge naturally and ineluctably from the way social science journal articles are structured and organized.

When students become adept at reading, they will begin asking themselves, "Will this assertion that is fraught with tension be resolved in the subsequent sections?" (WIL). Such questions arise because the reader has already anticipated several potential paths of the author's logic and her/his argument's possible itinerary. If the authors fail to connect logically related points, the reader will note that they missed an obvious theoretical, conceptual, and analytical connection to earlier works (MOP). Sometimes, the reader may "see" points that even the authors did not intend or anticipate. Such omissions in the text that you are reading do not point out any limitations and gaps; rather, the stated point could be used as a POC in a future paper – that is, Relevant Point to Pursue (RPP) and mine in another paper.

How to read the data and methods section

One of the primary objectives of the methods section parallels the hallmark of science – reproducibility. That is, those interested enough – for whatever reason – in a study ought to be able to recreate its conditions sufficiently so that the results can be challenged or confirmed. According to Jordan and Zanna (1999, p. 464), readers ought to pay attention to the following guidelines while reading methods sections: (1) how the independent and dependent variables are measured and (2) do the measures accurately reflect the intended concepts? This means that if a student wants to critique the previous literature (CPL) on methodological grounds, then the deficiency in the current article or literature is a limitation and a GAP that the student could exploit as a way of remedying the gap in the literature (POC).

Consider how Piquero et al. (2010, p. 157) measured "life failure" of men at ages 32 and 48 based on history of employment, relationships, substance abuse, mental health, criminal justice involvement, and self-reported delinquency. If the men at those ages scored high, they were considered failures in life; a low score indicated success in life. So what constitutes a high score? If the men kept an unclean apartment or home, or moved more than twice within the past five years, that would be counted as life failure. Furthermore, if the men were not living with a female partner, or had been divorced within the past five years, or did not "get along well with female partner," the men would have been counted as a life failure. If the men had self-reported offenses in the past five years (excluding theft from work and tax fraud), they would have been counted as life failures. There are six other measures of life success and failure. Although these are an established and accepted way of measuring psychopathy and antisocial personalities, I'm sure that readers could find a way to critique those measures. An astute graduate student can find a way to argue that the purported measures do not accurately reflect the intended concepts. The grounds on which you – the student – could critique the measures used illustrates a Point of Critique (POC). Or one could find issue with the statistical tests that are used. If a previous study used a single measure, your POC could be that only one measure was used, and that you will remedy that GAP by using multiple measures.

Jordan and Zanna (1999) provide detailed instructions on how to read quantitatively designed social psychology journal articles. However, social sciences journal articles are not exclusively composed of quantitative studies. There are qualitative – non-statistical – approaches to data and analysis. Reading qualitative social science journal articles, however, is somewhat similar to reading quantitatively-designed studies. Consider Stephen Lyng's (1990) article entitled "Edgework: A social psychological analysis of voluntary risk taking" which was published in the *American Journal of Sociology*. In this article, Stephen Lyng introduces a new concept to explain various forms of voluntary risk-taking activities (e.g., skydiving, motorcycle racing); he does so by drawing on a rich theoretical tradition in sociology (e.g., Marx, Mead). So how did the author arrive at the new concept? What data did he use?

> As a jump pilot, I was able to observe the most intimate details of the group's activities. These observations were recorded in the form of field notes written up at the end of most weekends at the drop zone (an area approved by the FAA for parachute drops) and after many sky-diver social events. The accuracy of participant-observational data was also checked in intensive semistructured interviews with strategic respondents. In these interviews, which totaled scores of hours, respondents were asked to describe the experience of dealing with the various risks associated with the sport. (Lyng, 1990, p. 856)

Lyng conducted semistructured interviews with skydivers. Based on the respondents' answers, the author identified recurring patterns in the data that led to three analytical categories: (1) various types of edgework activities; (2) specific individual capacities relevant to edgework; and (3) sensations associated with edgework. Note that no independent and dependent variables were measured. That's because in qualitative research, hypotheses are not tested as much as they are generated. In qualitative research – whether the form of the data is ethnographic text, transcriptions of interviews, or historical documents – the data are collated and classified into distinct analytical categories based on the principle of induction, also known as grounded theory (Strauss, 1987).

34

To develop a POC from the analytical categories, readers can question the validity of the theoretical concept the author introduces. Does the measure accurately reflect the intended concepts? That is, are the activities that Lyng lists as edgework sufficiently reflective of the concept of edgework? Moreover, readers can critique the fact that insufficient details were presented in the paper. Thus, how many participants did the ethnographer interview? How were the participants selected? How long did these interviews last? Were the respondents paid? And so on. These are all valid potential POCs that could be used to remedy methodological GAPs in the literature and as rationales (RATs) for another study.

As shown here, the abstract provides a brief synopsis of the main ingredients of an article in less than 200 words. The general introduction (not psychology introductions) elaborates on the main components of the article (SPL, CPL, GAP) hinted in the abstract in two to four paragraphs, but explicitly tells readers what it is the authors are going to do in the article (WTD). The literature review section (psychology introductions) will provide a much more extended SPL, CPL, GAP, and RAT (see Chapter 5). The methods section presents the material, method, and procedures used in the study. If a critique will be made on methodological grounds, it will revolve around the issue of measurement – measurement of independent and dependent variables and the accuracy and commensurability of measures intended to reflect a particular concept. During the act of reading, the code POC should be inserted whenever the reader finds either of the two issues questionable and debatable.

5

So What? How to Read the General Literature Review, Psychology Introductions, and Results Section

There is consensus in previous how-to books that the literature review is the most important component of any research paper, from master's-level theses to PhD dissertations. This point is true in journal articles as well, for it is here that authors review the work of others and make their proposed work relevant to previous works. Furthermore, the critique of the previous works provides a rationale for why our – your – proposed work is necessary and warranted. That is, before we can proffer our own "knowledge claims," (Vipond, 1996) we must tell readers which authors carried out similar studies and examined similar topics, and why our work is sufficiently different and contributes to the knowledge on a given topic.

If the literature is inadequately covered, then the ideas that we present in our papers – knowledge claims – might be framed as being too one-of-a-kind, often ignoring, unwittingly, the work that preceded ours; by doing so, we fail to acknowledge that other scholars have had similar ideas long before. In plain language, beginning graduate students often try to reinvent the wheel on a given topic. Academic writing, however, should not be conceptualized as wheel invention. Instead, it is more accurate to frame the proposed work as wheel modification. As Vipond (1996, p. 39) advises, do not "expect to develop your own knowledge claim without first examining and understanding those of other scholars. Claims are seldom completely original; instead, they are connected to, and grow out of, the claims of others."

One of the elementary mistakes that students make when writing research papers and drafts of theses is the failure to connect to the work of previous researchers – the literature. Out of deference, a fledgling student might leave out the name of a prominent scholar for fear of contradicting and disagreeing with a "big name"; or, the omission arises from insufficient reading. Students need to understand that citations are acknowledgements – good or bad – and they are the currency of academic life and business; omitting a relevant name/theorist from the literature review constitutes a slight of the tallest order. Therefore, do not be afraid to critique and disagree. Disagreements are better than omissions, witting and unwitting.

Others who have written books on how to do a literature review have lamented the fact that students simply rehash the work of others in a literature review. We might call this practice the making of a "laundry list." Rudestam and Newton (2001, p. 56) write that "many students erroneously believe that the purpose of the literature review is to convince the reader that the writer is knowledgeable about the work of others. Based on this misunderstanding, the literature review may read like a laundry list of previous studies, with sentences or paragraphs beginning with the words 'Smith found... Johnson found... Jones found...'." I too made this mistake when I finished my dissertation and submitted a chapter from it to a journal. Both reviewers noted that the literature review read like a laundry list. A laundry list literature review is a simple compendium of facts from previous works, author by author, year by year; it is cumbersome and tedious to read; in a journal article it takes up too much space. Most importantly, a laundry list literature fails to identify thematically parsimonious points of similarity across the literature. That's why creating a laundry list leads to the laundry list problem.

Previous literature must be organized in some logically connected way. Landrum (2008, p. 96) instructs students to "group research studies and other types of literature according to common denominators such as qualitative versus quantitative, objectives, methodology, and so forth." This advice simply means that the laundry list of authors has to be grouped in some principled way. Methodological distinctions are one way to group prior studies; conceptual distinctions are another. However, merely stating what others have said about a topic – author by author, year by year – constitutes only a quarter of a competent literature review. The other quarter entails a thematic and principled summary of previous works. The remaining half entails a thematically connected critique of the previous literature that identifies gaps in the knowledge base, which leads to the rationale for a study. Summarizing the work of others – the first half of the literature review – is represented by the reading code Summary of Previous Literature (SPL). SPL refers to sentences, paragraphs, or pages that describe a summary of the results from prior studies and works. SPL requires a tremendous amount of condensation, taking complex ideas and reducing them into paragraphs, sentences, and if the author is brilliant enough, one word (see Chapter 8).

How to read a literature review

The location of literature reviews in journal articles differs by discipline. In most psychology journals, the literature review is placed up front as part of the introduction; psychology journals therefore combine a general introduction (where the subcomponents of an article are briefly described) and an extensive literature review into one section. There is a separate section for literature reviews, usually under that very heading, in most sociology, criminology, and communication journals. No matter where literature reviews are located in a journal article, the work that is done in them is all the same: summary of previous work, critique of previous work that highlights a gap in the knowledge, and a rationale of why the proposed work – your work – is necessary. Consider how literature reviews are structurally organized.

There are 11 paragraphs in the introduction section of "Distinguishing juvenile homicide from violent juvenile offending" in DiCataldo and Everett's (2008) article in the *International Journal of Offender Therapy and Comparative Criminology*. The first sentence of the first paragraph reads, "*Homicide, particularly by means of firearms, among contemporary American male adolescents has been the focus of intense media coverage, social science research, and moral commentary*" (p. 158). This topic sentence provides a succinct yet broad overview of juvenile homicide as a topic. It introduces the reader to what the paper will be about. Moreover, it tells readers that the topic has been addressed by three different stakeholders as well. The rest of the sentences in that paragraph support and illustrate that first topic sentence. The first paragraph and first sentence would be an example of SPL. On the right margin next to this paragraph, the code SPL should be inserted after the paragraph is read.

The second paragraph begins with the following sentence: "*Juvenile murder is essentially a legal category defined within a state's criminal codes, statutes, and case law*" (p. 159). Readers ought to expect that the rest of the sentences that follow this topic sentence will be related to the various definitions of juvenile murder. In fact, the very next sentence reads, "*It is not a diagnostic term, like schizophrenia, or personality disorder*" (p. 159). The authors are introducing the distinction between a legal definition of murder and a clinical term used to diagnose offenders' psychological states. Notice that the second sentence supports and elaborates on the first sentence. The rest of the sentences in that second paragraph go on to differentiate between the two categories. So far what we have is SPL, and that code ought to be entered in the right margin next to the paragraph. Then the following sentence appears as the last sentence of the second paragraph: "*It remains an empirical question as to whether juvenile murderers are a scientifically valid category apart from their existence as a legal one*" (p. 159).

The last sentence clearly does not provide a summary of the previous literature. All of the preceding sentences, in one way or another, have provided support for the ways in which juvenile murder has been conceptualized, defined, and discussed (SPL). The last sentence, however, does not perform

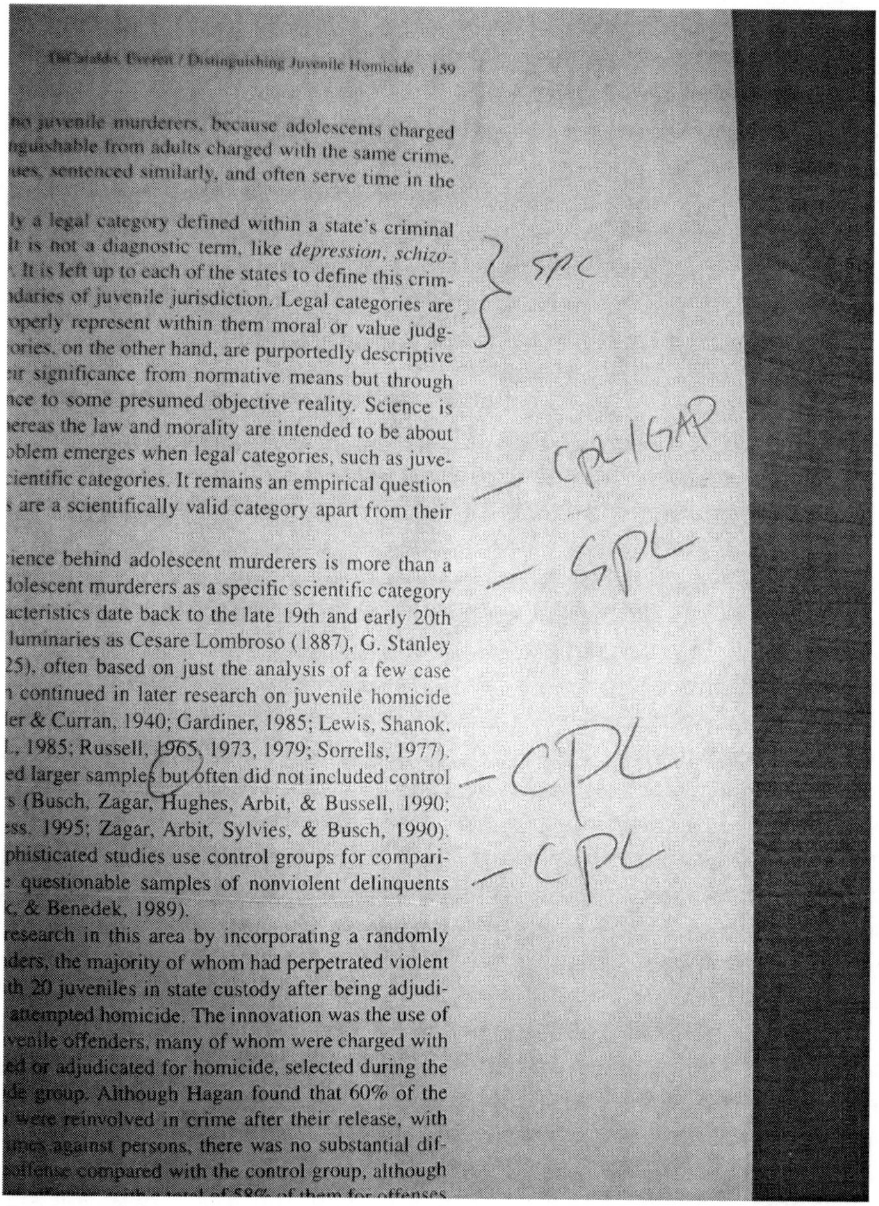

DiCataldo, Everett / Distinguishing Juvenile Homicide   159

no juvenile murderers, because adolescents charged
guishable from adults charged with the same crime.
ues, sentenced similarly, and often serve time in the

ly a legal category defined within a state's criminal
It is not a diagnostic term, like *depression, schizo-*
. It is left up to each of the states to define this crim-
daries of juvenile jurisdiction. Legal categories are
operly represent within them moral or value judg-
ories, on the other hand, are purportedly descriptive
ir significance from normative means but through
nce to some presumed objective reality. Science is
ereas the law and morality are intended to be about
oblem emerges when legal categories, such as juve-
cientific categories. It remains an empirical question
s are a scientifically valid category apart from their

ence behind adolescent murderers is more than a
dolescent murderers as a specific scientific category
acteristics date back to the late 19th and early 20th
luminaries as Cesare Lombroso (1887), G. Stanley
25), often based on just the analysis of a few case
continued in later research on juvenile homicide
er & Curran, 1940; Gardiner, 1985; Lewis, Shanok,
., 1985; Russell, 1965, 1973, 1979; Sorrells, 1977).
ed larger samples but often did not included control
s (Busch, Zagar, Hughes, Arbit, & Bussell, 1990;
ss. 1995; Zagar, Arbit, Sylvies, & Busch, 1990).
phisticated studies use control groups for compari-
: questionable samples of nonviolent delinquents
c, & Benedek, 1989).
research in this area by incorporating a randomly
ders, the majority of whom had perpetrated violent
th 20 juveniles in state custody after being adjudi-
attempted homicide. The innovation was the use of
venile offenders, many of whom were charged with
ed or adjudicated for homicide, selected during the
de group. Although Hagan found that 60% of the
were reinvolved in crime after their release, with
mes against persons, there was no substantial dif-
offense compared with the control group, although

} SPC

— CPL/GAP

— SPL

— CPL

— CPL

FIGURE 3

that summarizing function. It does suggest that there is a missing element in the existing literature on juvenile homicide: no one has yet to determine if juvenile killers are a "scientifically valid category." Another way of describing sentences like that would be to state that they are pointing out a critique (CPL) and a gap (GAP) in the existing literature. There is a gap because no one has addressed that topic; we could also state that that sentence is a critique of the previous literature (CPL) because, again, no one has addressed that question. The codes CPL/GAP should be inserted in the right margin next to that sentence/paragraph (see Figure 3).

So far, we have examined two paragraphs in one journal article. In those two paragraphs, the authors of the article have summarized the literature into two themes: (1) significance of juvenile murder as a topic; and (2) definition of juvenile murder. In the last sentence of the second paragraph, the possible shortcomings or deficiencies (CPL/GAP) in the literature have been suggested. A Critique of Previous Literature (CPL) provides a critique and a limitation contained in previous scholarship. CPL highlights the deficiencies in the existing works on a theoretical, methodological, and analytical level; CPL is conceptually related to GAP since GAP specifically identifies the shortcoming in the literature as well. And notice how those codes, SPL, CPL, and GAP, are structurally and logically connected. Before something can be critiqued, the content of that something has to be filled in first. In most, if not all, literature reviews, that's how a critique of the literature is done. The author(s) proffers a body of ideas, theories, and works of previous researchers; if this component is listed one by one, and presented that way in theses, dissertations, or journal articles, what we would have is a "laundry list" – the cardinal sin of any literature review.

But DiCataldo and Everett (2008) do not discuss the literature, author by author and year by year, in a way that resembles a laundry list. They have synthesized their readings and identified a recurring theme, and structured their literature review along those recurring thematic lines. If you are instructed to synthesize your readings, by definition, you must combine all of your assigned readings and form something new. No one can do that for you. You, the reader and author, must create those thematic categories from the readings you have done. That's what makes the research and writing process – scholarship – creative acts. In addition to developing thematic categories, DiCataldo and Everett (2008) have also begun to subtly hint at the missing dimensions of the existing literature. That is, they have tacitly begun the critique of the previous literature and set up an expectation of the rationale (RAT) for their own work. Structurally, then, SPLs precede CPLs and GAPs. When reading journal articles, CPLs will follow SPLs. This is one way to avoid unstructured reading. Readers should understand that ideas in journal articles are structurally and sequentially organized: summaries of literature introduce the reader to a topic in some thematic and principled way; critiques then follow. Again, one can't begin a critique out of nothing; there has to be something to critique. Film critics cannot – do not – exist if there are no films.

There are other grammatical clues to look for that CPL and GAPs are emerging in the text. The third paragraph of "Distinguishing juvenile homicide" begins with, "*The search for the clinical science behind adolescent murderers is more than a century old.*" The sentences that follow clarify in greater detail how that topic has been relevant for at least 100 years, the main feature of previous research being limited sampling. Then the following two sentences appear at the paragraph's end: "*More recent studies have examined larger samples **but** often did not included* [sic] *control groups of nonhomicide offenders. Some more methodologically sophisticated studies use control groups for comparison purposes **but** elected to use questionable samples of nonviolent delinquents*" (p. 159). Notice that phrases like "more recent studies" and "some more methodologically sophisticated studies" summarize previous works. In those types of sentence, the first clauses perform the work of SPL; the second clauses do the work of CPL and GAP. Coordinating the two contrasting ideas are disjunction markers. What do those do in a text?

Pretend for a minute that you are the recipient of the following words from someone you have a crush on: "I like you; I think you're great. You're sweet; you're funny and really nice ...[?]..." Even before I finish the rest of the sentence, I know that a lot of the readers will know the word that will appear next: "...BUT..." We know because some of us who have lost the parental lottery and have not received the cute gene have heard the painful phrases that follow. In fact, I suspect that when men and women hear a list like that – a series of complimentary assertions that appear independently and without any context or follow a strongly-encouraged request for a dialogue ("we should talk") – their gut (not intellect) already senses the bad news to come; the word 'but' confirms the initial suspicion; the actual bad news – "we should just be friends" – hammers the nail in the coffin.

That disjunction marker – but – coordinates the rejection to come – about why it would be better to be "just friends" than dating partners. In other words, words like "but," "however," "while," "albeit," and "although" do the work of highlighting and contrasting the consequent from the antecedent. Hence, in the preceding sentences discussed, SPL comes first ("I like you"; "more recent studies have examined larger samples"; "some more methodologically sophisticated studies use control groups for comparison purposes"), followed by the CPL/GAP ("we should just be friends"; "often did not included [sic] control groups of nonhomicide offenders"; "elected to use questionable samples of nonviolent delinquents"). That a CPL/GAP is on the way is signaled by the appearance of the disjunction marker such as "but." In the context of literature reviews, again, SPLs, as a rule, precede CPLs. Grammatical disjunction markers such as "but" and "however" are good indicators that the ideas proffered in the first clause or paragraph will be critiqued and qualified in the second. In addition to the structural locations of texts, looking out for grammatical markers that contrast ideas is another way to structure reading so that readers can anticipate critiques.

Does this pattern hold true in other disciplines besides criminology? Does SPL precede CPL and can disjunction markers serve as signs of GAPs to emerge? Consider the following from a well-cited and influential sociology journal article that was published in the *American Journal of Sociology*, one of the top journals in the field. The third sentence of the first paragraph reads, *"In this classic work, Shaw and McKay argued that three structural factors – low economic status, ethnic heterogeneity, and residential mobility – led to the disruption of community organization, which, in turn, accounted for variations in crime and delinquency. **However**, while past researchers have examined Shaw and McKay's predictions concerning community change and extralocal influences on delinquency* [citations omitted], *no one has directly tested their theory of social disorganization"* (Sampson & Groves, 1989, pp. 774–775). Again, notice that SPL emerges first in the text (discussion of Shaw and McKay's three structural facts that disrupt a community's organization) and then the CPL/GAP. The disjunction marker "however" provides a clue that the SPL will be critiqued in some way, and the authors go on to tell readers what the GAP is: no one has directly tested their ideas. That's a pretty significant deficiency in the literature that warrants remedy.

In the very next paragraph, the authors write, *"First, most ecological researchers inspired by Shaw and McKay have examined the effects of such characteristics as median income, racial composition, and residential mobility on crime rates* [citations omitted]. **While** *useful as a preliminary test, this strategy does little to verify and refine social-disorganization theory since it does not go beyond the steps already taken by Shaw and McKay"* (Sampson & Groves, 1989, p. 775). Again the first sentence describes the literature (SPL) and the second sentence critiques the literature (CPL). Sampson and Groves charge that the literature has moved little beyond what Shaw and McKay initially claimed. Again, a disjunction marker ("while") signals the approaching criticism in the text. The next two sentences in the same paragraph repeat that pattern: one sentence summarizes the literature ("As Kornhauser argues..."); a disjunction marker ("but") sets up the critique to emerge. By carefully reading the first two paragraphs of the literature review, readers already have a good idea of how the logic of the argument will unfold.

Readers should keep in mind that topic sentences of paragraphs perform a certain type of work in journal articles; they summarize previous literature (SPL) in some cogent way; these should be noted in the right margins of printed articles. Disjunction markers that appear after SPLs can serve as clues to the CPLs/GAPs to come. CPLs and GAPs also should be written at the margins. Does this pattern (SPL, CPL, GAP) hold for disciplines other than criminology and sociology?

In "Adolescent-limited versus persistent delinquency: Extending Moffitt's hypothesis into adulthood," published in the *Journal of Abnormal Psychology*, White, Bates, and Buyske (2001) extend Terrie Moffitt's theory of delinquency into adulthood. As noted, literature reviews occur early on in psychology journals. The first sentences of the first and second paragraphs read, (1) "*Some criminologists have argued that criminal propensity is attributable to stable individual differences established early in life*" (2) "*Moffitt has proposed that for some individuals, antisocial behavior is stable and persistent, whereas for others it is temporary*" (p. 600). Both sentences and paragraphs serve to introduce readers to a broad summary of the literature (SPL). The rest of the sentences elaborate on the themes developed. Then in the second sentence of the third paragraph, the authors write, "*The hypothesized neuropsychological, personality, and environmental risk factors have been useful in distinguishing early onset from escalating delinquency and childhood-to-adolescence-persistent from adolescence-limited delinquency* [citations omitted]. *Yet, little is currently known about the utility of this typology for differentiating adolescence-limited from adolescence-to-adulthood-persistent delinquency*" (p. 600).

As can be seen here, the pattern repeats again, with SPL occurring before CPL. Moreover, the disjunction marker "yet" again portends the CPL to follow the SPL. While there may be other techniques that scholars have to use to summarize and critique the literature, I have found that the structural organization of texts, and the grammatical markers that indicate conceptual transitions, are good heuristic devices to employ during the act of reading. Thus, without even elaborating on the content of the sentences, their structural location in the text, the grammatical clues proffered, and by examining only the form of the sentences, we can discern that the second sentence critiques the first – pushes against the ideas contained in the first sentence. Understanding the work that sentences and paragraphs perform in a journal article is the first step in organizing the information that one reads in the literature. Thus, without even reading the content of the sentence, we know that the first sentence in the literature review in the next section which begins with "*According to Moffitt...*" will be a summary of previous works (SPL). The disjunction marker "however" intimates that the rest of the words to follow will push against the preceding SPL. Similarly, sentences that begin with words such as "although," "despite," "yet," "unfortunately," "regrettably," and "sadly" connect the SPL and CPL by putting the disjunction marker first, but still abide by the SPL→CPL format. For example, "*Although neuropsychological functioning and personality characteristics have been found to differentiate early-onset from late-onset delinquents, few studies have examined their ability to differentiate those individuals who persist in delinquency beyond adolescence from those who do not*" (p. 600). Very few people have examined those who persist into adulthood from those who do not. In other words, there's a GAP – something is missing in the literature; that's why the proposed study is worth doing. That's why SPL, CPL, and GAP are logically connected. Although only heuristic, the reading codes represent simple guidelines to follow when reading social science journal articles.

Some journals (and authors and disciplines) organize summaries and critiques into separate and distinct sections. For instance, Dixon and Linz (2000) organize the summary of the literature into the following thematic categories: (1) overemphasis on white victimization; (2) indices of victimization; (3) intergroup comparisons of victims; (4) interrole comparisons of victimization; (5) utility of intergroup and interrole measures; and (6) inter-reality comparisons. Again, notice what the authors have not done. They have not listed the literature author by author and year by year in the manner of a laundry list. They have organized the voluminous literature on race, media, and crime into the aforementioned six categories, in a way that is meaningful for what they aim to do in their work. Dixon and Linz (2000, pp. 553–554) go on to provide a separate section for the limitations of previous literature section: "*This section attempts to overcome several of the limitations of prior works that examined race and victimization. In this section, we lay out three limitations of this prior research and how this addresses them.*" One could even anticipate what the criticism might be, based on the way the existing literature is organized and discussed. This type of structural format makes reading and organizing voluminous amounts of information easier, for we the readers are spared from acting like textual detectives. Even this type of format, however, follows the general rule stipulated here: SPL, then CPL. Again, that's because before we can critique a body of work, the reader has to know what that body of work is, so that the critique can be meaningful. The GAP emerges from this process. This process is what Vipond (1996) means when he states that new claims grow out of previous claims.

GAPs are conceptually related to RAT. The deficiencies in the present state of knowledge justify and warrant a study that will remedy the missing gap in the knowledge base – that's the rationale for why a study is necessary. So if someone asks, "So what? Why should anyone care about your work?" the answer ought to be a derivative of CPL and GAP. Thus, if someone asks you why anyone should care about your work (senior thesis, master's thesis, or dissertation), your hypothetical response should be something like the following: "My study is worth doing because (1) few have done it, (2) others who have done the type of work have used incorrect measures, used the wrong statistical tests, or incorrectly defined the problem, and (3) they have made little progress beyond what the seminal theorists have done." In journal articles, the answers to the "so what?" questions come in 3–5 carefully argued rationales (RAT).

Dixon and Linz (2000) list three answers to the "so what?" question that are logically connected to CPL and GAP: (1) Previous studies have used one measure. This sentence would be an example of CPL/GAP. So how will this gap be remedied? "This study uses multiple indicators" (p. 554). The use of multiple indicators is RAT #1. (2) "Very few studies have analyzed portrayals of Latinos on television news." This sentence would be an example of CPL/ GAP. So how will this gap be remedied? The current work analyzes Latinos. Analysis of Latinos on television is RAT #2. (3) No one has examined Los Angeles television news. This sentence would be an example of CPL/GAP. So how will this gap be remedied? Our current work examines television news in Los Angeles, where a lot of Latinos live. This is RAT #3. The three GAPs in the literature and their proposed remedies function as RAT – the rationale for the study. In a proper literature review, one must review and summarize the literature (SPL), and critique the literature (CPL) by finding shortcomings and deficiencies in the literature (GAPs); and the remedy of those gaps constitutes the rationale for the proposed study (RAT): SPL→CPL→GAP→ RAT. A competently done literature review – not a laundry list – generally follows the format outlined above.

Rudestam and Newton (2001) write that a literature review is more than a simple list of previous works. As argued here, that's only half of a literature review. A competently done literature review ought to transport the reader to the destination before arriving. In Rudestam and Newton's (2001, p. 58) words, "by the end of the literature review, the reader should be able to conclude that 'yes, of course, this is the exact study that needs to be done at this time to move knowledge in this field a little further along'." That "yes" moment occurs because the SPL→RAT process unfolds in a logical, thematic, and anticipatable way. And advances in disciplines do not occur by leaps and bounds; they occur incrementally, one study at a time. Each study modifies the wheel little by little. When readers finish reading the SPL, CPL, and GAP, they should be able to anticipate the RAT, the hypothesis to be tested, or argument being made. When students are writing, the logical structure of their papers ought to follow along the preceding lines so that readers can expect and anticipate the next item from the previous one.

For example, White et al. (2001, p. 601) examine the delinquent trajectories of adolescents into adulthood: *"On the basis of previous studies of childhood-to-adolescence persistence, we hypothesized that three different trajectories would be identified ... we also hypothesized that adolescence-limited and adolescence-to-adulthood-persistent delinquents would differ on selected measures of neuropsychological functioning, personality risk, and environmental risk."* How did the authors arrive at these two hypotheses? The key theorist in this area is Terrie Moffitt (1993a, 1993b), who claims that delinquency is temporary for most delinquents while for some it persists into adulthood (SPL). The authors organize the SPL (under the major heading "Differentiating limited and persistent trajectories of delinquency") into three themes: (1) neuropsychological dysfunction; (2) personality; and (3) environmental adversity. White et al. (2001, p. 601) go on to write, *"Yet, little is currently known about the utility of this typology for differentiating adolescence-limited from adolescence-to-adulthood-persistent delinquency. … **Although** neuropsychological functioning and personality characteristics have been found to differentiate early-onset from late-onset delinquents, few studies have examined their ability to differentiate those individuals who persist in delinquency beyond adolescence from those who do not"* (CPL/GAP).

White et al. summarize the literature (SPL), point out the limitations of previous works (CPL), and identify a deficiency in the literature (GAP); and by pointing out the shortcoming in the previous literature, the authors have provided an implicit rationale (RAT) of why their work is necessary and warranted. If someone were to ask them "so what?" they could answer by stating that no one knows the "utility of this typology" and that "few studies are able to differentiate life-course-persistent offenders from adolescent-limited offenders." Those answers to the "so what?" question are their way of remedying the gap in the literature. From this logical chain of reasoning, the hypothesis emerges. The emergence of the hypothesis is not an act of magic – out of the blue – for authors usually carefully set up the reader to anticipate the hypothesis and to see the logic of their reasoning by introducing her to the literature (SPL), its limitations and criticisms (CPL), and shortcomings (GAP). The hypothesis follows naturally and inevitably from the way the authors have crafted and organized their ideas. That's why, by the end of a literature review, the reader is able to "conclude that 'yes, of course, this is the exact study that needs to be done at this time to move knowledge in this field a little further along'" (Rudestam & Newton, 2001, p. 58).

How to read the results section

Results sections are probably the easiest to read, for authors simply lay out their main findings. In "Urban black violence: The effect of male joblessness and family disruption," Sampson (1987, p. 377) reports the following results (published in a sociology journal): *"while male joblessness has little or no impact on crime, it has the strongest overall effect on family disruption, which in turn is the strongest predictor of black violence.*" An assertion like the preceding one in the results section constitutes a "knowledge claim" and should be treated as such by marking on the right margin Result of Findings (ROF). ROFs describe the primary results of the article being read. This particular finding is significant given the author's summary and critique of the previous literature – previous theories that have explained black criminality in the US as a function of a subculture that condones and promotes violence. Sampson is arguing against such views in this article.

Moffitt et al. (1996) report in their results section (published in a psychology journal) that teachers rated life-course-persistent offenders as being more antisocial than adolescence-limited delinquents at ages 5, 7, 9, 11, and 13. Such a finding would support their theory of delinquency, which claims the existence of two distinct trajectories of offending. Those ROFs are found in the Abstract, Results, and Discussion and Conclusion sections; the main ROFs are what need to be marked and noted. Pritchard and Hughes (1997, pp. 58, 60) report in their results (published in a communication journal) that "the race of a homicide victim accounted for almost all of the predictive power of race," and that the "most consistent predictor of newsworthiness was whether the victim was a child or a senior." The ROFs are noteworthy because the authors are showing patterns in newspaper coverage that others have simply assumed. DiCataldo and Everett (2008, p. 167) report in their results section (published in a criminology journal) that "the non-homicide group had more significant delinquent histories than the homicide group on a number of the delinquency variables." Such an ROF is significant because it is counterintuitive and also supports previous literature. All of the significant and relevant – for your paper's aims – ROFs ought to be highlighted, underlined, or made salient in some way; the code ROF should be inserted on the right margin so that even if the reader wants to go back and look up the primary findings several months later, she can look at the ROF code and know exactly what it is that she is looking at.

Transitioning from ROF to SPL: Making the quarter turn

As I have shown here, the reading codes are meant to facilitate critical reading by understanding the work that sentences and paragraphs perform in a particular type of text, the social science journal article. By inserting the pertinent reading codes at the right margins, the readers are actively reading by summarizing (SPL), critiquing (CPL), identifying shortcomings (GAP), and cultivating points of critique (POC). Simply put, the general instructions that previous scholars have proffered to "read critically" and "think critically" have simply been condensed into operational codes that could be deployed during the act of reading. When it comes time for students to write their own literature reviews, for a research paper, thesis, or dissertation, they have to reproduce in their papers what they have read others do in those social science journal articles. The reading codes are meant to help students in the writing process by actively and critically engaging texts – precisely by summarizing, critiquing, identifying gaps, and cultivating their own unique contributions to the literature during the act of reading. For example, let's say that an undergraduate senior is writing an honor's thesis on personality and crime, and she has found 30 journal articles that have been published on that topic within the last ten years. How should she organize her literature review?

First, the ROFs from the 30 articles she has read will become SPLs of her paper. That's because the 30 articles she found on personality and crime while searching PsycINFO, or any other database, constitutes – is – the previous literature. The authors of those 30 articles will have read the seminal works of other researchers in the field, and the works they have read became the SPLs of their articles. The 30 authors identified CPLs and GAPs and proposed to remedy that GAP in the literature (RAT) by doing original studies. The results of those original studies constituted the ROFs of their papers. Therefore, the first step involves looking through the 30 articles and figuring out what common denominators exist in all of her ROFs because those ROFs will become her SPLs. Again, Landrum (2008) tells us to "group research studies and other types of literature according to common denominators such as qualitative versus quantitative, objectives, methodology" and so on. Second, the said student will have to look for common patterns that can be collapsed into several themes. What she cannot do is list the 30 authors one by one; then a laundry list problem is created. There is a way to mine the 30 articles you have read to assist you in your writing process.

Our hypothetical student who is writing her paper on personality and crime can begin by looking through the 30 articles and scanning the right margins and identifying all SPLs. She would then examine that sentence and/or paragraph and insert a sufficiently broad theme or a word on the left margin of the printed articles. For example, in DiCataldo and Everett's (2008) article on juvenile murder, there should be three words that summarize the three paragraphs we used as excerpts: (1) significance; (2) definition; and (3) time – or something along those lines. For the Dixon and Linz (2000) article, there should be six words/phrases that thematically summarize the paragraphs and sentences: (1) white emphasis; (2) victimization indices; (3) comparisons; (4) intergroup/interrole; (5) utility of measures and (6) interreality. Thematic code insertions can be done at the same time that reading codes are inserted, on the first act of reading, or saved for later. Doing both simultaneously, however, requires practice. Until the reader is familiar enough with the reading codes, and comfortable enough with the act of reading, the left margin insertions ought to be done after the first act of reading. When trying to come up with ways of organizing your own literature review, the thematic codes and summaries ought to serve as a guide in the preparation of your paper. Use the way previous SPLs are organized from your reading of the 30 articles as a way of framing and guiding your own SPL from the ROFs. We might call this turning the SPL a quarter turn. Why reinvent the wheel?

The second step in the writing process involves coming up with a critique of the previous literature so that you can justify your paper on personality and crime. You need to be able to answer the "so what?" question. How do you go about finding limitations and deficiencies in previous literature? Go through your 30 journal articles and identify all the GAPs. What patterns exist in your GAP collection? What Point of Critique (POC) can you develop based on those GAPs? POC is a deficiency in the articles you have read or the literature in general that you could use as a way of remedying a deficiency in the literature. POC is easily developed with experience; that's because POC is developed and refined over time – through years of continuous reading. First-time graduate students and upper-class undergraduates do not yet have the experience of cultivating POCs when they embark on their research papers. There is a way, however, for beginners to exploit their reading codes to cultivate their POC.

Go through the 30 articles again and scan for CPLs. As mentioned earlier, CPL is a critique of SPL. On what grounds did the previous authors – authors of the 30 articles you will have read – critique the SPL? That is, are there common denominators in the way that the authors of the 30 articles on personality and crime have CPLed the SPL? Usually, the answer is yes. Use those existing themes to cultivate your own POC. Moreover, look at the right margins again and identify all the Recommendations for Future Works (RFWs); these are signposts to the GAPs in the literature. That's why the authors put them in their conclusions – because there is still a GAP in the literature that needs to be remedied. RFWs, along with patterns and trends in the way SPL is CPLed, are a good way to mine for one's own unique way of organizing a literature review. Using that existing pattern that others have used as a way of framing your own paper might be called "making a quarter turn." Such turns do not invert or subvert the established ideas, theories, and critiques in paradigm-shifting ways; you are simply turning the SPL and CPL just enough to be different from previous studies while justifying the necessity of your own proposed study.

6

Becoming a Part of the Scholarly Community: How to Read the Discussion and Conclusion

In previous chapters, I noted that one of the elementary mistakes that students make when writing research papers and drafts of theses is the failure to connect to the works of previous researchers. Regrettably, this problem is not unique to students; freshly-minted PhDs and even seasoned academics fail to connect their papers to the relevant literature. I am no exception. I too have made this error, and continue to make it because I have not read sufficiently or widely. In previous chapters, I also argued that connecting to the work of others in the literature review entails doing two things: (1) summarizing the work that others have done (SPL), and (2) identifying shortcomings in the current state of the literature as part of a critique (CPL, GAP). Once previous works are discussed and critiqued, students have set up a rationale (RAT) for why their proposed work (e.g., honor's thesis, thesis, and dissertation) is warranted and necessary. The proposed work will be necessary because it will remedy the knowledge gap that exists in the literature. Once you – the student – are able to defend why your proposed study is necessary, you can begin the data collection process, analyze the data, and present the results of your study as part of an honor's thesis, master's thesis, and dissertation. As I have argued in this book, the social science journal articles that students have to read also follow the aforementioned general format (SPL→CPL→GAP→RAT). After authors have critiqued and provided a rationale for their studies, they have to provide a description of the data and methods used to analyze them. After the data and methods are introduced, authors present their findings in the results section. After the results are presented, then what? In most, if not all, social science journal articles, the authors provide readers with a discussion and/or conclusion section. This chapter teaches students how to read them.

In the discussion section, the results of findings (ROFs) are interpreted and explained in the context of the previous literature; results of findings (ROFs) from a study are significant given the author's summary and critique of the previous literature. In the results section, the findings are generally stated, without additional commentary or elaboration. If the literature review transports readers into the history of a discipline and a topic by bringing the past – previous scholars – to the present, the current study, then the discussion and conclusion take the findings from present research into the past and back to the future. In the literature review, the past is made relevant to the present by pointing out the limitations of previous works, which the current work attempts to overcome; in the discussion section, the present is made relevant to the past by interpreting current results in the context of past findings; moreover, the deficiencies in the current work are made relevant for other scholars who may want to remedy those gaps in the future. The discussion section thereby transports readers across three time periods – past, present, and future – by interpreting the present in the context of the past, and through self-reflexive criticism that sets up the RAT for future research.

For example, Glatthorn and Joyner (2005) instruct their writers (readers) to ask themselves what the study "means" when writing discussion sections. To do so, they provide helpful questions to follow when writing – and I would argue, reading – one's own discussion section: what is the "relationship of the current study to prior research?" and what are the "theoretical implications" of the study? Are there insights that the researcher could proffer? Are there unanticipated results that need to be reconciled and resolved? As Jordan and Zanna (1999) note, discussions can be "particularly interesting when the results did not work out exactly as the researchers anticipated." Furthermore, what are the limitations of the current research and what recommendations could be made for future and further research? If a competently executed literature review demonstrates its debt to the works of previous researchers and scholars by building upon their research, then the discussion and conclusion sections also perform a similar function by tethering the results of the current study to the past. That's why knowledge claims grow out of the claims of others: they are conceptually, methodologically, and temporally bound to the cyclical and historical character of academic scholarship. Knowledge claims do not – cannot – begin *ab initio*. Those types of questions that previous scholars have instructed writers to contemplate while writing discussion sections are also applicable to students who are reading journal articles. In this chapter, reading codes that are particularly related to discussions and conclusions (i.e., RCL, RTC, RFW, RPP) are taught and discussed.

How to read the discussion section

If there are minute differences in where the literature reviews are located in social science journal articles, discussion and conclusion sections almost always appear toward the end of an article – for the same reason that introductions have to appear at the beginning of an article. In the section below, select paragraphs from discussion sections are reproduced in order to teach students how to read the discussions and conclusions. To describe the function of the sentences in the discussion section, and for accessibility, clarity, and ease of reference, each sentence has been numbered consecutively. There are ten paragraphs in the discussion section of "Distinguishing juvenile homicide from violent juvenile offending" in DiCataldo and Everett's (2008) article in the *International Journal of Offender Therapy and Comparative Criminology*. The first paragraph of the discussion begins the following way:

> (1) This study set out to determine if adolescent homicide offenders could indeed be distinguished from a sample of violent nonhomicide perpetrators. (2) The overall findings contradict the predominant portrayals of adolescent homicide perpetrators in popular media outlets as the clinically distinguishable super-predator or cold psychopath compared with violent nonhomicide perpetrators, many of whom had been charged or convicted of murder. (3) In this study, the nonhomicide participants proved more problematic on many of the variables of analysis. (4) They often began their delinquent careers earlier, had significantly greater numbers of total offenses, and had more violent offenses. (5) The nonhomicide participants often had less stable early childhood histories, with more frequent placements out of the home and more frequent sibling delinquency. (6) They also reported being more likely to use knives in crimes of violence than the homicide group.

The first sentence of the first paragraph of the discussion tells readers the main research question that the authors have asked and attempted to answer in their paper. Sentences like it describe What They [authors] Did (WTDD). WTDD is a logical and historical cognate of WTD that appears in past tense in discussions and conclusions. Thus, there is temporal symmetry between WTD and WTDD, for authors instruct readers what they will do in the introduction and what they have done in the discussion and conclusion. The reading code WTDD should be inserted at the right margin next to that sentence.

The next sentence interprets and contextualizes the primary results of the findings (ROFs) from their study to the broader literature and culture.

The word "contradict" explicitly informs readers that DiCataldo and Everett's ROF was inconsistent with the popular notion of what it means to be a juvenile killer. Such sentences are best represented by the code RTC, Results To the Contrary, and that code ought to be inserted at the right margin. The rest of the sentences in the paragraph go on to elaborate on the ROFs from their study: that nonhomicide offenders were more problematic on several measures; and that they started criminal careers earlier than the homicide offender group, and had less stable lives at home. In the very next paragraph, DiCataldo and Everett (2008) note that the nonhomicide group had anger control issues and bad memories of their parents as well.

If the code RTC describes the way the ROFs contradict the findings from the literature, Results that are Consistent with the Literature (RCL) describe findings that corroborate and support results from previous studies. Thus, sentences like *"The homicide perpetrator's more frequent reports that they were intoxicated at the time of their deadly violent acts are consistent with recent research by Dolan and Smith (2001), who also reported that their sample of juvenile homicide offenders were more likely to report that they had abused alcohol at the time of their offenses than the nonhomicide offenders,"* and *"the homicide participants greater exposure to guns at home within their personal histories as a predisposing factor to their later homicidal acts is consistent with a recent report by Bingenheimer, Brennan and Earls (2005), who concluded that being exposed to firearm violence nearly doubled the probability than an adolescent would commit a serious violent act in the subsequent 2 years"* (DiCataldo & Everett, 2008 p. 170) in the third and fourth paragraph nestle their findings in the context and work of previous researchers. That is, rather than simply presenting their findings as new knowledge claims, they bind their ROFs within the context of work that others have already done. By doing so, DiCataldo and Everett (2008) join the community of researchers whose work corroborates a particular finding; they participate in the construction and reproduction of knowledge in the scholarly community – their claims become tied to the claims of others. Although their primary findings are RTC, other facets of their findings are consistent with the literature (RCL) on the topic, and next to those types of sentences, the code RCL should be inserted at the right margin.

So far, the authors have described how the findings from their research contradict and support the work that others have done. By linking their work to those of others, they are performing the very advice that writers like Glatthorn and Joyner (2005) have provided: answering questions like "what is the relationship of the current study to prior research?" and what are the "theoretical implications" of the study? The codes RCL and RTC describe two interpretive possibilities for ROFs of a study, and by elaborating on the relationship of the current ROFs to past ROFs the current findings are made meaningful and situated in the community of scholars who have carried out similar and related works. Although DiCataldo and Everett (2008) do not discuss the theoretical implications of their work, they do address the policy implications of their findings. They go on to critique the legislative changes that have occurred in the US which seek to treat adolescent killers like adults in the criminal justice system; such policies, they argue, are aimed at the wrong population, for their ROFs would indicate that nonhomicide offenders are much more psycho-socially problematic than homicide offenders. Again, by teasing out the implications of their research and findings for public policy, the authors make their research meaningful in the larger social context: they are able to contextualize their findings and make them relevant in the ongoing debate about crime and punishment; they are able to critique a social policy that may be targeting the wrong group and causing undue harm; more importantly, they can substantiate such criticisms based on empirical research. Those types of implications – theoretical, conceptual, methodological, policy – are teased out and pursued in the discussion section.

Their work, however, is not complete. In the first sentence of paragraph five, the authors write that "There exist a number of selection biases within this study that may account for the findings" (p. 170). They point out that "a differential processing of cases within the juvenile justice system may be operating that may alternatively explain the differences identified within this study" (p. 170). In other words, the authors are pointing out shortcomings – GAP – in their own work. That means that in future works someone could address those shortcomings of juvenile homicide research to overcome a GAP in the current state of the literature. Those types of sentences would illustrate Recommendations for Future Works (RFWs) and Relevant Point to Pursue (RPP). RFWs highlight the fact that the current paper is incomplete; the authors are providing a map of what is still missing (GAP) in the literature. Such POCs could be mined in a future paper by someone who is interested in the topic, and has the capacity to overcome those limitations. In the first sentence of the last paragraph, a similar sentence appears: "This study did not attempt to investigate the motivations or circumstances of the homicides for this sample of juveniles" (p. 172). This sentence again is a POC, for the authors tell the reader what was not done in the current paper; logically, the authors are pointing out a gap in the literature. Those GAPs could be used as POCs in another paper and represent RPPs and RFWs. Next to relevant sentences, the pertinent codes ought to be inserted at the right margin.

The last sentence of the last paragraph of the last page is even more explicit about how the shortcomings of the current paper can be remedied: "*Future research with this sample will progress toward a finer-grained, within-group analysis of the homicide perpetrators, coding the multidimensional contextual features of their acts of homicide by looking at the physical setting of the homicide, the interactional and historical relationships with the victims, the means and methods of homicide, the posthomicide behavior of the*

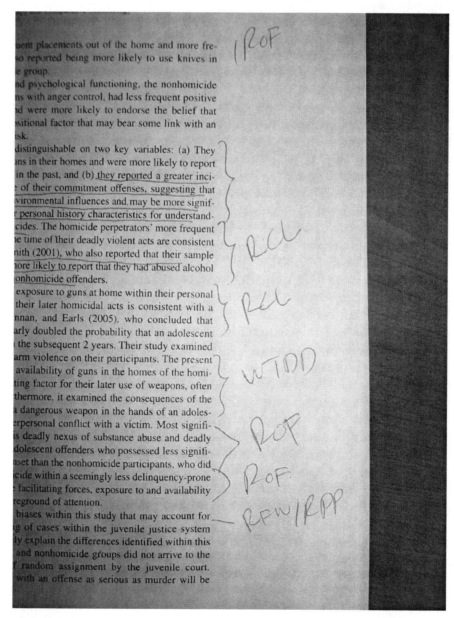

FIGURE 4

perpetrators, and the legal outcomes" (p. 172). In other words, the RFWs just mentioned illustrate the missing elements in the literature on juvenile homicide (GAPs) – they need to be addressed in the future. The code RFW should be inserted at the right margin of paper. That's five POCs and GAPs which the authors have provided in one sentence alone. That such GAPs and POCs are already contained in the articles being read is the reason why reading should not be treated as a secondary activity. The components of a future paper are already embedded in the current work. Writers do not necessarily have to come up with "new ideas," because they are already buried on the surface in the readings. Future writers just have to know how to find them during the act of reading.

In Sampson's (1987) article on "Urban black violence: The effect of male joblessness and family disruption" published in the *American Journal of Sociology*, there are six paragraphs that make up the discussion section under the heading "summary". The first two sentences of the first paragraph state: "(1) *The manifestations of the black 'underclass' have been discussed in recent literature but rarely empirically examined in a systematic theoretical framework, especially a structural one. (2) To redress this imbalance, the present study has attempted to link Wilson's theory of the structural determinants of black family disruption with a macrolevel perspective on communities and crime*" (p. 376). The first clause of the first sentence summarizes the literature (SPL); the first clause is coordinated with a disjunction marker that portends the contrast to emerge in the second clause (CPL). Then in the second sentence, the author tells readers the main research question he has attempted to answer – WTDD. This code should be inserted at the right margin.

Notice that even in the WTDD Sampson's research question is tethered to the claims of others. His work draws upon the ideas of William Wilson. How is Sampson's work related to that of Wilson? Sampson draws upon Wilson's research on black family disruption and uses it to examine its impact on crime and community. Readers can thus see that even the research questions that scholars ask and attempt to answer are not shaped in a vacuum; instead, they grow out of and arise from the literature itself – from the work of researchers in the scholarly community. Sampson goes on to connect his ROF to the work of previous scholars in the third paragraph:

(1) The consistent findings, that family disruption has stronger effects on juvenile crime than adult crime, in conjunction with the inconsistent findings of previous research on individual-level delinquency and broken homes (see Wilkinson 1980; Ross and Sawhill 1975) tends to support the idea that the effects of family structure are related to macrolevel patterns of social control and guardianship, especially regarding youths and their peers

(Sampson 1986b; Felson and Cohen 1980; Felson 1986). (2) However, it should be emphasized that definitive resolution of the mechanisms linking family disruption with crime rates must await further research, for direct measures of the hypothesized macrolevel mediating constructs (e.g., informal community supervision of peer groups, patterns of formal social control) are not currently available. (pp. 376–377)

Notice how the author connects his ROF to the ROFs from previous research in the discussion section. He begins his discussion section by pointing out how the literature on the impact of family disruption on juvenile crime has yielded inconsistent results; his ROFs, however, support ROFs from other works; that support is indicated through citations – RCL (i.e., Sampson, Cohen, and Felson). Again, the results from the current study are tied into the findings from previous research à la Sampson, Cohen, and Felson. Rather than presenting his findings as brand new knowledge claims, Sampson contextualizes the results from his study to those of others who have carried out similar studies. As such, the code RCL should be inserted at the right margin. Even Sampson's work, however, is incomplete, for he informs his readers that "direct measures of the hypothesized macrolevel mediating constructs are not currently available" (p. 377). Sentences like this illustrate a Recommendation for Future Works (RFW); Sampson is pointing to a GAP in the current state of the literature and proposing a way that it can be remedied in future works. Such an absence could be used as a POC to be pursued in a future paper, an RPP. In other words, the potential new ideas for future works are buried in the text being read, again illustrating the importance of learning to read critically through the use of the reading codes.

Eight paragraphs make up the discussion in Oliver and Armstrong's (1995) article on "Predictors of viewing and enjoyment of reality-based and fictional crime shows," published in *Journalism and Mass Communication Quarterly*. The first paragraph of the discussion begins the following way:

(1) The purpose of this study was to explore predictors of exposure to and enjoyment of reality-based crime programs. (2) Consistent with Zillmann's Disposition Theory, the results of this telephone survey suggest that these types of programs may be most appealing to viewers predicted to be particularly likely to enjoy the capture and punishment of criminal suspects who are often members of racial minorities. (3) Namely, this study found that reality-based programs were most enjoyed by viewers who evidenced higher levels of authoritarianism, reported greater punitiveness about crime, and reported higher levels of racial prejudice.

The first sentence repeats the main research question examined in the study; the code WTDD ought to be inserted at the right margin. The second sentence informs readers that the results of the study support the work of a previous researcher; hence, the code RCL ought to be inserted at the right margin. The third sentence provides the readers with the primary findings from the study: people who tend to be authoritarian, people who report greater punitiveness about crime, and those who tend to be racially prejudiced enjoy reality-based crime shows. The code ROF ought to be inserted at the right margin. The first paragraph is consistent with the form and structure of discussions that we have examined thus far: WTDD, ROF, RCL, RTC. Discussion sections are sites where the initial research question is repeated in the past tense, the primary results echoed, and then evaluated against the literature. Whether the reported results are consistent with the existing state of the knowledge, or contradict it, is played out in the discussion. Oliver and Armstrong (1995) do not explicitly tease out the social or policy implications of their work.

Simply noting if results support or contradict previous literature, as we have seen, is not enough. In the articles discussed thus far, the authors took time to bring to attention the limitations and deficiencies that exist in their own works. For example, Oliver and Armstrong (1995, p. 565) write that *"While the present investigation did not attempt to directly assess the relative beneficial or harmful functions of reality-based programs, the idea that these shows appeal to viewers with punitive, authoritarian, and prejudiced attitudes is worthy of further investigation."* Put another way, the present study did not assess the benefits or harms of reality-based programs; however, that such shows appeal to those who tend to be conservative in their political orientation should be pursued further. This means that there is a GAP somewhere in the literature. Again, the authors do not simply end there. They specifically provide four Recommendations for Future Works (RFWs) that are based on the presence of GAPs in their own works (pp. 565–566): RFW #1: *"future research may consider exploring reactions to these types of shows among a wider variety of respondents."* RFW #2: *"Further research may consider exploring the specific portrayals within this genre that appeal to viewers."* RFW #3: *"research could examine how long-term exposure may affect estimates of the prevalence of crime or the percentage of people of color who are involved in crime-related activities."* RFW #4: *"future studies may consider exploring how exposure to reality-based crime shows relates to perceptions and judgments about crimes witnessed or reported in other contexts."* Next to these sentences, the code RFW should be inserted at the right margin so that they are easily identifiable and retrievable. There are always GAPs in social science journal articles that could be used as POCs and already serve as RATs in a future paper.

There are eight paragraphs that comprise the discussion in White, Bates, and Buyske's (2001, pp. 606–607) paper entitled "Adolescence-limited versus persistent delinquency: Extending Moffitt's hypothesis into adulthood," published in the *Journal of Abnormal Psychology*. The first paragraph of the discussion begins the following way:

> (1) This study examined trajectories of delinquency from adolescence into adulthood. (2) Four different trajectory groups were identified, which partially confirms the hypotheses. (3) In accord with Moffitt's (1993a) model, an adolescence-limited and a persistent delinquent trajectory were both clearly differentiated from a non-delinquent trajectory. (4) In addition, a fourth trajectory group comprising escalating delinquents, who engaged in relatively little delinquency in early adolescence but whose delinquency increased from late adolescence into adulthood, was also identified.

The first sentence repeats the main research question addressed in the study. The code WTDD should be inserted at the right margin. The second sentence reports a main finding from the study, so the code ROF should be inserted at the right margin. The phrase "in accord with" suggests that the ROFs from this study were consistent with that of Moffitt; therefore, the code RCL should be inserted at the right margin. The fourth sentence presents a new claim, one that differs from previous findings. The code ROF should be inserted as well. The first paragraph of White et al.'s (2001) discussion thus parallels the ones we have examined thus far. In the next three paragraphs, the authors tease out the meaning of their results in the context of previous literature, proffering conjectures about the unexpected findings in their research which are inconsistent with previous works. In these three paragraphs, the authors do exactly what ought to be done in discussion sections: resolving tensions that exist in ROFs from current research to previous ROFs. Such tentative inferences are reflected in the language they use in their attempt to resolve the tension: "these results **may suggest** that... It is **possible** that... An **alternative** explanation is that..." (p. 607). Simply put, the authors proffer educated conjectures that are rooted in known and corroborated findings to explain what remains unknown.

The authors go on to admit some of the limitations of their work, and provide readers with several recommendations for future works. RFW #1 is that some of the adolescence-limited delinquents were "propelled" into the persistent category due to "snares" (e.g., receiving a police record, becoming involved in delinquent peer groups), and erroneously included in the persistent offender category. The authors state that this false positive identification was not examined, and recommend that future research resolve this issue. RFW #2 is that the specific executive functions assessed (e.g., problem solving, cognitive flexibility) may not be adequately relevant for identifying persistent offenders. Future research might use tests that are more reflective of concepts being measured. RFW #3 notes that some subjects may have been locked up and were unable to continue their rule-breaking behaviors. Future research could examine the continuation of rule-breaking while incarcerated rather than simply assuming that rule-breaking ceases once in a detention facility. Next to all of these types of sentences, the code RFW should be inserted. Later, when students are trying to critique and find GAPs in the current literature as a way of justifying their own work, these codes will facilitate the organization of an outline as part of the prewriting process.

How to read the conclusion section

Robert Entman's (1990) article, entitled "Modern racism and the images of blacks in local television news," published in *Critical Studies in Mass Communication*, examines how local news challenges conventional views of racism and facilitates it at the same time. There is no discussion section. However, three paragraphs make up the conclusion section of the article. In the first paragraph, the author summarizes the ROFs from the current study: showing blacks as offenders and victims makes them look ominous, thereby perpetuating a negative stereotype, while showing positive images of blacks in the news leads to the false impression that racial discrimination is no longer a significant problem. In the second paragraph, Entman goes on to explain the paradox of news as it relates particularly to blacks. He states that the constraints and market-driven and standard operating practices of TV journalism, rather than malicious intention, may account for the paradoxical outcome that local news produces. He ends the second paragraph by stating that "The implication of this research, then, is that local news is likely to continue the practices hypothesized here" (p. 343). In the third and final paragraph, Entman (1990, p. 343) writes:

> (1) To be sure, images of blacks in the local news are complicated and replete with multiple potential meanings. (2) And audiences bring to the news a variety of predispositions. (3) Social scientists have no more than a rudimentary understanding of how audiences perceive and process media messages [citations omitted]. (4) Nonetheless, the exploratory study provides ample support for a hypothesis that local television's images of blacks feed racial anxiety and antagonism at least among that portion of the white population most predisposed to those feelings. (5) Quantitative research on the impact of exposure to local TV news seems in order, as does extensive content analysis of large samples of local and network news. (6) Such work would also illuminate the ways that television helps to alter and preserve dominant cultural values and structures of power.

The main thrust of the conclusion is that local news carries several meanings; as the last sentence suggests, TV – local news – shapes and maintains culture and power. The paradoxical way that local news creates and debunks racism is again reflected in a much broader context in the conclusion. Moreover, the author's work is consistent with his initial hypothesis. His work, however, is not complete. He proffers two RFWs: (1) additional quantitative research of exposure impact, and (2) more content analysis using larger samples of local and network news. The code RFW should be inserted at the right margin. Although no discussion section is present, readers can see that certain components are essential elements of the conclusion. The larger meaning of the current study is teased out; limitations of current research and recommendations for future works are stated in the conclusion, despite the absence of a discussion.

It was noted that Sampson (1987) began his discussion section by connecting his ROF to the ROFs from previous research. His ROFs supported ROFs from other works. But Sampson is not finished there. He has yet to tease out the implications of his research and findings; he has yet to contextualize his ROF in the ongoing debate about crime, criminality, its causes, and consequences. He takes up that question in the conclusion: "The theoretical framework and empirical evidence from this study suggest that current social policy agendas are potentially quite misleading." Why is current social policy misleading? Because conservative politicians in the US have turned their backs on welfare while liberal politicians have ignored high black crime rates. Sampson's ROF suggests that "social policies be directed toward the structural forces of economic deprivation and labor-market marginality faced by black males and the resulting consequences for family disruption and community crime" (p. 378). Moreover, Sampson (1987) goes on to speculate that the current trend of mass incarceration of black males may lead to an ominous future for crime in inner cities, for the causes of crime remain unaddressed by throwing people in prison: "to do so will, in all likelihood, lead to continued repressive crime-control measures and escalating violence" (p. 378).

In the two discussion sections and one conclusion section we have read through, we have seen how the authors have made their ROFs relevant and meaningful by linking their works with past research; furthermore, we have seen how the authors have teased out the policy implications of their work – doing in their papers what numerous how-to books have instructed students to do. That does not mean that points of critique do not exist. In fact, the authors themselves might have Missed an Obvious Point (MOP) and this MOP can be used as a POC to be RPPed in a future paper. MOP should be inserted at the right margin. For instance, one of the implications that Sampson teases out is that black men face economic deprivation and labor-market marginality, which then leads to family disruption and crime. One of the scholars that Sampson cited, William Wilson, argues that black men face and have faced structural impediments to employment by being segregated in inner cities, that black men display characteristics that make them less attractive to potential employers, and that black men have been the first to lose their jobs in the deindustrialization that took place in rustbelt cities. That is, black men face cumulative disadvantage of sorts. So if an astute reader asks why black men have faced economic deprivation and labor-market marginality, how might Sampson answer this question? For a cogent and comprehensive answer, that reader will have to go outside of sociology and criminology to find an answer; the answer to that question lies in disciplines such as history and communication. Even the most influential articles published in the highest-tier journals, written by a highly-influential scholar teaching at one of the most prestigious institutions, can be critiqued; even such scholarship can be CPLed and used as a POC and RPP in a future paper. That process begins during the act of reading.

As argued throughout this book, the reading codes serve several purposes. First, they slow down the act of reading so that readers do not gloss over words and phrases; by enacting the role of a textual detective during the act of reading, readers are trying to figure out the function of a particular text in addition to processing its contents. Reading therefore occurs on two levels. Second, reading with codes leads to critical thinking during the act of reading. Rather than reflecting on the merits or limitations of an article after the reading is completed, the use of reading codes engages the reader with the text in real time, while the reading is taking place. Problems of recall and memory are thus minimized since observations and notes about the readings are made on the text itself. The use of reading codes thus structures the mind toward a purposive task with realizable objectives that can be accomplished, thereby avoiding unstructured – unproductive – reading. The use of readings codes leads to questions such as "What function does this sentence/paragraph serve in the article?" rather than "What did I just read for the last 15 minutes?"

By identifying sentences and paragraphs that perform a particular function (RCL, RTC, RPP, RFW, MOP) within a social science article, students are not only thinking critically and evaluating the paper's strengths and weaknesses, but also implicitly structuring their own papers to write in the future. That is, readers are identifying the relevance of current research to the past literature, and spotting deficiencies and gaps in the literature for their own exigent (e.g., end-of-semester literature review paper) and future-oriented tasks (e.g., thesis, dissertation). That is why reading cannot be treated as a secondary activity. Before a writer can even think about constructing an outline, the contents of that outline have to be filled in somehow. The left margin thematic codes along with the themes in the SPLs at the right margins proffer a starting point for an outline. As argued in this book, trying to recall the content of 50-plus articles and trying to organize it in some cogent way are daunting tasks; the reading codes facilitate the organization and management of information necessary for academic writing.

7

Highlighting and Organizing the ROF, SPL, CPL, GAP, RFW, and POC

One of the notable mistakes I have seen again and again when I check students' primary reading materials (e.g., books, articles) is the highlighted blocks of text in various colors. That is, rather than using a highlighter to emphasize useful and important points (useful and important defined as points that can be used toward easy retrieval and incorporation of pertinent information from the text into an ongoing writing project), students highlight entire paragraphs, sometimes even pages, falsely believing that entire paragraphs are sufficiently important to warrant their highlight. Simply put, students do not use highlighters appropriately. Highlighting entire paragraphs constitutes nothing short of highlighter abuse.

As I have attempted to demonstrate in previous chapters, and as notable composition teachers have noted (i.e., Strunk & White, 1979), pages and paragraphs are not organized in formless ways. The first sentences of paragraphs perform functions that differ from the rest of the sentences in them. First sentences introduce main ideas in a summarizing sort of way while the rest of the sentences that follow support them. I have argued in this book that readers can structure their reading so that the contents of their social science journal articles can be anticipated and classified along predictable and recurring patterns. Once this internal structure and logic of social science journal articles are understood, the blocks of texts – paragraphs that coalesce into pages – should be seen for what they are: as one ring in a logical chain of paragraphs. The authors that you are reading are trying to persuade you to their line of argumentation. They want to convince you that what they are trying to say in the articles makes sense; by the time an article appears in a peer-reviewed journal, the authors have persuaded two to three other academics that the paper has merit and ought to be published.

The tools of academic reading

We have all done it on Sunday afternoons. We have, at one time or another, sat back on the velvet-draped couch, put our feet up on the coffee table or slung our legs over the armrest, held up the book (usually a mystery or a romance novel) in mid-air with one hand, and lazily thumbed through the pages. This scene is pleasure reading at its best. In university libraries across North America, I have witnessed students mimicking this posture on wooden chairs and desks – putting their feet up on desks and curling up in institutional chairs as they would do at home. This attempt to reproduce idyllic Sunday afternoon reading in a library is bad for one's back and the absolutely wrong way to read. Such a posture ought to be reserved for pleasure reading where students do not have to worry about summarizing and critiquing the state of the literature as well as finding ways to justify the rationale for their projects. Reading social science journal articles is a purposive task; and like other goal-oriented tasks, the right tools and the right techniques are essential components of the reading process. In fact, the two are inextricably intertwined.

Reading social science journal articles – if I may – does not bring a sense of joy that one receives from reading, let's say, the Book of Ecclesiastes, the Book of Psalms, Shakespeare, or Pushkin. Reading social science journal articles, for most professional social scientists, and graduate and under-graduate students in the social sciences, is work. And as work, it ought to be treated like work. That means reading academic texts ought to be approached differently from pleasure-related texts. The first step in correct reading entails assuming the right posture. Readers ought to sit at a desk of some sort, preferably with a hard surface, and mentally and physically prepare to read actively. Trying to read academic texts as one would read a romance novel – curled up on a sofa – is apt to lead to meandering reading. By assuming a correct – working – posture, we dignify reading as work rather than something leisurely; by conceptualizing and executing reading as a form of work, we do it irrespective of our personal preference and taste. We do it because it is a job, and it needs to be done. That's why writing problems that other scholars have noted is not attributable to one of motivation. That is, police officers, nurses, and janitors do not have to be particularly motivated to answer 911 calls, take care of patients, and clean toilets; they do it to pay bills and eat. If academics treated reading and writing like other working-class people treated their jobs, there would be no motivation problems and writer's blocks.

Second, as I have instructed in the preceding chapters, readers should engage the text actively. Active reading is the opposite of meandering reading, just as pleasure-reading is the corporeal opposite of academic reading. As argued earlier, inserting reading codes during the act of reading facilitates cognitive boundary demarcation through a purposive task orientation – that is, reading with a concrete objective in mind and end in sight. This engagement is done actively in two ways: insertion of reading codes at the right margins and thematic codes on the left margins. Thus, rather than wrestling with the problem of memory and recall after the act of reading is completed, code insertions force readers to engage the text in real time during the act of reading, thus interrupting the meandering train of useless thoughts that creep in by corporeally engaging the body and the mind during the act of reading.

I have found that three tools facilitate the reading process: (1) ruler, (2) pen, and (3) highlighter (Figure 5). A ruler's primary function during the act of reading is to interrupt the series of jumps (saccades) our eyes make along a line by delineating the perceptual boundaries of texts (Rayner &

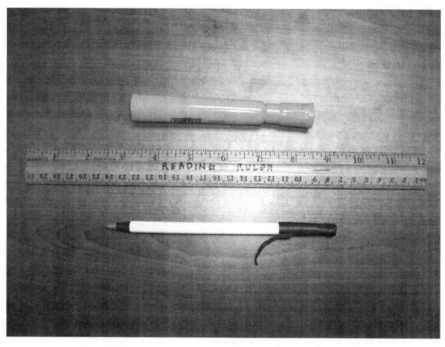

FIGURE 5

Pollatsek, 1989). That is, rather than becoming overwhelmed by the number of pages in an article and lines on a page that have to be read, the ruler demarcates sentence boundaries in order to contain the task of reading to one sentence at a time. This way, readers are forced to slow down the act of reading to prevent mindlessly jumping from sentence to sentence horizontally and paragraph to paragraph vertically – becoming lost in meandering reading.

Second, by using a pen to insert reading and thematic codes at the margins, readers again slow down the act of reading at the sentence and paragraph level by identifying the respective functions of sentences and themes in paragraphs. As I have argued in earlier chapters, directives to read "critically," although benign in intent, are useless without palpable instructions for students to follow. Inserting reading codes during the act of reading constitutes a critical engagement with the text and the author since readers are not passively imbibing the information contained therein; instead, the reader is summarizing, critiquing, and connecting the reading to the broader literature (e.g., RCL, RTC, MOP, POC); in that sense, inserting reading codes during the act of reading constitutes a literal and a dialogical performance of the "critical" in critical reading. As one can see, it is nearly impossible to use a ruler and a pen during the act of reading in a pleasure-reading posture, nor can a student read passively when doing critical reading. The reading tools mentioned in this chapter are meant to assist in that critical reading process.

Third, highlighters are meant to emphasize – highlight – important points in a text. So how should student readers decide what is important and what to highlight? In the context of social science journal articles, that choice is constrained by the structure, logic, and form that are inherent in texts themselves. If students employ the reading code sheet, they should never have to wonder what to highlight. As shown in previous chapters, social science journal articles are organized in logical and predictable ways. The highlighter abuse problem occurs because novice students have not understood the form of the journal articles. Once the functions of SPL, CPL, GAP, RAT, ROF, and POC are understood, deciding what to highlight also should not occur indiscriminately or randomly. ROFs are the primary claims that authors of social science journal articles are trying to make; the ROFs will become the SPLs in the papers that students are trying to write – they are the most important components of a journal article when reading. Therefore, the ROFs ought to be highlighted. GAPs are another important part of the writing process so they are also highlighter-worthy during the reading process. If a student uses one color to highlight all ROFs and another color to highlight GAPs throughout her literature review, the colors will make identification and retrieval much easier. Of course, another student may choose to use different colored highlighter for each reading code (e.g., red for all SPLs, blue for CPLs, etc.), but the rainbow of colors may lead to highlight overkill and create another type of highlighter abuse, thus vitiating its effectiveness.

Reading code management

In Chapter 5, we discussed how to construct a literature review. As part of crafting a literature review, it was noted that ROFs from the current literature will become the SPLs of the to-be-written paper. I also mentioned at length one of the cardinal sins of any literature review – the laundry list problem. To avoid that mistake, it was suggested that summaries of previous literature be synthesized – organized thematically, whether the theme was methodological, conceptual, or analytical – not author by author, year by year. Moreover, in addition to a thematic summary of the previous literature, a critique of previous literature leading to a GAP also had to be incorporated in a competently executed literature review. Using the reading codes to organize, cultivate, and develop themes in summaries and critiques was described as "making the quarter turn," for using the way the literature has been organized in previous studies and mining them for existing patterns and trends were techniques to be exploited to justify one's own proposed study.

Although such a strategy appears to be questionable and problematic, it is consistent with the business and practice of academic publishing. Again, professional academics are in the business of wheel modification, not wheel reinvention. A study, thesis, or dissertation does not have to be radically innovative; it just has to be sufficiently innovative to earn the affirmative votes of thesis and dissertation committee members. An article submitted to a journal to be considered for publication does not have to be paradigm shifting work; it just has to be sufficiently innovative to earn the affirmative votes of reviewers. While the aforementioned attitude may appear to plant the seeds of mediocrity, graduate students who have to worry about the expiration of their funding, and untenured assistant professors who have a gun pointed at their heads to publish or perish, do not have the luxury of working on a dissertation or paper until it is capable of shifting paradigms. Those days of luxury – working for years on end on a single paper or a book that radically shifts paradigms – if they ever existed, are long gone in academia.

To mine for patterns and themes to organize one's literature review, I recommended going through each article and identifying all SPLs, CPLs, GAPs, POCs, and RFWs by perusing through the left and right margins. By going through the SPLs and CPLs, themes and patterns in the way the literature and its critiques are organized can be used as reference points to organize one's own literature review. For small projects such as an undergraduate honor's thesis, looking through each and every article collected for the literature review is a manageable task. For literature reviews that require more than 40 articles, inspecting each and every article for patterns in the way previous SPLs and CPLs are organized is a daunting task, especially if one has to carry around the articles. This means that a much more centralized method of organizing the information gathered from the readings is necessary (see Figure 6).

The Reading Code Organization Sheet (RCOS) is meant to facilitate the identification and retrieval of requisite information gathered from the readings in order to cultivate a synthesis of the literature. Rather than looking through each and every article, page by page, the seven reading codes that are essential to constructing a literature review should serve as the starting point for academic writing for students. Obviously, RCOS will only be as useful as the information that is put into it. But assuming that there is correct input, the output should be more manageable than the traditional methods used (e.g., index cards, memory, intuition). Ideally, students should enter reading

Article #	Author, Year	ROF	SPL	CPL	GAP	RFW	POC/RPP
1							
2							
3							
4							
5							
6							
7							
8							
9 . . .							
100							

FIGURE 6   Reading Code Organization Sheet (RCOS)

codes into RCOS on the day the articles are read. So for example, if a student has set aside one day of the week for reading/writing and has used that day to read six journal articles, she should enter the reading code summaries into RCOS upon their completion. Realistically, for whatever reason, students may not be able to complete RCOS immediately upon completion of the readings. Should the same student return to her task a day or two later, after the exigencies of life have passed, she should not have to look through the articles to find out what their main claims are, what their shortcomings and critiques are, and what recommendations for future works the authors have made, because those important points will have been noted at the margins and highlighted. All that remains to be done is the mechanical act of entering the summaries of codes into the coding sheet. Such activities would count as prewriting. For example, a sample entry might look like that shown in Figure 7.

If a student searched the term "juvenile homicide" in an academic search engine, the article by DiCataldo and Everett (2008) will result in a "hit." In fact, one may get an unmanageable number of hits. Again, suppose that our hypothetical student who is writing a master's thesis on juvenile homicide narrows the number of relevant articles she has to read to 60. The fundamental problem I have raised and attempted to answer is how to manage the volume of information that she will gather from reading those 60 articles. Now, suppose that our hypothetical student entered the summaries of codes for the remaining 59 articles in RCOS. Undoubtedly, she will see common themes that emerge in the SPL category; that's because in order to discuss the works of previous researchers in the field, the 59 authors she will have read will also have read the same influential works (e.g., Bender, Busch, Corder, Cornell, Duncan, Ewing, Heide, Lewis, Russell, Zagar). That's why there's bound to be convergence in literature reviews. Moreover, if the ROFs

Article #	Author, Year	ROF	SPL	CPL	GAP	RFW	POC/RPP
1	DiCataldo & Everett (2008)	1. Non-killers had higher delinquency rating than killers 2. Situational forces (guns, alcohol) may explain outcome rather than psycho-pathological personality	1. Extensive interest 2. Definition 3. Cause 4. Method 5. Mental health 6. Substance abuse 7. Gun availability 8. Stereotype	1. Scientific validity of term 2. No control group 3. Questionable sample 4. No theory integration	1. Scientific validity of term 2. No control group 3. Questionable sample 4. No theory integration	1. Differential processing 2. Explore motivation and circumstances 3. Explore offense characteristics + offender characteristics	1. 67.9% of adol. non-killers had anger problems while 37.5% of adol. killers reported anger problems

FIGURE 7

69

from 59 other articles are examined, there's bound to be convergence as well. The ROFs from the 60 articles become part of the SPL in the literature review component of the thesis that our hypothetical student is writing. Taking those 60 articles, identifying recurring patterns and themes, and condensing them into 8–10 coherently and logically connected themes are what constitute a synthesis of the literature.

Notice again that if there was a collection of 60 CPLs and GAPs, a pattern will emerge. Those recurring GAPs ought to serve as the thematically grouped critique of previous literature (CPL) that follows the SPL. In addition to GAPs, the said student can mine through RFWs; these can serve as CPLs of her SPL. RFWs exist because previous scholars have not examined that aspect of the topic. For example, that DiCataldo and Everett (2008) did not examine offense characteristics of juvenile homicides and circumstances surrounding the killing can serve as GAPs in the literature that warrant remedy. If our hypothetical student wanted to examine the motivation and circumstances behind juvenile killings, that there is a GAP in that component of the literature can function as a RAT behind why her master's thesis is warranted.

Creating an outline for a literature review

Once the recurring themes in SPL and CPL/GAP are identified, the next step in the transition process from reading to writing is transferring those themes into an outline. Silvia (2007) notes that outlining should not be considered as a prelude to actual – real – writing. He observes that writers who experience trouble writing are the ones who do not form outlines: "After trying to write blindly, they feel frustrated and complain about how hard it is to generate words" (p. 79). He advises writers to "get thoughts in order" before trying to write. If we ask how the contents of those thoughts and outlines are to be filled in, we would be right back at where we started. Others have not shown how to make the transition from reading to outlining to writing in a methodical and operationally actionable way. Again, the reading codes are designed to facilitate the outlining and writing process.

In most academic writing that involves original research entailing data collection – honor's/senior thesis, master's thesis, PhD dissertation, a peer-reviewed journal article – the structure and format of those academic texts are essentially the same:

- Introduction: SPL, CPL, WTD
- Literature Review: SPL, CPL, GAP, RAT
- Data & Methods: Description of data and plan of analysis

are given a backpack and instructed to march forward. You are not told how far you must march; you are not told if you can stop and take breaks; you are not told the pace at which you should march; you are not told when your march will end. You are not told the destination. Similarly, imagine that your professor tells you to write a paper. She does not tell you what the topic ought to be; she does not tell you the paper's acceptable length; she does not tell you which citation style to use; she does not tell you how many references you need in your paper. She does not even tell you when the paper is due. Some might say that both conditions represent absolute freedom – freedom to do whatever the hiker or the student author wants: unbridled room for creativity.

However, like most things in life, the notion of freedom (and academic writing) does not exist in such indeterminate states. Although we westerners like to think that we exercise "free speech," we do not (Fish, 1994). We are constrained by what we cannot say legally, socially, and morally. That is, we can't walk up to a police officer and utter, "I'm going to kill you!" and expect to receive first amendment protection when arrested for making terroristic threats; nor can we yell out "fire!" in a crowded theater and claim free speech. Furthermore, we can't say whatever harmful, hurtful, and deceitful things we want about others without legal repercussions (e.g., libel); and if we uttered whatever honest thought that came to mind in our interpersonal interactions, we would lead a very lonely and solitary existence very, very quickly. As Stanley Fish would say, "there is no such thing as free speech and it's a good thing." But despite such constraints that are placed in what we can say and write, notice that such restrictions do not place limits on what we can accomplish with language. Creative expressions of comedy, wit, irony, and tragedy abound in written and spoken forms of language despite restrictions and constraints.

The same types of boundaries and constraints exist in academic writing. Academic writing in its most revered and valued form – the peer-reviewed journal article – suffers from an even greater constraint than other forms of writing (e.g., novel, book) for one simple reason: space. Most journals have a finite amount of space available in each issue of a journal; if you sent a 20,000-word essay to most social science journals, my guess is that it will promptly be returned. Most social science journals have word limits on manuscript submissions. Such restrictions are both positive and negative. Such a restriction is good as it provides boundary markers; authors know they can't exceed a certain word count and page limit; it is bad in the sense that it limits what authors are able to do in an article. At the extreme end, some journals are willing to accept a paper that is up to 15,000 words in length; most social science journals expect between 8,000 and 10,000 words in a single paper submission. For the purpose of illustration, I will use the lower word count. This means that in 8,000 words, the following components have to be covered:

1   Cover page: title, name, affiliation
2   Abstract
3   Introduction
4   Literature Review
5   Data & Methods: Description of data and plan of analysis
6   Results
7   Discussion & Conclusion
8   References

Some student readers may be wondering what 8,000 words translates into; they need to comprehend this word count in the context of countable pages. One single-spaced page of text in 12 point Times New Roman font will yield approximately 600 words; about 15–17 reference materials (books, book chapters, and articles) will fit into one single-spaced page of references, yielding about 300 words. Dividing 8,000 by 600 results in 13.3 or about 14 single-spaced pages. Authors have 14 single-spaced pages to introduce the article, do a literature review, describe data and methods, display results, and discuss the results and implications of their findings relative to those of others in the field – plus the reference section. If you look at it in that perspective, 14 single-spaced pages or 8,000 words is not all that much. In fact, first-time writers may want additional space. Such greed is not practical, for journals are generally bound and restricted in their resources. It is therefore incumbent upon authors to exercise creativity and innovation within an already existing set of restrictions and constraints – like "free" speech; and like "free" speech the possibilities are endless.

The task before us now is how to allocate the 14 single-spaced pages to the 8 sections of the 8,000-word paper. I have found that this task becomes more

Section	Textual Function in Article	Page Amount (in single space)
Cover page	Paper title, name, affiliation	x
Abstract	SPL, CPL, ROF, WTD	.5
Introduction	SPL, CPL, WTD	1
Literature Review	SPL, CPL, GAP, RAT	4–5
Data & Methods	Description of data and method of analysis	1.5–2
Results	ROF	1–2
Discussion & Conclusion	ROF, WTDD, RCL, RTC, RFW	2–3
References		3–5
	Goal	14

FIGURE 8

manageable if the reading codes are used to organize, identify, and fill in the contents of the sections (Figure 8).

Throughout this book, we have used sample social science articles as data to identity how they are structurally and textually organized. Abstracts tended to fall between 150 and 200 words; they were mini-reproductions of introductions in 150–200 words or less. If students need to write an abstract of their own, they should write sentences that resemble SPL, CPL, ROF, and WTD in 150 words or less. Introductions were composed of 2–4 paragraphs, generally not more than one single-spaced page that covered the SPL, CPL, and WTD. If students need to write an introduction for a paper that they are writing and thinking of sending to a journal, the students should write sentences that resemble SPL, CPL, and WTD in 2–4 paragraphs. Literature reviews and psychology introductions varied, but most would fall within a 4–5 single-spaced page range. Data and methods sections generally can be described in 1–2 pages, with results, 1–2, and discussion and conclusion, 2–3.

Rather than blindly reading social science journals for simple content, this book has made the articles themselves the objects of analysis. That is, I attempted to identify what functions the sentences in abstracts, introductions, literature reviews, data and methods, results, and discussions and conclusions perform. By doing so, it was intended to organize the information contained in the readings in such a way as to make the writing process more manageable. Furthermore, by breaking down the constitutive elements of a social science journal article, I have tried to show how graduate students can undertake the task of writing an 8,000-word paper – should they be inclined and motivated to do so. The format provided above is one place to start. Emulating the authors that students have read by following a textual function approach delineated by paragraphs and pages is one way to go about accomplishing that task.

What students should not wonder about is how to fill in the contents of an outline and the article itself. As I have shown here, social science journal articles are organized in logical and predictable ways. By employing the reading codes, students should be able to write an article or an article-length paper on their own. As I have argued in this book, the literature review is one of the most central components of an article. As shown here, introductions are small-scale reproductions of literature reviews executed in 2–4 paragraphs. Literature reviews are made up of a thematic synthesis of previous works (SPL), and their critique (CPL, GAP) in 4–5 single-spaced pages. One organizes a literature review by looking through the reading code sheet and mining for commonly recurring themes. Data and methods and results sections are fairly straightforward, as the student author describes the data and how they were analyzed, and presents the results of findings. When writing up the discussion and conclusion, one must interpret those results in the context of the findings from previous works (i.e., RTC, RCL). As shown above, all of those elements occur within an already existing set of confined space and words.

Out of the several components of a journal article, the literature review exerts the greatest amount of ecological force on the structural and textual organization of academic writing. The literature review also takes up the greatest amount of space in journal articles. That's why a competently done literature review is important. And to do a competent literature review, students must read the work of other scholars. Students are unable to write not because they have not formed outlines, but because they haven't read enough relevant literature to be able to even form a coherent idea of an outline. Trying to write a paper without sufficient reading is like trying to speak a foreign language without having learned enough vocabulary. One may know the syntactic structure and grammatical rules of a language, but without adequate vocabulary to apply those rules, one is unlikely to produce meaningful utterances. In order to even think about writing an academic paper, one must read sufficiently; to write an academic paper of professional quality, one must read critically and translate those critiques into a cogent rationale for why that paper is necessary. Then one can collect and analyze the data, and write them up.

When reading journal articles, the ROFs constitute the primary nuggets of information that are important. As shown in earlier chapters, those ROFs will become SPLs of the paper that a student is trying to write. When writing one's own paper, however, the literature review is the most crucial component of the journal writing process since it affects the backward (abstract, introduction) and forward (discussion, conclusion, reference) elements of a paper. Believe it or not, when academics are asked to review a paper for a journal, one of the first things that we read is not the abstract or the introduction – it is the reference section. By reading through an author's reference list, we can discern if the author has read enough and read the right stuff. Moreover, we can anticipate the logic of the argument to unfold in the paper to be reviewed.

By employing the reading codes during the act of reading, and entering the summaries of reading codes into the Reading Code Organization Sheet upon the completion of reading, the idea of how and what to write in a paper ought to emerge on its own. Once students read enough literature, read actively, and organize their readings into the organization sheet, the outline for an 8,000-word paper will almost emerge on its own and organize itself. If students are contemplating writing a professional-quality paper to submit to a journal, they should also consider another potential writing project that is considerably less intensive and demanding than the 8,000-word paper.

The structure of short reports, flash reports, and research notes

In most of the social scientific disciplines, there are articles that are shorter than the average length of 8,000–10,000 words. In sociology and criminology, these are called "research notes," which run from 12 to 20 printed pages. In psychology, shorter-than-average papers come in two forms, "short reports" and "flash reports." Short reports are research articles that are less than 5,000 words, flash reports less than 2,500 words. Despite their diminutive size, the work done in the three types of paper are essentially similar to the full-length articles we have seen thus far.

For instance, Usoof-Thowfeek, Janoff-Bulman, and Tavernini (2011, p. 1) carried out three studies to examine the role of "automatic and controlled processes in moral judgments." The article is six pages in print, much shorter than the 20–30 print pages of average journal articles. The article, consistent with the practice in psychology, places the literature review upfront, and in it the authors summarize previous works (SPL) in a succinct three pages before the following sentences appear in the fourth paragraph:

> (1) Haidt (2001, 2007) notes that moral "reasoning" often functions as a post hoc process that provides evidence to support our automatic reactions, but he also recognizes that rational deliberation can alter our intuitive responses. (2) To date, however, few empirical studies have explored the relationship between automatic and controlled processing in moral judgments. (2011, p. 1)

Again, notice that the disjunction marker provides a hint of the CPL/GAP to come in the second sentence. If three prior paragraphs have summarized the current state of the literature, the second sentence critiques it by pointing to a shortcoming within it. In the very next paragraph, the authors provide the rationale for the study: "*We believe that social harm may be a particularly important variable in understanding the relationship between automatic and controlled processes in the case of moral judgments*" (p. 2). Following this rationale, the authors go on to introduce three hypotheses they are testing in the study. The rest of the report follows a format recognizably similar: data and methods section that describes the materials, participants, and procedures used in the study; followed by a short results and discussion section particular to the first study. These processes are repeated for studies 2 and 3. A general discussion is proffered at the end of the paper that interprets their ROFs in relation to prior work.

In Cao, Adams, and Jensen's (1997, p. 368) research note, the authors ask and resolve one question: "The research reported in this article tests their

[Wolfgang & Ferracuti, 1967] black subculture of violence thesis." Before they can do so, however, they must first introduce what the subculture of violence thesis is, and critique it before they can claim the WTD. In this research note, published in *Criminology*, the literature review and introduction sections are collapsed into one section, similar to a psychology publication; and in it the authors discuss the work of Wolfgang and Ferracuti (SPL), before systematically stating the following points:

> The association between the subculture of violence among blacks and violent behavior remains largely inconclusive. (p. 368)

> While Dixon and Lizotte directly measured individuals' beliefs in practice, they did not control all of the independent variables proposed by Wolfgang and Ferracuti, such as employment and violent history. (p. 369)

> Thus, existing studies on the subculture of violence indicate that race has been seriously neglected in direct tests and that beliefs in violence among southerners have received attention. (p. 369)

Based on the preceding CPLs and identified GAPs, the authors answer the "so what?" question by explicitly stating how their work will remedy the existing shortcoming in the subculture of violence literature. One can readily see how the short reports are similar to and different from their full-length siblings. They are similar in that the structure of ideas begins with a summary of previous literature, then moves to a critique and a gap, which is then remedied. They are also different in that the topic addressed is very narrow, which constrains the literature to be reviewed into substantially fewer themes (and pages). This compression also reduces the ROFs derived and their interpretation proffered relative to previous findings in the discussion section. If general introductions are sort of small-scale rehearsals of literature reviews, then we can understand research notes and short reports as smaller-scale versions of full-length research articles, for the work done in them is less, but their form and structure are similar.

Once students are motivated enough to write and complete an article or a research note, it should definitely be reviewed by a faculty advisor before they send it to a journal; and before a journal is considered as a potential outlet for full-length papers or research notes, graduate students should consider another outlet – graduate student paper competitions sponsored by their respective disciplines. In some cases, the top prize paper is published in a journal if the disciplinary association is the one that organized and sponsored the competition, and the standards of judgment are likely to be less stringent than professional reviews. Graduate student paper competitions are good places to get one's feet wet before jumping into a pool with shark-like reviewers.

The first sentence does the work of critiquing previous literature (CPL) and pointing out a GAP in existing literature. Simply put, Owen states that although the writings of Stanley Fish contain ideas that are relevant for political theorists, they have been neglected as objects of inquiry. Political theorists have not closely examined the implications of Fish's works for their discipline. The word "neglect" hints that something is missing in the current state of the literature. The second sentence summarizes the work of one theorist; in fact, the writings of Stanley Fish are one of the main topics to be covered in the paper. Hence, as background material, sentence #2 counts as an SPL. The third sentence does the work of a WTD, for in it the author tells readers what he will do in the paper ("qualified defense of liberalism"), as well as point out another CPL in previous work ("he fails to do justice to liberalism"). Thus, in exactly 100 words, the abstract in Owen's article does work that is similar to the ones we have examined thus far in other social science journal articles. The abstract provides a brief summary of the literature, a critique of it, and what the author will do to remedy the deficiency in the literature.

Owen's (1999) article is also structurally organized in a recognizably similar form to the ones we have examined thus far as well. The paper is organized into five major sections, with headings which sufficiently describe the topic covered in that major section; in those five sections, the author discusses the work of previous researchers, critiques them, and identifies a GAP in their works which he proposes to remedy. This step is rehearsed first in the abstract and then in the two paragraphs that precede the first major section, and comprise what could aptly be called an "introduction." In the first paragraph of the introduction, Owen goes on to summarize those aspects of Stanley Fish's works that are pertinent for political theory (SPL); then toward the end of the second paragraph, the following sentences appear:

(1) Fish is an influential proponent of antifoundationalism, which maintains that all claims to knowledge are made from a particular and partisan perspective, are "socially constructed", and therefore are never impartial or objective. (2) Radical as this doctrine is in itself, the singular radicalness of Fish's critique is the result of his focus on a potentially explosive area that seems to have escaped the notice of many political theorists: the theoretical juncture between antifoundationalism and the liberal doctrines concerning religion, which are the basis of liberal constitutionalism (3) ... (4) This essay lays out Fish's critique and offers a limited defense against it. (Owen, 1999, p. 911)

Similar to the sentences that precede it, sentence #1 summarizes the main ideas of a previous scholar (Stanley Fish). In sentence #2, however, the phrase "seems to have escaped" provides a clue that there might be something missing in the current state of the literature. So what is that missing element in the research? An examination of the "theoretical junction between antifoundationalism and liberal doctrines concerning religion." That is, no one has examined how antifoundationalism as a school of thought might affect the intersection of liberalism and religion – "*a potentially explosive area.*" Such an assertion constitutes a GAP in the literature, and one sentence later, Owen tells readers how he will remedy that gap: lay out Fish's critique of liberalism (SPL) and offer a defense of liberalism (WTD). Readers can anticipate and expect that the rest of the article will do just that: offer a summary (SPL) of Fish's main ideas (Fish's critique of liberalism) before critiquing Fish's critique (CPL/GAP); then he will go on to defend the very thing that Fish has critiqued.

Sentence #4 constitutes a WTD, for the author tells readers what he will do in his paper. But notice what is missing: there is no sentence that can stand as an explicit RAT as we have seen in other social science articles. Readers are left to infer the necessity of a proposed work – rationale – by pointing out a GAP. One might call this practice "reading between the lines," for logically, the RAT lies between a GAP and a WTD. We might thus speculate that one unique feature of humanities texts might be that the reader is expected to do a bit more work; that extra work entails the work of inferring. Given proposition A then conclusion C, the process of inferring B that is unspoken is left to the reader – the paradigmatic structure of syllogistic reasoning. Unless one is explicitly taught this logical structure of arguments, or is sufficiently motivated enough to investigate this pattern, readers are apt to miss that hidden step in the reading process. We might tentatively state that this is one way that social science articles differ from philosophical texts. Social science articles leave little room for reader inference. The various elements of the reading codes – as signs of textual work being done in the text – appear again and again throughout a paper.

Notice also the triadic character of the scholarship process that binds social sciences and humanities. Fish's critique of liberalism constitutes previous literature, the preexisting body of ideas, and a summary of results of findings (in a social scientific sense) from previous works; in essence then, Fish's critique of liberalism is Owen's SPL. Owen describes previous works – the first major section entitled "religion and the demise of liberal rationalism" – as "sinuous." That word does a lot of work, for it traces the genealogical indebtedness of contemporary political and legal theory to philosophers such as Thomas Hobbes, René Descartes, Immanuel Kant, Frederick Nietzsche, John Stuart Mill, and John Rawls. Those names are practically a who's who of western intellectual history, and to say that their ideas are "interesting" would be a gross understatement. "Sinuous," however, eloquently and succinctly captures the winding, curving, and meandering course of western political philosophy in the past 500 years. That is to say, that before one can understand

Fish's critique of liberalism, one must at least have some background knowledge of what is liberalism.

The problem that political theorists have struggled to bracket is the differences in moral and philosophical views that lead to conflict between individuals and states. One can see why fundamental differences in moral, philosophical, and political views might be fraught with potential conflict. Differences and disagreements about notions of right and wrong, and about which god to worship and its methods of worship have led – continue to lead – to conflicts between nations and individuals – "*a potentially explosive area.*" Liberalism's objective since its inception has been to devise a way to create a stable political order in societies by focusing on how public goods (e.g., jobs, benefits) are distributed fairly (i.e., procedures, methods) rather than defining the constitutive features of that public good (content), precisely so that individual differences in religion, morality, and tastes do not affect political institutions. Fish's critique of liberalism is that once a person sets aside his/her most cherished beliefs and values (e.g., religious doctrines), those beliefs no longer can be claimed to be what they are: core values that constitute the religion that believers profess them to be. Fish's critique of liberalism is that it might as well be another form of the church (that is, not content-less), despite its claim to be neutral and procedural; his critique is that liberalism is incoherent and confused. So what is Owen's critique of Fish's previous work? "*The ramifications of his* [Fish's] *critique are therefore radical: Nothing, so to speak, can be ruled out – not religious orthodoxy or even theocracy*" (Owen, 1999, p. 913). Such sentences count as a CPL; there are others:

> Contemporary political theorists have debated at great length the consequences of the demise of liberal rationalism for politics, but a crucial aspect has been neglected. (Owen, 1999, p. 912)

> Little has been written directly on the significance of the demise of liberal rationalism for the liberal doctrines on religion... (Owen, 1999, p. 912)

> Following antifoundationalism all the way, Fish argues, means giving up on all such projects of overarching and neutral inclusion. What does this mean for religious freedom and the separation of church and state? (Owen, 1999, p. 912)

Sentences like the above provide a contrast to summaries proffered in preceding paragraphs. As shown in earlier chapters, CPLs follow SPLs, for before an idea, a body of results, or a school of thought can be critiqued, the contents of the things that are being critiqued have to be made available, for logical reasons. Again, before something can be critiqued, that something has to be introduced. That's the function of SPL. But if existing literature

83

was sufficient, then there would be no need to rehash what is already known. New articles and new books are written precisely because another author believes that s/he can reframe the debate, challenge obsolete findings, and provide a new way of thinking about a problem. And that's what CPLs do: they highlight limitations and deficiencies in previous works in some systematic and cogent way, which leads to a GAP. The excerpts above illustrate the CPL/GAPs shown in earlier chapters that function as a way of providing a rationale for the current paper without being as explicit as social science journal articles. How will Owen remedy the GAP that follows from the CPLs?

> I offer a limited defense of liberalism against Fish's critique. I will begin by showing how Fish reaches his radical conclusions. I will then argue that, despite his shockingly antiliberal conclusions, Fish remains entangled within the liberal worldview he is so intent on criticizing ... I conclude that Fish has underestimated the conceptual and moral power of liberalism. This underestimation is largely the result of mistakenly identifying neutrality as the essence of liberalism... (Owen, 1999, p. 913)

In the excerpt above, Owen provides readers with an itinerary of what he will do in the paper; therefore, that paragraph would count as a WTD, similar to the ones we have examined thus far in social science journal articles. The paragraph above captures the main (research) question that the author is posing in the text. In social science journal articles, those questions are resolved by collecting and analyzing data, then presenting the results. However, in certain review articles, theoretical articles, and philosophy articles, there are no palpable data that are analyzed. Instead, the new claims and results occur as a result of argumentation. Owen spends pages challenging Fish's presuppositions about liberalism, his conclusions, and the logical consequents of his claim if assumed to be true. In other words, Owen uses Professor Fish's writings as data and attempts to use them as POC, as a way of setting up his own argument to emerge. Owen's new "findings" will be comparable to the ROFs we have seen in earlier chapters, except that the claims emerge from the critiques of previous arguments rather than some "empirical" data. An argument is "any group of propositions of which one is claimed to follow from the others, which are regarded as providing support or grounds for the truth of that one" (Copi & Cohen, 1990, p. 6). What might those "results" look like? Consider the following sentences:

> We may say, then, that Fish's antiliberalism is just as tolerant, after a fashion, as liberalism. (Owen, 1999, p. 920)

> Liberalism may have a greater hold on Fish than he recognizes. (Owen, 1999, p. 921)

Fish does not adequately recognize that his antifoundationalism rests entirely on liberal presuppositions. Thus, however antiliberal his aims may be, he remains in the grip of liberalism in subtle yet powerful ways. (Owen, 1999, p. 923)

Fish thus significantly mistakes the degree or manner of liberalism's opposition to religion. (Owen, 1999, p. 923)

It is partly for the benefits of such protection [that religion provides to liberalism] of the private sphere that liberalism is worth defending. (Owen, 1999, p. 923)

Thanks to liberalism, "culture war" has replaced civil war. For this we must be grateful. (Owen, 1999, p. 923)

Even one who recognizes the radical limitations of liberalism with a view to the ultimate truth remains morally obligated to uphold liberalism in the absence of a better practicable alternative. (Owen, 1999, p. 923)

Sentences like the ones above do not point out a critique of prior works, nor do they point out a gap or a rationale of sorts. They all declare something. We might even call such preceding statements conclusions, for such propositions are "affirmed on the basis of the other propositions of the argument" (Copi & Cohen, 1990, p. 6). This something is the product of the criticisms he has pointed out in previous writings on the topic. Grammatically, the arrival of conclusions is signaled by conclusion markers such as "therefore," "hence," "thus," "as a result," "for such reasons," etc. The claims Owen makes are new – claims that emerge and grow out of the previous claims made by Fish, whose own claims emerge out of those who asserted prior claims. This type of process – claim→critique of claim→new claim – is what the business of academia and scholarship is all about, for disagreements about and challenges to a claim spur on others to modify and remedy the initial claim (Fish, 1980). This constantly evolving cycle of claims-making is aptly described as a dialectical process, for ideas emerge out of other ideas. *Ex nihilo nihil fit.*

Seven paragraphs constitute the introduction in Wyller's (2005) article entitled "The place of pain in life," published in *Philosophy*. Before we examine the introduction, one of the notable points about this article is the absence of an abstract. There is no 100–150-word synopsis of what the article is about, a pattern that appears to be rather common in philosophy journals. Readers have no way of perusing the article to discern if indeed it is pertinent to a topic that a student might have chosen to write about. A reader has to wade through the introduction to find out if the article should be included in her literature review.

The second notable observation about articles in philosophy journals, again, is the absence of data and methods, results, and discussion sections.

That absence might be explained by the fact that political theory, literary criticism, and philosophy are disciplines that generally do not collect and analyze data in a social scientific sense. If "data" are analyzed, they are likely to be texts. Thus, literary critics tend to use the actual writings of novelists, philosophers, and other authors as the corpus of data to be analyzed. And because no "data" exist in the sense that social scientists are accustomed to, the character of the "results" that are produced is likely to be different. The "results" found (what I have termed ROF in social science articles) are more likely to be arguments that an author makes to challenge the arguments made by a previous scholar, thus building on previous knowledge and providing a new claim. This pattern was evident in the previous article we examined. Rather than Result of Findings (ROF), we could anticipate that philosophy's equivalent of an ROF might be Result of Argumentation (ROA). But aside from the absence of an abstract, data and methods, results, and discussion sections, are there other similarities and differences between articles in philosophy journals and articles in social science journals?

To illustrate how articles in philosophy journals are organized, I have chosen to work backwards this time, much like the way a homicide detective works backward to reconstruct a crime scene and discern a victim's last-seen-alive location. Like a particularly difficult logic problem or a murder investigation, sometimes we have to assume the conclusion to be false and then proceed to attempt to prove it as a way of finding the truth.

So what does Wyller (2005) want to claim as the "news" in "The place of pain in life"? What is the new claim that he is making in his paper, in a way that is sufficiently different from previous scholars who have written on the topic of pain? The answer emerges in the very end. Wyller begins the last paragraph by returning to the principal author he is pushing against (much like the way Owen pushes against Fish) and critiquing in his paper – John Hyman – and uses the idioms Hyman used as a backdrop for his claims: *"(1) I have an itch in my toe; (2) I have a headache; (3) my leg is hurting."* Wyller then goes on to write: *"I accept the structural equivalence ... but I do not agree that (3) is more transparent than (1) and (2)."*

There are two points that need to be elaborated. First, that the concept "transparency" will be meaningful in how the second claim (Wyller) differs from the first (Hyman) one. We might anticipate that the Result of Argumentation (ROA) will revolve around the issue of transparency. Second, the two phrases, "I accept" and "I agree," although characteristically different from the language of social science journal articles, perform a similar kind of function noted in previous chapters. "I accept" is another way of saying that the results (of findings, of argumentation) are consistent with previous findings. Thus, some of the ROAs that Wyller proffers are consistent with claims that previous scholars (e.g., John Hyman) have made. Again, although no "results" in the social scientific sense are presented, there is conceptual equivalence if we substitute "findings" with "argumentation."

In philosophy, one does not generally collect data like social scientists do; instead, the data are the texts and arguments that previous scholars have made. Therefore, the phrase "I do not agree" should be seen for its fraternal resemblance to Results to the Contrary (RTC). If we substitute "argumentation" for "results," then we can see that Wyller is presenting an argument that contradicts and is inconsistent with previous findings. So what is Wyller's new claim? He writes, *"If I had to choose, I would say (1) and (2) are more transparent; making explicit what is implied by (3) as well: a feeling person."* Then in the last sentence, readers are finally treated to a new claim, an ROA of sorts: *"Thus whereas Hyman takes pains to be modes of person's limbs, I propose we understand them as modes of persons located in their limbs."*

As one might suspect, the difference between the two assertions appears to be minute; but then again, I am not in a position to assess the merits and significance of such assertions, for I am insufficiently trained in that discipline to be able to even appreciate the magnitude of the difference. But, if we presuppose that *"modes of person's limbs"* and *"modes of persons located in their limbs"* are not that radically different, then Wyller has done what social scientists also do in their journal articles: present a claim that is sufficiently new – not a paradigm-shifting one – to warrant peer reviewers to accept its contribution to the literature by voting to publish the paper. One might say that Wyller simply made a quarter turn.

We began by working backwards. We already know Wyller's conclusion. But what question did he ask in order to arrive at his conclusion? Wyller (2005, p. 385) begins the article in the following way: *"I take a hammer, drive a nail into the wall and suddenly hit my left thumb. I spontaneously withdraw my hand, screaming. Where is the pain located?"* Wyller contextualizes that primary question in the work of John Hyman's article entitled "Pains and places," and it is against that previous work and theorist that Wyller is pushing. He also critiques Hyman's work as a way of justifying the necessity of his own paper: *"However, I believe he overstates his point to the effect of excluding some natural allies. Hyman is right that the pain of my thumb is in my thumb. But Wittgenstein expressivists are also right that it is where I, the whole person, am."*

Wyller's contention with previous work is that it insufficiently locates the experience of pain (CPL); he wants expanded coverage of where pain is located and experienced. And by turning *"our attention to the fact of embodied consciousness,"* Wyller will propose in his current paper to remedy the limitations that exist in the philosophy of pain literature. This is the rationale (RAT) of his paper. But notice that such justifications and itineraries are not stated explicitly; the reader, again, must do the work of inferring one or two steps in the reading process, work that does not have to be performed in social science journals. Without a sufficient background understanding of the pain literature, or a sound understanding of the extra work that readers have to perform, an undergraduate student reading this type of article is apt to get lost in the inference that has to be made during reading.

The term "embodied consciousness" not only provides an implicit rationale of his work, but also hints at the literature to be reviewed as a way of setting up his argument. As a way of summarizing previous literature (SPL), and true to the identity of the discipline, the author begins his set up of connecting parts to the whole by introducing the work of Aristotle; he then connects the concept of autopoiesis to Aristotle before presenting the material basis of consciousness. The author then brings in Kant and Wittgenstein as a way of prepping the reader to his line of argumentation: "*I thus suggest we take the autopoietic whole/part relation as the key to understanding phantom pains*" (Wyller, 2005, p. 393). Consider why phantoms would be problematic, and the most difficult test for the question he has asked. Explaining pain in one's thumb as a result of an accidental hammer blow can be accounted for, whether the pain is located in the thumb, the mind, or the nervous system. The pain is "real." It really hurts. Phantom pains that occur from missing limbs, however, are a bit problematic to explain. He has to show that answer through argumentation rather than data collection:

> Within today's natural sciences one encounters definitions of "life" in terms of physiology, thermodynamics, information theory, biochemistry and genetics. No unified conception is to be found. However, this also makes it a legitimate task for anyone to reflect upon which one among the vast definitions best captures the distinction we naturally draw between living and non-living things. (Wyller, 2005, p. 387)

That's why Wyller has to incorporate all of the preceding hard sciences in order to answer his question. Trying to account for pains in missing limbs is much more difficult to do than trying to explain the pain in an attached thumb. To provide sufficient background knowledge (SPL), the author has to go outside of the discipline and draw on the work done in natural sciences to buttress his claims. Whether one goes outside of a discipline or stays inside, synthesis of the literature prior to a critique of it entails a tremendous amount of reduction and condensation. Writers have to find a way to boil down numerous themes that a topic has been grouped into and repeat that process for one's own work. Synthesis in philosophy also occurs along a parallel line. One must consult and review canonic authors, and apply their obscure ideas to suit one's aims in a paper. This practice of finding new concepts and then explaining and justifying their relevance for the proposed work is one way in which theoretical papers differ from research papers. In such papers, existing ideas are redefined, reframed, and commandeered to produce a new idea, much like the way Wyller uses biological concepts to define concept of life, and then apply it for his purposes in his paper on pain. In research papers, the "new angle" is the empirical data that are analyzed, not novel ideas.

There is also one final noteworthy difference between social science articles and philosophical articles. In the former, authors begin the process of future scholarship in the present by proffering the limitations of their own studies and works. Such self-critique paves the way for future research that can be carried out by others. As we have seen, Recommendations for Future Works (RFWs) also perform a similar task of suggesting a path of improvement for future scholars and research; in the philosophy articles we examined, we have seen that the reader must come up with a POC and RPP without much help from the author. There are no benign recommendations that are made to future authors in the philosophical works we have seen thus far. Scholars have to read between the lines to find the GAPs and CPLs, and come up with an implicit RAT. This difficulty is compounded by the lack of repetition of essential components.

Readers are left on their own. For an undergraduate or a beginning graduate student trying to read between the lines for the first time, that is a tall order.

So far, I have argued that there are parallels in social science texts and philosophy texts for the simple reason that scholarship tends to be dialectical in character. We have seen throughout this book that social scientists, political theorists, and philosophers begin their works by introducing a body of previous thoughts (SPL) which is then critiqued (CPL) as a way of highlighting some missing dimension in the literature (GAP). This absence, explicitly and implicitly, provides a paper's necessary existential justification (RAT). In this section, I want to apply the reading code to one of the books that shaped my undergraduate education. Will the reading code be applicable to one of the most influential philosophical works in the past 100 years, thereby buttressing the claims I have made in this book, or will the reading code fall flat on its face and show it to be nothing more than feces smeared on the walls of the academy?

Rawls (1971, pp. vii–viii) begins the preface to his book *A Theory of Justice* in the following way in the second paragraph:

(1) Perhaps I can best explain my aim in this book as follows. (2) During much of modern moral philosophy the predominant systematic theory has been some form of utilitarianism. (3) One reason for this is that it has been espoused by a long line of brilliant writers who have built up a body of thought truly impressive in its scope and refinement. (4) We sometimes forget that the great utilitarians, Hume and Adam Smith, Bentham and Mill, were social theorists and economists of the first rank; (5) and the moral

doctrine they worked out was framed to meet the needs of their wider interests and to fit into a comprehensive scheme. (6) Those who criticized them often did so on a much narrower front. (7) They pointed out the obscurities of the principle of utility and noted the apparent incongruities between many of its implications and our moral sentiments. (8) But they failed, I believe, to construct a workable and systematic moral conception to oppose it. (9) The outcome is that we often seem forced to choose between utilitarianism and intuitionism. (10) Most likely we finally settle upon a variant of the utility principle circumscribed and restricted in certain *ad hoc* ways by intuitionistic constraints. (11) Such a view is not irrational; (12) and there is no assurance that we can do better. (13) But this is no reason not to try.

How do we make sense of a block of text like this? What is the author trying to do in this paragraph? Sentence #1 appears to do the work of a WTD, but we are not sure exactly what Rawls will do in his book. So what is he trying to do? Sentence #2 introduces what the paragraph will be about. Moreover, Rawls tells readers that one particular form of philosophy has been the "predominant" one. Sentences #2–5 provide what is aptly termed an SPL, for Rawls is summarizing previous works; sentences #3–5 elaborate on the prior scholars who have written on the topic (Hume, Smith, Bentham, Mill), their influence, and prior attempts at constructing a "comprehensive" scheme of sorts. Sentences #6–7 provide an SPL of the CPL that has been made in previous works as well; that is, Rawls provides readers with a thematically organized classification in SPL form of the Critique of Previous Research (CPL). So what is that critique?

Rawls notes that the implications of utilitarian theory are not consistent with a person's own sense of morality. What does this mean? If, for example, we had to kill one innocent person to save the lives of a hundred people, would that decision be morally justifiable? In its most simplistic version of utilitarianism, the guiding principle of greatest good for the great number of people would justify that decision to violate the fundamental rights of one person. In its most obtuse form, that's what utilitarianism and democracy are. And from sentences #1–7 what Rawls has done is provide an SPL and a thematically organized SPL of the CPL – a summary of previous works and critiques.

But beginning in sentence #8 the words "but they failed" suggests that he will provide a CPL of his own. As we saw in previous chapter, such disjunction markers portend contrasts to emerge (e.g., "I like you, but..."). So what is Rawls's critique of previous literature (CPL)? That there is an absence of a systematic method to oppose the morally unpalatable outcomes illustrated in the hypothetical example. Such an assertion constitutes a GAP. If the dominant form of philosophy has been utilitarianism, and according to its tenets, distasteful outcomes are justified on practical and democratic grounds, and there is no cogent and systematic moral argument that could be made against such practices, except a nagging sense of intuition that such practices violate some preexisting sense of morality, and only "*ad hoc*" ways of settling such questions exist, then what ought to be done? Can Rawls do any better than intuitionism and *ad hoc* ways of countering such outcomes? He says there's no guarantee, that there is "No assurance that we can do better. But this is no reason not to try."

The preceding declaration is not a very forcefully argued rationale (RAT). Imagine if someone asked Rawls why his *A Theory of Justice* was necessary. He has obviously identified a GAP in the literature, but rather than assuredly pronouncing the necessity of his work, he provides the response noted above. Another way of illustrating the rhetorical equivalence of Rawls's answer is to imagine a girl who demands of a teenage boy that he provide her with a good rationale as to why she should go out with him. His answer is: "If you don't want to go out with me, that wouldn't be irrational. There is no assurance that I can do better than your previous boyfriends. But that is no reason not to go out with me." Such an answer is tentative, weak, and something that only a George McFly would utter. One would be tempted to donate money to such a person so that he can go buy a loaf of self-confidence. Or, perhaps, Rawls is just being humble. Consider how the next paragraph is organized:

(1) What I have attempted to do is to generalize and carry to a higher order of abstraction the traditional theory of the social contract as represented by Locke, Rousseau, and Kant. (2) In this way I hope that the theory can be developed so that it is no longer open to the more obvious objections often thought fatal to it. (3) Moreover, this theory seems to offer an alternative systematic account of justice that is superior, or so I argue, to the dominant utilitarianism of the tradition. (4) The theory that results is highly Kantian in nature. (5) Indeed, I must disclaim any originality for the views I put forward. (6) The leading ideas are classical and well known. (7) My intention has been to organize them into a general framework by using certain simplifying devices so that their full force can be appreciated. (8) My ambitions for the book will be completely realized if it enables one to see more clearly the chief structural features of the alternative conception of justice that is implicit in the contract tradition and points the way to its further elaboration. (9) Of the traditional views, it is this conception, I believe, which best approximates our considered judgments of justice and constitutes the most appropriate moral basis for a democratic society. (Rawls, 1971, p. viii)

If one uttered the semantic equivalent of a spate of talk like the preceding paragraph on the street, it would, necessarily, have to be followed by an "Oh

Snap!" or "Three snaps in a circle!" Here's why. If Hume, Bentham, Smith, and Mill count as the previous authors who have championed utilitarian theories of the social contract (SPL), then Locke, Rousseau, and Kant constitute the previous authors who might be classified as influential proponents of a deontological theory of social contract (SPL). Rawls is summarizing and critiquing two of the most influential schools of thought in western philosophy for the past 500 years. Rather than relying on "*ad hoc*" explanations and "intuitionism," as others before him have done (CPL), Rawls is proposing that he can come up with a theory of society that is general (as opposed to intuitionistic) and systematic (as opposed to *ad hoc*) (RAT). He is proclaiming that his theory of society and justice will be "superior" to those of prevailing utilitarianism and of a "higher order" than previous theories proffered by theorists such as Locke, Rousseau, and Kant. That is like a rookie boxer telling Mike Tyson, Muhammad Ali, and Joe Frazier that he can box better than them. Either one is crazy to say stuff like that, or Rawls really has an unrivaled left hook.

In sentence #4, when Rawls states that his new theory is "highly Kantian in nature," and in the very next sentence he claims that "leading ideas are classical and well known," he is introducing the reader to the background literature (SPL), for those three words (leading, classical, well known) mean nearly the same thing in the preceding sentence. And because Rawls is using ideas that already exist in one form or another, perhaps that's why he humbly disclaims any originality. But notice how the form and movement of Rawls's ideas have been shaped by prior research. Political theorists throughout the centuries have attempted to provide a coherent narrative of how a society secures a unified and stable social order composed of free and equal citizens despite fundamental differences in their moral, philosophical, and religious views. Such a task is easy when a society is composed of angels, for values such as equality, piety, and justice would be abundant, and blindly assuming them as a necessary psychological precondition is not problematic. Governments would require minimal use of coercion.

The problem for political theorists has been that such benign assumptions have to be set aside and the empirical realities of a pluralistic world have to be presupposed from the beginning. That is, robbers, thieves, and murderers would also dwell in the midst of angels, and they would have to be included in any theory of the state in order for it to be truly universalizable and logically consistent – *reductio ad absurdum*. Hence, Kant assumed as a premise for his political (and ethical) theory a state that could be constructed through mutual agreement even by a "nation of devils":

> In order to organize a group of rational beings who together require universal laws for their survival, but of whom each separate individual is secretly

inclined to exempt himself from them, the constitution must be so designed that, although the citizens are opposed to one another in their private attitudes, these opposing views may inhibit one another in such a way that the public conduct of the citizens will be the same as if they did not have such evil attitudes. (Kant, [1784] 1991, pp. 112–113)

To accommodate the existence of such vagaries of character and disposition in the self and theoretical framework, political theorists since the time of Locke, Rousseau, and Kant have pursued a definition of justice that is devoid of substantive content, and toward a purely formal and procedural account of justice (Fish, 1999). When Rawls states that his theory is "highly Kantian," he is summarizing, compressing, and reducing Kant's idea of mutual consent as a legitimating principle, the principle of self-interest, and the categorical imperative as all necessary preconditions for a theory of a social contract in one word – "Kantian." If readers do not understand the weight of the word "Kantian" and its impact, they are likely to miss other connections to previous theorists in the chapters to come. One word does all that work.

What does Rawls mean when he says, "I have attempted to generalize and carry to a higher order of abstraction the traditional theory of the social contract"? This tendency toward abstraction and generality is evident in Rawls's notion of the "veil of ignorance" within "the original position." The original position is, according to Rawls (1971, p. 12), the "appropriate initial *status quo*" and serves as a theoretical underpinning of the two principles of justice that would be chosen by all rational persons. In this fictitious account, subjects are to devise social and public policy that would be mutually agreed to by all members of society. The aim is to recreate one of the fundamental moments in the origins of society and the social contract; to address the problem of difference and self-interest, to prevent any one subject from choosing policies that show preference for one group within society, the subjects are hidden behind a veil of ignorance where any identifying markers such as race, class, and gender, hence bias and preference, would exert little influence on the adoption of public policy. The "simplifying devices" he refers to in sentence #7 describe conceptual tools he has modified and developed from previous scholars.

One can see the genealogical and conceptual debt that Rawls owes to previous scholars. In a way, Rawls's work is the culmination, synthesis, and apogee of western philosophical thought, for he draws upon Descarte's ([1641] 1951) epistemological certitude as a metaphysical attribute and mooring for his "reflective equilibrium"; he relies on Mill's (1997) principle of utilitarianism as a second principle of justice ("maximum minimum"); he presupposes difference as a potential cause of conflict that ought to be set aside in public domains *à la* Locke or curtailed through the despotic pronouncements of a bureaucratic Leviathan à *la* Hobbes; he uses logical consistency, universalizability, and mutual consent as necessary criteria for a rule's applicability (Kant, [1784] 1991). The word "sinuous" captures the winding history and summary of political thought quite well. Another word sums up Professor Rawls's *A Theory of Justice*: brilliant.

If Professor Rawls's final argument is brilliant, the general method of arriving at that destination is less so, for the road that he traveled is a road that all academic writers must traverse. As Professor Rawls admits, he does not have original ideas of his own. That's partially true. He has simply borrowed and modified the previous ideas to make his argument. He wrote the book because he saw that there was a GAP in the existing state of the literature in political philosophy, and he could remedy that gap. That GAP served as his rationale (RAT). But before he could remedy that GAP, hundreds of pages are spent summarizing (SPL) and critiquing (CPL) the previous scholars who have written on the subject. Then the results of his arguments (ROA) are presented. In this sense, the form of the arguments made in humanities and social sciences is not that different. They have an underlying structure and form.

The form of the reading codes

As I have argued in this book, social science journal articles tend to be organized along the paths I described. Again, before the author can write an article or a book, he/she must be able to justify why his/her proposed work is warranted. That rationale is shaped by the deficiencies in the current state of the literature. If there are no flaws, deficiencies, or limitations – perfection – in the knowledge base (literature), why would anyone try to improve it? Perfection, by definition, necessitates no change. Academics and scholars do so because they believe that they can improve the state of the knowledge by redefining and reframing the research questions posed in the discipline, or by challenging the methods and procedures that a previous researcher used. At times, the improvement that results is spectacular and paradigm shifting; the agents of such change become superstars in their disciplines. However, most of the time, the improvement is minute, but sufficiently innovative to warrant publication. I think I have also shown that this general pattern holds in non-social science as well.

I must admit that trying to use the reading code on a 500-page text is a daunting task. However, if readers use the highlighter and pen to highlight the important parts of a book, then the task becomes a bit more manageable. I argued that in social science journal articles, the ROF and GAP are two of the most important nuggets of information that ought to be highlighted, for the simple reason that the ROF readily provides an answer to the question "what did they find?" and ROFs become SPLs in a future paper. GAP is important for the reason that it answers the "so what?" question. If an author can't answer that question, then that paper ought not to be attempted, or the author should read more. But I presume that students reading this book, for the most part anyway, will not have to worry about applying the reading code sheet to a 500-page book. Even I would not assign such an asinine task to my students.

I would, however, assign students to read a 20–30-page journal article and verify their correct application of the reading codes. As I have argued again and again, this project was motivated by the simple fact that I saw recurring errors in students' papers; when I looked back on my career as a student, I noticed that I had made the same errors. I just wanted to find a way to correct them. Although I began with the assumption that writing problems can be remedied by sending students to writing centers, I found this not to be the case. Students' writing problems existed on several levels. Writing problems that were rooted at the conceptual level affected papers on a structural level, which then seeped into mechanical details. Simply fixing sentences and grammar did not work to improve students' writing at all. Rather than examining badly-written papers to try to fix them, I changed my assumptions and decided to examine well-written papers to learn how to write them so that I could teach those techniques to students. *Where would I find well-written papers?* I thought to myself. Then I looked around my office. Duh.

I began to read social science articles and attempted to understand the text at two levels: (1) what is the author trying to do in this paragraph, this sentence? and (2) how is this article structurally organized? Once I started asking those questions, I began to notice a recurring pattern in the way the journal articles were written. Readers will have noticed that the reading codes are represented in a rather odd combination of – sometimes vowel-less – consonant clusters: WTD, ROF, SPL, CPL. Those codes serve as evidence that I had indeed asked the first question as a guiding principle in the current project. I began the reading code by writing out "what they do," "result of findings," "summary of previous literature," etc. at the margins and found them to be too cumbersome to write each and every time. So I just started using the acronyms of the functions performed in the text. After about two years of reading, I began to see a pattern in the way the articles were structurally organized. SPLs generally preceded CPLs and GAPs; RTCs and RCLs generally appeared in the back parts of articles rather than in the front, and so on. I also noticed what the authors weren't doing in their papers. For example, some authors I was reading Missed an Obvious Point (MOP) in their discussions; I noticed that the authors claimed something that ought not to have been claimed, and those became Points of Critique (POC)

I could use in a future paper. Sometimes, the points that an author missed was a Relevant Point to Pursue (RPP) in a future paper. These became the reading strategy codes.

Once I formulated a preliminary reading code sheet, I asked several of my colleagues to try it out on a journal article. For about a year, I pleaded, entreated, and begged them to try it on their own readings. After little success, I did what most professors would probably do: I made the undergraduate students try reading with the code sheet. I spent two hours reading one article with the entire class to demonstrate how it worked. I think the codes worked. In the final research papers that students submitted, I did not find gross structural problems in their papers. There were other typical errors (e.g., capitalization, fragments, semicolon abuse, etc.) but those were problems that could now be fixed rather easily. Encouraged by the success, I tried it with a graduate class. I was met with moderate success. A colleague who was teaching a professional seminar asked me to talk about my ongoing research. I asked if I could share with the students the reading code. He obliged. Afterwards, he suggested that I write a book. I thought he was joking. As of this writing, I am on a second set of undergraduate students who are reading with the reading codes and who will be writing research papers – not book reports.

9

Concluding Remarks

Although I have heard the phrase "television makes you stupid" countless times, I have never heard the phrase "reading makes you stupid." In the latter, reading makes you stupid only if you read stupid stuff. But even in this view, the act of reading is not dismissed as a worthless activity. The two phrases, however, serve as a good contrast between the two media through which people know. One is word-based and the other is purportedly picture-based. One requires audiences to process and digest syntactically complex sentences, and follow a linear and carefully crafted sequential flow of ideas, propositions, and arguments, the other a couch.

The two types of medium – television and book – are what Postman (1985) refers to as *telegraphic* and *typographic* forms of epistemology. The telegraphic mind requires plain language to understand and enjoy television, language that is syntactically simple, with minimal logical propositions, assertions, and arguments. Such discourse is illogical, emotional, and expressive; it is banal in every sense of the word, and pollutes public communication. The typographic mind, on the other hand, requires language that is logical, sequential, linear, and orderly. Such language is the language of Shakespeare, Aristotle, Plato, and the rest of the great western Classics authors. Consequently, literary language is aesthetic, a pleasure to read, and fertilizing. But more importantly, it produces virtuous traits in the reader.

Postman values the typographic mind over the telegraphic one because of the types of minds that reading literary words produce. Reading requires that readers follow a linear and carefully crafted sequential flow of ideas and arguments. And for Postman (1985, p. 51), that is what reading does: "uncover lies, confusions and overgeneralizations, to detect abuses of logic and commonsense." For Postman a culture that is "dominated by print" is predisposed to a mind-set characterized by "coherent, orderly arrangement of facts and ideas" in its public discourse (p. 51). Pictures, images, and plain language needed to understand television, on the other hand, do not require complex sentences and logical argumentation, for "discourse is conducted largely through visual imagery, which is to say that television gives us conversation in images, not words" (p. 7).

Postman's charge is that television makes too much information available, hence, renders it useless. Postman argues that superfluous information is useless because newly received information has no relevance to the audience's immediate life: information becomes context free, not bound to anyone's particular history, setting, and time, but free-floating, with no clear mooring, captured in catchy phrases and bites. According to Postman, TV is primarily for entertainment; it has nothing to teach us, in form or content; moreover, it does so in a plain and vulgar way: "what we watch is a medium [television] which presents information in a form that renders it simplistic, non-substantive, non-historical and non-contextual; that is to say, information packaged as entertainment" (p. 141).

Postman argues for television's evilness because of the type of minds it creates; people who watch TV want constant amusement, and that desire for a never-ending good time is likely to lead to "death." The death is probably not literal, but it is accurate in another sense. Those who watch excessive amounts of television, Postman would say, do not read; moreover, they rarely do anything else, such as play sports, go out for walks, or do chores around the house. The word reserved in our culture for such persons is "couch potato." And if Postman's characterization of television is right, then in the long run, this culture would breed nothing but couch potatoes; but more significantly, people would turn into mental couch potatoes as well because not only would they lack the physical capabilities to exercise their bodies, but also the muscles that work the mind would have atrophied owing to inactivity. The death in Postman's work is mental and intellectual – in the mind – but it is every bit as scary as physical death.

Postman is interested in the effects of language. The effects he wants are virtuous ones, and in reading literary "printed words," the effects are twofold: one benefits from the activity of reading itself since it teaches the reader to "uncover lies, confusions, overgeneralizations, to detect abuses of logic and common sense"; the other benefit is that readers undergo a profound aesthetic experience. According to Postman, reading literary works leads to critical thinking and aesthetic appreciation. Postman is correct to point out that reading produces a certain type of mind; however, the texts that are read as a way of cultivating one's mind or for enjoyment do not give birth to themselves. The authors of those texts, wittingly and carefully, craft a linear and sequential flow of ideas and arguments, or unwittingly scatter their texts with lies, confusion, and abuses of logic and common sense.

This is to say that although the reader and the writer may be separated by time and distance, they stand face to face in intimate ways. They are bound to one another because writers are engaged with their readers from the moment they think about a potential writing project to the time they compose it and complete it. Linear and logical arguments do not emerge on their own; they are created by writers who assume the role of readers, who, although invisible and absent, exert exponential force in the shape of an author's argument (Eco, 1979). Good writers anticipate readers' reactions and rebuttals even before they emerge, and craft their ideas with such a response in mind. That type of sensitivity and care can be seen in the way paragraphs are organized, for responsible authors lead their readers to "see" their train of thought and the logic that got them there; those types of paragraphs flow "tightly" and can't be undone by simply moving one paragraph to another location. If one of those paragraphs is moved, then the entire argument would collapse under its own weight. Irresponsible writers, on the other hand, are similar to bad lovers, for they are inconsiderate of their partners during their intimate acts. Both do as they please without an iota of thought for their bored partners.

As I have shown in this book, some authors prepare their readers much better than others – by logically and sensitively guiding them through abstract points and tricky curves. For such reasons, reading and writing are intersubjective acts, for readers and writers enter into a mutually pleasurable yet arduous task of creating and reading texts together. Writers have readers in mind when crafting their ideas and structure of arguments; readers have the authors in mind as they attempt to understand the intent, purpose, and aim of a particular block of text. That's what makes reading and writing dialogical and intersubjective acts, for authors are trying to persuade their readers to see their point; similarly, readers are trying to discern an author's argument and logic as to why s/he organized the text in a particular way or chose a certain word to describe something when another would have sufficed. Texts that are constructed and interpreted in a particular way are not random outcomes. They are collaboratively and reflexively produced by the reader and writer alike – across time, history, and geography – even if they meet for the first time in 500 years. Television requires no such dialogical imagination.

Hence, I have argued that reading and writing, although usually done solitarily, are intersubjective acts. When scholars read the work of a previous scholar, the reader is, in essence, engaged in a silent dialogue with the writer; conversely, the author is engaged in an invisible dialogue with the reader, trying to figure out how best to persuade him to her point of view and accept the validity of her argument. That's what authors are thinking when they are writing. Such a process is aptly termed dialogical. Those types of internal debates that occur between readers and writers are rarely boring and never lonely. I have heard some students and academics complain that scholarly work is lonely, but such a conclusion is drawn because they have conflated solitariness with loneliness. They are not the same things.

Reading for pleasure is done solitarily, primarily for intensely selfish and philosophical ends. The literary critic Harold Bloom (2000, p. 24) advises that before readers engage in activism of any kind – the 10,000-isms that populate university campuses catering to the just-awakened moral palates of college students – as a result of reading a particular text, they ought to set aside such defiant notions until the author is first discovered: "Do not attempt to improve your neighbor or your neighborhood by what or how you read." That is Bloom's second principle of reading. And for Bloom, and other literary critics of his variety, we ought to read in a "quest of mind more original than our own" (p. 25), to strengthen ourselves. Pleasure reading in such a view is not social. One might even call such an act the epitome of antisociality.

In the context of social science reading and writing, however, I have argued for their intersubjectivity purely on formal grounds. Throughout this book I have also argued for the intersubjective character of social science writing by demonstrating how the very contents of social science articles exemplify and reify that sociality. We saw this tendency in the front and rear of journal articles. Authors entered the scholarly community by introducing and discussing the work of previous researchers in abstracts, introductions, and literature reviews. The very research questions asked are shaped by the history of a discipline. This practice, in and of itself, attests to the heavy intellectual down-payments scholars have to pay in order to establish residency in a community of scholars. Again, even before scholars can present their own findings, even before they can justify why their proposed works are necessary, the work that preceded theirs must be acknowledged and critiqued before a deficiency in the current state of the literature is remedied. By recognizing, including, discussing, and critiquing previous works, we enter into the socio-moral order of scholarship, for we acknowledge our conceptual debt to those who preceded us in the form of paragraphs and citations.

Discussions and conclusions also illustrated that order and dialogical character of academic work, for results of findings were rarely interpreted and discussed in absolute terms, but always relative to the past findings of previous scholars. Moreover, our contribution is shaped by previous scholars in the discipline who have asked similar questions, used similar methods to answer those questions, and interpreted those results in accordance with a canonic school of thought. That's why knowledge claims grow out of the claims of others: they are conceptually, methodologically, analytically, and temporally bound to the dialectical character of academic scholarship. Knowledge claims do not – cannot – emerge from nothingness. Such debt is paid in the form of citations.

Finally, social science writing embodies and cultivates a selfless moral virtue. That value is manifest in the outward critique in the front of journal articles and an inward one near the end. As we have seen, most, if not all, authors of social science journal articles discussed the limitations of their own work, as well as making recommendations for future works. As I argued in this book, those types of assertions dramatize the gaps in current knowledge. Such self-critiques also illustrate the tenuous and indeterminate character of knowledge claims and knowledge in general in the social sciences. That is to say, there is always room for improvement. Such a humble and skeptical outlook is desirable, for it reifies and parallels professed values in science (not literature), and stylistically prevents an accidental death that hubris might cause (i.e., Icarus). That such a noble moral value is encoded in the structural organization of social science texts sets it apart from other genres (e.g., romance novel, poetry). The moral trajectory of scholarship in the social sciences bends toward humility, and the structure of social science journal articles provides that constraint. That's not a bad thing.

The typographic mind may be desirable to achieve, and colleges and universities are mandated to do it, but there may be less frustrating ways to reach that desirable end, especially in the social sciences. Rather than expecting a desirable trait as an incidental byproduct of the reading process, as Postman does, critical reading ought to be taught to students; they ought to be given tools to spot "a linear and carefully crafted sequential flow of ideas." Using social science journal articles and a limited number of non-social science texts, I have shown that academic writing is organized in a very particular way, in a way that is expectable and anticipatable. The sequential, linear, and orderly organization of ideas in social science writing (and non-social science texts) can be canonically formulated as SPL→CPL→GAP→RAT, for that process embodies the structural flow of ideas in social science texts. And rather than simply telling students that there is a pattern in the texts, I have advocated revealing the structure of this pattern in texts so that students can see it, understand it, and – with cautious hope – emulate this pattern in their own writing – before they can be confident enough to overcome their diffidence, and pronounce their own scholarly voice.

As I have argued in this book, reading is not secondary to writing in the social sciences. Reading is half – if not more – of the writing process. The other half entails creative and moral work on the part of students, for they have to find ways of collating, classifying, and organizing previous ideas into highly-compressed yet cogent thematic categories before they can critique and provide a rationale for their own work. Only then, after the task of organizing and connecting previous ideas is done, can students compose unique – but limitless – ways of translating those themes into sentences. That task is not easy if the student is honest or obsessively compulsive, and remarkably easy if the student is guileful. As one can see, scholarly writing is a creative and a moral act. But then again, such exercises of the mind are what a university is principally for – in addition to the cool parties, sports, and, uh, other things best left unsaid.

I began this book with the assumption that writing problems are related to poor reading skills and information management. After ten years of trying to figure out why students were making the types of errors they were making on their papers (e.g., literature reviews, drafts of theses, etc.), I came to the conclusion that students did not have an adequate understanding of the idea of *criticism*. Simply asserting whether one likes the assigned reading or not, or finds it boring, is not a critique. Those are opinions. And it is impossible to critique an opinion. Criticisms, on the other hand, are not opinions; they are assessments of a work – whether the work is a painting, film, novel, philosophy book, or a social science article – that are grounded in the normative standards of judgment which are internal to that discipline. Thus, a test of logical consistency would not – I presume – be particularly relevant for assessing the merits of an oil painting or urban photography; however, for a book on philosophy, it would be a relevant criterion. Similarly, methodological rigor (e.g., random sample selection) would be a poor criterion to use to evaluate the literary merits of a historical novel, but absolutely appropriate for a social science journal article.

That was the problem I noticed again and again in my students' work. They had trouble critiquing the work of the authors they were reading. They were able to summarize, but the idea of critique was not adequately developed. Again, trying to teach critical reading to students who do not know how to do it by telling them to "read critically" is like trying to instruct aspiring bodybuilders on bodybuilding by telling them to go "build bodies." The advice is ridiculously absurd. One would have to tell someone who wants to be a bodybuilder to perform compound movements – exercises that require multiple joints – to develop a solid foundation for the first year or so; then begin to specialize body parts by rotating and cycling training schedules so that each muscle group is targeted a minimum number of times per week. The novice would be instructed to consume one gram of protein or more per pound of body weight, followed by adequate sleep and water intake. Oh, and, uh, avoid alcohol.

Notice the difference in the quality of instruction that exists between "go build bodies" and "perform compound movements, specialize, rotate and cycle, eat proteins, and rest." The former is completely useless unless one already knows what the directive entails and knows how to do it. When I consulted how-to books to improve writing (literature review), I noticed that the general advice that was proffered resembled directives such as "go build bodies" (SPL). If there were other specific directives that were offered, they were unwieldy and difficult to implement (CPL). I saw that a better way to teach students could be devised (GAP). Consequently, I developed the reading codes as a way of introducing a structure and pattern to the text that students were reading as a way of getting them to engage with it critically (RAT #1). Rather than simply telling students to be "critical," this book has provided a way of reading and coding that constitutes the very performance of "critical reading" others have presupposed (WTDD). I also wanted to find a way for students to organize the information they gathered from the reading codes in some principled and methodical way as a way of getting them to think about the writing process during the act of reading and prewriting, not after (RAT #2). This book has been an attempt to demonstrate and persuade readers that the reading codes are a relevant and useful heuristic device for critical reading and management of information (WTDD).

I have argued in this book that words, sentences, and paragraphs in social science journal articles perform a particular rhetorical function (ROF), in a way that is expectable and anticipatable according to the structure and logic that is inherent in social science journal writing (ROF). Once readers see this pattern, I argued, they would be able to read in a way that the contents of what they have read can be organized and classified in easily identifiable and retrievable ways. That pattern was introduced as a way of providing textual, cognitive, and conceptual boundaries so that readers did not engage in mindless and meandering reading filled with "cant" (Bloom, 2000). By identifying the function of texts and inserting codes into margins, I wanted readers to do three things: (1) slow down the act of reading; (2) organize the contents of the reading into recurring themes (e.g., SPL, CPL, GAP, ROF) that can be easily retrieved for writing purposes; and (3) identify potential GAPs so that the reader could anticipate the RAT from the given CPL and GAP for use in their own papers. The advice provided above, I argued, is the reading equivalent of "perform compound movements, specialize, rotate, cycle, consume protein, and rest."

The recommendations made in this book are neither radical nor new. I have simply fleshed out what previous writers (e.g., Cone & Foster, 2006; Glatthorn & Joyner, 2005; Rudestam & Newton, 2001; Vipond, 1996) were already doing and have presupposed in their practice (RCL). I have simply reduced their practice and advice into operational and deployable reading codes. This is hardly an innovation. In fact, some professors will claim that they already do something like this in their classes. I wouldn't be surprised. That's what my teachers did as well, although they did not call it SPL, CPL, RAT, RCL. Again, that's why I can't take credit for any of the ideas stated here.

Rhetoricians and literary critics – if they read the book at all – will most likely clutch their bellies with near-fatal laughter at the obtusely simplistic analysis of text that I have done here. But then again, I am not a literary critic trying to break new ground. I may also have forgotten to cite and discuss some of the relevant previous scholars in this area as well. That omission is not attributable to arrogance as much as pathological ineptitude. And that I have not been able to provide self-critiques and recommendations for future works should not mean that they do not exist. It's just that I am not smart enough to be that critical or reflective. If I were that smart, I'd be a marine biologist or an architect with Vandelay & Associates. But I'm only a teacher.

As a teacher, I have simply attempted to teach students how to read social science journal articles as a way of improving their writing. And because I am a teacher, I have a professional obligation to my students, to my institution (employer), and to the discipline to do what is best for my students, irrespective of my personal desire, preference, and inclination to do otherwise. I simply do not matter. That's what being a professional means. For this project, students are and have been the only invisible audience I have had in mind. I hope they will find the reading codes useful and learn to disregard the odor.

References

Bingenheimer, J., Brennan, R., & Earls, F. (2005). Firearm violence exposure and serious violent behaviour. *Science* 308, 1323–1326.

Bloom, H. (2000). *How to Read and Why*. New York: Touchstone.

Bui, Y. (2009). *How to Write a Master's Thesis*. Thousand Oaks, CA: Sage.

Burg, B. R. (1982). The sick and the dead: The development of psychological theory on necrophilia from Krafft-Ebing to the present. *Journal of the History of the Behavioral Sciences* 18, 3, 242–254.

Cao, L., Adams, A., & Jensen, V. (1997). A test of the black subculture of violence thesis: A research note. *Criminology* 35, 2, 367–379.

Cone, J. D. & Foster, S. L. (2006). *Dissertations and Theses: From Start to Finish*. Washington, DC: APA.

Copi, I. & Cohen, C. (1990). *Introduction to Logic*. New York: Macmillan.

Descarte, R. ([1641] 1951). *Meditations on First Philosophy*. New York: Macmillan.

DiCataldo, F. & Everett, M. (2008). Distinguishing juvenile homicide from violent juvenile offending. *International Journal of Offender Therapy and Comparative Criminology* 52, 2, 158–174.

Dixon, T. L. & Linz, D. (2000). Race and the misrepresentation of victimization on local television news. *Communication Research* 27, 5, 547–573.

Dolan, M. & Smith, C. (2001). Juvenile homicide offenders: 10 years' experience of an adolescent forensic psychiatry service. *Journal of Forensic Psychiatry* 12, 2, 313–329.

Eco, U. (1979). *The Role of the Reader: Explorations in the Semiotics of Texts*. Bloomington, IN: Indiana University Press.

Ehrenreich, B. (2001). *Nickeled and Dimed: On (Not) Getting By in America*. New York: Owl Books.

Entman, R. (1990). Modern racism and the images of blacks in local television news. *Critical Studies in Mass Communication* 7, 332–345.

Fink, A. (2010). *Conducting Research Literature Reviews: From the Internet to Paper* (3rd edn). Thousand Oaks, CA: Sage.

Fish, S. (1980). *Is There a Text in This Class? The Authority of Interpretive Communities*. Cambridge, MA: Harvard University Press.

Fish, S. (1994). *There's No Such Thing as Free Speech ... And It's a Good Thing*. London: Oxford University Press.

Fish, S. (1999). *The Trouble with Principle*. Cambridge, MA: Harvard University Press.

Fish, S. (2008). *Save the World on Your Own Time*. New York: Oxford University Press.

Glatthorn, A. A. & Joyner, R. L. (2005). *Writing the Winning Thesis or Dissertation: A Step-by-Step Guide*. Thousand Oaks, CA: Corwin Press.

Gruenewald, J., Pizarro, J., & Chermak, S. (2009). Race, gender, and the newsworthiness of homicide incidents. *Journal of Criminal Justice* 37, 262–272.

Jordan, C. H. & Zanna, M. (1999). How to read a journal article in social psychology. In R. F. Baumeister (ed.), *The Self in Social Psychology* (pp. 461–470). Philadelphia: Psychology Press.

Kant, I. ([1784] 1991). *Perpetual Peace: A Philosophical Sketch*. In H. Reiss (ed.), *Political Writings* (pp. 93–130). Cambridge: Cambridge University Press.

Keppel, R. D. & Birnes, W. J. (1995). *The Riverman: Ted Bundy and I Hunt for the Green River Killer*. New York: Pocket Books.

Keppel, R. D. & Birnes, W. J. (2003). *The Psychology of Serial Killer Investigations*. San Diego, CA: Academic Press.

Landrum, R. E. (2008). *Undergraduate Writing in Psychology: Learning to Tell the Scientific Story*. Washington, DC: APA.

Lewis, C. S. (1955). *Surprised by Joy*. New York: Harcourt Brace.

Locke, L., Silverman, S., & Spirduso, W. (2010). *Reading and Understanding Research* (3rd edn). Thousand Oaks, CA: Sage.

Lyng, S. (1990). Edgework: A social psychological analysis of voluntary risk taking. *American Journal of Sociology* 95, 4, 851–886.

Mickleburgh, R. (2010). Internal police strife delayed Pickton arrest, former officer says. *The Globe and Mail*, August 9.

Mill, J. S. (1997). On liberty. In A. Ryan (ed.), *Mill* (pp. 41–132). New York: W. W. Norton.

Miller, A. B. (2009). *Finish Your Dissertation Once and For All: How to Overcome Psychological Barriers, Get Results, and Move on With Your Life*. Washington, DC: APA.

Moffitt, T. (1993a). Adolescence-limited and life-course-persistent antisocial behavior: A developmental taxonomy. *Psychological Review* 100, 4, 674–701.

Moffitt, T. (1993b). The neuropsychology of conduct disorder. *Development and Psychopathology* 5, 135–151.

Moffitt, T. E., Caspi, A., Dickson, N., Silva, P., & Stanton, W. (1996). Childhood-onset versus adolescent-onset antisocial conduct problems in males: Natural history from ages 3 to 18 years. *Development and Psychopathology* 8, 399–424.

Muir, W. K. (1977). *Police: Street Corner Politicians*. Chicago: University of Chicago Press.

Noland, R. L. (1970). *Research and Report Writing in the Behavioral Sciences*. Springfield, IL: Charles C. Thomas.

O'Hara, S. (2005). *What Can You Do With a Major in Psychology?* Hoboken, NJ: Wiley Publishing.

Oliver, M. B. & Armstrong, G. B. (1995). Predictors of viewing and enjoyment of reality-based and fictional crime shows. *Journalism & Mass Communication Quarterly* 72, 3, 559–570.

Owen, J. J. (1999). Church and state in Stanley Fish's antiliberalism. *American Political Science Review* 93, 4, 911–924.

Piquero, A. R., Farrington, D. P., Nagin, D. S., & Moffitt, T. E. (2010). Trajectories of offending and their relation to life failure in late middle age: Findings from the Cambridge Study in Delinquent Development. *Journal of Research in Crime and Delinquency* 47, 2, 151–173.

Postman, N. (1985). *Amusing Ourselves to Death: Public Discourse in the Age of Show Business*. New York: Penguin Books.

Pritchard, D. & Hughes, K. D. (1997). Patterns of deviance in crime news. *Journal of Communication* 47, 3, 49–67.

Rawls, J. (1971). *A Theory of Justice*. Cambridge, MA: Harvard University Press.

Rayner, K., & Pollatsek, A. (1989). The Psychology of Reading. Hillsdale, NJ: Lawrence Erlbaum Associates.

Reichhart, D. (2004). *Chasing the Devil: My Twenty-Year Quest to Capture the Green River Killer*. New York: Little, Brown and Company.

Rosman, J. & Resnick, P. (1989). Sexual attraction to corpses: A psychiatric review of necrophilia. *Bulletin of the American Academy of Psychiatry & the Law* 17, 2, 153–163.

Rudestam, K. E. (2007). *Surviving Your Dissertation: A Comprehensive Guide to Content and Process* (3rd edn). Thousand Oaks, CA: Sage.

Rudestam, K. E. & Newton, R. R. (2001). *Surviving Your Dissertation: A Comprehensive Guide to Content and Process*. Thousand Oaks, CA: Sage.

Sampson, R. J. (1987). Urban black violence: The effect of male joblessness and family disruption. *American Journal of Sociology* 93, 348–382.

Sampson, R. J. & Groves, W.B. (1989). Community structure and crime: Testing social disorganization theory. *American Journal of Sociology* 94, 774–802.

Shumaker, D.M. & Prinz, R. (2000). Children who murder: A review. *Clinical Child and Family Psychology Review* 3, 2, 97–115.

Silvia, P. (2007). *How to Write a Lot*. Washington, DC: APA.

Strauss, A. (1987). *Qualitative Analysis for Social Scientists*. Cambridge: Cambridge University Press.

Strunk, W. Jr. & White, E. B. (1979). *The Elements of Style* (3rd edn). Needham Heights, MA: Allyn & Bacon.

Usoof-Thowfeek, R., Janoff-Bulman, R., & Tavernini, J. (2011). Moral judgments and the role of social harm: Differences in automatic versus controlled processing. *Journal of Experimental Social Psychology* 47, 1–6.

Vipond, D. (1996). *Success in Psychology: Writing and Research for Canadian Students*. Toronto, CA: Harcourt Brace & Company.

White, H. R., Bates, M. E., & Buyske, S. (2001). Adolescence-limited versus persistent delinquency: Extending Moffitt's hypothesis into adulthood. *Journal of Abnormal Psychology* 110, 4, 600–609.

Wyller, T. (2005). The place of pain in life. *Philosophy* 80, 313, 385–393.

Index